About Island Press

Island Press is the only nonprofit organization in the United States whose principal purpose is the publication of books on environmental issues and natural resource management. We provide solutions-oriented information to professionals, public officials, business and community leaders, and concerned citizens who are shaping responses to environmental problems.

In 1999, Island Press celebrates its fifteenth anniversary as the leading provider of timely and practical books that take a multidisciplinary approach to critical environmental concerns. Our growing list of titles reflects our commitment to bringing the best of an expanding body of literature to the environmental community throughout North America and the world.

Support for Island Press is provided by The Jenifer Altman Foundation, The Bullitt Foundation, The Mary Flagler Cary Charitable Trust, The Nathan Cummings Foundation, The Geraldine R. Dodge Foundation, The Charles Engelhard Foundation, The Ford Foundation, The Vira I. Heinz Endowment, The W. Alton Jones Foundation, The John D. and Catherine T. MacArthur Foundation, The Andrew W. Mellon Foundation, The Charles Stewart Mott Foundation, The Curtis and Edith Munson Foundation, The National Fish and Wildlife Foundation, The National Science Foundation, The New-Land Foundation, The David and Lucile Packard Foundation, The Pew Charitable Trusts, The Surdna Foundation, The Winslow Foundation, and individual donors.

Managing Tourism Growth

Managing Tourism Growth

ISSUES AND APPLICATIONS

Fred P. Bosselman, Craig A. Peterson,
and Claire McCarthy

ISLAND PRESS
Washington, D.C. • Covelo, California

ISLAND PRESS is a trademark of The Center for Resource Economics.

Library of Congress Cataloging-in-Publication Data
Bosselman, Fred P., 1941–
  Managing tourism : issues and applications / by Fred P. Bosselman,
Craig A. Peterson, and Claire McCarthy.
    p.   cm.
  Includes bibliographical references (p.   )
  ISBN 1–55963–605–X (paper)
  1. Tourism—Management.   I. Peterson, Craig A.   II. McCarthy
Claire.   III. Title.
G155.A1B63   1999   99–10999
338.4'791—dc21   CIP

Printed on recycled, acid-free paper

Manufactured in the United States of America
10 9 8 7 6 5 4 3 2 1

Contents

Preface

Tourism is by many measures the world's largest and fastest growing industry. It provides a myriad of positive benefits to hosts and to visitors. At the same time, destination communities must not be sanguine about the effects of tourism. If poorly managed, tourism can have serious, adverse impacts on the environment, physical appearance, economy, health, safety, and social values of the destination community.

Our overall purpose of this book is to analyze and evaluate methods by which communities can successfully "tame" tourism by carefully managing its growth so that it brings to the destination community the benefits the community wishes and minimizes the impacts that the community deems harmful.

In Chapter 1 we offer a number of actual examples of how uncontrolled tourism can adversely affect destination communities. Some are very far reaching, such as a broad array of negative impacts seen by the Tourism Authority of Thailand in that heavily visited country. Others are more circumscribed (although very significant), such as temporary fecal contamination of the swimming water off the Philippines island of Boracay. But despite these and many other examples of problems, we remain persuaded that destinations should not avoid tourism growth out of a conviction that it will bring only difficulties. Rather, we believe that tourism development can be successfully managed for the benefit of hosts and tourists alike.

Chapter 2 is oriented toward the process of creating an effective strategy, with special emphasis on the methods successfully employed in a wide range of tourism settings. We recommend that in deciding how and to what extent to manage tourism growth, communities should adopt strategies that (1) minimize any long-range negative impacts of tourism on the destination ("sustainability"), (2) maximize the aggregate benefits of tourism to the tourists and the destination ("efficiency"), (3) allocate the benefits and burdens in a way that is perceived as fair by as many people as possible ("equity"), and (4) are adaptable to future changes in conditions ("resiliency"). These ideas grow out of the concept that "tourism resources"—anything that attracts tourists—are very often "shared" by both the host community and the visitors. The quality of the water and sand at a beach destination and the vista of meadows and mountains are common examples. These shared resources should be used by all persons in mutually beneficial ways and with due concern for the needs of later generations, who will certainly want to enjoy those shared resources in the future.

Successful tourism management systems, as well as a new body of academic research and analysis called "common-pool resource" studies, strongly suggest that successful shared tourism resource management systems should include six components. They should (1) define resource boundaries clearly (i.e., identify the resources and their location); (2) identify the "players" affected by the system (i.e., specify those individuals and entities that are entitled to use the resources); (3) let the players make the rules (i.e., take into account the perspectives of the users of the resources so that they are more likely to comply with and enforce the rules necessary to manage the assets); (4) localize the rules as much as possible (i.e., provide very tailored rules that reflect the special nature of the resources); (5) give the players a sense of permanence (so as to enhance the likelihood that they will obey the rules); and finally, (6) monitor and mediate rule violations efficiently but effectively (i.e., persuade users that the rules will in fact be enforced, thus improving the chances that they will be complied with).

Chapter 3 addresses growth management techniques. Some of our ideas about the substantive aspects of managing tourism growth derive from the experiences of a number of places (especially the United States) to manage population growth generally (as opposed to a focus on tourism growth). In considering a growth management (and, more specifically, a tourism growth management) strategy, it is critical to understand the considerable interaction of free market economic forces, local norms that govern behavior, and legal mechanisms (necessary for ensuring that a selected tourism growth management system is properly embodied in enforceable legal enactments). Successful strategies often involve elements of all three.

Destination communities should also be aware that the nature of the resources being protected should determine the appropriate level of management: resources such as air present complex regulatory problems and therefore might well be best managed at a global or national level; while resources presenting much simpler challenges (such as the open space between one hotel and another) could best be determined locally. In a sense then, smaller, more local systems protecting local tourism resources can be thought of as being "nested" in larger, broader systems guarding more complex resources.

In the following chapters we describe and evaluate in detail types of strategies that are available for communities to use to manage tourism growth. Chapter 4 analyzes three strategies that control the "quality" of development: quality differentiation, performance standards, and trade-off strategies. Chapter 5 analyzes three approaches to managing the "quantity" (i.e., the rate or amount) of development: preservation rules, growth limitations, and incremental growth strategies. Chapter 6 analyzes four ways to enhance the "location" of development: expansion, dispersal, and concentration strategies and identification of new tourism resources. Each chapter presents numerous case studies from a broad range of settings that can guide destination communities as they consider the alternative legal and regulatory measures, management techniques, and incentives that can be combined into a strategy tailored to suit their local conditions.

The final chapter (Chapter 7) briefly describes the elements of successful strategies— in terms of both process and substance—as a checklist for readers to consider as they begin the planning process to develop a tourism growth management strategy for their community.

1

The Benefits and Risks of Tourism

Contemporary tourism is a vast and rapidly expanding industry that claims to be the "largest industry in the world, measured by gross output, value added, capital investment, employment and tax contributions."[1] The principal reasons for its exploding growth are all late twentieth century phenomena: increased wealth (especially the emergence of larger middle classes); changed demographics (an increase in the number of retired persons with additional time to travel, especially in the developed countries); greater mobility (increased car ownership); transportation improvements (especially the increased size and number of large airplanes, combined with the reduced cost of travel); technological changes (improved communications); and maturation of the tourism industry (as evidenced, for example, by creation of more consistent standards and methods of service delivery and the proliferation of package holidays).[2]

Whatever the reasons, the recent growth is staggering in its scope. By 1992, tourism was the fastest growing economic segment of many industrialized countries.[3] Even more current statistics and projections reflect the growing scale of global tourism. In 1996, over 10 percent of the world's population of 5.7 billion took at least one international trip (this, of course, excludes more common in-country trips); those numbers are expected to increase by 2020 to a breathtaking 1.6 billion international travelers, over 20 percent of the expected total world population of 7.8 billion. According to the World Tourism Organization, the phenomenon is equally impressive from the economic standpoint.[4] (See Table 1-1.)

The Symbiotic Relationship of Host and Tourist

The statistics leave no doubt that tourism is a phenomenon of increasing significance throughout the world. Certainly judging from the vast number of people who choose to spend their time and money on travel, many of us enjoy being tourists. Given the ever increasing number of communities and countries trying to attract their share of the exploding tourist market, many of us assume that tourism development will bestow benefits on the hosts as well as the visitors.

The symbiotic relationship of host and visitor has a long history. Tourism in some form has been around for thousands of years. Formal travel narratives are often said to have begun around 1900 B.C. with the Babylonian *Epic of Gilgamesh,* and continued with Homer's majestic *Odyssey,* even though "(t)he travels narrated (there) are god-decreed and thus not wholly voluntary nor pleasurable."[5] History tells us that special places have

Table 1-1 Tourism Economic Statistics (U.S. Dollars)

	1995	2000 Estimate[a]
Tourism spending	3.4 trillion	4.2 trillion
Capital investment	645 billion	828 billion
Tourism employees	232 million	250 million

[a] World Tourism Organization.

attracted visitors from the earliest days, and that enterprising locals have long provided their visitors with shelter and sustenance, transportation and guides—all at a price. Myths and stories teach us that the interaction of host and traveler goes far beyond a mere commercial transaction, however, and can often be an enriching experience for both.

The face of tourism has changed,[6] however, in the last half-century. With the tremendous growth in the number of people traveling throughout the world, the impacts—both positive and negative—of visitors upon their host communities have been magnified. The challenge for the tourist is to find the "perfect spot" for a weekend getaway or summer vacation. For the host community, whether long-established as a popular tourist destination or embarking on tourism development for the first time, the challenge is to find a way to manage tourism growth in an equitable and sustainable way so that the benefits it confers will outweigh the burdens it imposes.

This book looks at ways by which host communities can ensure that tourism brings as many benefits and as few risks as possible. By focusing on ways that tourism can be effectively managed and regulated, we do not mean to detract from the role of the tourism industry itself in promoting beneficial types of tourism. Efforts of private enterprise to integrate principles of environmental sustainability are growing rapidly. The World Tourism Organization, headquartered in Madrid, and the World Travel and Tourism Council in London have vigorously championed this goal, publishing informative articles on sustainable tourism practices and recognizing successful programs.[7]

Nevertheless, we think a study of ways in which governments have managed tourism should be as helpful to industry professionals as to community representatives. Regulation has usually come about in response to problems that were perceived to have been created by members of the tourism industry. An understanding that regulation often follows negative impacts may be an incentive for businesses to act in ways that minimize harmful impacts. Careful and thoughtful management of tourism growth seeks not only to minimize negative impacts, but also to increase the benefits that tourism can bring to host communities and visitors, and thus to the tourism industry as well.

The Benefits of Tourism

The primary benefit of tourism to travelers is a measure of personal pleasure, and there seems to be a tourist offering to fit every taste and individual interest. (See Photo 1-1.) Some just want to lie on a beach. Others may seek exposure to the arts, architecture, cuisine, crafts, traditions, or lifestyles of a different culture. Others wish to visit a place of exceptional natural beauty or a location that offers specific recreational activities, or to study a particular topic. Whatever the focus—whether going white water rafting or taking an architectural tour or photographing native flowers—it is an activity chosen to bring enjoyment to the tourist.

Photo 1-1 Tourist photographing nature on Sanibel, Florida

The most obvious potential benefits that tourism can bring to destination communities are economic. (See Photo 1-2.) For developers of successful tourist attractions and facilities, the major benefit is profit. For governments and citizens, it includes increased employment opportunities; an expanded tax base; access to markets for locally produced goods; the infusion of foreign exchange, investment (see Photo 1-3), and expertise; an ability to finance infrastructure improvements and pollution control measures that they might not otherwise be able to afford; and an improved standard of living.

Tourism growth is often a catalyst for jobs not only in the tourism industry, but also in fields that supply goods and services to tourist developments: construction, agriculture, entertainment, some manufacturing, arts and crafts. Job opportunities for women often expand with tourism development. In communities where tourism operators teach skills to local residents, these skills can often be transferred to other sectors, thus increasing productivity throughout the economy in the long term. Destination communities often embark on tourism development solely with the aim of securing such economic benefits.

When oil industry profits plummeted in the 1980s, the town of Corpus Christi in southeast Texas lost 5,000 jobs and unemployment soared to 12.2 percent.[8] With few other visible options, the city determined that tourism was its best shot at adding jobs and reviving its sagging economy. A beach town on the Gulf of Mexico, Corpus Christi has no spectacular scenery or historical claim to fame to attract visitors. Instead, it is focusing its efforts on creating new attractions to draw a larger share of the convention delegates and three million Mexican tourists who visit Texas annually.

The city has gone about its tourism development carefully and methodically, ordering economic impact studies prior to expending any public funds. Before building a new aquarium, it analyzed the financial costs and annual revenues of Baltimore's aquarium. Before purchasing a famous World War II navy ship, it studied the experiences of six other

Photo 1-2 A multitude of tourism uses in Queenstown, New Zealand

Photo 1-3 Small convention center and bar/restaurant under construction in Ambergris Caye, Belize

cities that promote former war ships as tourist attractions. Corpus Christi now has replicas of the *Niña, Pinta,* and *Santa Maria;* a zoo and botanic garden; a greyhound race track; an Asian Cultures Museum and a Museum of Science and History; and a life-size bronze statue of Selena, the murdered Mexican singer.

The economic results from such thoughtful planning have been impressive. Since 1986, tourist numbers have increased almost 140 percent to a total of 5.5 million in 1997; hotel revenues have doubled; tourism-related jobs have doubled to 10,200; and tourism-related payroll came close to tripling. The average visitor, who used to stay one day, now stays for two and a half days. The city is also working to form cooperative relationships with San Antonio, Laredo, the port of Corpus Christi, and Monterrey, Mexico, to attract even more tourists.

Sometimes the economic benefits of tourism growth far exceed the expectations of a destination. Lake Powell in Arizona was created when a dam was built in 1963. Since then, to almost everyone's surprise, it has become the second most popular camping spot in the entire United States, attracting over 2.5 million recreational visitors a year. Environmentalists (including some who originally proposed building the dam) now want to drain the enormous reservoir to restore Glen Canyon to its natural splendor. But most residents of Paige, the town closest to Lake Powell, want to protect the lake from the environmentalists, as do electricity users dependent upon it as a source of energy, those cities that rely on it for water, those involved in the US $500 million tourism industry, and the Navajo nation, who fear a loss of jobs if the lake is drained.

Economic benefits also accrue directly to individual residents in terms of increased wages and a higher standard of living. A farmer in Nusa Dua, Bali (see p. 232), described the economic impact of tourism development on his life: "Before the project (in 1973), I had a hectare of coconut groves, and I couldn't afford to feed my family. If people from (my village) wanted to buy rice, we had to take a boat over to Benoa harbor and walk to Sanur. There was no road, no market, nothing. Just coconuts and the sea."[9]

As the farmer's statement implies, tourism development has broader benefits than merely economic impacts. Properly managed, tourism can have important social and cultural benefits for destination communities as well. It can spark renewed pride in local crafts and traditions, and in some instances has spurred a revival of waning skills in traditional carving, jewelry design, weaving, embroidery, pottery making, painting, music, and dance. This has been the case with whale bone carving among the Maori of New Zealand, pottery and tile painting in Turkey, rug weaving among the Navajos of the American southwest, fiddle playing in Scotland, and aboriginal painting in Australia.

The interest tourists evince in a destination can also foster a greater appreciation of local historical structures, landscapes, and cultural heritage, resulting in conservation measures to protect these important assets. Recent restoration of the ancient Roman baths in the English spa city of Bath, and current reparation efforts in the medina of Fez in Morocco, have both been fueled in part by tourists' interest and their dollars. The serpent eagles, lemurs, and leaf-tail gecko lizards on the island of Madagascar have piqued the interest of tourists, and now the government is working to protect the rain forests that sustain the animals.[10] Poaching of wildlife and such endangered species as the mountain gorilla in many portions of Africa has been drastically reduced by the realization (combined with formal and informal sanctions) that the animals bring much greater economic benefits to the region as tourist attractions than as a source of income for individual poachers.

Sometimes tourism development replaces a more harmful activity. New roads are being built to previously inaccessible Mayan ruins like Calakmul and Uaxactun in Central

America. While no one is positive of their precise environmental impact, it is expected to be far gentler on the land than the current slash and burn practices of the local residents.[11]

Often infrastructure improvements that are made in order to support tourism growth—such as pollution control and environmental protection measures, improvements to roads and transportation systems, enhanced recreational and leisure facilities—also benefit the host community. The development of the Huatulco Bays in Mexico (p. 262) brought running water and electricity to poor villages for the first time. In some cases, tourism development also revitalizes commercial areas and expands the range of shops, restaurants, and entertainment facilities for residents as well as tourists.

Many of the potentially greatest benefits of tourism attach equally to both hosts and visitors. In any cross-cultural exchange there are opportunities for mutual education and the breaking down of cultural barriers. Even within countries, particularly large countries like the United States, tourism increasingly creates contacts among people of widely varying backgrounds.

As hosts and visitors have a chance to relate to each other as individuals (especially those who are interested in understanding other peoples' lifestyles, values, and cultures),[12] they may begin to reconsider their stereotypes and question the accuracy of their preconceptions. Exposure to new ideas makes both host and visitor less parochial. Travel has the potential to lead to a lessening of prejudices and a promotion of a new understanding of "foreigners" for both the hosts and the visitors.[13] At some level, tourism can even serve to increase international understanding. (See Photo 1-4.)

Photo 1-4 Tourists at the Kremlin, Moscow, on anniversary of V-E Day during the Soviet Era

Another educational benefit of tourism has been the growth of interest in learning foreign languages. Jobs in the tourism industry often require that employees be able to speak a second or third language in order to serve tourists. Although visitors are rarely as fluent in the language of their hosts, the number of tourists clutching their Berlitz guides to French or Spanish or Chinese suggests that many are at least trying to master a few helpful phrases.

The Risks of Tourism

Unfortunately, these benefits are not the only or inevitable result of tourism growth. Expected economic benefits do not always materialize. When Long Beach, California, used its oil well revenue to build a massive convention center, it anticipated attracting a steady stream of trade shows and conventions. But the worldwide growth in convention center space has far outstripped its demand, and Long Beach has wind blowing through its vacant parking lots far more often than the city expected.

The construction of costly infrastructure to serve future tourists can also be a chancy endeavor. In the 1980s, the British government built an airport and paved roads in the Turks and Calicos Islands in the West Indies at a cost of some £6.11 million, with an understanding that Club Med would build a major resort. The expectation was that the benefits that would accrue from the tourism development would allow the islands to become economically independent. Unfortunately, it was years before Club Med even signed a contract for a much smaller resort.[14]

In some cases, even successful attractions don't generate the expected economic benefits for the host community. The ever-popular New Orleans has found that of the 16,000 workers in the tourism industry, the vast majority are working in low-paying jobs. Industry experts estimate that for a major hotel employing 700 people, 92 percent of the employees earn under US $15,000 per year.[15] A study by Loftman and Nevin of the International Convention Center, in Birmingham, England, reported that only 7 percent of permanent jobs went to local residents.[16]

A World Wildlife Federation study of ecotourism[17] in the Royal Chitwan National Park in Nepal showed that despite a 1994 visitation rate exceeding 60,000 tourists, the economic impact on household income was minimal and limited to villages closest to the main park entrance. "Of the estimated 87,000 working age people living near the park, less than 1,100 were employed directly by the ecotourism industry. Only 6 percent of the surveyed households earned income directly or indirectly from ecotourism; the average annual salary of these households from ecotourism was $600."[18]

In some communities, international organizations seem to dominate the trade in ways that appear to exclude local entrepreneurs. A recent study by a group at the University of Arizona concluded that whale-watching tours off the Baja peninsula of Mexico returned less than 1 percent of the tourists' expenditures to the Mexican economy.

The risks that destination communities face from tourism growth are not just that expected benefits will not materialize, but also that there may be adverse impacts that are not anticipated. These negative impacts are not generally envisioned or planned by members of the tourism industry, the destination community, or the tourists themselves. By carefully analyzing potential impacts in advance of additional tourism development, and then adopting and implementing a suitable management strategy, host communities can either avoid or substantially mitigate adverse impacts. But have communities in fact been harmed by inadequate management strategies? The answer, unfortunately, is a resounding "yes."

Our computer database searches of thousands of English language publications throughout the world since 1995 produced thousands of articles reflecting adverse impacts from tourism,[19] in situations where appropriate mitigation strategies were either not in place or not adequately implemented. The breadth and seriousness of most of these reported impacts are distressing, although perhaps not surprising in light of many highly publicized problems—overbuilding of the Costa Brava, Spain, coastline; water pollution in the Bay of Acapulco, Mexico, and in the Adriatic Sea; and unhealthy air pollution and major traffic problems in Katmandu, Nepal. Other examples are discussed in more detail on the following pages.

Thailand

An unusually candid 1993 government memorandum[20] from the Tourist Authority of Thailand (TAT) discussed a disturbing litany of adverse impacts on the natural,[21] as well as the social and cultural environments, throughout Thailand that resulted from poorly or unmanaged tourism growth.[22] These "problematic conditions" were generated over thirty years of economic and social expansion, when strong growth of the tourism industry was a key element of the government's approach to national development. In fact, recites the memorandum, "(t)ourism has become and been deservedly recognized as the economic activity that generates the highest revenue in foreign exchange earnings for several consecutive years."[23]

The TAT memorandum very pointedly categorized the negative impacts brought upon by unchecked tourism in Thailand.[24]

1. *Deterioration of tourist destinations and pollution.* Visitor sites became dirty and degraded. Pollution in many forms abounded: water degradation, discolored beaches, and stench from garbage and traffic, all of which were "injurious to the visitors' health and induced psychological distress and displeasure to them. Tourists left with a negative impression and had no wish to make a repeat visit."

2. *Encroachment on public land.* Commercial tourism development was located on public mountains, islands, beaches, and forests without valid legal title or permission. Additionally, some developers improperly expanded existing tourism uses onto adjoining public lands.

3. *Buildings and structures.* Scenic integrity and quality were compromised by illegal building that did not comply with code requirements as to height, quality, and open space, particularly around two popular beach regions and one culturally attractive city in the north. Some buildings were illegally and insensitively sited in locations where they were out of scale and disfigured the natural contours and features of the land. Additionally, building had "mushroomed in complete chaos, resulting in a jumbled sea of eyesores"; examples included beer bars in the previously peaceful beach areas of Phuket and Ko Samui, as well as shopping stalls and arcades next to Chiang Mai temples and archeological sites.

4. *Development of infrastructure and facilities without regard to the environment.* This set of problems involved improper filling of waterways, roads constructed too close to the coastline or through mangrove forests, and soil disturbances (e.g., excavation) causing subsidences and silt accumulations to the detriment of natural ecosystems and geography.

5. *Commercial sex.* Tourism growth triggered substantial increases in this industry, even

though it "has been with the Thai society for a long time." The increase in such activities brought with it disease (e.g., STD and AIDS), drug use, crime, and child prostitution.

6. *Crime.* Urban communities experienced increasing crime against tourists.
7. *Unequal emphasis on area development.* Improvements to infrastructure and facilities, such as electricity and roads, were provided to tourist hubs rather than to nontourist locations.
8. *Other negative impacts.* There were a number of other problem areas related to or caused by unmanaged tourism growth: unfair exploitation of tourists (e.g., extortion and unconscionably high prices); manipulation of traditional culture (e.g., neglecting the "intimate meaning" of cultural elements and instead presenting the culture in "outward, dazzling display and performance"); decline in the quality of artifacts and handicrafts; and occasional hostility between tourists and the local population where tourists behaved in ways that are offensive to residents.[25]

These negative impacts illustrate the types of problems[26] that can occur in the absence of an effective tourism growth management strategy, especially in a destination experiencing significant growth. Failure to mitigate the negative impacts of tourism is not limited to developing countries, however. Nor is it limited to suddenly popular destinations. We turn now to other examples of negative impacts, not because we believe them to be inevitable, but only to illustrate briefly the breadth of potential problems that destination communities frequently face.[27]

Gatlinburg, Tennessee

One of America's most visited natural areas (ten million visitors in 1997) is the Great Smokey Mountains National Park in North Carolina and Tennessee. An excellent study of commercial development in communities near national parks, *Balancing Nature and Commerce in Gateway Communities*, addressed the degradation of the gateways to the "Smokies":

> Haphazard development of private land in the shadow the Great Smokey Mountain National Park also takes its toll on the region's magnificent scenery and natural resources. The roads into the Smokey Mountains are lined with bumper-to-bumper traffic and hundreds of billboards. In Gatlinburg (Tennessee) views of the Smokies have been marred by an observation tower, scores of high-rise condominium developments, an aerial tramway, and a fifteen-story hotel, which, while boasting of its "spectaculars views," spoils the view for everyone else. . . . Worse are the impacts that development has on the park's wildlife—the original attraction for visitors . . . the rush to find building sites near the park has sealed off important migration corridors necessary for the bears to reach feeding grounds.[28]

Pequot Reservation, Connecticut

The gambling casino that the Native American Mashantucket Pequots have built on their reservation in Connecticut attracts some twenty-five million visitors per year, mimicking the effect of a twenty-four-hour shopping mall. Despite the casino's success resulting in reduced unemployment rates, fewer applications for food stamps, and enormous income for the tribe, there have been unanticipated negative economic impacts. There has been a 300 percent increase in traffic around the casino, and public safety, traffic, and legal expenses have all increased. The Pequots have had to pay for road-widening and sign projects on state roads; create a public transit system to shuttle employees as far as ten miles from home to work as well as to carry visitors from the train and ferry stations on the coast; and establish police, emergency, and fire department resources.[29]

Fort William, Scotland

Fort William, Scotland, has faced annoying noise pollution from pubs blasting Gaelic songs to attract passing tourists. Town elected officials unsuccessfully sought to pass a new local ordinance banning all loud music, which would include this noisy form of advertising, but local pub owners asserted that the officials were undermining the Gaelic culture: "What an insult. All we're trying to do is to promote the Gaelic and that was the response we get from the town council. The tourists love hearing the music belting out, that's why they come to the Highlands—to get a taste of the culture."[30]

Fort Lauderdale, Florida

The city of Fort Lauderdale, Florida, for many years was invaded by huge crowds of rowdy college students on Spring Break from college. They often slept four or five in a single motel room, drank to excess on the beaches and elsewhere, failed to place garbage in receptacles (or found that the trash barrels were filled), resisted efforts of local police to keep order, and generally overwhelmed the city. This understandably caused the flight of quieter, older, and more affluent tourists. Finally the influx abated, partly as the result of city efforts and partly because of changes in what the fad-conscious students regarded as the trendier destinations (e.g., South Padre Island in Texas and Cancun, Mexico).

Moab, Utah

The Utah town of Moab, population 5,000, has undergone profound transformation as the result of exploding tourism. Cliffs, canyons, and buttes characterize this high desert area, which (especially when the county in-season population grows to 16,000) well deserves its sobriquet as "mountain biking capital of the world." But the negative impacts have been considerable.

Behavior of some visitors has been appalling: in what is now known locally as the "Sands Flat Massacre" in 1993, thousands of drunk college students used parkland trees for firewood and a group of boaters needing wood to roast hot dogs, destroyed roof beams of an ancient Native American dwelling. Major crime increased by 155 percent from 1982 to 1995. There are many accommodations and food service outlets, but few stores selling such essentials as children's clothing. The cost of living, including property taxes, has increased greatly (partially, of course, as the result of a increase in property values, which local residents should find beneficial). In view of all of these impacts, one might well agree with an elected official who in 1995 remarked, "Community leaders went fishing for a little tourism to revive and diversify our economy, and they hooked a great white shark. This monster has swamped the boat and eaten the crew.[31]

Taming Tourism by Managing Its Growth

The goal of any sensible community should be to maximize the benefits and minimize the risks of tourism. We believe that this can be done and that tourism can be "tamed" by carefully managing its growth. Every community is unique, and no tourist destination is a replica of another. The combination of qualities that attract visitors to one destination is never precisely duplicated anywhere else. But the goals of each destination are the same: to secure those benefits that the community most desires; to avoid those impacts that the community deems harmful; to share the benefits and burdens in an equitable way; and to be resilient enough to adapt the chosen strategy to future changes.

Before we proceed with our analysis of how destination communities can achieve these goals, we need to clarify what it is we mean by "tourism," "tourist," and the "host" or "destination community."

Scholars working in the many subspecialties of tourism studies have for years devoted time and thought to an issue of only modest import to travelers themselves: how properly to define the term "tourism." Numerous technical articles and books have sensibly pointed out that analysis of tourism (including its statistical measurement) must be grounded on a baseline understanding of what is being analyzed. It is not our role here to enter the academic fray of definitional disagreements. For our purposes, we adopt the early definition of "tourism" offered in an influential 1982 work by leading academics Alister Mathieson and Geoffrey Wall entitled *Tourism: Economic, Physical and Social Impacts:* "Tourism is the temporary movement of people to destinations outside their normal places of work and residence, the activities undertaken during their stay in those destinations, and the facilities created to cater to their needs."[32]

The issue of which persons should be regarded as "tourists" is an exercise undertaken more recently by tourism consultant Thomas L. Davidson. He regards a "tourist" as "a person travelling outside of his/her normal routine—either normal living or normal working routine—who spends money."[33] Included in that definition would be the traditional leisure traveler (whether on a group tour, individual trip, or family vacation) as well as business and convention visitors outside their normal territory. We view the term "tourist" in a similarly broad context.

As to "community," sociologists and other academics have for years and in many different contexts addressed how to define and analyze the nuances of this term. We do not wish to add to the ongoing scholarly debate but merely to clarify how we are using the concept in the context of strategies for managing tourism growth.

We begin with the notion of a tourism "destination," which is itself susceptible to multiple interpretations.[34] We adopt the definition of Canadian geography professor Peter Murphy: "To be a destination an area must attract non-local visitors, people who have traveled some distance from their homes to see the attractions or use the facilities."[35] Thus, in the geographical sense, a "destination" can be national or regional in scope but will, in most situations, be smaller and local in scale.

We use the term "community" to mean the persons and public and private bodies who are potentially affected, both positively and negatively, by the impacts of tourism development[36] within the boundaries of the destination area.[37] How to determine the boundaries of a destination area and how to identify the groups that make up the destination community are issues addressed more fully in the following chapter.

2

Planning for Tourism Growth

Consider the community of Whistler, British Columbia. Until the early 1970s it was a remote backwoods outpost. Today it is one of Canada's most successful tourist destinations. The process by which it reached its current status provides an example of how one community developed a plan for tourism growth. Over more than twenty years, an active community participation process evolved to develop a strategy to manage tourism growth in Whistler, to monitor the efficacy of the strategy to mitigate the impacts of continuing development, and to amend the strategy to respond to changing conditions.

From Outpost to Destination

The scenic beauty surrounding Whistler, located about seventy-five miles north of Vancouver, has been attracting visitors for almost one hundred years. Early tourism was limited largely to Canadians who enjoyed trapping and fishing, were willing to ride in on horseback or take the train, and were content to stay in one of the small boarding houses, cabins, or lodges scattered around the lakes or at the base of the Coast Mountains. Then in 1965, the highway connecting Whistler with Vancouver was completed and the first ski lift was constructed. Since then, the resident population has grown from a modest 250 to over 7,400; and Whistler has become a world-class, year-round destination mountain resort, with approximately 1.5 million tourist visits a year.

Soon after the dramatic growth began, residents of what was then known as Alta Lake, including those involved in businesses serving tourists, grew concerned about the tourism pressures facing the area in and around Whistler and the neighboring Blackcomb Mountains and the potential impacts of unmanaged growth. Local lobbying efforts led to the incorporation of the Resort Municipality Whistler in 1975. The new 12,630 hectare (31,209 acre) municipality was granted broad powers to regulate land-uses within its borders, including tourism development. Since that time, Whistler has set a remarkable example of a successful relationship of process and substance. The municipality has for over twenty years had an active and evolving public community participation process that has resulted in a carefully crafted, and continually monitored, growth management strategy that responds to community needs and goals. We will discuss here the process used in Whistler, and in Chapter 5 (p. 162) we will look at the substance of the strategies Whistler has adopted to manage its dramatic growth.

In the early 1970s, the population was relatively small (five hundred), with few distinct constituencies. There was thus a generally uniform desire to adopt a mechanism for controlling the pace of growth and for channeling development into a high-quality tourist product. These were the very goals that had prompted the lobbying efforts for incorporation. In 1976, the first Official Community Plan reflected the wishes of the fairly homogenous Whistler community. The few objections to the plan focused on the moratorium it placed on development in areas other than what would become the center of development, Whistler Village. Even this limited opposition abated, however, when the municipality offered trade-off opportunities to the affected landowners.

As Whistler grew, second-home owners, resident-entrepreneurs, and seasonal workers created new constituencies whose interests diverged to a greater degree than when the population was more homogenous. The municipality responded to these changes by expanding the forums for public participation in an effort to ensure significant levels of participation by all affected parties. By the 1980s, the municipality undertook a Community Facility Requirement Study. Based on the results of the study, the municipality built an ice arena, a swimming pool, a library, and medical facilities.

By the early 1990s, the municipality was providing additional opportunities for public involvement in the planning process: public information meetings, public hearings, small group meetings, "living-room" discussions, workshops, and open houses. The greatest expansion of channels for community participation came with the 1994 Official Community Plan, which essentially provided that new development would be approved *only* if it (a) provided substantial benefits to the community and resort; (b) was supported by the community; and (c) would not cause unacceptable impacts on the community, resort, or environment. In order to evaluate the existing condition of the community and to be able to determine which impacts from proposed developments might be unacceptable and which might provide desired benefits, the 1994 plan instituted a formal public consultation process that included two new elements: the community and resort monitoring program and the annual town hall meeting.

The comprehensive monitoring program was designed to "provide the information that allows the community to measure how it is changing and, more importantly, to predict how it will change in the future if there is additional population growth, development, and visitation."[1] Each year the program gathers a wealth of data concerning residential and commercial development; social aspects of the community; quality of the environment, community facilities, and infrastructure; the tourism and business market; transportation; resident and visitor satisfaction;[2] and regional trends. Information on specific measurable indicators for each of these topics is included in the report.[3] Statistics are included for previous years (often back to the 1980s), providing even more information.

An extensive resident survey is hand delivered to all residents (over 2,200 households) with a high return rate in 1995 of 30 percent. Its main objective is to monitor social and attitudinal changes of residents. Developed in conjunction with academic experts, the survey covers such topics as evaluations of aspects of community life in Whistler, ratings of community services, attitudes toward tourism issues, level of support for development, and development priorities. Responses to each question are broken down between permanent residents and second-home residents.

This information, along with the other findings, is made public in the final report of the monitoring program. An important section of the report highlights the findings and identifies significant issues for the community to consider. Based on community feedback, refinements are made to the monitoring program itself. In 1996, for example, the monitoring system included requested information on trail line counts and fish and wildlife habitat inventories and undertook new studies concerning affordable housing and unique land acquisition. The community also embarked on a "community visioning process," an exercise that has now been incorporated into the monitoring program.

A well-attended annual town meeting is held each October to discuss the findings of the monitoring program, the related policy implications, and the directions the community might take in the following year. At the meeting, the community addresses four primary questions: (1) whether any additional development is appropriate and in the best interests of the long-term vision for the community and the resort; (2) what is the single most important short-term issue facing Whistler; (3) how to improve the monitoring system and the town meeting process; and (4) how to measure and ensure that protection of the natural environment is actually achieved. The community also decides whether any new development should be approved in return for community amenities. If necessary, a second town meeting is held later in the year to discuss implementation of the priorities agreed upon for the municipality over the next few years.

Whistler's community participation process has evolved to ensure a continuous—and well publicized—flow of information among those parties with an interest in managing tourism growth in the municipality: the government, the residents (including second-home owners), developers, employees, and visitors. Information that comes from the process then informs the substance of the strategies and regulatory mechanisms that the municipality adopts.

One of the most significant results of the wide dissemination of shared information has been that Whistler's planning efforts have attained a high degree of community confidence. People know that they have specific and objective information on which they can make their own judgments; they have the opportunity to participate in making decisions about what tourism development will be permitted (based on whether the benefits it brings are important enough to the community or whether its impacts are unacceptable); and they have the opportunity to recommend changes each year to amend either the process or the substance to respond to changing circumstances. The community appears to believe that the process is both fair and effective.

Tourism Resources

Whistler is a good example of a community whose planning process demonstrates an appreciation of the community's tourism resources. Tourism resources can be defined as whatever attracts tourists.[4] What attracts tourists to Whistler? A good highway, ski lifts, and modern hotels are obvious answers. But they aren't the complete answer. You can't get lots of tourists to visit every place that provides these facilities, as many communities have learned at great cost.

Whistler provides more. It has beautiful scenery, favorable climate, aesthetically harmonious appearance, friendly service, clean air, and an ambiance that is very hard to define but easy to like. Unlike the hotels, the ski lifts, and the highways, these assets of Whistler are not owned either by the public or private sector. They are "common-pool resources," shared by all but owned by no one.

Most tourism destinations have learned through experience which resources seem to attract tourists.[5] Watch their ads. Advertising agencies design their material on the basis of experience with the things that motivate tourists to visit a place. Looking at tourism advertising makes it apparent that many of the resources tourists seek are neither private nor public, but are common-pool resources that are shared by everyone.

Advertisers assume that visitors to Tahiti, for example, prize crystalline water, sparkling air, and the languorous atmosphere of the tropics. These three resources are essential to a successful tourism industry in Tahiti, but no one owns them in the conventional sense. They are assets shared by all. Similarly, Britain is currently seeking to revise the image it presents to tourists. The current government objects to the emphasis on aristocratic history and seeks to promote "mod" images such as trendy design and rock music. But both the old and new images are neither privately nor publicly owned—they are assets broadly shared among all the British people.

Tourism is highly dependent on these kinds of common-pool resources.[6] Because the word "common" has so many meanings, we sometimes prefer to use "shared resources" or "shared assets" in describing common-pool resources.[7] Some shared resources are national or even worldwide in their scope (for example, think of the ozone layer).[8] But most tourism resources are quite localized. The attractive features of Sorrento, for example, are quite different from those of the Amalfi coast or Capri, even though they are only a few miles apart.

The tourism industry develops resources like these: the view of the Amalfi cliffs, the memories of the Beatles, the lazy image of Tahiti. The idea of development of resources usually brings to mind the conversion of iron ore to steel or the harvest of lumber and paper from a forest. The tourism industry uses steel, wood, and paper as well, but above all it develops the less tangible aspects of a place that give it whatever special appeal it has.

Development of resources means making them more useful to humans. It is said that the facility to develop resources is a genetic trait that distinguishes the human race from other forms of life. But the ability to manage the development of resources in an efficient and sustainable manner is something that needs to be learned. And some people, in some places, have learned a lot more easily than others.

Because most tourism resources are of a localized nature, strategies to manage tourism growth should be locally based. And because so many tourism resources are likely to be common-pool resources rather than public or private property, experience with the management of such resources is essential to local communities seeking to develop a management strategy.

In analyzing tourism resources, it is important to remember that the common-pool resources that attract tourists are usually also valued highly by the local residents. People who reside in a place typically choose to live there because they like the "quality of life," a term that covers everything from the color of the sunset to the regularity of pickup football games. Residents and tourists need to share these resources in a mutually beneficial way, which requires a cooperative attitude on both sides. In the book *Vacationscape*, Clare Gunn notes that tourism developers often forget that many of the things that they create will be used by both visitors and residents, and that to "satisfy both requires considerable communicative exchange and often diplomatic compromise."[9] Moreover, the sharing needs to be intergenerational as well.[10] The residents need to see how tourism can help make the place better for their descendants. And the tourists ought to leave with the hope that their children and grandchildren might someday enjoy the same experience that they have had.

It has frequently been observed, however, that the sharing of resources held in common isn't easy. The difficulties are sometimes described as a "tragedy of the commons." In 1968, California ecologist Garrett Hardin wrote one of the most influential articles ever written in the environmental field—a short essay for *Science* magazine entitled "The Tragedy of the Commons," calling for international cooperation to reduce world population growth. He compared by analogy the problem of overpopulation to an inevitable failure of peasants to prevent overgrazing of common lands because each individual peasant would stand to benefit by grazing one more cow, despite that cow's contribution to the overall malnutrition of the herd. From his parable, Hardin drew the conclusion that we must "explicitly exorcize" the "invisible hand" when dealing with problems involving commons. For those commons that could not be privatized, he favored "coercion."

Hardin was not the first person to call attention to the problems of resources held in common. Economists had occasionally commented on the issue earlier, but their work had attracted little attention among economists or other social scientists. Hardin's essay, however, struck a chord among both scholars and the public. Few metaphorical creatures have proved to be more powerful than Hardin's poor peasants and their cattle. They have become the players in one of the most commonly quoted parables of our time. Almost everyone familiar with these issues knows about the tragedy of the commons.

But Hardin's thesis has been challenged by recent studies of the management of commonly owned property. Researchers have sometimes found a lot of fat and happy cattle grazing on common lands. Was Hardin wrong?

Studies on Common-Pool Resources

All kinds of common-pool resources, whether used for tourism or any other purpose, present certain similar management problems. A new field of research into the management of shared resources has grown up in the last decade or so. This research tries to overcome the difficulties that have historically attended the management of common property. Beginning in the 1980s, scholars in a variety of fields began to undertake extensive empirical research into the operation of common-pool resource systems. In some cases they found that Hardin's tragedy had indeed occurred, but in other instances they found systems of managing common property that appeared to be working well.

For example, a study of common grazing lands in Morocco found a highly complex body of rules that had evolved out of agreements to resolve conflicting claims of nearby villages and tribes. By strictly limiting the seasons of use, the rules allowed the surrounding Berber communities to maintain a highly productive and sustainable resource in common ownership.[11]

Similarly, ocean fisheries have long been cited as a classic example of the tragedy of the commons. Fish are common-pool resources—shared assets that are available to all. Examples of disastrous overfishing are all around us, and the fact that ocean resources are held in common has aggravated the problem. Nevertheless, despite the continuing seriousness of the worldwide problem of overfishing, in some coastal communities the management of ocean fisheries has provided sustainable yields and prosperous fishing businesses. In Alanya, Turkey, for example, the fishermen all gather in the coffeehouse each September and draw lots for one of a series of numbered fishing spots along the shore. During the forthcoming season, each participating fisherman moves each day to the next location to the east, thus giving each an equal opportunity at the best sites.[12]

Many of the common-pool resource studies have looked at third world locations where customary law has been predominant. But other studies have found similar examples in highly developed countries such as Switzerland.[13] In the Alpine regions, effective rules for the management of common grazing land have been adopted through the highly formal processes that are characteristic of the Swiss system with its emphasis on direct democracy.[14] Other studies reached similar conclusions in modern American settings. For example, a study of several groundwater systems in semiarid portions of California concluded that locally accepted and managed regulations can sometimes control sharing behavior effectively.[15]

Systems of common-pool resource management not only span the globe, but they also span the centuries. For example, Richard W. Judd's recent history of common land in New England cites many such systems that date back to the first half of the nineteenth century and earlier.[16] It is not the systems that are new, it is the study of them in a coordinated manner.

Empirical research involving currently operating shared resource management systems has now attracted the attention of social scientists of many disciplines. But most of this research is still in an early stage. The authors of studies of these systems include James M. Acheson, Arun Agrawal, Fikret Berkes, William Blomquist, Daniel W. Bromley, Susan J.B. Cox, Jere L. Gilles, A. P. Lino Grima, Susan Hanna, Gary D. Libecap, Bonnie J. McCay, Margaret A. McKean, Mohan Munasinghe, Ronald J. Oakerson, Elinor Ostrom, Samuel G. Pooley, C. Ford Runge, Shui Yan Tang, Glenn G. Stevenson, Ralph E. Townsend, and Michael D. Young. (See the endnotes for citations to specific works.) These works include such disciplines as anthropology, ecology, economics, geography, marine biology, political science, and sociology.

Most of this research began within the last ten or fifteen years. It is somewhat premature for a definitive summary of the research findings, but some tentative conclusions can at least be drawn from those published to date. In the United States' experience to date with growth management systems, some strategies for common-pool resource management have proved to be successful, while others have played out the tragedy that Hardin anticipated. So the tragedy of the commons is a possible—even frequent—result when resources are held in common, but it is evidently not a necessary result.

To say that the studies found that some of the systems for managing shared resources were successful raises the question of how one should define success. Different research programs have defined success in different ways, sometimes only implicitly. We propose a four-factor test that is generally consistent with the objectives identified by most of the research programs.

Management Objectives for Common Resources

The goal of a successful common resource management system can be achieved if the following objectives are attained: equity, sustainability, efficiency, and resilience.[17]

Equity

An *equitable* system is one that is perceived as fair by most potential participants. Users of common-pool resources have a natural tendency to worry about what other users are doing. To create a perception of equity, a management system must overcome these worries. As Elinor Ostrom puts it, each individual must be assured "that he or she will not be the 'sucker' who cooperates" while others do not.[18]

And to understand people's perception of equity, Daniel Bromley reminds us that we need to be aware that history may give certain people more reason than others to suspect that the system is inequitable.[19] Past legacies of discrimination may mean that it will take real effort to convince some groups that a system is fair. Ostrom cites a study of an irrigation system that was poorly managed. The downstream landowners were uncooperative because they believed that the upstream landowners were taking more than their share of the water.[20]

On the other hand, Gary Libecap has pointed out that groups who believe that their past successes in appropriating common resources reflect their greater diligence may believe that such diligence should be recognized. Resolving such disputes may be made more difficult by unequal access to relevant information and by puffing on both sides.[21]

Considerations of equity in tourism planning vary greatly with the makeup of the local population, as the case studies illustrate. But in places as diverse as Bermuda (p. 144), and Aspen, Colorado (p. 167), planners have successfully dealt with issues of equity in developing strategies for managing tourism growth.

Sustainability

A *sustainable* system is one that protects the resource for future generations. The idea of sustainable growth is supported by people of many differing views because the concept is so loosely defined. In general, a system is sustainable if it is "basically conservative in the way resources are utilized" with an emphasis on "taking what is needed" and "social sanctions against excessive individual gain."[22]

Sustainability can be tested by observing changes in the quality or quantity of the resource, although such changes may be heavily influenced by changing environmental conditions that are beyond human control. But attitude is what counts. Michael Young and Bonnie McCay call for a "strong sense of stewardship" through which "resource users prefer potential long-term benefits to short-term, opportunistic gains."[23] Zbigniew Mieczkowski argues that the creation of a symbiotic relationship between tourism and natural resources promotes sustainable resource use.[24]

The communities discussed in the case studies in Chapters 4–6 have all give consideration to the need for sustainability. Examples worth particular note are Sanibel Island, Florida (p. 137), and South Pembrokeshire, Wales (p. 254).

In general, the necessary attitude is a recognition that resources are not purely private. Carol Rose postulates that if the users of a resource recognize that it has elements of a "public-good," they may develop a system of careful common management that "permits some individual consumption at an appropriately low level but aims primarily at conserving the bulk of the resource as a whole, for the common benefit of the entire collectivity of users."[25]

Efficiency

An *efficient* system is one that produces enough value for the effort expended that it results in considerable economic benefit, though perhaps nowhere near perfection on an economist's typical scale of efficiency. It is often impossible, notes C. Ford Runge, to "do the precise technical and economic calculations necessary to determine whether aggregate use of the commons is optimal," particularly because the "costs of obtaining collective action" may suggest "that some degree of suboptimal use may actually be efficient."[26] Ostrom's study of irrigation districts in the Philippines has shown that landowners may often reject incremental improvements in efficiency where the transaction costs of achieving them seem too burdensome.[27]

Forecasts of the economic impact of tourism are notoriously unreliable, and a pessimist might argue that in many countries the prospect of dramatic economic improvement is so remote that "perhaps we should not worry overly much about improving incomes" but about "preventing incomes from continuing to decline because of resource degradation."[28] Nevertheless, most communities have at least some reason to hope that tourism growth may bring economic benefits that outweigh its costs.

Many case studies illustrate a wide variety of ways to promote economic efficiency in tourism management, from dispersal (the Republic of Maldives, p. 215) to concentration (Bruges, Belgium, p. 237).

Resiliency

A *resilient* system is one that has demonstrated a capability to respond to changing environmental conditions. Resilience is an ecological concept that can also be applied, Young and McCay suggest, to "the capacity of an institutional system to continue to function in the face of new and different circumstances."[29]

The prospect of potential climate change, together with unpredictable fluctuations in the global economy, makes long-range planning difficult. Decision makers, says Susan Hanna, need to have "the appropriate incentives" to take into account "equilibrium shifts" and "make the appropriate trade-off between the social costs and benefits to society at large."[30]

To be resilient, a management system needs good procedural rules for changing the substantive rules. For example, McCay's historical study of oystering in New Jersey illustrates the difficulty of maintaining workable systems for managing common resources that are particularly susceptible to random or cyclical changes in the environment.[31]

Many of the case studies in this book illustrate resiliency in the management of tourism growth. The Lake Tahoe Regional Planning Agency (p. 91) and the Great Barrier Marine Park in Australia (p. 115), for example, have continuously adapted their management strategies to changing environmental conditions.

These objectives are far from precise, and there is room to argue about their exact meaning and about whether additional objectives should be considered. However, there seems to be sufficient agreement on the general outlines of these objectives that they can be used to evaluate tentatively what works and what doesn't.

No attempt has been made to quantify the extent to which systems having the characteristics discussed in the next section meet these objectives. Judgment about the kinds of systems that seem to work are merely hypotheses that will undoubtedly be revised as research progresses, but at this stage they seem to be shared by most of the people familiar with the field.

Characteristics of Successful Strategies

Most of the research in successful strategies for common-pool resource management contains common elements important to success. A review of these conclusions suggests that successful strategies for managing common-pool resources are likely to have the following six components (which we will apply to tourism management strategies in the next section).

Define the Boundaries Clearly

Strategies for managing common-pool resources must clearly identify the resources and their location. For purposes of analysis, some set of physical boundaries must be posited, says Ronald Oakerson, even if ambiguous, and the boundaries should "derive from nature and technology" rather than being imposed by legal rule.[32] Only if the boundaries are "consistent with the natural boundaries of the ecological system" will decision making be fully effective, Hanna suggests.[33]

Boundary definition may need to be temporal as well as spatial. Jere Gilles and his colleagues, who studied the use of common pasture land on the slopes of Morocco's Atlas Mountains, concluded that the key to success was the setting of strict seasonal entry and exit dates for use of the pasture because these rules preserved the sustainability of the pasture and were easy to enforce.[34]

Identify Permitted Users of the Resource

Those individuals who have a right to use the resources should be clearly specified. For example, in a study conducted in six villages located in the middle Himalayan ranges in Northern India, Arun Agrawal examined how small councils of farmer–leaders regulated the use of fodder and fuel wood in community forests. He concluded that "rules that limit who can use a forest" are among the most important components of a workable system.[35] Agrawal concluded that strong institutions were needed to administer "boundary and authority rules determining who can use how much from a resource."[36]

Rules that define permitted users must be clear and well understood. Resource users will not have an interest in cooperative management, says Elinor Ostrom, unless they know that they can enforce limits on the number of people who can use the resource.[37] All successful strategies for managing shared resources, Fikret Berkes found, "are characterized by the presence of arrangements for allocation of the resource among co-owners."[38]

Encourage Repetitive Users

When participants in a system of sharing resources know that they are going to be dealing with the same people again and again, they are more likely to obey the rules. One of the prerequisites for "major, long-term collective action," Ostrom states, is "extensive common knowledge" about "the types of individuals with whom they would be interacting over the long run. . . ."[39]

Repetitive users will be more concerned about sustainability. When "the biological limits of the resource have been learnt [sic] by experience" of repeated users, the "community has a built-in incentive" to stay well within those limits.[40] While if "assurance to future claims to resource benefits is absent, no incentive exists to limit current use."[41]

Game theory postulates that players who anticipate that a game will continue indefinitely will be more likely to cooperate with each other than those who perceive their participation as temporary.[42] Ostrom's game-playing simulations of common-resource problems found that the ability to communicate continually with other repeated players resulted in even more cooperative behavior than game theory had predicted.[43]

Let the Users Participate in Making the Rules

Users of common-pool resources typically have their own perspective that needs to be taken into account. If all users feel that they are represented in the process of managing the asset, they are more likely to comply with and enforce the rules necessary to manage the asset. As Margaret McKean pointed out in her study of common lands in Yamanashi Prefecture, Japan, "the villagers themselves invented the regulations, enforced them, and meted out punishments. It is not necessary, then, for regulation of the commons to be imposed coercively or from the outside."[44]

User participation helps efficiency as well as equity. In Hanna's economic terminology, user participation can improve efficiency by providing "supplemental nontechnical knowledge" that reduces information costs and can improve compliance by creating a sense of "management legitimacy."[45]

Localize the Rules as Much as Possible

Because any particular resource is likely to differ from any other, even within the same category, the rules applicable to each shared resource should be tailored to local conditions to the greatest extent possible. For example, Bonnie McCay found that "the 'turn and turn about' customs of the shad fishers of the Delaware are examples of particular and enduring solutions to conflict and congestion problems, sanctioned by the Legislature but clearly local and crafted by the fishing industry."[46]

Localizing rules increases resiliency. When conditions change, local rules can be adapted to the new conditions more quickly than rules applicable to larger areas. Berkes points out that a recognition of the need to localize rules to reflect "ecosystem and social-system variation" implies a willingness to decentralize administration. This "involves a major shift in the role of resource-management agencies and bureaucracies unaccustomed to sharing power." Nevertheless, he argues, such a change in attitude may be necessary if the advantages of user participation are to be realized.[47]

Monitor and Mediate Rule Violations

If rules are to be workable, people must know both that they will be enforced and that disputes about their application can be resolved without undue expenditure of time and money. Equity requires, says Berkes, mutually agreed upon rules that provide an efficient means of conflict resolution with a minimum of internal strife or conflict.[48]

In Agrawal's Himalayan study, he concluded that in addition to the need for "(1) boundary rules . . ." (discussed above), there was a need for "(2) effective monitoring of rules, (3) sanctioning of violators who break rules, and (4) arbitration of disputes among monitors, users, and managers." The villages that best conserved their fodder and fuel resources had such rules, whereas the least successful ones "did not create appropriation rules that could prevent users from overexploiting and degrading resources." Nor did they create adequate institutions to monitor and enforce what rules they did have.[49]

Where the users of a resource have participated in making the rules for its use, they are often the most reliable monitors and mediators to administer the rules. Shui Yan Tang found that where irrigation projects use unpaid and part-time local farmers for enforcement, they "are more proactive and rule conformance is more predictable than when full-time external government agents are the guards."[50]

Lino Grima and Fikret Berkes suggest that the research on common property management has produced a broad agreement on monitoring and enforcement methods, although it is often masked by terminology differences. "Regulation, monitoring, policing and enforcement—all these are elements of 'mutual coercion.' The rhetoric of the ecological romantics and the hard-nosed economists differ; the instruments for allocating rights-to-use are quite similar."[51]

Processes Tailored for Community Tourism Planning

Our examination of the efforts of hundreds of places to manage tourism growth has led us to observe that although each strategy is "tailor made" to the needs of a specific destination community, the processes by which successful strategies evolve have common characteristics, and these characteristics are similar to those identified by the studies in common-pool resource management discussed earlier. The processes that are most successful in producing equity, sustainability, efficiency, and resiliency are those that (1) define clearly the boundaries of the affected area; (2) identify the players; (3) let the players make the rules;

(4) localize the rules as much as possible; (5) give the players a sense of permanence; and (6) monitor and mediate violations of the rules efficiently but effectively.

Define Boundaries Clearly

Any strategy for planning tourism resources needs a clear definition of the resources and their location so that well-recognized boundaries can be drawn. Meaningful planning is not possible if the boundaries of the planning area are forever changing. For example, a community that seeks to preserve historic areas that are attractive to tourists needs to clearly identify those areas in which the historic character needs to be maintained. In Whistler, British Columbia (see Chapter 5), the bowl into which geography placed the community created the logical planning boundary, but sometimes the definition of resource boundaries is more complex. The case studies in Chapters 4–6 will illustrate the way that boundary selection often proves to be an important factor in devising a solution to a problem.

Identifying tourism resources is the first step. To define manageable boundaries, it is important to understand the special qualities of the area that attract tourists. Sometimes, the attractive qualities of an area are obvious, but not always. The art deco buildings in Napier, New Zealand, went unnoticed for many years until a group of citizens recognized their potential as a tourism asset. Sanibel Island, Florida (p. 137), has had a particularly difficult time pinpointing the resources that make it so attractive. Its wide beaches with their abundant seashells, its easily accessible wildlife refuge, and its favorable climate are obvious attractions. But to many seasonal visitors these assets are secondary to the peaceful lifestyle that results from factors less easily identified. Similarly, tourists to Ambergris Caye in Belize (p. 178) appear to be drawn by the sandy roads of San Pedro and the laid-back atmosphere of the island just as much as by the scuba diving, snorkeling, and cooling tradewinds.

Identification of areas impacted by tourism development will help determine appropriate boundaries. In some instances, enlarging the boundaries of the resource area led to a solution. In Canterbury (p. 211), for example, the problem of overcrowding in the cathedral was seen, not just as a problem to be solved within its walls, but as a problem for the historic district as a whole.

In other situations, narrowing the area's boundaries has led to the desired result. In the Indonesian government's plan for Bali (p. 232), the boundary selection process served the purpose of narrowing the scope of the impacted area rather than broadening it. The assets to be shared with the tourists were the beaches and the climate, but not the privacy of the Balinese. By concentrating tourism in Bali in a particular district, the plan reduced the impact of the tourists on the traditional lifestyle of the Bali residents.

New laws may sometimes be needed to resolve boundary issues. For Lake Tahoe, defining the boundary of the planning area was the crucial decision that made it possible to define a plan that preserves the key resource. Prior to the creation of the Tahoe Regional Planning Agency (TRPA), with a jurisdiction limited to the watershed of the lake, the lake served merely as the boundary for a group of large California and Nevada counties. No single county was the seat of power or held a concentration of population within the Tahoe Basin, so the lake was largely ignored until the Tahoe Regional Planning Agency was created with a jurisdiction limited to the basin (p. 91).

Interlocal agreements may be used to define boundaries for new planning areas that do not conform to any existing jurisdictional or zoning borders. When Park City, Utah, was experiencing development pressure, it entered into an Interlocal Planning Agreement with

Summit County that allows Park City to annex additional land and creates cooperative planning arrangements for any remaining unincorporated land in the area requiring regulation (p. 79). The town of Jackson and Teton County joined in a similar cooperative effort after they had begun independent planning processes. Both town and county came to the realization that growth and its impacts on transportation, air and water quality, affordable housing, and wildlife habitats do not respect jurisdictional boundaries. Recognizing their interdependence, the two worked together to develop a joint comprehensive plan (p. 85).

Identify the Players

Studies of the allocation of common-pool resources have concluded that those individuals who have a right to use the resources should be clearly identified. If a "tragedy of the commons" is to be avoided, people need to develop confidence that the value of the resources will not be so diluted by an ever-expanding pool of users that there is no point in conserving resources for the future. For tourism development to be sustainable for future generations, the negative impacts of tourism development must not be so severe that the destination community loses the very qualities and assets that attract people to live and visit there.

There is no scientific method for identifying who should be included in the community planning process. The legitimate players vary from community to community and from culture to culture. In parts of Asia where respect for authority and the wisdom of the elderly is a societal value, it would be an affront to the customs of the community for younger individuals or "informal" groups to expect to be part of the tourism planning process. But in many American cities and towns, where there is a tradition of community organizing, special interest groups and small cadres of neighbors may demand to be treated as equal players with larger, more formally established groups. In some Islamic countries, the religious authorities are regularly consulted by private developers, and their views are afforded great weight.

Location will identify some players. Certainly the developer of any proposed project will play an active role. Close neighbors of a development will almost always want to be involved. The boundaries of a planning area will also help to identify affected parties: those living or working within the borders are, after all, the people who use the affected area the most.

As in boundary selection, identification of the impacts—both burdens and benefits—will indicate some of the appropriate players. Perhaps the economic benefits will accrue to businesses that cater to tourists, resulting in closures of small stores serving locals. Outsiders may get hired for all the "good" jobs, while locals fill the slots of chambermaids and busboys. Some residents may be forced to relocate to make room for new tourism development or may see the character of their neighborhood change completely. Access to a popular recreational spot may be lost due to development. Those who believe that they will bear the brunt of the burdens are likely to feel that their interests are not being given due consideration.

A similar problem arises when the benefits of tourism growth are seen to accrue to only a small segment of the community, even though community-wide resources are being committed to tourism development. Perhaps scarce public resources are being diverted from improving community facilities serving a larger population, for example, to building amenities for tourists in only a limited area. Those who believe that the benefits of tourism development will be unfairly allocated may well oppose any plan that is developed unless they can be assured that their views have been heard and their concerns taken into account.

An additional reason for an inclusive approach to identifying the players is purely practical: solutions arrived at through consensus tend to be more successful than those imposed from the outside. Examples of failed top-down solutions to tourism problems are numerous. In the Florida Keys, for example, initial attempts by the state to impose standard solutions for problems unique to the Keys produced local revolt and ineffective controls. Only after the state created a local office with experienced personnel did cooperation begin. Similarly, the Maltese government decided to promote the medieval walled city of Mdina as a major cultural and historic attraction as part of an effort to broaden Malta's appeal from that of only a seaside destination, extend the visitor season, and increase revenues. Unfortunately, the three hundred or so residents of the Mdina had not been included in the decision-making process and resented the number of tourists (seven hundred and fifty thousand in 1993) who poured into their narrow streets and sometimes into their homes as well.[52] Their frustration at the loss of privacy and dissatisfaction with the changes in the character of their community meant that visitors no longer felt welcomed or comfortable. Tourism declined and the situation steadily worsened until the government worked with the Mdina residents to develop ways to alleviate the most troublesome of the tourist pressures.

The type of development being considered will also affect who is sufficiently motivated to become involved. In the United States, for example, efforts to permit riverboat gambling casinos are inevitably met by the organized opposition of certain religious groups. Similarly, proposals for increased development in environmentally sensitive areas may evoke the protests not only of local people but of national organizations as well. When the tourism resources are perceived as belonging to the patrimony of people well beyond the boundaries of the planning area, local decision makers may find themselves facing broader coalitions.

In 1991, Colorado voters approved a measure to allow limited gambling in the old mining town of Black Hawk. The impetus for the measure was to save the dying town and its old mid-nineteenth century houses. By 1997, the main casino grew so popular that it wanted to expand its parking lot onto the site of the 1863 historic landmark Lace House. The casino offered to move the Lace House two blocks away into a new "historic village," and the Black Hawk Town Council voted six to one to approve the move. Preservationists across the state fulminated against the vote; Colorado Preservation, Inc. drew up a list of the state's most endangered places, with Lace House heading the list; the Colorado Attorney General successfully filed a court injunction to stop the move; the Colorado Historical Society brought suit to forestall relocation or demolition; and a historian at the University of Colorado planned to lead a protest. The National Trust for Historic Preservation used the episode as a cautionary tale to persuade other communities not to use gambling as a tool to save historic towns.

Similarly, development that is perceived as insensitive to the community's culture and heritage may draw fire from a variety of constituencies. Disney's plans to build a theme park on a three thousand acre parcel near the historic Civil War battlefield at Manassas, Virginia, pitted the entertainment giant against what at first was a small group of residents who objected to the proposal. They were soon joined by an impressive array of historians and scholars. The media coverage led to a widespread public perception that Disney was exploiting America's Civil War heritage and desecrating the site where more than twenty-two thousand soldiers died. Eventually, Disney ultimately abandoned the project, in large part because it had failed to predict the degree of opposition its plans evoked.

Participants in the planning process are usually self-identified and become involved because they feel directly affected by potential development. Acceptance of such players into the process is essential if an equitable result is to be achieved. If there are some who find these democratic ideals unconvincing, they may need to be reminded of a practical reason for inclusiveness: excluded people cause trouble later! So efficiency, resiliency, and sustainability all benefit from inclusive participation.

The case studies in this book suggest that this inclusive approach is appropriate for communities of any size, although it is obviously easier for a small town or village to seek such participation than it is for larger and more diverse communities. In the early stages of Whistler's development as a resort, the population was relatively small and homogeneous, but as it grew it needed to expand its process for encouraging participation to involve new groups in the planning process.

Regional developments bring their own challenges. The management plan for the Saguenay-St. Lawrence Marine Park in Quebec involves two governmental units (national and provincial), nongovernmental organizations, residents of over fifteen separate municipalities, Native communities, as well as the fishermen who use the waters (p. 120). Often, the larger the affected community, the greater the number of constituencies that exist, the less cohesion there is among the constituencies, and the more subtleties there are to the distinctions among each constituency. All these nuances can make it difficult to reach consensus concerning who the legitimate players are. Often, but not always, the conundrum will be resolved by the practicalities of participation: it takes time (and often money as well, for professional advice and other services), and only those sufficiently interested and invested in the outcome will take part in the process.

Adding Players

Communities will sometimes need to make special efforts to promote the inclusion of other relevant players who do not become involved on their own initiative. This may be particularly necessary in cases where there are cultural barriers. In developing tourism in the poor villages of the Oaxaca valleys, government planners faced the challenges of working with multiple ethnic groups with distinctive dialects and cultures (p. 190). The New Zealand case study (p. 196) shows how the government provided for participation by Maori people and a wide range of other groups.

Sometimes the job of identifying legitimate players involves the enlistment of people who hadn't given much attention to the potential benefits of tourism. The goal of the South Pembrokeshire Partnership for Action with Rural Communities (SPARC) is to improve the economic and social life of the local people in that southwest area of Wales. SPARC worked with local people in thirty-seven villages to identify the problems and opportunities of their own communities. It was only after a series of discussions that villagers identified rural tourism as a potential source of economic growth and became involved with tourism planning (p. 254).

At other times, a commitment to an inclusive process means inviting potential adversaries to the same table. The current Lake Tahoe regional plan developed from several years of "consensus building workshops" that brought together representatives of sometimes conflicting constituencies: conservation and property rights groups; federal, state, and local governments; utilities and other businesses; and the general community (p. 91). In Door County, Wisconsin, the "Future Search" process fostered communication among groups that often clash: environmentalists, builders, property owners, farmers, and government officials. Both these approaches were effective in part because the inclusive process fostered collaborative problem solving. Had any one of these groups been excluded from the process, they may have withheld support from any final plan (p. 173).

A final group that is often added in an advisory capacity is the consultants that communities hire to provide expertise. Peninsula Township, Michigan, secured the help of the American Farmland Trust and Michigan State University students who created comprehensive resource maps of the peninsula (p. 129). SPARC in South Pembrokeshire, Wales, secured expert assistance from such organizations as the Swansea Institute and the Dyfed Archaeological Trust.[53]

LIMITING THE PLAYERS

Although the planning process itself should focus on including all legitimate players, the area's assets are often such that they necessarily limit the number of people who can beneficially *use* them. Nantucket, for example, has only limited supplies of water. Until new technologies are developed to provide increased water supplies, the island will need to limit the number of potential users. Similarly, the "calm" of Westminster Abbey is an asset that cannot exist for an unlimited number of users at the same time. By rerouting visitors and charging admission fees, the Abbey has protected the quality of the experience for those who are willing to pay a modest amount for the privilege.

The residents of Ambergris Caye, Belize, worry that rapid tourism growth will mean immigration of newcomers attracted by tourism jobs, with the result that the local population will be quickly outnumbered.

Limiting those who can share tourism resources affects residents as well as visitors. Bermuda, for example, controls the impact of tourism through limits on who may open hotels, serve as entertainers or tour guides, etc. Similarly, on the Great Barrier Reef in Australia, the number of people who may operate facilities for tourists on the more convenient islands has been limited by grandfathering in existing facilities and refusing licenses for new ones. Bonaire in the Netherlands Antilles is considering reevaluating existing unused licenses to build tourist accommodations, and revoking some of those licenses. The government of the Republic of Maldives has adopted a policy of developing resorts on unoccupied islands to insulate the local population from adverse foreign influences (p. 215).

Let the Players Make the Rules

Our study of the tourism planning process indicates that if strategies for the allocation of tourism resources are developed by one group without the participation of other affected parties, they are rarely successful. When a community is considering ways to manage its tourism development and the use of its shared resources, it needs to create a process for meaningful participation by disparate parties with different objectives. In modern planning parlance, this is often referred to as a "shared vision" theory of planning or even, to the disgust of language purists, as "visioning."[54]

There is no easy formula for devising an effective process for participation. What works for one community will not necessarily work in another. The culture of the community will always govern what kind of process will be successful. The process, however, should be perceived by the players as inclusive and fair according to local standards. Whatever the process ends up looking like, it will need, in its own way, to address the following issues.

THE CONVENER

Who initiates the process and invites the players to participate? Frequently it is the government, which is facing uncontrolled, or inadequately controlled, development and seeking to impose regulatory mechanisms. The Whistler experience is a particularly good example of the evolving role of a government convener. In the 1970s and 1980s, the governing municipality simply instituted formal public hearings to elicit community response to proposed plans. Today, it uses a wide range of community-wide surveys, data gathering and analysis, and large public meetings to achieve the same objective.

Environmental groups may be the catalyst when seeking to protect a special place they believe to be endangered by existing or potential tourist pressures. In the Czech Republic, a group known as "Greenways–Zelene Stezky" promotes eco-friendly tourism. It develops hiking and biking trails, linking formal gardens, farms, forests, castles, and even a UNESCO Biosphere Reserve. The organization works with communities, encouraging them to participate in the Greenways program. Any number of towns, particularly in Moravia and Bohemia, have joined the program, using local volunteers to maintain the trails, and adapting existing buildings as small hotels and restaurants rather than constructing new tourist facilities.

Business interests are sometimes the initiators of community discussions. For example, a group of owners of small hotels near the Monteverde cloud forest in Costa Rica[55] has undertaken efforts to limit the number of tourists who visit the forest because of its ecological sensitivity. The cloud forest, located in the mountains between the Atlantic and Pacific Oceans, is an area of astounding biological diversity. It is home to the legendary quetzal as well as the beautiful blue Morpho butterfly. Because of poor access and rain, which often turns the single mountain road into a series of ruts and mud holes, Monteverde is difficult to reach, even with four-wheel drive vehicles. Local dairy farmers would like the road to be paved to increase their access to markets. Some villagers want a better road to make it easier for them to get to areas where there are more job opportunities. The hotel owners and conservationists want the road to remain in its present state to serve as a barrier to increased tourist pressure on the delicate ecology of the cloud forest. The hotel owners have joined together in a cooperative effort and have voluntarily agreed not to expand their facilities. (The case study of Door County, Wisconsin, provides another good example of a planning effort stimulated by the local business community.)

In some instances, the process begins with grass root efforts of local people who want to attract tourists to their community. The "Book Villages" of Hay-on-Wye in Wales, Redu in Belgium, and Montolieu in France were largely created by the efforts of single individuals, who convinced others to invest in bookstores, bookbinderies, and galleries, and to market the towns to the bookworms of the world (p. 249).

Occasionally the convener is an international organization that is addressing economic development issues. The United Nations and the World Tourism Organization, for example, are involved in efforts in numerous "undeveloped" nations to create sustainable tourism projects in rural areas as a means of improving economic and living conditions. In St. Lucia, for example, studies conducted by United Nations agencies established the need for new policies for the location of tourism facilities.

The most important issue is not who convenes the players, but the perception that the convener is not using the power of the position either to exclude any legitimate player or to limit genuine participation in the decision-making process. If the players view the convener as manipulating the process, whatever plan is adopted may be crippled by the lack of broad-based community support.

FORUMS FOR PARTICIPATION

Creating a process that promotes real participation in decision making by all the relevant players is not an easy task.[56] Some groups, such as developers of proposed projects, will surely participate in discussions, as will neighbors who feel threatened by potential developments, some "community activists," and possibly special interests groups whose mission is involved. The challenge is to attract (and maintain) the participation of the broader community—the equivalent of "getting out the vote" on a cold, rainy morning. Discussions concerning a "shared vision" or "community character" sound numbingly boring to some and frighteningly abstract to others, while assessing the impacts of potential tourism development is a daunting prospect to any nonspecialist.

Organizers must recognize that any successful process for public participation will need some techniques for dealing with such potential problems as low interest levels, apathy, lack of knowledge, limited time availability, and variable levels of commitment. There will always be a significant fraction of the population who choose not to participate, and that choice must be respected. The most common method for addressing these problems is to offer a spectrum of opportunities for people to participate.

Whistler, British Columbia, offered public information meetings, formal public hearings, small group meetings, "living-room" discussions, workshops, extensive community surveys, open houses, and well-attended annual town meetings. For many years, Whistler has also conducted surveys of visitors to understand why they did choose Whistler and whether their expectations have been met. Aspen, Colorado, included more than 400 individuals in its latest public participation process, using interviews, surveys, community meetings, smaller focus groups, and neighborhood meetings. Five formal citizen committees drafted the "Action Plans" that guide implementation of the community plan. The town of Jackson, Wyoming, divided itself into seven neighborhood planning areas for "small-area" meetings, while Teton County provided public forums, one of which drew more than three hundred participants. Santa Fe held some of its public meetings to discuss a draft general plan in local malls: parking was easy; people could combine shopping errands and civic obligations in one trip; passersby could drop in to the meeting on their way to another destination in the mall.

Planning for large regions presents difficult logistical problems. In the Florida Everglades, where a massive and complex planning effort is underway, planners have been posting complex hydrological and ecological models on a web site and receiving comments from scientists all over the country. The planning agencies for both Yosemite National Park, California (p. 150), and Milford Sound, New Zealand (p. 201), submitted draft documents with alternative proposals to the public for comment. Milford Sound received hundreds of comments at public meetings throughout the Southern Lakes District, while Yosemite garnered more than four thousand comments from workshops it held throughout California, its large mailing list, and its web site.

Some forums are more appropriate for providing information, while others are better geared to eliciting community opinion, and still others to sharing and generating ideas. Regardless of what forums are used, there should be sufficient variety and flexibility to meet the needs of both disparate constituencies and different individuals within those constituencies. Inevitably, there will be some members of the community who will never actively participate, and the process should include a variety of techniques to solicit their feedback. This is particularly important if large segments of the community are remaining aloof from the process.

The goal in all these cases is to elicit the opinions and perceptions of the broadest range of players as possible. It can require enormous time and effort to secure involvement of at least a representative sampling of the community, but it is essential if the final strategy is to reflect the values and vision of the community.

THE FOCUS OF DISCUSSIONS

Before any destination community can fashion a suitable management strategy for tourism development and use of the community's tourism resources, it needs to define the goals of such a strategy. Organizers need to plan a method for structuring discussions to arrive at a consensus concerning goals.

These types of discussion are often referred to, particularly in the United States and Canada, as creating a "shared vision" for the future of the community that will guide all decisions concerning further development.[57] This is often the easiest time in the planning process to achieve consensus, because this step involves an identification of shared pleasures: the special qualities of the place that make people want to live, work, and visit there. These may include such elements as the ambiance, the cultural amenities, the friendliness of neighbors, the open spaces, the natural beauty, the sense of history, the architecture, the good schools. These are shared assets that the community will want to protect or enhance.

In Park City, more than three hundred residents met with city staff, City Council members, a Citizens Advisory Committee, and planning consultants to redefine their vision for the future of the city. The resulting *Community Vision,* which established as goals the preservation of the mountain resort, the historic, small-town character of the city, its environmental quality and open space, was the starting point for the revision of the city's general plan (p. 79).

The Town of Jackson and Teton County participated in a Successful Communities program, where residents split into ten randomly selected groups, each one of which developed a vision statement.[58] These ten statements were then fused into a single vision by a workshop organizer. The process continued over a period of two years of workshops and moderated roundtable discussions, often with consultants. The final vision emphasized preservation of the unique, small-town, western character of Jackson and the rural setting and outdoor recreational opportunities of Teton County.

The villages of South Pembrokeshire, Wales, used a different vocabulary but had similar discussions. Members of those communities went through a process of "Community Appraisals." Almost all final appraisals included two elements: they stressed maintaining the "quality of life" and rural character of their community, and they highlighted concern for the environment and the heritage of the area. When they targeted tourism as a means of economic development for the region, they stressed that it must be consistent with the goals they had identified: tourism must be small-scale and rural in character, providing an experience based on enjoyment of the culture, countryside, and heritage.

In Bermuda, the Department of Planning organized "Working Groups" to identify those characteristics that defined the "quality of life" in Bermuda. All groups included elements of the physical environment, often with a visual and aesthetic emphasis (e.g., "Bermuda architecture" and "pleasant views"). This led to detailed surveys of residents and visitors identifying the specific visual elements of the island that contribute to its aesthetic quality and to new planning policies to protect and enhance those elements (p. 144).

While the case studies in this book present numerous examples of communities that have successfully moved from goal-identification discussions to strategy development, the transition is not always smooth. Organizers need to establish clear objectives for "visioning" exercises (or "community character" analysis or "community appraisals"). Without such definition, participants may well feel that they have not achieved their purpose until they have unanimous agreement on every potential issue. In order to be efficient, processes also need a time table for reaching consensus. With no deadlines, there is little impetus for compromise. Interminable talks will exhaust the enthusiasm of most players and achieve little.[59]

Organizers also need a structure for linking the planning process to action. In some instances the political decision makers are not invested in the process, so that there is little impetus for them to initiate whatever actions are necessary to meet the goals set by the community. In other cases, participants feel their role is finished when they have created the vision, and they withdraw from the process before difficult decisions are made concerning what strategy to adopt to foster that vision of the future.[60]

POWER DISPARITIES
There are inevitable distinctions among the skills and resources of various constituencies.[61] Large business interests often have access to far greater financial resources than do small community groups. Experts can be enormously persuasive and usually testify for whoever can afford them. Access to the media and the knowledge of how to use it effectively can shape public opinion.

Local residents, on the other hand, may have a big advantage over outsiders because of their familiarity with local traditions and relationships. A history of working relationships with government officials and influential business and community leaders can mean that one constituency's voice may be heard in private as well as in public conversations.

Occasionally, neighborhood groups may exercise such dominant control of local elected officials that they can kill most development proposals simply through extended delays. In some communities, neighborhood organizations are able to demand cash from developers for the purpose of hiring consultants to advise them about the developer's proposed project.

Lengthy processes often turn in favor of one party or another. A developer may not be able to afford to hold on to a piece of property while community opponents clamor for more and more public hearings. On the other hand, community members may not be able to sustain the high level of energy and commitment required to show up at evening meetings month after month to counter the positions articulated by a well-paid staff of business interests.

Such imbalances are inevitable, and no process can level the playing field between emergent groups and conventional power holders. The greatest threat these disparities pose is not that one group will outmaneuver another, but that the entire process will be seen as favoring one constituency over another. Being open to all affected parties is not enough; the process must also be seen to treat all parties, whatever degree of power and influence they have, in an equitable fashion.[62]

In some places the difficulties of obtaining cooperation among antagonistic groups may appear almost insurmountable. The old city of Jerusalem is a classic example of a place in which widely disparate interests need to participate if the amicability needed for optimal tourism is to succeed. For years, the former mayor, Teddy Kollek, labored mightily to reach a consensus on development issues with at least some success. Sadly, the present administration seems either less adept at or less interested in building a consensus.

Localize Rules as Much as Possible

Studies of common-pool resource management have particularly emphasized the need to tailor solutions to local conditions instead of trying to impose "model" solutions. Because any particular combination of tourism resources is likely to differ from any other, even within the same category, the rules applicable to each situation should be tailored to local conditions to the greatest extent possible. Even in a string of beach communities, such as Spain's Costa Brava, each community has an individual character that is not submerged in the identity of the area as a whole.

Failure to give adequate consideration to the human and financial resources of a destination often results in failed plans. An extremely detailed and impressive "Tourism Action Program" was prepared in 1989 for Bangladesh under the auspices of the World Tourism Organization. The plan included, in a scaled-down version, conservation and marketing of a world heritage site that had been previously outlined by UNESCO. It also included recommendations for small-scale, up-market developments with great specificity concerning location, costs, amenities, and possible sources for funding. Then in 1992 the government adopted a "National Tourism Policy," identifying tourism as "an industry of due priority" and outlining steps the government would take to encourage and facilitate tourism development. As of the date of writing, the situation has barely changed: the country lacks the financial resources and the necessary level of skill to implement the plan.[63]

A similar problem occurred in Nepal, where officials are eager to develop Lumbini, the birthplace of Buddha, as a tourist destination. A master plan, funded by the United Nations, ambitiously proposes three-mile square zones. However, only 20 percent of the recommendations have been implemented because Nepal is far too poor to fund them and outside resources have been limited.

In some cases, failure to take local conditions into account may spawn organized protests, disruption of proceedings, and refusal to participate further. The Iguaçu Falls in Brazil, designated by UNESCO as part of the World's Patrimony, is that country's most popular tourist attraction. Shortly after the designation, part of the surrounding Iguaçu National Park, home to jaguars, monkeys, armadillos, and butterflies, was declared a wildlife refuge. To protect the park and the refuge, a thirteen-mile-long road was closed in the late 1980s. Then in 1998 a bitter dispute arose, with local businessmen and residents clamoring to have the road opened. They maintained that families at either end of the road are now forced to drive one hundred miles to visit each other, and that many businesses have fallen into bankruptcy. Residents, along with the local Rotary Club, seized a piece of the park and opened the road and once again started operating a ferry across the river at the end of the road. Demonstrators apparently threatened to set fire to the park at one point; conservationists called for a worldwide boycott of the Iguaçu Falls until the demonstrators were ousted; and one environmental official threatened to call in the military. In an election year, many politicians were carefully avoiding making decisions.[64]

Sometimes the problem is less one of confrontation than it is of indifference to or disregard for whatever plan or regulations have been adopted. On the French Polynesia island of Bora Bora, the mayor pursued a policy of strict environmental protection measures in order to promote the growing tourism element of the economy. The focus was primarily on water quality of the island's famous lagoon with its own color name, "Bora Bora Blue." But many local citizens who traditionally support themselves by subsistence farming and fishing resisted these governmental efforts. Mayor Tong Sang asserts that "(m)y greatest problem has been to get the residents to accept tourism. By the year 2000, tourists will choose their destinations because of the environmental condition of the place, and I'm betting on Bora Bora. Without hotels there would be no employment; without Mother Nature there would be no destination."[65]

The case studies in this book provide numerous illustrations of communities that emphasized their individuality in the development of their plans. The residents of Teton County, Wyoming, identified the "rural and Western character" of the area as its most important feature. After a long process, the residents of Aspen, Colorado, identified a series of local objectives that included maintaining specific physical attributes (such as the small scale of buildings and important viewscapes) as well as unique social factors (such as the diversity of the population). Both the Maldives and Bali have a goal of isolating tourists to protect the local population from foreign influences.

The case studies show that communities not only localize objectives, but they also localize techniques for reaching those objectives. When some landowners opposed the moratorium on development imposed on some areas in Whistler, their protests abated when the municipality offered specific local trade-off opportunities. The complex rating system devised for Lake Tahoe includes procedures for frequent reanalysis of environmental conditions for parcels to allow reasonable changes to the ratings, as well as trade-off mechanisms.

Bruges, Belgium, used "target marketing" to encourage visits from overnight tourists, who provide more economic benefit than day-trippers (p. 237). Bermuda's ads seek to attract high-income overnight visitors, while they limit the number of cruise ships that can discharge passengers for daytime excursions (p. 144). The Times Square Business District pays for quick removal of graffiti and garbage collection, to the delight of both residents and visitors (p. 241).

Give the Players a Sense of Permanence

If participants in a system of common-pool resource management know that they are going to be dealing with the same people regularly in a system that is going to be around for a long time, informal social sanctions can often be used to enforce rules. It is people who have or will put down roots in the local community who can develop this kind of cooperative spirit. For example, shopkeepers who feel that they are a part of the community are less likely to rip off customers in ways that will damage the reputation of other merchants. For all of the players, a sense that the system has permanence makes them less likely to grab for short-term advantages. A sense of permanence includes agreement on long-term objectives and confidence in the ability of the system to adapt to changes that are likely to occur over time.

Family ties are often an important factor in promoting a sense of permanence. If participants can envision benefits from the system for their sons and daughters, they will value long-range sustainability instead of narrowly calculated present interests. Residents of the Galápagos saw jobs for their children as tourist guides and park rangers as a positive benefit of the Ecuadorean government's policy of restricted tourism, but an influx of mainland Ecuadoreans to the islands has raised doubts about the permanence of those benefits.

The need for continued community involvement does not end with the initial implementation of a tourism management strategy. As any tourism development progresses through stages, its impact upon the community will change; as tourist numbers in a community grow, those impacts will multiply. The community itself will also change over time and will need to adapt its tourism management strategy so that it continues to address the needs and desires of a changing community. This requires a continuing relationship among all of the players.

One example of the development of an ongoing relationship among groups that participate in the tourism planning process is the South Pembrokeshire Partnership for Action with Rural Communities (SPARC; p. 254). SPARC forged working relationships with educational institutions and various public agencies, which provided expertise and financial and technical assistance, offered training to small businesses, cooperated in developing and marketing the tourism program, and continued to be involved in the process over the long term rather than as one-time consultants. The partners' continued participation not only enhanced the tourism program that developed, but also assured the villages of South Pembrokeshire that they would continue to receive the assistance they needed to improve and sustain their tourism management approach.

Community organizations can be created in ways that emphasize their permanence. The British "Tarka Project" (p. 250) operates through a coalition of members and groups that intend to work together indefinitely for the purpose of making the project work. The Business Improvement District (BID), which was such a catalyst to the Times Square redevelopment, continues to fund projects, oversee development, and work cooperatively with the city government on issues facing the district.

Laws can also be structured to foster continuing relationships. New Zealand emphasizes the ongoing roles of particular groups and agencies by requiring that they be consulted as part of the resource consent process. California's Environmental Quality Act (CEQA) similarly fosters ongoing relationships among groups that regularly comment on development proposals.

Because developers who maintain a long-term presence in a community are likely to be more respectful of local needs than those who intend to build and leave, some communities, such as Jackson, Wyoming, try to attract quality developers by limiting speculation in development approvals. To make it unlikely that someone will obtain development approval with the hope of selling the approval to the highest bidder (an all too common practice), they strictly limit the time period in which the approval must be exercised (p. 85). The Tahoe region is a good example of an area in which controversial and restrictive regulations needed to reduce deterioration in water quality have finally been relatively well accepted by those who live and work in the community. Most of the objections come from outsiders who bought lots for speculation or future use and are not long-term participants in the activities of the area (p. 91).

Places like Stewart Island, New Zealand, which are at an earlier stage of implementation and depend heavily on outside consultants paid by the central government, will have a much harder time gaining people's confidence that tourism policies for the island are likely to be in place for a long time. Still, with its small population and obvious interest in maintaining tourism quality, the people of the island may be able to assert control of its ongoing planning if they can form a consensus around long-term objectives (p. 221).

The development of long-term relationships may be hampered where a local community lacks the full panoply of skills needed to manage a successful tourism program, with the result that many jobs are initially filled by consultants and temporary workers who may lack interest in the community's long-term objectives. To achieve a cohesive approach that maximizes long-range sustainability, it is important to develop locally a wide range of tourism-related skills.

Training programs may be desirable to ensure that the community has the skills both to manage tourism development and to participate in the tourism program itself. The SPARC program provided business training so that local residents could become small entrepreneurs and training in restoration skills to local craftsmen so that they could perform the necessary work on historic buildings and sites. Ambergris Caye, Belize, has imposed incremental growth restrictions on tourism development in part because it recognizes that in order for local people to be able to hold jobs in the tourism industry, they will require job training and better education.

In some cases the business community may not have the required investment capital or access to it. In the Oaxaca Valleys of Mexico where the state government was working with villagers to establish central market places to sell locally made crafts, residents could often not afford the cost of constructing even relatively simple stalls and shops. The government would sometimes provide financing if villagers provided labor or would share the costs of construction with a few families.

The 1997 proposed Tourism Plan for Bonaire identifies a shortage of adequately trained staff, combined with a strong resistance to further immigration to supply skilled workers, as a particular challenge to successful tourism development on that Caribbean island.[66]

Even established tourist destinations can have continuing training needs. With the economic downturn that affected much of Asia in 1997–1998, Thailand lost most of its traditional market from South Korea, Japan, and Hong Kong. At the same time, the relaxation of both travel restrictions in China and visa requirements in Thailand meant that it was much easier for Chinese to visit. Suddenly, the Bangkok Handicrafts Center needed sales clerks speaking Mandarin, and tour guides who spoke Japanese or Korean needed retraining.

Availability of information is another key issue which often needs to be addressed specifically in a process for tourism planning. In order for a community to have confidence in the legitimacy and permanence of any shared asset management program, there must be a perception that relevant information has been, and continues to be shared with all the players. Clear information, particularly concerning potential negative impacts, should be made available to community members. If the community is prepared for these impacts, and decides that they will not be unduly damaging, most individuals will not resent having to put up with them.

In situations where visitors will come from different cultures than the hosts, sharing information can do much to explain what might otherwise be viewed as bad manners or disrespectful behavior. A recently developed five-year tourism management policy for the Cayman Islands was coupled with a tourist awareness program to help the local population understand tourists' expectations and behavior and their own role in making the tourism product successful.

In some situations, an important element of information relates to the responsibilities of the host community. The ruins of a Mayan city were discovered in Tekax, on the Yucatan Peninsula of Mexico, during cleanup efforts following Hurricane Gilbert in 1988. Recognizing the potential for tourism development, the local and national government, together with the tourist administration, undertook excavation of the site and, together with local people, developed a tourism plan. This included a major education component: convincing the community of the importance of protecting the Mayan site. Often members of the local community need to recognize that their own behavior can negatively impact tourism development.

Details about a proposed strategy need to be shared with all the members of the destination community. In Peninsula Township, Michigan (p. 129), a group of citizens, who had banded together as "Concerned Citizens in Support of PDR," became the core group of volunteers who coordinated a community-wide campaign to circulate information that led to passage of a referendum approving an increase in property taxes to support a development rights purchase program. The effort was successful in part because the networks used and the spokespersons chosen were designed to appeal to the local community.

For the players to feel confident that a plan is sustainable and resilient over the long term, the sharing of relevant information needs to continue on a regular basis. Whistler is an example of a place in which the planning effort has attained a high degree of commu-

nity confidence. An important element of that success has been the development of information about the community and its options and the wide dissemination of that information throughout the community. In Nantucket and Martha's Vineyard, the present structure for tourism planning dates from the adoption of special legislation for the islands in
1973. The process includes detailed data-gathering and effective distribution of the information. Although not without controversy, the planning process has proved its staying
power and created a sense that it will be in place permanently.

Even when the issues are technical and complex, modern technology has increased the
ability to disseminate information effectively. The web posting of detailed models for the
Florida Everglades, referred to earlier, enabled planners to get comments in much faster
time than would otherwise be possible. This is one of the techniques used by the National
Park Service in Yosemite as well, both to share information about its draft alternatives for
growth management in the Park and to elicit public comment.

Monitor and Mediate Violations Efficiently but Effectively

Users of common-pool resources who have participated in making the rules for their use
are often the most reliable monitors and mediators to ensure that the rules are followed.
Successful systems of common-pool resource management often use informal penalties,
such as exclusion of violators from social occasions, to control minor rule violations. When
informal sanctions fail to control players' behavior, however, a relatively quick and inex-
pensive method of arbitrating disputes is important.

MONITORING

Monitoring efforts to ensure compliance with the rules are often the responsibility of the
government. Enforcement of building codes, design guidelines, various performance standards, zoning ordinances and maps, tax regulations, and environmental standards is normally delegated to a specific public entity. Voluntary associations often develop their own
monitoring systems to guard against rules violations.

Monitoring can ensure that a sustainable tourism management strategy is being
achieved and that a resilient strategy is being adapted as necessary to meet changing circumstances.[67] Tourism, in most cases, will grow, and that growth may result in unexpected
impacts on the community. The charming village of Clovelly on the Devon coast of
England has one cobblestone pedestrian street, lined with stone houses bright with gerani-
ums, leading down a steep incline to the sea. At the height of the season, the street is
crammed with tourists wending their way down past the shops and houses, or struggling,
panting, back up. No one originally predicted how popular this picturesque village would
become. The strategies it has now devised weren't needed fifteen years ago.

The impacts of growth were clearly visible in Clovelly. Sometimes monitoring is needed
to determine precisely what effects increased numbers of tourists are having on a destination.[68] Golfo Nuevo, a bay on the southern coast of the Peninsula Valdes in Argentina, is a
major breeding ground for the southern right whale. Tourist numbers have recently grown
to one hundred and twenty thousand a year, and additional growth of 25 percent per year
is expected. Most visitors to the Gulf arrive on cruise ships, resulting in fifty busloads of
tourists unloading in the small port town of Puerto Piramides (population 104) in a single
day. Some environmentalists have been concerned that the increasing number of tourists
has been adversely affecting the sea lions and elephant seals in the area, and that whale
watching boats have been disturbing the southern right whales. A new monitoring program has established ways to measure site-specific, quantifiable negative impacts from

tourism growth. If such impacts are found, the World Tourism Organization is recommending establishing the peninsula as an ecological reserve.

Sometimes tourist markets change in unpredictable ways, with unexpected changes in economic and social impacts on the destination community. Places that initially appeal to one type of tourist, later may appeal to a totally different category of visitors. Because of cheap excursion fares, the Greek isle of Corfu is now inundated by package tours from Britain, traveling the island on large buses, buying English tabloids at kiosks, and eating at tavernas that now serve fish and chips instead of moussaka. Areas once visited only by a few adventurous backpackers are now destinations on up-scale "exotic" tours. One can tour the Sahara and travel the Silk Road in air-conditioned buses with the assurance of a firm bed, bottled water, and specially catered meals.

No matter how well thought out tourism programs are, there usually develop at least some unforeseen occurrences, which the community has no control, that significantly alter how that tourism progresses. Strategies adopted one year may not address the problems faced in future years. Hurricanes have periodically devastated numerous Caribbean islands, turning successful destinations into shambles. Communities that were basking in the glow of tourist dollars/marks/yen suddenly were having to seek loans to rebuild themselves and then tourist confidence that they were safe to visit. The "green algae" in the Adriatic caused visitor numbers on the Italian coast to plummet.

Political disturbances can be as disastrous as natural ones. Reports of attacks by bandits have scared tourists away from visiting the Mayan ruins in Guatemala, and bombings of tourist buses in Cairo have dampened tourist enthusiasm for that destination. And of course economic fluctuations in the world financial markets affect people's travel plans. Hawaii and many other destinations that depend heavily on Asian markets have been badly hit by the Asian recession that developed in 1997. Once a community has embarked on tourism development, no matter how small and controlled, it needs continually to monitor how that tourism is impacting the community and how the community may be changing.

Monitoring can also help communities determine whether they are achieving the benefits that they expected from tourism development. Chepstow, a market town in southeast Wales, wanted to increase its level of tourism primarily to generate economic growth.[69] Over a five-year period its monitoring program included research on (1) annual pedestrian counts and attitude surveys of both residents and visitors; (2) the economic impact of visitors on local commercial establishments; (3) the costs to local government and agencies of visitors; (4) economic and environmental analysis of costs, benefits, and multiplier effects; and (5) analysis of market trends. On the basis of the information gleaned from the monitoring program, Chepstow amended its strategy each year in ways aimed at increasing the economic benefits of tourism.

Sometimes, of course, monitoring can be so effective that nothing happens at all. For years the redevelopment program for Times Square was critiqued so intensively that it was implemented only in a very limited fashion. In the end, however, the critics proved to be right, and a much-revised plan has now proved to be much more popular and workable.

One important element in monitoring that is sometimes overlooked is visitor satisfaction. Every destination community needs to ensure that it is offering a high-quality visitor experience, so that tourists will return. Whistler, British Columbia, discussed earlier, includes an annual visitor satisfaction survey in its monitoring program. Bermuda took a survey of residents and visitors to identify "the principal visual elements which contribute to aesthetic quality in Bermuda." The results were used to guide policy to protect visual and environmental quality on the island. The survey was a response, in part, to the sense that the changes Bermuda was experiencing could lead to a loss of the island's appeal to the specific type of tourist it desired.

In general, private enterprises are much more apt to pay attention to visitor satisfaction than destination communities. The Ritz Carlton Hotel chain has instituted complex quality management programs that focus on enhancing visitor value, with the goal of retaining 100 percent of its customers. One practical result of the hotel's "quality conscious culture" is that the chain generally leads the industry in generating revenue per available room.[70]

The Shangri-La Hotels have pursued quality in another arena. This chain has incorporated any number of environmentally responsible systems into their daily operations, which are used to educate guests about "green" habits, to create a separate "identity" for the hotel, and to attract guests back. The Shangri-La Kowloon in Hong Kong encourages hotel guests to participate in a variety of measures to minimize the environmental impact of their stay without endangering the quality of their hotel experience.[71] Destination communities could adapt many of the attitudes of successful businesses in the tourism industry concerning visitor satisfaction to their own long-term benefit and incorporate this element into their monitoring programs.

MEDIATION

Any realistic process for managing tourism resources should involve some mechanisms, based on local norms and values and agreed upon early in the process, for negotiation and conflict management. Sometimes this involves securing the assistance of either an experienced, disinterested third party who can act as mediator or an organization that specializes in alternative dispute resolution. An experienced mediator, vested with the needed authority, can often bring opposing camps to agreement, foster better communication among disparate groups, and identify areas of congruence. In those instances where one party's goal is to derail the entire process rather than find a mutually acceptable solution, failure to cooperate with the mediator may effectively marginalize that party and destroy its credibility in the community.

On some occasions it is possible for a government official, a convener, or another involved player to be accepted in the role of mediator or binding arbitrator. Volunteers from among the users of the resource often act as mediators. In a community like Carmel, California, the unpaid local zoning board spends much of its time resolving disputes over rules designed to regulate tourism.

Sometimes groups that have opposed each other can reach an accommodation without formal mediation. The beach at Parker River Wildlife Refuge on Plum Island, Massachusetts, was closed in 1991 to protect the endangered piping plover. The local Chamber of Commerce fought the closing, less worried about the plover than about lost revenues through decreased tourism. After more than four years of contentious struggle, the business community is now cooperating with the Massachusetts Audubon Society. The Chamber decided to promote the Refuge to ecotourists as a sanctuary for migratory birds, hoping to expand its market to Europeans interested in bird-watching and to attract visitors in the winter as well as summer. Some residents still oppose the access restrictions, but most have come to see the plover preservation as good for tourism business.

Sanibel, Florida, has also been able to maintain consensus on the need for development limits by ensuring that decisions are made by permanent residents of the community, rather than development interests whose goals were short-range profits. Sanibel's plan has now existed for twenty-five years and serves as an anchor for tourism policies that are widely perceived as permanent, but continued monitoring and mediation are essential elements of the plan's resiliency.

Common-pool resource research suggests that a forum in which disputes about the rules can be mediated cheaply and easily is important if confidence in the system is to be maintained. Agencies, like the Vieux Carré Commission (p. 51) and Whistler's annual town meeting illustrate this type of forum.

Legal Implementation of Common-Pool Resource Management

Many studies of systems of the management of common resources have emphasized the importance of legal sanctions for the enforcement of rules governing the resource. Lino Grima and Fikret Berkes suggest that the "legal specification of user rights at the community level lowers management costs and helps solve implementation problems."[72] But legal rules imposed from the outside without an adequate appreciation of local conditions may have a negative impact.

Legal scholars have only recently begun to realize the valuable implications of research in common-pool resource management. By observing the way people reach agreements among themselves about common property, lawyers can model the needed legal rules on those that have been developed through the process of "customary law." Books like Yale law professor Robert Ellickson's *Order Without Law* have focused on the ways in which cohesive groups are able to manage potential property-right conflicts through the development of internal norms.[73]

Procedural changes in legal systems are paralleling the research results. Proposals that encourage the participation of well-defined interest groups in negotiated rule making emphasize clearly bounded group participation, a characteristic that has been observed in successful strategies for managing common-pool resources. And dispute resolution strategies rely on trained facilitators to promote informal communication among potential adversaries within local communities; the importance of communication networks in developing and implementing informal norms has been seen in the shared asset management studies.

Law plays an essential role in managing tourism resources. If there are no enforceable rules that will effectively control development so as to avoid unacceptable impacts, then the profit-centered behavior of private parties can and often does create consequences that are contrary to the public good. Markets by themselves are inadequate protection for common-pool resources. We have noted a few such examples in Chapter 1; unfortunately, there are many others that could be identified.

Most tourism destinations are too large, and too closely tied into even larger networks, to rely solely on informal norms to manage shared assets. The more legal jurisdictions involved, the more complex the problem. The study of fishing in Chesapeake Bay by Susan Cox[74] illustrates the problems caused when the legal boundaries of the governing jurisdictions do not match the boundaries of the resource (an issue that will be discussed in the next chapter).

Some studies of common resource management have found that self-organizing institutions have successfully replaced poorly functioning legal mechanisms. These situations deserve careful study for designers of legal mechanisms, but it is important not to obey the nostalgic impulse to conclude that "primitive is better." Duncan Snidal's analysis of the literature led him to conclude that decentralized enforcement is more fragile (i.e., less resilient) than when enforcement is "rooted in external authority."[75] But Snidal also recognizes that external authority can be given to decentralized systems by the appropriate legal rules. Ralph Townsend and Samuel Pooley suggest that legal mechanisms, rather than self-organizing institutions, can best create equity and resiliency:

> Spontaneous and indigenously organized institutions may certainly have a credibility that centrally sponsored institutions lack. But self-organizing institutions also have significant limitations. Most obviously, there is no guarantee that a self-organizing institution will arise in any particular situation. If an organization does self-organize, it may not necessarily be representative of the entire set of local interests. And finally, a self-organizing institution may also self-disorganize, which would cause a renewed void in governance.[76]

The legal rules that contribute to management of shared assets often do so indirectly. Ellickson points out that the laws that promote planning for future generations of a family promote sustainability. "Laws that authorize inheritance by kin, disposition of property by will, and perpetual (fee simple) interests in land all encourage a living person to manage capital assets as if the game of life were infinite in length."[77]

It is helpful for our purposes to define the term "law" very broadly. The most obvious examples of law are legislative enactments at the national, regional, state, and local levels. Such binding enactments normally are the products of political compromise—an appropriate method for arriving at a fair, balanced consensus on how to advance important public values. Another category of law is rules adopted by executive officials pursuant to a power conferred by legislation. And in "common law" countries such as the United States, the term "law" also includes the body of judicial appellate opinions (there are thousands of written opinions in the United States involving land-use disputes among landowners, governments, and/or objecting private parties). Most countries have another less obvious type of "law": the system of judicial and administrative adjudication of disputes among private parties and/or governmental units. Still another form of "law" is a system of monitoring and enforcing compliance with established rules.

Generally, public interests are best protected from harmful activities by legal regulation. In the specific context of tourism development, law should play a central role in the management of tourism resources. But these legal systems can be most effective if they parallel systems for controlling common-pool resources that have shown that they can be efficient, equitable, sustainable, and resilient. In the next chapter we will review growth management systems used in the United States as background for our later examination of specific case studies of the management of tourism growth.

3

Managing Growth

From the perspective of a local community, tourism development is simply one of many kinds of land development. Consequently, the strategies a local community uses to manage tourism development will be interrelated with its comprehensive plans and policies for land use and development. In the United States, local communities have been managing land development in various ways for over a century. In modern terminology, the various techniques used are known as "growth management."[1]

Growth Management Strategies

A leading text by David Godschalk and David Brower defines growth management as a "conscious governmental program intended to influence the rate, amount, type, location, and/or quality of future development within a local jurisdiction."[2] For our analysis, we can collapse their five objectives into three: "type" is subsumed in *quality* of development; "rate" and "amount" relate to the *quantity* of development; and the third is the *location* of development.

A growth management strategy can work toward all three of these objectives, but many put the emphasis on one of the three.

1. Some strategies focus on the quality of development, usually with the objective of encouraging only development that meets certain standards.
2. Other strategies manage the quantity of development by regulating the rate of growth or ultimate capacity for development.
3. And many strategies emphasize the location of development by expanding or contracting existing areas that attract growth or by diverting the growth to new areas.

Sophisticated communities may consider all three of these objectives in managing growth, but in most cases one objective or another tends to take precedence.

It is important to note that the term "management" does not imply a negative attitude toward growth.[3] Some growth management strategies encourage development to take place; others emphasize limitations on development. The term "management" is intended to be neutral in that respect. But growth management strategies all emphasize the need to balance economic growth and environmental protection.[4]

The extent to which local growth management strategies can influence the nature of tourism development depends on the way the responsibilities for managing growth have been distributed by law among (1) private law: rules that affect the relationship of various parts of the private sector; (2) customary law: rules enforced by legal processes but derived from local norms and traditions; and (3) public law: rules administered by various levels of government agencies.

Before addressing the management of tourism development specifically, a brief and non-technical review of growth management in the United States will be helpful to set the stage.

Quality

Today, Americans are so accustomed to a wide array of programs designed to maintain the quality of development that these programs are largely taken for granted. Protection against toxic dumping, poisoned water, and unhealthy smog has produced a substantially cleaner environment than that of twenty-five years ago. Building and zoning codes have so successfully protected neighborhood property values that we are often barely conscious that the codes exist.

This current backdrop of quality controls is a product of gradual evolution. The medieval idea of "nuisance" has been replaced with more sophisticated regulations that reflect changing ideas of quality, increasing scientific understanding of impacts, and a growing need to manage human relationships in more crowded conditions.

Early in the twentieth century, zoning began to be used to control quality by segregating land uses in ways designed to encourage high-quality development. New York City's initial zoning tried to protect Fifth Avenue's expensive housing from too close contact with the burgeoning garment industry. Countless suburbs used zoning to insist that large areas be limited to single family housing on a lot of a certain size.

Gradually communities began to expand on the kinds of quality standards they enforced. Architectural controls became common in some communities, particularly where the maintenance of a particular historic character was desired. Landscaping requirements also became popular, as did regulation of signs and billboards. And the construction of public facilities was increasingly seen as an opportunity for aesthetic improvement through public art and beautiful parks and gardens.

The concern about nuisance increased and was channeled into a wide range of pollution control regulations, both at the state and local level. After Congress enlarged the federal presence in the 1970s, businesses and industries were required to install particular technologies to limit the dumping of waste materials into the air or the surface or underground waters. State and local governments supplemented the required federal regulations with a wide variety of their own programs tailored to local conditions.

The more we understand health and safety hazards, of course, the more amorphous the idea of "nuisance" becomes. Hazard is typically a question both of likelihood and harmfulness. Mosquito bites in Alaska have a high likelihood but are only moderately harmful. Grizzly bear bites are much less likely but much more harmful. Any process of risk assessment must try to quantify both the likelihood and the degree of harm and the cost of safeguards. Moreover, safeguards associated with tourist development may produce not only a reduction in risks but positive benefits as well. Thus, for example, widening a road may not only reduce the likelihood of accidents but may save everyone time through faster travel.[5]

The process for more carefully deciding whether to build things is called environmental assessment. Conceived in the late 1960s and incorporated into the law through the National Environmental Policy Act (NEPA),[6] the idea was deceptively simple—that the impact of development on the environment should be analyzed in some formal manner before the development took place.[7]

The process of impact analysis has pointed to the difficulty of predicting impacts even on familiar issues such as public health. Assume, for example, that the introduction of tourism into a new area will bring with it imported food that will also then be available to the local population. Will the improved food supply reduce chronic malnutrition, as it has in some parts of Alaska? Or will it induce local people to give up a healthy diet for imported foods loaded with sugar and fats and create a serious risk of diabetes and heart disease, as it has in parts of Micronesia?[8]

The environmental analyses required by NEPA also raised public consciousness of some types of environmental impact that had often been ignored. For example, awareness of the impact of development on wildlife, and particularly endangered species, led to a growing interest in biodiversity.[9] And the loss of wetlands to development highlighted an increasing recognition of the valuable functions that wetlands perform.[10]

But in the United States and many other developed countries, the most omnipresent source of discontent about the quality of new development is simply its impact on vehicle traffic. The public has gradually come to realize that rapid growth can lead to critical congestion that defies any cure. Adding more lanes of highway simply attracts more vehicles, creating time-wasting delays and unhealthy air quality. Increasingly, efforts are being made to manage traffic cooperatively through coalitions of local businesses that stagger hours and combine car pooling efforts, but traffic remains a very common cause of opposition to new development proposals.[11]

As scientific knowledge has increased, communities have begun to recognize that certain types of land should be developed only in ways that will protect the natural attributes of the land. Development on hillsides, for example, is now frequently regulated to protect lower areas from erosion and mudslides. Maintenance of wetlands' natural functions, such as absorption of pollution and floods, often requires that development meet strict quality standards. More and more environmental regulations have become location-dependent, and thus involve both quality and location controls.

Despite these scientific advances, to a great many communities the quality of a potential development is still measured primarily by the amount of tax revenue it will contribute to needed local services and facilities. Such "fiscal zoning" is commonly denigrated, but in states where local governments are under strict legal restrictions on revenue raising methods, the competition for those few revenue sources that are available seems inevitable. In California, where a succession of ballot initiatives has hamstrung local governments, strip malls (which generate sales tax) often demand "payola" from a local government for moving into its jurisdiction.

Insofar as tourism development is concerned, many communities have decided that they want such development only if it meets certain standards of quality. The economic benefits and environmental impacts of various kinds of tourism development vary greatly. The case studies in Chapter 4 illustrate techniques by which communities implement strategies designed to maintain desirable qualities.

Despite all of these quality controls, which drive developers crazy with their complexity, the public is often unhappy about the results of the land development process. This has led some communities to conclude that they need to control the quantity of development as well.

Quantity

Strategies to manage the quantity of development are not new, but until recently communities have usually wanted more and more development rather than less. Many places throughout the United States and the world are still desperate for almost any kind of development that will bring enough jobs to the local community to keep normal services and amenities alive. How many times has one heard the laments of industrial workers whose jobs have moved to low-paying areas? Or the rural families who complain that there is nothing in the community to keep their children there once they have grown?

Many such communities have long had economic development programs, designed to attract more development to the area. These programs are not indiscriminate about quality—try locating a waste disposal site if you are in doubt of this. But within certain quality limitations, the primary objective of economic development programs is to *increase* the quantity of development in the area. State governments often spend very large sums of public money in support of these programs to attract economic development.

In the third world's early post-colonial period, many countries viewed tourism development in a similar light. Seeking a quick fix for the economy, they saw tourism as requiring small and easily financed capital outlays that would generate rapid improvement in the balance of payments. But as pointed out in earlier chapters, sometimes uninformed and desperate players made bad bargains that depleted shared tourism resources with little overall benefit to the communities in which they were located.[12]

More sophisticated communities, in both developed and developing countries, have been successful in promoting sustainable beneficial tourism development through strategies that emphasize quality and location. But until recently, few strategies emphasized a desire to attract tourism development while limiting its quantity. This reflected the fact that few communities had experience with any form of quantity-limiting growth management.

Environmental analyses under NEPA contributed to the recognition of quantity as an issue. Assessing the impact of a series of small, gradual changes in natural systems raises an issue that cuts across all categories of impact analysis but is particularly difficult in the ecological context—the question of cumulative impact: if the change caused by any individual development proposal seems minor, but it can be seen that a major impact will take place when the impacts of many projected developments are aggregated, to what extent should each development bear the costs of safeguarding against this impact?[13]

As a technical matter, it is much easier to devise needed safeguards if one can accurately predict the total amount of development that will take place and the time frame during which it will occur. In real life, however, those factors are likely to be speculative projections that are subject to considerable debate. The early developer will have a strong incentive to use estimates that reduce the costs assigned to the initial proposal. Even when agreement can be reached on the degree of safeguards needed and the appropriate share for each participant, legal and financial considerations may make it very hard to implement methods of providing such safeguards if there is no way to project the quantity of development accurately.

Beginning in the late 1960s, some communities in the United States began to adopt policies to limit and/or control the quantity of increases of their resident population that would otherwise occur. Since that time, states and localities have adopted many growth management programs that emphasize thoughtful coordination of the quantity of land development.[14]

Many quantity-oriented growth management programs are based principally upon environmental protection grounds. Other programs seek to reduce the cost of public services and facilities. Often the community really worries about less easily quantifiable objectives, such as avoidance of overcrowding and maintenance of an existing "character" or ambiance.

The late arrival of these quantity limitations reflected lingering doubts about their legal validity in the United States. Early enabling legislation for land-use controls did not contain specific authority for regulation of the rate or amount of development. Initially, the legal support for quantity limitations grew out of the local practice of adopting a "moratorium" on development when confronted with a development proposal that caused public outcry. When the outcry reflected serious public concern about the impact of the proposal on, for example, the adequacy of sewage treatment or the protection of scenic views, the courts allowed communities to halt all development for a reasonable time while they formulated a regulatory strategy.[15]

Once the legal validity of these time-based regulations became established, some communities began to develop more sophisticated use of time factors in their growth management strategies. Some set a limit on the number of dwelling units to be permitted in the community each year. A widely publicized example was Petaluma, California's, phased growth plan that was adopted in the 1970s and approved by an appellate court. That program limited the number of building permits to 500 per year (with a "point system" for allocating those permits). It also imposed a moratorium on annexations and on extensions of such services as sewers to land adjacent to the city boundaries, and it established capacity limits on water and sewerage on the basis of the needs of a 55,000 maximum population.

Quantitative limitations on growth have been widely accepted when the limits are correlated with programs to expand public services or facilities.[16] In the states of Florida and Washington, for example, the term used for this correlation is "concurrency." New development is supposed to take place at the same time as the public facilities necessary to serve it are built.[17] Concurrency, like sustainability, sounds great but is hard to define. Difficult timing issues arise over when facilities are deemed to be complete. Is it when financing is assured? Or when construction has started? Or when facilities are open for business? But the concept itself has wide support despite, or perhaps because of, its indeterminacy.

Strategists who use quantity limitations need to make difficult policy decisions. How do you decide if the level of service demanded by a community reflects realistic objectives? If the local voters continually refuse to vote money to upgrade schools or roads, can they legitimately deny development because these facilities are too crowded? On the other hand, if Los Angeles runs low on water, does it need to build desalinization plants in order to accommodate growth?

Limiting the supply of development without reducing the demand has a natural tendency to increase the price that buyers must pay for the product being developed. Where is the line to be drawn between public services that everyone traditionally has a right to receive, such as education and police protection, and scarce resources that can legitimately be conserved by pricing policies?

One early celebrated example of a strategy that placed limits on the number of new dwelling units until particular essential facilities or services were in place occurred in Ramapo, New York. Developers of residential units had to apply for and receive a "special permit" that would be granted only if the development had fifteen "development points," calculated by reference to the current availability of sewerage, drainage, parks, schools, roads, and firehouses. If a development company did not want to wait until the municipality had installed those elements necessary for it to be awarded the minimum fifteen development points, then it could "earn" the points by installing sufficient infrastructure to reach that point level.

Another technique currently in increasing use employs mapped "urban growth boundaries." Lines are drawn on a map to delineate where growth will be permitted or encouraged and, conversely, where it will not. Although this technique is location-based (see the next section), it is often used as a practical means for regulating the quantity of development as well. Oregon, and more recently Washington, have adopted policies at the state level encouraging such boundaries, and of course such boundaries have been effectively employed in many European countries for many years.

Urban boundaries are designed to contain growth to places where costly infrastructure services can reasonably be provided and to preserve from development those areas outside of the line that are rural in character. Douglas Porter's recent book discusses such programs in such diverse places as Clackamas County, Oregon; Fort Collins, Colorado; King County, Washington; Lexington/Fayette County, Kentucky; Portland, Oregon; and Sarasota County, Florida.[18]

There are many other kinds of growth management mechanisms for quantity control, many of which are variations of the principal types just discussed. Porter suggests that effective quantity-based strategies have certain key elements in common. First, he notes that the process should be "dynamic"; instead of a plan of action, it should be "evolving and ever changing" as to objectives and methods. We have referred to this characteristic as "resilience." Second, successful programs anticipate growth and seek to accommodate it without undue stress in an efficient yet sustainable manner. Third, there should be an equitable "forum and process" to allow for a fair and effective balancing of public and private interests. Finally, Porter emphasizes the importance of localities being aware of the regional nature of many problems,[19] a point we will return to in the last section of this chapter.

Most of the programs Porter discusses are designed to mitigate the adverse impacts that the community believes will occur if unchecked population growth is permitted. But there are many other local strategies that seek as much development as possible and view quantity as a minimum to be achieved rather than a maximum to be avoided. In many cases, these communities see no need for maximum quantities because they anticipate that they can avoid adverse impacts of the new development by managing both for quality and for location.

With tourism, the quantity is often very important. Unless a certain volume of tourism builds up, neither the private nor the public sector can afford to provide the services and facilities that tourists expect. But if the quantity becomes too great, it may not be possible to expand support systems without destroying the resources that attract the tourists. Management strategies that regulate quantity are illustrated by the case studies of tourist destinations in Chapter 5.

Location

Many growth management programs encourage new development to locate in particular areas. A wide range of techniques is available to communities that seek to attract development to, or to divert it from, specific parts of the community. These location-oriented management techniques generally fall under the umbrella of land-use planning. Communities identify areas that are appropriate for particular uses and plan to provide the public facilities and services needed by the projected type and quantity of development.

Capital improvement programming, under which a community develops a list of infrastructure improvements and a time schedule for their construction, can guide the placement and timing of development. The location of new streets and highways determines where new development will take place. Sewer and water line extensions are often necessary to make housing subdivisions feasible; timing those extensions and deciding where they will go has a large impact on development patterns.

Open space protection through regulatory strategies has been a more recent phenomenon. As many courts began to approve limitations designed to protect agricultural land uses, communities began to design greenbelts as a way of protecting such uses from urbanization.

Farmers may like to farm but they don't like to see their land values limited by regulation. Often the perceived inequities to rural landowners are being ameliorated by programs for the purchase or transfer of development rights. Even so, the success of greenbelt programs in the United States remains spotty in comparison to European countries, many of which maintain much more strict boundaries between urban and rural uses.

Certain locations tend to require special management strategies because of their physical characteristics. The coastal zone is the most prominent. Federal, state, and local laws often set particular standards for coastal development on the basis of considerations of public access, water quality protection, aesthetics, protection of wildlife habitat, and a wide array of other considerations. Here, as in the wetlands and hillsides discussed in the section of this chapter on quality, considerations of quality and location are tightly intertwined.

But location-oriented growth management is by no means dominated by negative attitudes toward growth. Many communities have identified parts of their area that they think are particularly appropriate for development, and they focus their strategy on means for increasing these areas' desirability to developers. This strategy is sometimes known as "nodal development."[20] Communities can offer various financing mechanisms to lure new development to, for example, industrial parks. Special assessment or taxing districts can help developers defer costs, and many communities offer tax abatement for the most attractive kinds of development. State governments compete actively to provide subsidies to builders of automobile or chemical plants.

Subdivision regulations may play a key role in directing development into patterns that will be compatible with surrounding property. Communities will often finance a wide range of local improvements for attractive types of development if they locate in the right area. State and regional agencies may also help to extend public services into rural areas in order to hasten their urbanization.

Zoning can also help attract development to a particular area by keeping out incompatible uses. For example, by barring housing from agricultural or industrial areas a community can help ensure that the desired uses will not be harassed by unhappy neighbors. And despite the traditional kid glove treatment for agriculture, more and more communities are realizing that uses such as hog factories are capable of blighting a wide area in a way that precludes other development.

Some communities seek to attract development by intensifying the use of already developed areas. Sometimes a critical mass is necessary to attract particular types of development, and this can be accomplished by encouraging higher densities in areas in which such development is already taking place. A few places like Waikiki and Las Vegas seem to thrive on crowded conditions that most communities would find wholly unacceptable.

Redevelopment is the strategy often used by older cities. Vacant land within older industrial areas is being rehabilitated by "brownfield" programs. Local governments in the United States have the authority to use land acquisition powers to facilitate redevelopment for a wide array of uses.

Other communities try to create wholly new areas to which "greenfield" development will be diverted. The construction of highway systems and trunk sewers often serves as the trigger to attract development into a new area. Often financing will be facilitated through special taxing districts.

Tourism development is subject to the same three rules (pardon the cliché) as other real estate: location, location, location. Sometimes the strategy is to locate the tourists in a separate area away from the local population, as in the Maldives (see Chapter 6), while in other places the strategy is to concentrate the tourists in the heart of town, as in Bruges. The case studies in Chapter 6 illustrate a wide range of strategies for managing the location of tourism development.

This discussion of growth management skims only the surface of a topic of increasingly creative experimentation.[21] One issue that cuts through all of these programs, however, is a debate over basic methodology. The debate is among those who would like to emphasize (1) market-oriented strategies, (2) local vision-sharing and mediation, or (3) legal equity and predictability. In formulating strategies for managing tourism development, communities need to keep these issues in mind.

The Role of the Market, Local Norms, and the Law

In evaluating potential growth management strategies, consideration must be given to three strikingly different approaches to management. One emphasizes reliance on the market's invisible hand to produce an efficient balance of goods and services. A second focuses on the development of community norms that will influence behavior in desirable ways. The third relies heavily on legal processes to prevent violation of appropriate standards.

We believe that it is a mistake to adopt strong ideological preferences for or against any of these three management opportunities. The market regulates many things very well and some things quite poorly. Local norms can be highly effective in some situations but may break down in others. And the law can be effective, but only if it takes into account the working of the market and the beliefs and standards of the community.

The Market

Earlier chapters have described a number of communities that were or could have been dramatically harmed by unchecked tourism. There is no inherent problem with allowing and even encouraging tourism businesses to flourish; indeed, the industry has and continues to benefit thousands of destination communities, especially economically. But if the private conduct of revenue-seeking parties is allowed to deplete the area's shared resources for tourism rapidly, to the detriment of both the destination and the visitors, then the market has failed.

Economists readily acknowledge that the market is incapable of preventing the tragedy of the commons, for the reasons summarized in Chapter 2. When there is open access to a common resource that cannot effectively be privatized, normal market behavior will often cause the resource to be gradually appropriated by private individuals until the resource is destroyed.

Many economists argue, however, that we too often accept the proposition that a common resource is incapable of privatization. Interesting experiments with conversion of common resources into private allotments are underway, and many more deserve investigation. But it must be recognized that while some of these experiments have succeeded, many have not.

One cause of failure is the treatment of units of a resource as a fungible commodity despite the fact that the public recognizes important distinctions among them. The widely touted Environmental Protection Agency (EPA) program for the trading of sulphur dioxide air emissions is a case in point. The program allocates equal credit to the elimination of a ton of sulphur dioxide wherever it may be located and allows industries to trade pollution units as if they were completely fungible. But local communities can easily figure out that when a local utility trades pollution rights to an upwind polluter, it is the equivalent of spitting into the wind. Long Island Lighting Company has recently agreed to limit trades in pollution credits because of local pressure. In fact, the entire program of trading credits has languished because of fear of such local opposition.

Transfer of development rights is another way of turning a common resource into individual allocations, but such programs have only been successful in places where the public has provided the long-term support for the concept necessary to assure potential buyers and sellers of the program's sustainability.[22]

These two examples illustrate the complexity of designing workable market-based growth management strategies. Unless the process of creating units to be traded truly creates units that are perceived as equal over both space and time, programs to trade those units may be seen simply as opportunities for political manipulation. But the difficulty of the task shouldn't deter the attempt. When market-based strategies work, they tend to have low administrative costs and adaptability to changing conditions, which make them both efficient and resilient.

Local Norms

As discussed in Chapter 2, many of the recent studies of common-pool resources have focused on places in which community norms and customs provided the standards by which the sharing of resources is allocated and enforced. In some instances, these norms counteracted both the normal market behavior that economists would have predicted and the established rules that lawyers had drafted.

The success of these informal systems for sharing resources has led some observers to wonder whether the influence of both law and economics may not be less powerful than often assumed. While this observation deserves considerable attention, it must be noted that many informal resource sharing systems have failed as a result of outside economic forces or because the scope of the system outgrew the effectiveness of nonlegal enforcement mechanisms.

Micronesia provides one example of the breakdown of traditional systems for sharing resources when economic conditions change. A society that had long maintained a healthy lifestyle and clean environment on the basis of the shared use of local resources broke down when foreign governments introduced processed foodstuffs and welfare programs. High market prices obtainable in some Asian countries for live reef fish induced local individuals to poison the reefs, which produces one big haul of fish and then none.[23]

The breakdown of customary legal systems in the face of outside pressure also is familiar throughout history. A few centuries ago the English fen people operated the country's wetlands as a thriving economic operation, cutting reeds for thatch, harvesting fish and game, and digging peat according to customary rules that had maintained a sustainable economy for centuries. But increasing wool prices and the growing political power of large landowners led to changes in the laws that took away the rights of the fen people and resulted in the conversion of virtually all of the wetlands to grazing or crop land.[24]

Informal systems of norms can provide useful models for determining the characteristics of management strategies that will be perceived as equitable, efficient, sustainable, and resilient. But if they are to be applied to large-scale, complex situations, they usually require a degree of enforceability that only formal law can provide.

The Law

Each of the growth management techniques discussed in this chapter is adaptable to the management of tourism development. All that is needed is the appropriate legal authority to undertake the desired measures. Just as effective planning requires appropriate legal authority, effective management also requires such authority.

But legal techniques that ignore the market and local norms can also prove to be unworkable. The laws criminalizing the use of marijuana have proven no more enforceable than earlier laws prohibiting the consumption of alcohol, because of the low market price of the product and its broad acceptability in many segments of the community. Similarly, rigid enforcement of 55-mph vehicle speed limits proved to be impossible in the face of both community norms that made faster speeds not only acceptable but also fashionable and of economic pressures to reduce time spent getting from place to place.

Countless other examples could be cited of laws that have failed to overcome economic pressures and community norms. The risk is particularly great when shared resources are involved because of the low success record in managing such resources in the past. Growth management strategies need to be cognizant of the appropriate role of the market, the local norms, and the legal system.

Hierarchies of Management Strategies

The geographical breadth of tourism resources varies greatly, as noted in the previous chapter. Some tourism resources are worldwide in scope—the average temperature of the world's climate,[25] for example, while others may be highly localized, such as Jerusalem's "wailing wall." The nature of the resource being managed should determine the appropriate levels at which it should be managed.

With complex resources, this often involves hierarchies of strategies that could involve international, national, provincial, local, and even neighborhood levels. If properly organized, each strategy should be designed to allow various aspects of these resources to be managed at the lowest possible level consistent with the goals of equity, efficiency, sustainability, and resiliency identified in the previous chapter. Thus, a neighborhood level strategy is typically "nested" within other strategies operating at larger scales, but these strategies allow the more localized system considerable autonomy.[26]

Global Scale

Some resources can be brought under control only by actions at the global level. If current predictions of climate change hold up, the long-term value of many tourism destinations will be disrupted by future climate change in the absence of some treaty enforced at the international level.

An existing global treaty that protects many tourism destinations is the international convention to reduce chlorofluorocarbon usage, which has often been cited as one of the major successes of international environmental law. The troposphere, home of the ozone layer, is of vital importance in the long run to any community that relies on sun-seeking tourists. It is of most immediate importance to places near the Antarctic ozone hole, such as Punta Arenas, where people are already taking measures to avoid the summer sun.

Other globally shared resources are badly in need of international cooperative management. Fishing villages of the Canadian Maritime Provinces have been tourist attractions, but the fishing fleets are idle because the fish are gone. Attempts to regulate ocean fishing internationally are continuing, but with limited success.

The tiger reserves of India are threatened by widespread poaching. The poaching is bankrolled by the international trade in wild animals and their parts. Some aspects of the CITES treaty, which attempts to control that trade, have been controversial, and the treaty has not solved the problem completely, but it has had an impact.

Bilateral

Bilateral agreements among nations are effective means of regulating some shared tourism assets. Thus, duck hunting in North America has long depended on migratory bird treaties among the continent's nations that protect nesting and wintering sites.

Acid rain has been a serious problem for the forests of Ontario and Quebec, which have long been favorite destinations for summer tourism. The sulfates are damaging the trees and acidifying the lakes, reducing the population of game fish. Most of the sulfates originate in the United States. Treaties between Canada and the United States, implemented by the Clean Air Act of 1990 and additional regulations proposed in 1997, should reduce the problem over a period of time.

The few remaining European wetlands are a major attraction for birding enthusiasts. European community rules now require member countries to protect key wetland sites. And water pollution standards at the regional level have improved water quality in the wetlands.

National

Some tourism destinations rely on national controls of shared assets. The Maldives, for example, impose national regulations that limit development on many of the nation's islands to only one hotel.

Even very large countries have resources that are shared among the entire nation. The primary attraction of the Grand Canyon is the awesome scale of the canyon as viewed by a person standing at the edge. In recent years that view has increasingly been obscured by haze originating outside Arizona. Special applications of the Clean Air Act have been made by the Environmental Protection Agency and the Interior Department in an attempt to reduce the buildup of haze in the Grand Canyon.

Breton, in northern France, has few remaining examples of the beautiful, wild landscape that has attracted tourists to the area. The French government bought up many small parcels of private land at La Pointe De Raz in order to recreate one of the finest wild areas.

British history has long provided a common framework of interest that has attracted English-speaking travelers to Britain. The national government imposes strict requirements for the preservation of "listed buildings" to ensure that the visitor can obtain a visual perception of historical conditions.

State, Provincial, and Others

Many communities depend on state or provincial authorities to allocate their key assets. California has created a special commission to ensure that development along its beautiful coast is appropriately designed and located.

The Everglades, a unique sawgrass marshland, is a major attraction for visitors to South Florida. The ecology of the glades has deteriorated badly as a result of inflows of heavily fertilized agricultural runoff and invasions of exotic species. The voters of Florida have directed the state to develop methods to restore the natural environment.

Over a century ago, the voters of New York state adopted a constitutional amendment declaring the forests of the Adirondack mountains "forever wild." The Adirondack Park Agency, a state board with regulatory powers in the Adirondacks, works with local governments to try to create a balance of a healthy tourist industry with an emphasis on winter sports while retaining the wilderness ambiance that is so rare in the Eastern United States.

The Bungle Bungle mountains, located in the state of Western Australia, have important religious significance to members of the local Purnululu Aboriginal Council. A management plan developed with the cooperation of the state and the council restricts most permanent structures in favor of camping and limits access in fragile limestone areas.

Local

Most commonly, local communities undertake their own efforts to preserve their shared assets. Oxford, one of England's most popular tourist destinations, uses it local planning powers to try to protect its historic character while accommodating a profitable traffic of visitors.

Residents of the suburban area outside Washington, D.C., became concerned that urban sprawl would overwhelm all of the picturesque farming activities of the traditional landscape. One county, Montgomery County, Maryland, developed a program of transferable development rights for the protection of farmland, requiring developers to contribute to the protection of farmland as a condition for the approval of new developments.

In Boston, the historical setting that attracted tourists had been lost in many places by mixture of new and old structures. The city created a very powerful local agency (BRA) with both the power to control development and the power to buy land and resell it, enabling the city to deal with very fragmented ownership in the Faneuil Hall area and thus create a successful tourist destination.

Neighborhood

Neighborhood groups, formal or informal, often play a key role in protecting shared assets. The game parks around Victoria Falls, for example, have been relatively well protected by informal networks of local residents who recognize the economic benefits that they bring to the tourism-based economy.

In Canterbury, where the Cathedral attracts huge crowds of tourists, the city had many other picturesque and historic sites that were being ignored. A local public–private corporation has been created to reach agreement on alternative local sites to which some of the tourists might be diverted.

New Orleans is the only major community in the United States to have been established by settlers from France. The Vieux Carré, or French Quarter, retains many of the structures dating from this period and reflecting the architectural styles then prevalent in France. For more than fifty years the local landowners, through the Vieux Carré Commission, have required new construction in the quarter to harmonize with the original character of the area.

In the 1970s, the reputation of Miami Beach had declined significantly. Vacant buildings were commonplace and the crime rate was high. At the instigation of a few entrepreneurial builders who admired the art deco style of the South Beach area, special taxing districts were created by which property owners in the area could raise funds to redevelop the area, which has once again become a popular tourist destination.

The Case Studies

The following chapters explore a variety of strategies to manage tourism growth. Most of the examples of successful strategies involve legal components, because regulation is often needed to ensure the preservation of shared resources, which are highly vulnerable to degradation. The beautiful vista that is blocked by highrise hotels; the crystal clear water that is polluted by sewage from tourism facilities; the serenity and seclusion of a small medieval village lost to the hordes descending from tour buses—all require the protection of law.

We divide these strategies into three broad categories: (1) quality control, covered in Chapter 4; (2) quantity management, addressed in Chapter 5; and (3) location enhancement, discussed in Chapter 6. These are not necessarily exclusive strategies and can often be used effectively in combination.

In each chapter, we first discuss these strategies in general terms and then describe in greater detail specific techniques that can be used to implement them. We illustrate each technique in a series of case studies drawn from throughout the world. Almost all of them involve strategies planned during the 1990s. "Closing Comments" note special strengths and possible weaknesses of the community's approach. The case studies are as follows:

Southern Lakes Region, New Zealand (p. 196)
Stewart Island, New Zealand (p. 221)
The Republic of Maldives (p. 215)
The Tarka Project, England (p. 250)
Teton County, Wyoming (p. 101)
Times Square, New York (p. 241)
Whistler, British Columbia, Canada (p. 162)
Yosemite National Park, California (p. 150)

Following each set of case studies, we describe potential constraints on the usefulness of the approach. In the concluding "Final Observations" section of each chapter, we analyze some lessons to be learned from the case studies, highlighting important issues that destination communities should address as they consider these strategies for managing tourism growth.

4

Quality Control Strategies

"Quality"—everyone's in favor of it; but just as with "truth" and "beauty," no two people mean exactly the same thing by it. The Paris that twentieth-century tourists love, with its grand, tree-lined boulevards radiating from the Place de l'Étoile and the Arc de Triomphe, was created by Baron Haussmann during the 1850s at the behest of Napoleon III. But his wholesale demolition of the crowded streets of the medieval city was met with outrage at the time. A contemporary corollary is the resistance that was initiated by I. M. Pei's pyramid at the Louvre and more recently by the new Guggenheim Museum in Bilbao, Spain, designed by Frank Gehry. Standards for judging what is attractive vary not only from generation to generation, but also from culture to culture. English cottage gardens, the interior gardens of the Alhambra, the rockeries and water of Chinese gardens, and the newly popular prairie grass gardens of the American Midwest present starkly differing concepts of beauty (as well as differing climates).

Issues of quality, of course, are not limited to questions of aesthetics. Many tourists from developed nations have expectations concerning amenities that contrast with standards that are acceptable to those living in other parts of the world. American tourists know that they need to drink bottled water in Mexico, but many are shocked to learn that their charming hotel does not provide air conditioning. Visitors to India may be prepared for the onslaught of beggars, but be terrified by their first ride on a dilapidated, speeding bus. An otherwise intrepid traveler to Laos may be eager for treks to distant ethnic villages, but unnerved by the sounds of scurrying rodents in hotel walls. Even Venice can stun visitors, when the image of a gondola ride on the Grand Canal collides with the reality of the summertime smell of garbage drifting through the waters.

It is not just tourist expectations that can be frustrated. Destination communities often have their own fantasies. They may anticipate a new resort on the outskirts of town that will blend seamlessly into their style, attracting tourists much like themselves, and posing few problems. What they may get is something quite different: a massive development that is out of scale with the rest of the town, generating noise at night and traffic during the day, overloading their infrastructure, and changing the character of their community. They may be hoping for a sedate and elegant retreat and instead find a tacky theme park next door.

Protecting Quality

When tourists visit places that don't offer the quality they seek, they can leave early or never return. Usually, the worst that happens is a disappointing vacation and a misspent holiday budget. But for a destination community, tourism developments and their impacts remain part of the community for years. Any measures that can be taken to ensure that proposed developments meet high-quality standards can offer long-term protections to the community and its shared assets.

Inherent in any approach to quality control, however, is the threshold question of whose standards are used to determine "quality." A destination community, for example, may reasonably expect that a new hotel will be visually attractive. Whose standards of attractiveness should apply? Those of the developer, who will be paying for and own the development? Those of a cutting-edge architect? Those of the residents of the community, who may not be schooled in the aesthetics of architecture or landscape design? Or those of the tourists, who presumably won't pay money to stay in (or return to) a hotel they find ugly, uncomfortable, or inconvenient?

In reality, it is the destination community that imposes regulations and adopts management techniques to control quality. If it imposes requirements that are too onerous—for example, demanding such expensive materials for construction that a developer does not believe there will be a reasonable return on its investment and abandons the project—then the community will lose all the potential benefits that it expected to flow from the tourism development. Slightly less rigorous regulations may still have significant effects. Developers may pass on their costs to customers, and regulations that require substantial expenditures by developers may result in higher charges to tourists, which may well reduce the potential tourist market and the prospects for success.[1] Failed projects, no matter how attractive, will be a blight rather than a benefit.

Similarly, if the destination community imposes too specific quality controls, it may restrict development to a cookie cutter approach so that each hotel resembles every other hotel, offers precisely the same amenities, is located in the same vicinity, and appeals to exactly the same type of tourist. Such a heavy handed approach could stifle tourism development.

Other restrictions may make development less appealing to visitors. If communities have as a high priority maintaining open space and low density, for example, regulations might require large parcels for all tourist accommodations. In an already built-up community, this could effectively permit development only at the outskirts of town. Tourists, however, may find it inconvenient not to be in walking distance of restaurants and shops and decide to go elsewhere.

The essential point is that every destination community should recognize that while its own conception of quality is important, if it does not mesh to some extent with what developers are willing to offer and visitors are seeking, there may well be no tourism development.

The goal of quality control strategies is to strike a sensible balance: to promote tourism development and activity that meet the level of quality the community expects, that provide long-term profits to the tourism industry and the community (a "sustainable" development), and that attract tourists who will enjoy their experience. The goals are hardly incompatible. For example, Napier is a small city on the east coast of New Zealand's North Island. It was devastated by an earthquake and fire in 1931. Largely rebuilt in 1932 and 1933, the city is a treasure trove of Art Deco buildings. They fell out of style and in the late

1980s and early 1990s, a few were demolished to make way for new construction. A group of citizens who appreciated the architectural interest the Art Deco buildings gave their downtown, banded together to mount an educational effort to convince Napier citizens to protect their architectural heritage. Largely through voluntary agreements and community pressure, Art Deco buildings have been renovated, restored, and repainted. Napier now advertises itself as the "Art Deco City," offers architectural walks, shows videos of the effects of the earthquake and rebuilding of the city, and draws a whole new segment of the tourist market. There are more bed and breakfasts, restaurants and cafes, and a lively downtown pedestrian shopping area. The "quality" of the tourism product has benefited the community, businesses, and tourists in Napier.

There are a variety of mechanisms that communities can use to control quality in tourism development. Three principal strategies involve mapping, performance standards, and what we call "trade-off" opportunities, often used in conjunction with each other. All of these approaches have been used in nontourism contexts, and each is the subject of extensive (and often quite helpful) academic and practice-level literature. While the strategies cannot ensure that tourism developments will be "beautiful," they *can* ensure that developments will meet at least a minimal standard of quality. They cannot erase past mistakes, but they can provide protection against similar failures in the future.

Districting Strategies

Mapping is a widely used technique that, when properly applied, allows a community to define the boundaries of an area on the basis of particular attributes. Although usually initiated at the local governmental level, mapping can also occur at regional or national levels. Sometimes the technique applies to all land within a particular jurisdictional unit (for example, a town or a county); occasionally it applies to a single, large site (for example, a national park or historical area); less often, it identifies only limited areas to which special regulations may apply (for example, areas where scientific research is permitted). Mapping becomes a strategy for quality control[2] when it defines districts with the intent of promoting or enhancing their special qualities.

In its most familiar role in the United States, mapping is an element of a zoning system that regulates permissible land uses by applying different rules to various districts in order to further the policies of the community or, less frequently, a region or nation. In such a system, a map embodied in a legal enactment divides the land area into separate sections, and the accompanying zoning text sets forth the different regulations that will govern the uses (and other aspects of development) in each of the districts.

The first step in the process often used to create a zoning regime is to establish the goals. These could include—to list just a few examples—preserving prime agricultural land, protecting residential neighborhoods from incompatible development, encouraging affordable housing, or preserving historic districts. (In general, see Chapter 2 for an analysis of the elements that contribute to a successful process for determining goals and setting policy preferences in a shared asset context.) An equally important precursor to development of a zoning ordinance (including both text and map) is a careful study and analysis of existing land-use patterns, land characteristics, potential for future land-use change, ecology of the area, and a host of other relevant factors. Because of the specialty nature of these types of studies, communities often retain consultants who are trained and experienced in designing and executing planning studies to work with local government staff.

Armed with the results of whatever preliminary studies have been done and a consensus concerning goals, the governmental body is now in the position to create or amend (again often with the assistance of consultants) a comprehensive plan (required in a few states) to guide future governmental decision making. Whether or not a plan is adopted, in most places the government then develops a map and designs specific regulations for each zone that will further stated public policies. Once adopted into law or promulgated by decree, both the map and the textual rules governing uses become legally enforceable.[3]

Mapping can also be used as a planning tool to encourage future action. A government might identify special districts on the basis of their need for infrastructure improvements, prioritize areas for "clean-up" of environmental degradation, or draw boundaries around those areas where it will devote public funds for economic development. The boundaries of such special districts may have little or no relation to those on a map that is part of a zoning ordinance, because the purposes of the districting are so disparate.

The goals of a districting strategy often determine the level of sophistication required for drawing the map. Maps that include special overlay districts (see, for example, the Great Barrier Reef, p. 115) are more complicated to draw, especially when they are based on typographical or environmental factors that must be clearly identified. In unusual instances, districting requires three-dimensional capabilities. The Saguenay-St. Lawrence Marine Park in Canada (p. 120) is subject to districting regulations that are described in a vertical dimension, identifying the portion of the water column and seabed where activities are either permitted or prohibited. In general, the more complex the regulations and the greater degree to which special physical and environmental aspects of the land are being taken into consideration, the more sophisticated the map will need to be.

One of the most appealing aspects of a districting strategy to manage tourism growth is its general availability: virtually any local, regional, or national government can adopt this type of approach to further a broad array of goals and policies. In the United States and other countries that grant zoning powers to governmental bodies, mapping buttressed by zoning regulations can be used to control the location and intensity of development in order to minimize conflicts between tourism and other legitimate uses and to protect special qualities of a destination from threats posed by tourism growth.

For example, if a community wishes to protect the quality of certain open spaces—recreational, scenic, or agricultural—then it can use districting to prohibit tourism or other development in those areas. Districting can separate seemingly incompatible uses (for example, neighborhood residential areas from commercial tourism development); protect environmentally sensitive areas, perhaps a shoreline or a mountain ridge, from hotel and condominium development; reduce density in visually significant locations; create greenbelts or corridor zones to provide buffers between conflicting uses; and encourage tourism development in areas where its impacts will be most easily absorbed.[4]

The World Tourism Organization encourages the use of the zoning technique of districting tourism areas. "Application of zoning regulations is an important technique to ensure compliance with local area land use plans such as for resorts, towns and other types of tourism development areas. . . . Zoning is also important to control development near tourism development areas so that it is compatible with tourism. Zoning of all types of land uses in the area helps maintain overall environmental quality."[5]

A Classic Model of Districting: The Vieux Carré, New Orleans

One of the oldest U.S. examples of districting to protect the character of a geographical area is the Vieux Carré ("Old Quarter"), New Orleans, Louisiana. (See Map 4-1.) More than sixty years ago, legal enactments established an administrative system to ensure the

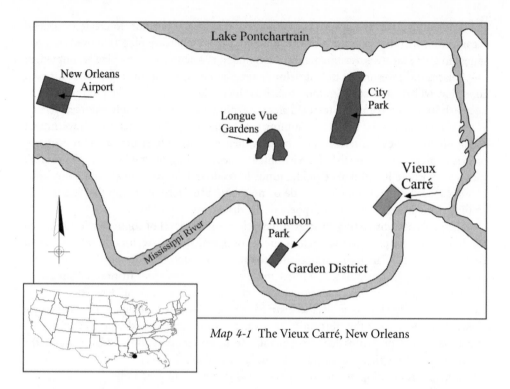

Map 4-1 The Vieux Carré, New Orleans

continuation of the distinct historical character of a ninety-block area, whose structures were almost all constructed during the eighteenth century, when New Orleans was a French-Spanish colonial city. That system, with minor adjustments, is fully in place today.

The Vieux Carré protections are designed specifically to preserve the special architectural character of the quarter. Buildings throughout the neighborhood are low, attached structures with interior patios, balconies with intricate wrought iron railings, no front yards, often painted with compatible exterior colors of browns and reds.

Created by state constitutional amendment in 1937, the Vieux Carré was the second historical district mapped within the United States (the first being Charleston, South Carolina, established in 1931).[6] Implementing the amendment is a local ordinance, which requires administrative approval for a number of proposed activities on buildings located within the mapped Vieux Carré area: "Before the commencement of any work in the erection of any new building or in the alteration or addition to, or painting or repainting or demolishing of any existing building, any portion of which is to front on any public street or alley in the Vieux Carré Section, application by the owner for a permit therefor shall be made to the Vieux Carré Commission, accompanied by the full plans and specifications thereof so far as they relate to the proposed appearance, color, texture, of materials and architectural design of the exterior. . . .[7]

Members of the commission itself are, pursuant to the local ordinance, appointed by the mayor with the consent of the city council, from a list of nominees recommended by specified institutions or groups of architects, historians, and businesses. It is composed of nine persons. The commission applies broad criteria[8] and its own internal guidelines in ruling upon landowner applications. Although the ordinance provides for review by the city council of decisions by the commission, in practice this is uncommon.

There have been six legal attacks on the Vieux Carré that were taken to courts of appeal; four decisions upheld the validity of the regulations, including one case upholding the ordinance standards as being sufficiently precise. One decision favored the landowner because the city had not enforced other regulations similar to those under attack. The other decision favoring the landowner was not surprising: the city had sought to expand the area of the district beyond that originally set forth in the state constitutional amendment. (See Chapter 2 on the need to define resource boundaries carefully.)

One shortcoming of the program is that although the ordinance imposes on the commission the duty to preserve "such buildings (as) have architectural and historical value and which should be preserved for the people," some buildings have fallen to the wreckers' balls. Thus, for example, there have been a few modern, tall structures built with special permission.

Another difficulty with the administration of the protective system relates to the sheer numbers of tourists that visit the Vieux Carré. More than a million visitors clog the narrow streets annually, with many coming to the festivities at Mardi Gras. The commission's daunting task is balancing the pressures of visitors (and the commercial interests desiring to serve them) with the legally mandated preservation goals. Architect and activist Malcolm Heard remarked in 1987 that "(i)f the first 50 years of the Vieux Carré Commission succeeded in getting the physical aspect of the Quarter under control, then perhaps during the next 50 years it could concentrate on the idea that the Quarter remains a viable neighborhood—a place where people work, live and tourists come."[9]

The pressures brought on by tourism growth have continued well into the 1990s. By 1994 there were about 120 T-shirt shops in the Quarter, some "complete with blazing lights and T-shirts bearing obscene messages," and many having skirted regulations mandating distance requirements between such shops.[10] Over the years, citizens have offered proposals to require the city to identify which commercial uses have become too prevalent (other than T-shirt shops, some citizens complain about the number of guest houses and other tourist-related uses) and to require new competitors to seek special permission in order to enter those businesses.[11] Proposals for new forms of businesses with potential negative impacts also spring up regularly. In late 1995, a local newspaper sought to install an elevated, 24-hour-a-day camera on famous Bourbon Street so it could broadcast tourism revelry on the Internet round the clock.[12]

Despite these and other challenges, the Vieux Carré historical district has been sustained for sixty years. Without this successful system, the mapped eighteenth-century neighborhood would long ago have lost its special character and would have been adversely altered with inappropriate modern elements.

Special Sites

Although districting is most often applied to large areas with a variety of residential and commercial uses, it can also work well to conserve a large site where a single use predominates. Often these are sites that because of their cultural, religious, or environmental significance merit special protection. Borobudur in Java, Indonesia, is an impressive eighth-century Buddhist monument.[13] By the 1970s, it was suffering severe degradation, particularly from water damage. To upgrade and conserve the monument, to attract tourists and provide them with necessary facilities, and to encourage the development of the surrounding community, the government created the Borobudur National Archaeological Park. It then adopted special regulations that applied only to the area within the mapped boundaries of the Park. The districting scheme worked so well that the Park project achieved the 1994 Grand Golden Award for Heritage and Culture from the Pacific Area Travel Association. Unfortunately, implementing the zoning approach required the relocation of 800 families.

NATIONAL PARKS

Use districts in national parks have been commonplace in many countries for years. The United States National Park Service uses a districting system to protect its parks, as does Australia. Parks Canada[14] uses a five-district system: (1) special *preservation districts* for preservation of rare or endangered species with some limited public use with limited access upon grant of a permit; (2) *wilderness districts* for dispersed human activities such as hiking; (3) *natural environment districts* for "intermediate levels of outdoor recreation" with some motorized access at the periphery, serving as a buffer between the preservation and visitor access goals of the parks; (4) *recreation districts* for visitor activities and supporting facilities, with some preservation of wildlife and landscaping; and (5) *park services districts* for essentially urban service and administrative areas.

Use districting is particularly well suited to national park settings, because it provides a "method for differentiating between conflicting uses and goals, by separating them into distinctive areas. . . . As such (it provides) a way to reduce conservation–tourism conflicts and operate within apparently incompatible mandates."[15] Although the disparities among the differing qualities of differing areas may be most apparent in national park settings, they exist in most communities to a lesser degree. Districting is a viable technique to minimize the negative impacts of potentially conflicting uses.[16]

Case Study: Indonesia

A national map divides all of the land into zones, imposes regulations governing the type of development that will be encouraged, identifies the infrastructure needs of various locations, and describes the appropriate target market for each zone.

The Republic of Indonesia consists of a group of approximately 18,000 islands lying between the mainland of Southeast Asia and Australia.[17] The Archipelago is the largest in the world, stretching from the Malay Peninsula to New Guinea. The largely Islamic population of two million people is spread over an area of approximately two million square kilometers. The climate is generally tropical with heavy rainfall from October through March. Although the official language is a form of Malay, there are roughly 600 other languages and dialects spoken in Indonesia.

Tourism is extremely important to the national economy. In 1995 there were 4.3 million visitors, and project planners estimate that there will be close to 9.4 million tourists by the year 2005. Indonesia has adopted a complex national approach to develop facilities to support that visitor level and simultaneously to accomplish a number of other policies. In the early 1990s, it adopted an initial national tourism development plan[18] and then in March of 1997, a supplemental plan. The initial plan covered a period of fifteen years and focused on development, promotion, and marketing of a tourism product; investments; and mitigation of environmental impacts. It also identified Tourist Destination Regions and Selected Strategic Areas for tourist development. The 1997 supplemental plan addressed strategic directions and infrastructure improvements at the regional and local levels.

An extensive planning staff developed these materials and focused on a number of issues such as the unwillingness of some local areas to accept tourism, the need to extend the economic advantages of tourism to less prosperous communities (what we have referred to in Chapter 2 as "equity"), the need for better integration of services and planning, and the need for increased environmental consciousness. The staff also identified another very significant problem: the disparity of growth and economic advantage between the western regions of the country and the eastern regions, and among groups within each of those two regions. Although the eastern area of Indonesia is well situated for tourism development, private investment has been concentrated in the western area (e.g., Sumatra, Java, and Bali). This is due, in part, to the lack of infrastructure and facilities in the east.

The Indonesian System of Spatial Tourism Planning

Indonesian planners have developed an elaborate, complex system of spatial planning. It designates as many as seventeen Tourist Development Regions; any number of Tourist Destination Areas (stratified in a hierarchy of main, second level, third level, and fourth level areas); various Tourism Supporting Areas, composed in turn of Main Tourism Supporting Areas and Second Tourism Supporting Areas scattered throughout the provinces. (These elaborate designations are not surprising, given a similar approach in nontourism planning. Cities in the National Space Area are designated as Centers for National Activities, Centers for Regional Activities, and Centers for Local Activities. There are also a number of mapped Leading Areas—thirteen in the eastern segment of Indonesia—that are identified as areas expected to develop at a rapid rate.)

Even though this spatial designation system is very complex, there is one aspect of the program that is of considerable interest: the establishment of a limited number of tourism zones, each accorded different development policies and funding opportunities, dependent upon their current state of tourism development, their natural amenities, and the potential for growth.

Six Tourism Zones

Indonesia's mapping system divides the country into six zones, A–F (see Map 4-2), going generally from west to east. The 1997 Master Plan for National Tourism Development states that each zone is expected to become self-reliant, with its own market opportunities; that the zones will not compete with one another but rather mutually support one another; and that particular types of attractions present in one zone will be designed to complement and reinforce similar attractions in other zones.

In Zone A, which includes the westernmost islands of Indonesia and Sumatra, the main tourist attractions are nature, the mountains, and the Malay culture. This area is at present crowded with domestic tourists. The goal of the Master Plan is to maintain these current numbers and to promote increases in the growth rate of foreign tourists. The supporting infrastructure is generally available, but there will be some limitations on growth because of size and carrying capacity issues. (In general, see Chapters 3 and 5.) Since most tourism is currently concentrated in two areas within Zone A, the basic strategy for development is to encourage tourists to visit other areas. This will necessitate significant improvements in access and transportation infrastructure.

Zone B, which includes the islands of Java, Bali, and Lombok, is a heavily visited tourist area, with the important city of Jakarta as its center. Government planners believe that sev-

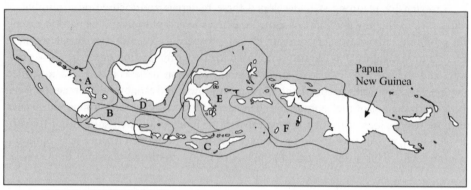

Map 4-2 Indonesia Tourism Zones

eral locations in this zone cannot support any increase in tourism numbers, but that many other areas could accommodate a measure of tourism growth as long as supporting infrastructure and facilities were provided. The overall strategy for Zone B is "intensification and consolidation," coupled with efforts to increase the carrying capacities of the region.

Zone C is a widespread and diverse area, overlapping Zone B on the west and Zone E in the north. It includes the central archipelagic area of Indonesia, with numerous islands that have important natural and cultural attractions. Government planners regard this area as unsuitable for mass tourism, but a perfect target for increased domestic tourism. The Master Plan expresses concern over the small number of domestic visitors who travel to Zone C, since they are the most obvious market for exposure to their own history, nature, and culture (each of which is available in abundance throughout the zone).

The western gateway section of Zone C (part of Java, Bali, and Lombok) already has a stable market, while the infrastructure is so poorly developed in the eastern portion that only modest tourism can presently be accommodated there. The government plans to develop touristic products emphasizing the zone's diversity and its unique natural and ethnic elements, recognizing that it will need to improve infrastructure and facilities throughout much of the zone.

Zone D, which encompasses a number of small islands and Borneo in the South China Sea just south of Malaysia and Brunei, is likely to experience substantial tourist growth and provide significant economic benefits to Indonesia. The fact that foreign tourists are now permitted to enter the zone with their own cars at the border with Malaysia is expected to dramatically increase the number of visitors. Regional cooperation among the Association of South East Asian Nations (ASEAN) members should also have a positive impact on the number of tourists in this zone. The government recognizes that because natural conditions of the area are the principal attractions, sustainable development practices are essential. Special interest tourism (especially adventure tourism and river tourism) has particular potential.

Zones E and F contain most of the islands in the north and eastern portions of Indonesia, stretching all the way to Papua New Guinea. Although there are a variety of ecosystems on the islands with interesting flora and fauna, the marine resources are the major attraction for most tourists. Government planners have determined that mass tourism would be inappropriate in most locations; therefore, tourism development is to be directed only to cities and the few already established touristic areas.

Closing Comments

Each of the six tourism zones has been mapped with reference to its existing and potential qualities, its present degree of tourism development, and its ability to sustain additional tourism growth. Each zone has been targeted primarily for one or more development strategies, on the basis of the type of tourist attracted by its special qualities. It remains to be seen how effectively the government will implement the zoning plan over time, especially in light of its great complexity and nationwide scope, as well as the political upheavals of 1998. National or regional staff and other officials may not be sufficiently familiar with local conditions to render sensitive decisions on development proposals. A similar, centralized decision-making approach has not worked well in Greece (another country composed of numerous islands, many of which have limited access and infrastructure), but perhaps there will be some decentralization in practice as implementation goes forward.

Indonesia is a huge and diverse country that has attempted to map the entire land area and provide regulation by way of separate books of detailed rules for each of a number of zones. Santa Fe, New Mexico, presents an example, on a much smaller scale, of a proposal to augment the existing plan with a multifaceted mapping approach to protect those qualities of the community that residents value.

Case Study: Santa Fe, New Mexico: A Plan in Progress

A draft General Plan seeks to enhance the quality of life by managing growth, promoting the development of neighborhoods, conserving natural resources, and fostering a Santa Fe tradition. One of the principal techniques the plan proposes is districting rules.

Located on the Rio Grande River in a valley of the Sangre de Cristo Mountains, Santa Fe has a rich heritage influenced by Pueblo, Spanish, Mexican, and American cultures. The city has long appreciated the diverse elements that have shaped its personality and has sought to preserve their imprint on its physical development. The very first city plan in 1912 proposed maintaining the winding, narrow streets that lent "charm and distinction" to the city. Santa Fe now has five separate Historic Districts, three Archaeological Review Districts, four National Historic Landmarks and over 100 sites registered at the national or state level for their special qualities. Santa Feans are not the only ones who find their city appealing. Tourists now flock to this chic oasis, admiring what has become known as "Santa Fe style"—a unique blend of such components as adobe architecture, desert coloration, Spanish tiles, Mexican furniture, silver and turquoise jewelry, Native American pottery, and an acclaimed contemporary cuisine.

Background

Since Santa Fe last passed a General Plan in 1983, there have been two trends that concern residents: tourism is on the rise, as is second home development. Tourism brought in over US $1.5 million to Santa Fe in taxes on hotel rooms in 1988; by 1993, that number had more than doubled to US $3.4 million. Along with the economic benefits, however, came some negative impacts that the residents wanted a new plan to address. First, the downtown plaza area, which had been the physical heart of the community since the early seventeenth-century Spanish colonial period (see Photo 4-1), was turning into a tourist center, filled with an ever-expanding number of boutiques selling designer denim, fringed leather, and squash blossom necklaces. The residential population there was declining, and most of the community-oriented businesses had relocated to peripheral areas, where the rents were lower.

Second, the increase in tourist-oriented land uses and the growth in second home development meant that real estate prices were rising. Fewer people who worked in Santa Fe could now afford to live there, and the resident population was losing its socioeconomic diversity. Third, second home development was resulting in a loss of open space. Fourth, because of the escalating number of workers who now lived outside Santa Fe, there was a sharp growth in the number of commuters, with a resultant increase in traffic congestion and parking problems. Finally, the population growth had a direct impact on natural resources, particularly on the water supply. Santa Feans were concerned that they were outgrowing the availability of water in their arid environment.

After three years of work, with active community outreach and participation, city planners and officials completed a final draft General Plan in September 1997. Reflecting community concerns, it has three major goals, to:

Photo 4-1 Plaza in Santa Fe, New Mexico (Courtesy of "Buddy" Lucero, Planning Director, Santa Fe)

- enhance the quality of life by ensuring that development is sustainable and that social equity, physical growth, redevelopment, and natural resource conservation and protection are balanced;
- foster a Santa Fe tradition which enriches everyday life by providing urban space conducive to public life and establishes an ecological basis for urban design, while continuing to build and preserve in accordance with the history of Santa Fe; and
- promote a compact urban form that creates affordable housing, reduces automobile dependence, provides a mix of land uses in all areas of the city, diversifies the economy, and enhances the unique personality, and sense of place and character of Santa Fe, while maintaining a regional growth management perspective.[19]

District Differentiation

The major technique applied by the draft plan to achieve its goals is the use of mapping along with quality promoting regulations. A variety of zoning measures encourage certain types of development and severely restrict others, with the objective of enhancing the different qualities of different districts.

Special Districts

Special zoning districts protect certain areas of the city from the impacts of incompatible development. Historic and Archaeological Review Districts include many examples of Santa Fe's architectural and cultural heritage. The plan recommends the establishment of a "transitional zone" around the Historic Districts that would serve as a buffer between these areas and large-scale, commercial development. Neighborhood Conservation Areas protect the ambience of older neighborhoods that were built up prior to 1940 from the intrusion of business uses. Two arts and crafts districts within these older residential districts allow an interesting mix of uses without generating heavy traffic or new construction. Regulations limit development in Resource Protection Areas and Sensitive Resource Areas in order to protect the viability of special wildlife habitats. Corridor Protection Areas provide a visual and physical boundary between urban areas and surrounding rural areas and highways.

Designation of an Urban Area

To control the location of future growth, the draft plan recommends that the city establish a clear urban boundary based on existing physical barriers, such as major highways. New development would be focused within this designated Urban Area, as would most infrastructure projects. The plan also recommends that Santa Fe annex large amounts of the surrounding land (and whatever land within the Urban Area that is not currently within city boundaries) so that it can control development more effectively. Without zoning authority over peripheral areas, Santa Fe would not be able to direct the location of future growth but instead would merely push development outside its borders, where it would be less closely regulated. (See Map 4-3.)

Density Increases

To promote the compact urban form that the plan envisions and to encourage the provision of affordable housing, the plan increases density in certain areas of the city. It permits greater massing of residential and commercial uses on specifically identified infill lots within already developed areas and in urban areas within a few miles of the downtown core

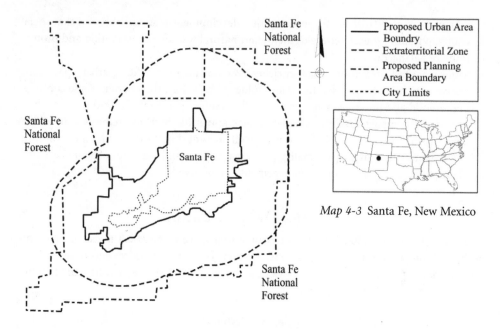

Map 4-3 Santa Fe, New Mexico

that have been identified for future growth. This strategy channels growth to areas away from the periphery of the city, which is largely rural, thus preventing suburban sprawl. This strategy also permits the development of more multifamily dwellings, which should produce more affordable housing for Santa Fe's employees and generally aging population. This in turn should promote a more balanced socioeconomic blend in most neighborhoods of the city. Finally, these measures also encourage growth where there is already infrastructure to support it.

Neighborhood Centers

The draft plan also includes measures designed to build and preserve neighborhoods, rather than subdivisions. The vision is of a city made up of a network of neighborhoods, each with a mix of housing types, with a blend of essential neighborhood services, and a pedestrian-oriented focus. In areas identified for future development, a centrally located commercial core, often designed around a plaza, would be surrounded by residential uses. This neighborhood center would permit such neighborhood serving establishments as drug and grocery stores, a post office, medical and dental offices, bakeries, hardware stores, and restaurants. To ensure that the neighborhood centers are pedestrian oriented, the plan restricts them to a size that can be walked across in ten minutes or so, with additional restrictions on the square footage of nonresidential uses. Neighborhoods themselves are relatively small scale, with greater densities permitted closer to the neighborhood centers. The goal is to ensure that between 35 and 40 percent of residential units in future developments will be within one quarter mile of the neighborhood core, and thus within walking distance of shops and transportation. A further benefit of the neighborhood center zone is that it also provides employment opportunities for neighborhood residents.

Protection of the Downtown Plaza

Another goal of the plan is to protect the downtown plaza area as the heart of the city. To ensure that no other commercial area competes with the downtown in size or scale, the plan spreads other commercial development throughout residential neighborhoods and limits their scope. It also allows strip commercial developments at only two existing locations and generally prohibits large-scale commercial uses that could encroach on neighborhoods and overwhelm the city's visual character.

Other techniques provide new support for the downtown plaza area. The draft plan proposes development of a "Public Marketplace" in the downtown area, which would include parking facilities, community-oriented retail stores, and small office space. The plan restricts the height of the Marketplace to that of adjacent buildings, so that it would not be visually incompatible with existing structures. The plan also identifies particular locations disbursed throughout the downtown area for zoning as community-oriented retail only. At the same time, tourist-oriented retail is restricted to an area within a few blocks of the downtown core, to ensure that it will not spread into residential districts. To lure residents back to the downtown area, the plan proposes that residential uses be permitted on second and upper floors of many downtown buildings. In a final effort to bolster community-oriented businesses in the heart of the city, the plan recommends consideration of a program that would provide economic incentives to help local-serving businesses afford downtown rents.

Reducing Density

In addition to proposing increased density in some districts, the plan also recommends reducing density in outlying areas of Santa Fe that are visually important to the community. Santa Feans do not want their views of the surrounding mountains to be marred by large-scale second homes and condominium developments on every ridge line. The technique the plan proposes to achieve this goal is a transfer of development rights, often referred to as TDR. (See the discussion of trade-off strategies later in this chapter.) Owners of mountain property identified on the map for decreased development could exchange the now restricted development capability of their land for the right to develop land in a separate area identified on the map for future development. The city of Santa Fe owns 2,500 acres of vacant land that it could use for these transfers.

Incremental Growth Restrictions

In conjunction with the variety of district regulations that the draft plan employs, it also includes an incremental growth strategy. Regulations direct the location, scale, density, and timing of all new development. Unlike some other communities, Santa Fe does not have a growth rate ordinance that specifies the number of building permits that may be granted in a single year. Instead, the plan relies on a variety of regulatory methods to control undesirable growth and to encourage growth where it will fulfill the goals of the plan.

Design guidelines and standards for residential neighborhoods, neighborhood centers, and commercial development govern the scale and appearance of new development. Timing is regulated in part by a carrying capacity tie-in: new development is to be approved only upon proven water availability and adequacy of the distribution and treatment system. Additionally, future residents and businesses are to bear the cost of providing water to the development where they are located, largely through the imposition of impact fees. These requirements would be waived for affordable housing development in infill areas.

The incremental growth approach includes an additional technique to guide the timing of future development: three Urban Area Staging Plans. These plans delineate which areas identified for future growth should be developed during three separate time periods. The first staging plan covers the period until 2005; the second is for 2005–2010; and the third, 2010–2020. Based upon such considerations as population growth projections, the ability of the city to extend infrastructure to areas without adequate existing infrastructure, and a desire for a geographic balance to new growth, the plans schedule the sequence and timing for development at each location identified for future growth.

Each staging plan also identifies the various studies the city will have to complete prior to development approval; these include regional waste management plans, environmental documentation, capital improvement plans, expansion of alternative transportation systems, and plans for such public and human service facilities as schools, libraries, and senior centers. This will ensure that there is adequate infrastructure in place (or that it would be paid for by developers) prior to new growth.

Neighborhood Planning

One of the fundamental concerns of the plan is to preserve and enhance neighborhoods throughout Santa Fe. The various mapping rules that foster mixed residential uses, affordable housing, neighborhood commercial centers that are easily accessible to residents, and clustering of residential and commercial uses to protect natural resources and open space are all designed for this purpose.

An additional strategy the draft plan provides is neighborhood and community planning. In 1989, Santa Fe formally adopted criteria for preparation of neighborhood plans, prepared by local residents and neighborhood associations. The draft General Plan envisions grass roots planning by local residents with greater authority to design guidelines and standards for the conservation and enhancement of their own neighborhoods. These plans could, for example, accommodate new development for infill sites or provide for the gradual elimination of uses that are deemed incompatible with the character of the neighborhood.

The draft General Plan also proposes a new process for the creation of Neighborhood Conservation Districts, which would be based on community consensus. These would include, among other things, a description of what the neighborhood envisions as its future character. This vision would then guide the city when making decisions regarding future development.

Finally, the draft General Plan also proposes that a process be established that would allow citizens, city staff, and officials to develop Community Area Plans. Each area plan would address the needs of a cluster of neighborhoods, allowing citizens to address issues that need to be planned for on a smaller scale than the entire city, but on a larger scale than an individual neighborhood. This might involve community services such as schools, parks, and transportation.

Closing Comments

The draft General Plan for Santa Fe addresses the negative impacts of tourism and second home development with a variety of regulatory techniques ranging from an especially impressive array of special districts to a transfer of development rights program to the imposition of impact fees. The plan is geared to addressing the concerns of residents, and includes proposals for continued citizen participation in planning and monitoring of development.

Realizing that growth in Santa Fe will have an impact on the broader region, the city recognizes the need for cooperative planning with other jurisdictions. While this regionalism is a significant element of the draft plan, it is an area that poses potential problems for the success of this or any other plan attempting to manage growth in Santa Fe. The strategy of designating the three urban areas for staggered growth will only be effective if there is a variety of agreements in place between Santa Fe and those bodies exercising jurisdiction outside the city (since the urban areas extend beyond Santa Fe's current borders). The city and the county in which it is located entered into a Joint Powers Agreement in 1981, and jointly adopted an "Extraterritorial Zoning Ordinance," governing the areas immediately adjacent to the municipal boundaries. Under the agreement, certain zoning powers of the city were delegated to the Extraterritorial Zoning Commission, while both the city and the county retained control in other areas.

While this sharing of authority is part of a serious attempt to cooperate in planning and administration, it has its own potential shortcomings. In a series of public meetings held in 1994 and through a survey, more than 1,000 residents of the extraterritorial zone (EZ) voiced concern and "anxiety about the lack of coordination among what they see as three jurisdictions affecting their lives and their property—the city, the county, and the Extraterritorial Zoning Authority/Commission."[20] There are often different policies and standards among the three jurisdictional bodies on such varied issues as preservation of open space; infrastructure planning, construction, and maintenance; water and environmental resource protection; subdivision regulations; and annexation. Many residents in the region regard the County Commissioners (who have effective control over land development decisions outside the city) as "pro-development" and view the City Council as responsive to voter pressures on existing conditions rather than permitting large-scale change.

Further complications arise from the fact that there are additional bodies with authority over land within the extraterritorial zone: the U.S. Forest Service, the U.S. Bureau of Land Management, the State Land Office, and Native American Pueblos. The ability of the city to annex the land required for implementation of the Urban Area Staging Plans will rely upon its ability to negotiate agreements with almost all of these separate entities.

There is the additional question of whether the residents of Santa Fe and those who live in the extraterritorial zone can forge a compatible vision of what they want the future to bring. Surveys taken in 1994[21] indicate that although there are many areas of agreement (for example, the importance of cultural heritage and traditions, the environment, and the landscape), there are significant areas where the two groups of residents diverge. Santa Feans value the character of their city, while those in the EZ wish to maintain the rural character of where they live. Those living in the urban area identify affordable housing as the top priority; EZ residents are most concerned about uncontrolled growth. Urban area residents are concerned about overcrowding at schools and economic development, while EZ residents are concerned about water quality and environmental protection. If the two groups cannot reach a level of consensus, it is unlikely that there will be widespread support for any plan.

As of the time of writing, the draft plan has not yet been adopted or amended, so it is too early to judge its efficacy.[22] Its combination of districting and growth management strategies provides an integrated approach that attempts to mitigate what the Santa Fe community perceives as the negative impacts of increased tourism. If the plan is adopted, whether these techniques will be able to revive the downtown as the heart of the Santa Fe community as opposed to an upscale, architecturally appealing shopping mall for tourists, create new pedestrian-oriented neighborhoods, and attract new, affordable housing development will be a major challenge. Whether the city will be able to forge the necessary agreements with the multiplicity of bodies with decision-making authority over land in the extraterritorial zone is an even greater one. Whether the residents of the city and the EZ will be able to work together as a single "community" to support any growth management strategy and plan is a final hurdle.

Limitations of Districting Approaches

Districting strategies are widespread because they can be adapted to almost any situation. Used in conjunction with other techniques—performance standards, trade-off opportunities, carrying capacity analyses, growth limitations, incremental growth restrictions—they can be remarkably successful at achieving specific community goals.

The major problem associated with districting strategies is that because they are relatively simple to use—often not requiring sophisticated scientific studies or costly consultants—communities may rely on them exclusively. However, adopting a map and related rules is just one element in an overall strategy to control the quality of tourism development. Planning should not stop once a district is defined and rules are promulgated. This situation could well produce undesirable rigidity—simplistic adherence to the established zones even when the environmental conditions, visitor needs, or economic circumstances of the community change.

A secondary problem associated with districting techniques is that they are sometimes imposed with little regard to the multiplicity of factors that may relate to different areas. For example, if a community wishes to preserve an area with historic buildings, it may map that area and impose separate protective regulations for it. However, the historic district regulations may impose financial burdens on owners of buildings that make it impossible for some lower-income residents to maintain their homes according to newly imposed standards. In Edinburgh, Scotland, stringent regulations governing the rehabilitation of the elegant Georgian houses in the squares and crescents of what is known as the "New Town" were designed to protect the splendid architectural heritage of the city. Instead, the requirements were so financially burdensome that few people could afford to rehabilitate the buildings, many of which fell into major disrepair.

Similarly, districting that drastically reduces permitted density in some areas while increasing permitted density in others has long-term financial implications for the owners of affected land (the "wipeout" and "windfall" effects). It may also have significant social implications. The map and regulations that protected the Borobudur National Park in Indonesia also required 800 families to relocate. Botswana is planning a tourism project in the central Kalahari that will force out some native Bushmen. Hotel development permitted along the Sinai coast in Egypt has closed off access to the shore for many Bedouins who traditionally fish there. Districting can have an enormous impact on people when the lines are drawn and the rules suddenly change. Those who make the decisions need to be aware of how many diverse elements there may be to consider in each situation.

Performance Standards Strategies

Performance standards systems are legal restrictions that regulate a physical or measurable aspect of development. They are a means by which a community can mandate that the physical characteristics of a development meet certain standards and also that a development not generate certain measurable impacts.

The design of a performance standards strategy begins with identification of broad goals—for example, the preservation of open space. Usually, these are goals agreed upon at the local community level with active citizen participation; sometimes, however, they are regional or even national goals. The next step is for the appropriate governmental body to select particular land development policies that will promote the goals. For example, a municipality may adopt a policy to require large lot zoning for single-family residential districts to foster the preservation of open space. Finally, the governmental body enacts clear and precise technical standards that describe the policy in measurable terms. Standards for large lot zoning, for example, might specify what percentage of open space will be required on a five-acre parcel, and whether that percentage will vary with the size, shape, or other characteristics of the site; how much flexibility the landowner may have in deciding where to place the open space on the site plan; and whether there will be any incentives offered (e.g., an increase in the number of permitted units) if the landowner voluntarily chooses to leave more open space than the prescribed percentage.

Types of Performance Standards

Performance standards are generally viewed as supplementary regulations, often embodied in a zoning ordinance, that can be used to address both what a community wants in development and what it seeks to avoid. Some performance standards are based on environmental factors relating to the parcel of land proposed for development. The primary concern is the ability of the land to sustain development, a consideration that will determine the type and degree of development permitted. These types of performance standards are usually applied to environmentally sensitive land where any development is potentially harmful: steep slopes, shorelines, wetlands, wildlife habitats.

Performance standards are more often used by communities to ensure that development that is of a general type permitted by an underlying zoning ordinance will, in its design and operation, meet certain expectations of the community. These standards customarily govern the appearance and visual impact of the development. Among the most commonly used performance standards establishing desired conditions are regulations that allow flexible review of a proposed development in any of a number of important categories.

Development density. These regulations limit the number of dwelling units permitted on a hectare, acre, or square meter of land on the parcel. In tourism settings, low density usually allows single-story structures, such as cottages, and preserves open space in a rural setting; high density permits multiunit buildings with less open space and landscaping, generally in an urban setting. In a parcel near water, a low density designation might be appropriate to protect the natural setting.

Floor area ratios and lot coverage. These factors control the bulk of buildings in relation to the lot size (their "footprint") and thus help determine the character of the project and the amount of open space.

Building height. This factor is important in creating the "character" of the development. For example, some destinations limit tourist developments to the height of a mature palm tree to ensure that they do not appear intrusive.

Building setbacks. Suitable setbacks help create privacy and provide open space and areas for landscaping around buildings. On environmentally sensitive parcels, larger setbacks can reduce risks (along coastlines, for example, setbacks guard against severe erosion or storm flooding) and minimize the intrusion of structures into the natural setting. Park

City, Utah (p. 79), increased setback requirements in certain areas to preserve sweeping, scenic vistas and to ensure that its entry corridors did not appear confining.

Building standards. These very technical standards, common in many countries, require that all construction meet a minimal standard to ensure public safety. There are often additional regulations that apply to any construction in areas that may pose special hazards: earthquake zones, flood plains, coastlines, etc.

Architectural and design standards. These regulations may cover everything from the style of the building, to the materials used for construction, to the exterior colors. They are usually imposed to ensure a uniformity of appearance that will be in keeping with the rest of the community. In Bermuda, for example (p. 144), the specific "Bermuda Style" is mandated for all tourist developments. Seaside, Florida, is one of the most famous designed communities, with strict regulation of exterior appearance and construction materials for all residential development.

Landscaping. These standards often require buffers to separate more intensive uses from less intensive ones. In some cases, trees of a specified height (taller than the structure) may be required and types of vegetation listed (usually indigenous rather than "exotic") to ensure congruence with the rest of the community. Revegetation is sometimes required in areas disturbed by construction. In environmentally sensitive areas, regulations may require developers to build raised walkways to minimize disturbance of existing vegetation.

Sign controls. These very common regulations are designed to ensure that signage is in keeping with the appearance of the community. The flashing neon that is appropriate to Times Square would not blend in at Colonial Williamsburg in Virginia.

Viewscape controls. These are regulations that limit development in areas that are important viewscapes. In Oxford, there are height and location restrictions on construction that would interfere with an important view of the church and college spires that create Oxford's unique skyline. In the Big Sur area of California's coast, there are restrictions on building that would interfere with the view of the Pacific Ocean from Highway 1, a world famous drive. In Japan, there are restrictions on construction that would interfere with another building's access to sunlight.

Utility line controls. Regulations often require utility lines to be underground for aesthetic as well as safety reasons.

Noise regulations. These do not mandate desirable aspects of development so much as they set limits for behavior with negative impacts. By setting measurable limits for noise, these types of regulations control everything from usage of loud garden machinery (many American communities do not permit noisy leaf blowers to be used before 8 A.M. or during the summertime) to the level of noise at outdoor concerts.

Performance Standards Systems and Zoning Controls

In the United States, performance standards are often incorporated into zoning ordinances. In combination with such traditional regulatory controls, performance standards constitute a "wonderfully simple and elegant formulation"[23] by providing a measure of flexibility to zoning. The underlying zoning ordinance still governs the use of the land, but application of the performance standards to individual development proposals allows decisions concerning density and dimension to be made on the basis of the specific attributes of the parcels at issue. This can be particularly useful when the environmental sensitivity of land varies from parcel to parcel, or within larger, individual parcels, requiring finer distinctions than mapping and zoning regulations can provide.

This type of flexibility is nicely illustrated by a local ordinance, described in detail in a 1992 U.S. court opinion upholding the legality of the enactment.[24] The Township of Upper Mount Bethel, Pennsylvania, wanted to require sufficiently large lots for residences so that the lots themselves would not be placed at environmental risk and also to protect "adjoining lot owners and groundwater in general from pollution and contamination due to sewerage and/or water problems." To accomplish those laudable goals, the government adopted a complicated method for calculating the minimum lot size that would be required for development, depending on objective conditions at the proposed development site.

The minimum lot size in a particular zone (for example, three acres) could be increased by application of a mathematical formula based on performance criteria relating to the character of the land and the availability (real or potential) of water and sewer services. This formula was expressed in a matrix. Along the horizontal axis were the types of water and sewer: on-site water, on-site sewer, central water, and central sewer. Along the vertical axis were land characteristics that were relevant to the ability of the land to sustain safely a dwelling without adverse impact to itself, neighbors, and groundwater in general: slope percentage, seasonal high water table at surface, seasonal high water table 1–3 feet, shallow depth bedrock 0–3.5 feet, and depth to bedrock 3.5 feet or more. Several of these factors applied to the litigant's land, with the result that the formula increased the minimum size of permitted lots and thus reduced the number of permitted lots in the proposed subdivision from six to three.

In a thoughtful and detailed exposition[25] of a specially conceived performance standards method for land-use controls, American land-use consultant Lane Kendig and others proposed eliminating "conventional zoning district designations and (replacing) them with far fewer and more important district distinctions." Uses and structures would be permitted based upon the "particular, and frequently measurable 'by-products' that each use is likely to have." Most of our book relates to residential development, but the concepts have applicability to broader contexts as well, including commercial tourism development.

While it is difficult to summarize such a detailed and comprehensive regulatory system, in essence this approach contemplates calculation of a "net buildable site area" for any project, by subtracting from the overall lot area any legally required open space. The required open space for any particular piece of potentially developable land is the total of the minimum level of recreation land the parcel must provide as well as any "resource protection land" required because of environmentally sensitive features. Once the "net buildable site area" is established, then the government applies a number of performance standards relating to floor area ratio, nonresidential open space ratio, impervious surface ratio, and permitted density to determine what development will be permitted.

This performance standards system also employs "bufferyards" of plantings, fencing, and berms to mitigate negative impacts that could result from "very intense uses abutting considerably less intense ones" (for example, a factory next to a multifamily residential use). A buffer may not be required if the landowner chooses to locate the proposed structures on the site in such a way that the buffer is not needed. Finally, the system includes development bonuses for certain specified socially or environmentally favored components of the project, such as the provision of moderate- or low-income housing.

One of the interesting aspects of Kendig's model ordinance is that it establishes measurements for testing compliance with each of his four basic performance standards. For example, a townhouse with two bedrooms should not exceed on-lot impervious coverage of 52 percent of the total area of the parcel, and the floor area ratio should not be greater than 57 percent if there is on-lot parking. This provides an objective measurement that can be included in the regulations to guide both developers and government personnel when evaluating proposals. Of course, a government might well choose different numbers to accomplish identified community goals. If there is a policy to retain open space, for example, a municipality might decrease the allowable floor area ratio for different types of structures to ensure less lot coverage by buildings and thus increase the amount of open land. The significant factor is that the standard can be both measurable and objectively applied.

Performance Standards and Tourism Development

Although performance standards usually apply to general residential and commercial development, they can be used just as effectively to ensure quality tourism development. The World Tourism Organization emphatically supports consideration of performance standards techniques: "Establishing facility standards is an essential aspect of developing tourism because they influence both the satisfaction level of tourists and the overall quality and character of the environment for residents. Many of these standards determine the extent to which the tourism development is integrated into the natural and cultural environment and does not generate environmental problems."[26]

One of the greatest strengths of performance standards strategies is that they can be applied in virtually any setting: local, regional, or national; rural or urban; industrialized or agricultural. Because they are able to address so many varied issues of "quality"—from the requirement to provide terracing on hillsides to minimize erosion in Park City, Utah, to the stipulation that certain tourist accommodations on the Caribbean island of Belize include verandahs—they can be used effectively by communities with very different needs and goals.

Case Study: New Zealand

The national government enacts a Resource Management Act that embodies performance standards to promote sustainable management of New Zealand's natural and physical resources.

The Lonely Planet guide to New Zealand begins with a paragraph perfectly encapsulating the visitor appeal of that biologically and culturally diverse country: "Fresh air, magnificent scenery and outdoor activities are the feature attractions of New Zealand. It's not a big country but for sheer variety it's hard to beat. As soon as you reach New Zealand, you quickly see that its reputation for being 'clean and green' is well deserved. Visitors who come expecting a pristine, green, well-organized little country are not disappointed." (See Photo 4-2.)

The tourism industry produces around 20 percent of New Zealand's export earnings. Those earnings are growing rapidly at approximately 6 percent per year, and it is estimated that by the year 2000 the industry will support 100 and 85,000 jobs and generate NZ $9 billion in foreign exchange earnings. The governments (national, regional, and district) and the industry itself recognize the importance of maintaining the natural resources of the country. Accordingly, there is in place an elaborate system of impact assessment and gov-

Photo 4-2 Bay in Urapukapuka Island, Bay of Islands, New Zealand

ernmental permitting to guide appropriate development of all activities (including tourism activities) that use environmental resources.

The Resource Management Act of 1991

The national government enacted the Resource Management Act (RMA) in 1991 with the principal purpose of achieving "sustainable management" of New Zealand's "natural and physical resources," defined as land, water, air, soil, minerals, energy, plants and animals, and structures. The statute establishes three essential goals for sustainable management: (a) to sustain the potential of the natural and physical resources to meet the needs of future generations; (b) to safeguard the capacity of air, water, soil, and ecosystems; and (c) to avoid, remedy, or mitigate any adverse effects of activities on the environment.

The RMA embodies the notion that control over the effects of activities that use resources is preferable to control over the activities themselves. The system is impact based, with permits (called "Resource Consents") granted only after consultation with affected parties and often subject to conditions to mitigate potentially adverse impacts.

Issuance of Resource Consents

Subordinate to the national government in New Zealand are Regional Councils and District Councils. Each has a role under the RMA, depending on the type of activity proposed by an applicant. The Regional Councils have authority over three types of permits: first, coastal permits to take water, discharge wastes, or build within a mapped coastal marine area; second, water permits to take, dam, or direct water; and finally, discharge permits to discharge water. The District Councils decide on Consents relating to specified land-use matters, structures, subdivisions, and building applications. Conditions that limit the activities often accompany the grant of these permits. Dissatisfied applicants and also persons who have submitted comments on the application have a right of appeal to a specialized "Planning Tribunal."

The criteria for deciding on applications for Resource Consents are contained in the "policy statements" and "plan" of the relevant Regional Council and the "plan" of the relevant District Council. These planning documents contain listings of activities and describe how the impacts of those activities will be assessed. Activities are classified in the plans along a continuum of relative permissibility: permitted, controlled, discretionary, limited or restricted discretionary, noncomplying, or prohibited. The two extreme categories are easily described: "permitted activities" may be conducted provided that the standards set forth in the plan for the activity are met; on the other hand, "prohibited activities" may not be granted a Resource Consent (although an affected party may seek an amendment to the plan itself to change the activity from the prohibited classification). Activities that are "controlled" on the basis of either the nature of the activity or its location will receive a Resource Consent, but conditions may be imposed upon that grant, relating to such issues as building design, site plan, access, and parking. "Discretionary activities" may receive Resource Consents but only after full evaluation of the environmental impacts, again subject to conditions, such as lot coverage and height.

Consultation

Before applying for a Resource Consent, the applicant is expected to have engaged in "consultation" with persons "interested in or affected by" the proposal (i.e., those persons we described as "players" in Chapter 2). The governing statute itself requires the applicant to specify the nature of such consultations, the identities of the consulted parties, and other information. This process embodies the notion of good faith dialogue to share views and attempt to resolve differences. Of course, meaningful pre-application discussions (accompanied in some cases by adjustments in the proposal itself such as a reduction in density or location of structures) will often soften outside criticism during the decision-making process, especially if a public hearing is convened.

A comprehensive 1996 publication jointly issued by the government and the tourism industry, *Tourism's Guide to the Resource Management Act,* strongly suggests that tourism developers have extensive consultations with a broad spectrum of groups that would be affected by the development. This list of "whom to consult" is broad: "local (indigenous leaders), local and regional authorities, Department of Conservation, adjacent land owners, local residents/community groups, Historical Places Trust, special interest groups, utility service providers, Transit NZ, recreational groups, environmental groups, NZ Tourism Board, NZ Tourism Industry Association, . . . Maori Tourism Federation, (and, if relevant) recreational fishers, commercial fishers, boating clubs, local education facilities."[27]

The guide also includes a special section addressing the cultural differences that a developer needs to understand in order to effectively communicate with the indigenous people, the Maori. This includes familiarity with Maori "protocol and decision-making dynamics."[28] The guide is a fine example of the type of sensitivity that is required to encourage effective and meaningful participation by culturally distinct constituencies.

Impact Assessment for Resource Consent Applications

The RMA statute requires applicants to conduct or commission an impact assessment of the proposed activity. Tourism-related developments should be analyzed carefully. In the words of the *Tourism's Guide:*

Impact assessment is a critical part of your consent application. You will need to work out what effects your proposal is likely to have on the environment. As a guide, the amount of detail to include in the environmental assessment should be commensurate with the scale and significance of the actual or potential effects. An assessment must show how environmental factors have been included in your proposal and identify any remedial action to be taken. If the scale of your proposal and the potential adverse effects are great, seek technical advice from experts in preparing an impact statement.

As noted, there is no statutory requirement of retaining professionals to conduct elaborate environmental impact assessments; indeed, the RMA contemplates that smaller projects will be evaluated by the applicant for impacts at a level of detail commensurate with the scope of the project. Not all small project proposers, however, believe that the system is sufficiently streamlined. A restaurant owner on the east coast of the Coromandel Peninsula gave up his quest for a District Council Resource Consent to reconfigure and expand his kitchen service facilities to allow for easy outdoor dining, after spending NZ $5,000 for plans and the cost of governmental inspections.[29]

The publication concludes with a "Model Application for Resource Consent," a helpful example regarding many areas of RMA compliance, including particularly preparation of environmental impact analyses. In general, the Resource Consent application should include "an assessment of any actual or potential effects the activity(s) may have on the environment, including social and economic factors, and the ways in which adverse effects could be mitigated." More specifically, in almost all cases, the assessment should include such matters as socioeconomic and cultural impacts on the neighborhood and community; physical impact, such as landscaping; effects on the ecosystems; effects on special value resources such as natural formations with historical or aesthetic significance; any discharge of contaminants; and any risk to the neighborhood, community, or environment based upon natural or introduced hazards.

Successful Resource Consent Applications

Included in the *Tourism's Guide* are several illustrative examples of fact patterns that culminated in a conditioned grant of a Resource Consent.

Luxury Resort Lodge on Promontory

One proposal sought to construct a twelve-unit resort lodge on a promontory reaching out from the North Island's rugged and famous Coromandel Peninsula. The project was to include a restaurant, bar, and numerous recreational activities including walkways down the beach areas. Construction would involve discharge of stormwater from newly created impervious surfaces, vegetation removal and reconstruction, soil disturbance, and building of culverts and pedestrian bridges.

The lodge construction itself was within the local jurisdiction of the District Council, whose staff was consulted as a first step. The Regional Council had jurisdiction over other elements of the proposal, such as structures to be located over and in the coastal water. All together, the development would require five Resource Consents, two from the District and three from the Regional Council. The respective Council staffs studied the application and its required environmental assessments, in light of a number of policies and rules set forth in the District and Regional Plans. Most significant in this review were aspects of the development bearing upon the natural character of the coastline; the disturbance of existing vegetation; noise; on-site erosion and slope stability; public access to the coastal environment; traffic effects; site utility services, including stormwater drainage and sewerage facilities; and projected increases in employment opportunities.

In granting its permit, the District Council found that the site was suitable for the proposal and that the design elements were well adapted to the coastal setting. The Regional Council also approved the application as in full compliance with its stated rules and policies, including appropriate means of dealing with otherwise undesirable impacts (for example, the use of pedestrian footbridges over watercourses and the immediate re-vegetation of cleared areas, using native rather than "exotic" plants). In fact, the Regional Council decided because the impacts within its jurisdiction were so minor and the applicant had very broadly consulted with interested parties, it would not convene a public hearing.

Construction of a Hiking Trail in a National Forest

A second successful application sought to create a hiking trail and overnight hut system. Since the trail would cross land managed by the Department of Conservation, the proposal required a Resource Consent. In this case, the huts would have sewage disposal equipment and thus under the RMA, Regional Council approval was required. District Council approval was required for the building of the huts and other elements of the proposal.

There were a number of considerations that led to a successful application. The proposal situated the huts to avoid natural hazards, to protect natural, landscape, and amenity values, and also provided adequate waste treatment. The hiking trails were routed to minimize damage to flora and fauna, protect geological stability, promote recreational usage, and respect indigenous people's cultural associations with the area. The proposal also enhanced public access to the coast and protected the natural character of the coastal environment.

Resource Consents Granted with Many Conditions for Boating Facility

The owner–operator of a boat rental and excursion business sought four Resource Consents. The Regional Council had jurisdiction because of the water-based nature of the uses. In examining the proposal, the Council considered, among other things, "impact upon public access, water quality, marine habitat and wildlife values, security and longevity of structures, navigation and impacts on other users of the area." In approving the Resource Consents, the Council imposed a number of conditions designed to mitigate what it regarded as minor impacts. These conditions imposed public access, limited the number of boats to be rented out, required a fuel spill containment plan, specified the maximum height of the ticketing office, and reduced the noise of operations. The applicant's success was appealed to the Planning Tribunal by neighbors who had previously offered formal protest to the application, but the appeal was denied.

Closing Comments

New Zealand's Resource Consent system has a number of very attractive features. The program sensibly allocates authority between two different levels of government. (See the discussion concerning hierarchies of management strategies in Chapter 3.) The Regional Council is empowered to decide on matters of regional scope such as waste disposal, water, and coastline; and the District Council handles more localized concerns. Applications must include detailed impact assessments and proposed solutions to adverse impacts; if complex, as will often be the case, the applicant should retain expert technical assistance in making those assessments.

Resource Consents often include binding conditions imposed to solve special problems caused by the proposal. The governments expect good faith and active pre-application consultations with affected persons and organizations. This is an excellent concept in view of the tendency throughout the world for vocal opposition to controversial proposals, which might be avoided or reduced through meaningful discussions between the applicant and other interested parties.

The New Zealand program is national in its reach and is designed to protect a very broad array of natural and physical resources. Performance standards often operate on local levels to address the particular situation of an individual community. In the following case study, a performance standards strategy was adopted to protect environmentally sensitive areas from the threat of spreading development.

Case Study: Park City, Utah

A "Sensitive Lands" ordinance embodies a performance standards approach to tourism management.

Park City, Utah, home to that state's largest ski area, is rapidly becoming a year-round resort area. Located in the Wasatch mountain range 36 miles southeast of Salt Lake City and its 350 daily flight arrivals, Park City has been selected as a primary location for the Olympic Winter Games in 2002. It boasts three large ski resorts, a new US $25 million Utah Winter Sports Park for United States Olympic sports team preparation, as well as facilities for public bobsledding and ski jumping. It is also the popular site of the world-renowned Sundance Film Festival founded by film star, director, and producer Robert Redford for professionals and entrepreneurs in the independent film industry.

Promoting itself as "The Greatest Snow on Earth,"™ Park City at present has approximately 3,500 overnight accommodation units including hotels, condominiums (the largest number of units), and simple bed and breakfasts. In addition to outdoor activities, the former turn-of-the-century mining town offers art galleries, live theater, shops, restaurants, bars, and clubs, as well as a two-hour tour of an abandoned silver mine. The heart of the town is historic Main Street, served by a free shuttle trolley system on a twenty-minute schedule from 7 A.M. until 12:30 A.M. Demand for housing is strong, especially for condominium complexes and prices are high. According to the Dow Jones Real Estate Index, the average 1997 sale price of a single-family home in Park City was $568,400—one of the highest averages of any area in the United States—far higher, for example, than such other popular vacation sites as Maui, Hawaii ($295,000), and Hilton Head Island, South Carolina ($275,000). Not surprisingly, increases in resident and tourist numbers have brought on rapid commercial growth as well; the quantity and variety of the town's many shops and restaurants increase each year. At the same time, there has been a social cost: the difficulty of maintaining a "laid-back" and carefree lifestyle.

Background

By the 1980s, many Park City citizens and political leaders were concerned about excessive development pressures, especially those associated with tourism and vacation homes. Almost all areas that were fairly flat and easy to build upon had by that time had been largely developed. Additional building proposals were being reviewed by city staff for possible construction on ridges and hillsides, which at that point were among the remaining vacant sites.

After considering the scope of the problem, the City Council adopted a number of general principles for protecting as yet undeveloped areas. Following the adoption of those principles, the city appointed a Citizens Focus Group, composed of representatives of citizen groups and organizations, to develop ideas for a legally enforceable ordinance.[30] This group then worked with the Planning Commission throughout the drafting of the Sensitive Lands Ordinance. A separate seventeen-member Citizen Advisory Committee provided a "sounding board" for the City Council.

The goal of the ordinance was to further the protection of those attributes of Park City that made it a unique and desirable place to visit and live. "The long-term viability of the community depends on its success as a year-round tourist destination and as a desirable place to live and work. Park City must maintain its identity to preserve and enhance its appeal."

1992 Sensitive Lands Ordinance

The City Council created a special overlay zone to protect several categories of "sensitive areas": steep slopes, ridge lines, entry corridors, wetlands, and streams. Basically, the city drew a line on the city map around those areas of the city that were already built up. All of the parcels lying outside the boundary line were deemed to be within the new "Sensitive Areas Overlay Zone" (SAO). (See Map 4-4.)

The SAO included some land that was beyond the jurisdictional boundaries of Park City, and where the city therefore had no regulatory authority. In June 1994, Park City and the surrounding Summit County entered into an Interlocal Planning Agreement to establish joint planning areas and to identify suitable areas for future annexation to the city. This agreement serves as a basis for negotiation between the city and the county concerning application of the SAO regulations to land outside the municipal boundaries.

For land within the city limits, any development proposed within the SAO would be subject to rigorous environmental analysis paid for by the landowner. The analysis must include extensive information on the status of any potential "sensitive areas" within the parcel—for example, a steep slope. The analysis may be more limited than that generally called for in the ordinance if the city staff at its discretion decides that the nature of the land or proposal does not demand such rigorous analysis. After city staff has reviewed the application and accompanying environmental analysis, it makes a formal "Sensitive Area Determination," which, in turn, triggers a number of requirements, depending upon the type of sensitive area present on the parcel.

The interaction of the SAO regulations with zoning and building regulations is one of a hierarchy based upon degrees of restriction. Every parcel within the SAO is governed by the rules of the zoning and building codes, except where these are less restrictive than the SAO requirements, the SAO regulations govern. In practice, the administrative methods in

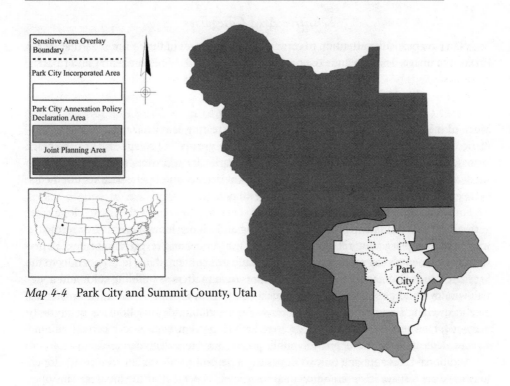

Sensitive Area Overlay
Boundary

Park City Incorporated Area

Park City Annexation Policy
Declaration Area

Joint Planning Area

Map 4-4   Park City and Summit County, Utah

place to interpret and enforce these regulations are an essential component of a land use control system.

Under Park City's SAO program, the first step in staff evaluation is to analyze the development submission to ensure that it correctly uses the criteria for delineation of sensitive environmental areas as outlined in the regulations. For example, the regulations provide that qualified professionals must conduct the analysis and address a great many features and conditions. By way of example, all ridge line areas (to include crests of hills and steep slopes) must be identified with precision; the analysis must also include the type and density of vegetative cover. A great many other categories of information are listed in the ordinance, and the staff has discretionary authority to require additional studies to be undertaken on such matters as "visual assessment," soil investigation, geotechnical reports on geological features, fire protection, and hydrologic and wetland/stream corridor resources.

The discretionary requirement of a visual assessment study is especially interesting and is fully consistent with the goal of the City Council to protect both natural sensitive areas and also visually sensitive areas. To that end, the SAO ordinance identifies several local "vantage points": positions where visitors and local persons find particular visual pleasure. This visual assessment must consider such elements as the proposed location, design, and other visual features of the project, based on study of the site along with sketches, renderings, and computerized images to determine whether there would be adverse aesthetic impact from the overall development or even some aspect of it. Once staff reviews the often broad array of information provided by the applicant, the officials then formally and in writing delineate all sensitive areas on the parcel, which in turn becomes "the basis for all calculations of open space, density, buffers, set backs and density transfers permitted or required" by the ordinance.

Sensitive Area Categories

The plan pays particular attention to certain physical features of the community that define Park City's image. These include the mountainsides and ridge lines and entry and riparian corridors.

STEEP SLOPES

Much of the land within the SAO area is very hilly, creating safety hazards and raising aesthetic concerns for inappropriate development. The greater the steepness (in percentage terms), the greater the risk. Therefore, under the Park City approach, regulated slopes are subdivided into two classifications having different density and open space requirements: between 15 percent and 40 percent and above 40 percent.

Some development standards apply in the same way to each of those two slope categories, such as requirements concerning grading and filling slopes, benching or terracing, street and road placement, retaining walls, and landscaping and revegetation rules. All private developments must meet specific design standards contained in a long appendix to the Sensitive Lands Ordinance. Special rules address such matters as building color and material; windows and glass; roof top mechanical equipment; roof pitch, color, and materials; height; dwelling size; and utilities. Incentives offer building density bonuses of up to 10 percent for owners of sloped areas greater than 15 percent who, under certain circumstances, dedicate open space, provide public access, or restore degraded areas.

Additional rules applying only to slopes of 15 percent to 40 percent require developers to reserve open space in an amount equal to at least 75 percent of the lot area. This open space requirement is softened somewhat by a sophisticated ordinance provision. If the city staff determines that the proposed overall building density, building design, and efforts to mitigate adverse impacts warrant relief, then the applicant is permitted to transfer 25 percent of the underlying density (i.e., the zoning ordinance allowance) on that open space portion to another area of the site. Slopes between 15 percent and 40 percent are also governed by a site-planning requirement that the development must be placed on the lot in its "least visually sensitive location."

Where the slope exceeds 40 percent, no development is permitted at all. However, there is a very limited density transfer provision: 10 percent of the underlying density of that slope area may be transferred to another part of the parcel whose slope is less than 40 percent, again subject to determination by the city staff that the placement of structures would be suitable in light of such stated criteria as overall density, building design, and mitigation of adverse impacts.

RIDGE LINES

Prior to adoption of the SAO ordinance, citizens in "focus group" meetings identified the most visually appealing ridge lines. The ordinance bars development within 150 feet from the crest of these designated ridge lines. These and other restrictions are designed to ensure that developments proximate to ridge lines blend in with, and do not disturb, the natural contours of these aesthetically pleasing landforms. The city was concerned that structures not create silhouettes against mountain backgrounds or the skyline, as viewed from any of the nine designated vantage points identified as having particular significance to community members and visitors.

A somewhat complex aspect of the ridge-line rules provides for certain density transfers. When a development is proposed in a ridge line area, a density transfer of up to 25 percent of the density permitted by the underlying zoning designation may be allowed if the city makes a "suitability determination" that the proposal will not have any adverse impacts on adjacent properties or development. Such a determination must take into consideration the overall density of the entire parcel, design features, and mitigating measures such as landscaping and screening. There is an incentive available to applicants whose plans further public interests: in addition to the potential 25 percent density transfer, the staff may recommend, and the planning commission grant, up to a 20 percent increase in transferable densities if the applicant donates open space, provides public access to trails, restores degraded environmental areas, or makes significant environmental improvements.

ENTRY CORRIDORS

Transportation approaches to a destination such as Park City are often through "gateways," the aesthetically important entry points. Park City was very concerned about maintaining the attractiveness of its entry ways: "To protect the image of Park City as a mountain community with sweeping, attractive vistas, it is the intent of this section to maintain the visual character of all designated entry corridors into Park City including open space and meadows located in the entry corridor protection areas, views of hillsides and ridge line areas and nature areas, such as streams and wetlands. This objective can be attained by eliminating or mitigating visually obtrusive development and ensuring that significant portions of meadows remain in open space."

The ordinance identifies three entry corridors and limits development on lots adjacent to or within 250 feet of the nearest right of way to these corridors. There are restrictions on creating new direct roadway access from parcels (favoring instead existing city streets joining with the corridor roadways) and measures to encourage common driveways between adjoining properties. Regulations require building setbacks of at least 100 feet from the corridors. Significantly greater setbacks are imposed to preserve "open meadow vistas" and areas with special visual impacts. Building setbacks on any given parcel are to be determined so as to "enhance and frame important views"; they are designed not to be uniform, but instead to vary and thus create a "walled effect." Other regulations encourage rear parking lots; require berms and earthwork screening to be graded and planted so as to create visual interest; specify the type of fencing to be used; and impose strict height controls. The general design standards referred to are also applicable in these entry corridor areas, and developers must submit a landscaping plan for approval by the city.

WETLANDS AND STREAM CORRIDORS

The Park City ordinance imposes a number of prohibitions and restrictions in order to protect wetlands and stream corridors because "Park City finds that the wetlands and stream corridors provide important hydrologic, biological and ecological, aesthetic, recreational and educational functions. Important functional values of wetlands and streams have been lost or significantly impaired as a result of various activities and additional functional values of these important resources are in jeopardy of being lost. The following requirements and standards have been developed to promote, preserve and enhance these valuable resources and to protect them from adverse effects and potentially irreversible impacts."

Essentially the regulations bar disturbances in any wetlands or stream corridors. An applicant for development approval must hire a professional approved by the city to determine whether there are wetlands or stream corridors on the parcel, using U.S. Environmental Protection Agency standards. If there is such a condition, then the developer may not "disturb, remove, fill, dredge, clear, destroy or alter (such) area," with some minor exclusions. The rules prescribe setbacks from wetlands and stream corridors and require that the project include appropriate run-off control to minimize sediment or contaminants to any adjacent wetlands.

Closing Comments

Park City's quality control strategy combines mapping and zoning techniques with detailed performance standards. The central Sensitive Lands Ordinance includes many well-conceived and drafted components. Of the many potential environmentally sensitive conditions on land, the ordinance identifies and regulates only those selected by the city as particularly significant to that community, especially in relation to its determination to maintain its essentially rural character, while providing many outdoor amenities. The ordinance calls for landowners to retain qualified professionals to identify and map the locations of these sensitive areas on each parcel on which development is proposed. One of the elements the ordinance protects is often overlooked: visual access to attractive vistas. These are important to residents and visitors alike and help define the aesthetic character of the community.

The ordinance also provides meaningful density bonuses to landowners who elect to exceed minimum open space requirements, grant public access, or restore environmentally degraded areas. Other provisions attempt to ensure that areas supporting increased densities will have landscaping or other buffers to mitigate any negative impacts. Finally, specific regulations cover a variety of design, appearance, and construction aspects of development to ensure that developments meet expected community standards of quality.

The strategy Park City has adopted is aimed at minimizing the negative impacts of growth both within and beyond its jurisdictional boundaries. The joint city and county planning agreement, the clear identification of areas for future annexation by Park City, and the coordinated efforts to apply the SAO regulations appear thus far to be managing growth outside Park City's municipal boundaries in compliance with the goals of both the county's and the city's comprehensive plans. (Park City's General Plan, however, wisely recommends reviewing the effectiveness of the Sensitive Lands Ordinance to determine whether amendments to the ordinance are necessary.)

However, residents of the city have voiced concerns—in community meetings, during public debate at the time of City Council elections, and in surveys—about population expansion, continuing loss of open space, and adjacent land uses. In response to these concerns, Park City's General Plan, adopted in 1997, includes recommendations aimed at improving regional planning and increasing city control over land beyond the municipal borders. Park City hopes to strengthen the Interlocal Planning Agreement with Summit County; develop a similar agreement with another neighboring county; develop consensus with these two counties on appropriate development patterns in areas immediately adjacent to the city; secure significant open space in annexation agreements; and acquire key parcels with critical environmental areas, important vistas, or desired public access.

Whether Park City and the surrounding counties will continue to "achieve common objectives for land use planning and urban development"[31] is yet to be seen. As growth progresses, there will be greater pressures on infrastructure and increased demand for public facilities and services, with financial implications for both the county and the city. The question of whether the residents of the rural areas outside the municipal borders will wish to be annexed to the city, especially as development continues and open space is lost, is a major one. Park City has begun the process of establishing good working relationships with its neighboring counties, but forging mutually beneficial solutions to regional issues is a continually challenging task.

New Zealand and Park City, Utah, have both seen steady growth over the past few decades. Both have instituted a combination of zoning regulations and performance standards to protect the natural and physical resources that are so important to each. Both are controlling the quality of all future development, much of it tourist development.

In some communities, there is a single land use that heavily influences the character of that community. Such a dominant development poses special problems but also offers regulatory opportunities not available in other situations. A major resort, for example, may have significant off-site "spill-over effects," often referred to by land-use planners and economists as "externalities." As the following case study demonstrates, these "blockbuster" uses can be treated in special ways under a performance standards approach.

Case Study: Jackson, Wyoming

Future expansion of a large resort must meet performance standards and comply with a Master Plan prepared by the developer, reviewed jointly by the town and county, and acted upon by the town.

Wyoming is justly famous for its scenery, wildlife, and national parks—attractions that have generated explosive growth of resident and tourist populations in several communities. (See Photo 4-3.) One of these is the town of Jackson, located at the southern end of

Photo 4-3 Sunrise on the Tetons in Jackson, Wyoming

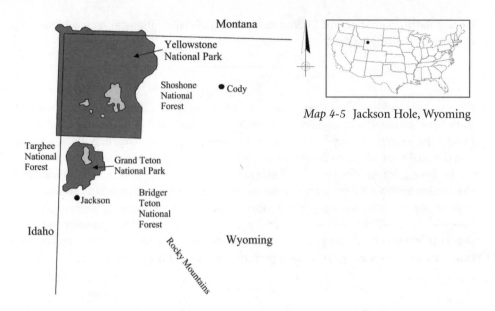

Map 4-5   Jackson Hole, Wyoming

the environmentally sensitive, 50-mile long and 10-mile wide Jackson Hole Valley. Both world famous Yellowstone National Park and Grand Teton National Park lie to the north of the town. (See Map 4-5.)

The town of Jackson has approximately 5,000 residents and has grown dramatically, as has Teton County, in which the town is located. From 1970 to 1980, for example, the combined population of the town and county increased 94 percent, while between 1980 and 1990, it grew an additional 19.4 percent. The number of dwelling units in the town and county has also burgeoned; during the eleven years 1980 through 1991, there was a 57 percent increase in dwelling units. Between 1989 and 1991 alone, more than 1,100 new dwelling units were built. The greatest number of winter and summer visitors to the valley stay in Jackson. As of 1992, there were approximately 10,000 lodging units available during the summer, and approximately 4,000 available in the winter (the numbers vary considerably because many of the overnight facilities, such as campgrounds, close during the winter).

Skiing is the principal recreational attraction of Teton County and the town of Jackson, although efforts are under way to expand summer season tourism. Almost all of the skiing and much of the summer activities take place at three large resorts, each of which has great potential for expansion. One of those resorts—the Snow King Ski and Summer Resort—is within the land-use control authority of the town and is subject to Jackson's Planned Resort District regulations. The other two large resorts in the area are outside the town's jurisdiction but are subject to a very similar set of performance standards established by the county government, which has authority over those resorts. The town and county planning departments and governments cooperated extensively in developing the respective guidelines for resort expansion and consult with one another with respect to ongoing administration of the rules.

1994 Town of Jackson and
Teton County Comprehensive Plan

An exhaustive Comprehensive Plan, in development for five years, was adopted jointly by the town of Jackson and Teton County in 1994. That plan addressed such areas as community vision; population; economy and growth; community character; natural and scenic resources; affordable housing; commercial and resort development; community facilities; transportation; intergovernmental coordination; and agricultural resources.

The planners who developed and governments that adopted the Comprehensive Plan were vitally interested in preserving the special qualities of the area. The plan begins with reference to the importance of "community character" and includes the significant observation that social and economic diversity (both of the population and the type of interaction taking place in a small town) are important aspects of the community character. The plan continues by noting that a resort community such as Jackson runs the risk of becoming homogeneous, thus losing its special characteristics. That risk is serious because "(i)t is a joy to encounter places that preserve, enhance and celebrate those things that set them apart and give them a meaning and personality all their own."

The Comprehensive Plan sets forth several "guiding principles" designed to balance growth with other values held by local residents. One of those four guiding principles is particularly relevant to tourist pressures: "The intent of this plan is to create conditions for a sustainable visitor-based economy not dependent upon growth, and an economy that reflects the unique small-town, Western character of Jackson, and the outdoor recreational opportunities of Teton County as key components of the visitor experience." To that end, the planning process to be implemented following adoption of the Comprehensive Plan was to include "establishment of planning capacity guidelines, providing a range for each resort's ultimate development, within which each resort can develop its own master plan."

The planners and community rejected a regulatory system for resort growth that was "strict (with) uniform standards and requirements" for all resorts. That rejection reflected a judgment that, although all three resorts share the common characteristic of high expansion potential, each faces different constraints and challenges, particularly in terms of the environment and their location. The 1994 Comprehensive Plan opted instead for a performance based master plan approach:

> A better regulatory strategy is to recognize the differences among the county's resorts. Any regulatory approach should be flexible, because of the differing limitations and opportunities exhibited at the existing resorts, in order to address the wide range of potential uses, functions, and scales of resort development. But above all, regulations should incorporate standards and criteria which require each resort to formulate a master plan for its future development in a community-wide context, considering both town and county concerns.[32]

Town of Jackson Planned Resort District

It took the town of Jackson two years after adoption of the Comprehensive Plan to develop and adopt a key implementing ordinance designed to carry forward the plan's contemplated regulation of resort expansion. This land-use control ordinance, which establishes a new Planned Resort District, by its terms applies only to the Snow King Ski and Summer Resort, whose physical location is mapped and described within the ordinance itself. The purposes and intents of the new Planned Resort District are broad and interactive:

- to encourage activities that rely on natural attributes of the area and contribute to community character;
- to provide high quality tourism by providing flexibility for planning and development;

- to establish a collaborative process between land owners and the town and county in developing resort master plans that are sensitive to the circumstances of that resort;
- to encourage winter and "shoulder" season tourism;
- to provide mixtures of land uses and transportation modes and to promote pedestrian walkways;
- to ensure consistency of resort planning with the 1994 Comprehensive Plan;
- to establish maximum potential size and character of each resort location to permit long-range planning by developers and the governments;
- to maintain a balance between tourism and the community while ensuring that the community character as a rural western location is not diminished; and
- to promote other attributes of the community.

Procedural Aspects of the
Planned Resort District Ordinance

The Planned Resort District Ordinance provides a very detailed procedure for securing governmental approvals of master plans prepared by the resort. In general, the process calls for preparation of a master plan by the affected land owners "to establish the development standards and serve as a guide to all future development," but it does not require technical specifications such as engineering plans or architectural drawings.

Once approved, the master plan is recorded in the public deed records, together with any conditions of approval and additional standards or agreements relating to future development or landowner responsibilities. This is a crucial aspect of the ordinance because the legal requirements of compliance with the filed plan and governmentally imposed conditions will thereafter "run with the land" and be binding upon all future owners of the resort. Of course, any potential purchaser of the resort or a portion of it would be on legally "constructive notice" of the limitations and undertakings embodied in the filed documents. Also, interested neighbors and citizens generally would have full access to the legally binding documents by visiting the deed recording office and inspecting the language. This is salutary from many standpoints, including conveyance of information useful in planning investment decisions and providing "transparency" of governmental decision making that has an impact on many within the town of Jackson.

The Planned Resort District Ordinance very effectively addresses a concern that has vexed many communities: how to enhance the likelihood that a development applicant will maintain its represented construction schedule and complete it in compliance with legal requirements. Some communities have faced the problem of approvals that are not followed up in a timely manner or by stoppages after construction has begun (often because of private lawsuits or financial problems).

There are a number of techniques to cover these risks that can be incorporated into a land-use control ordinance. Jackson's ordinance stipulates that the master plan will expire three years from the date of its approval unless the land owners have by that time submitted an application for a "Final Development Plan" for a particular phase as called for by the master plan (and containing more detailed information on the building of the project than the more general outlines set forth in the master plan itself). The ordinance also requires prompt construction of the expansion project: the master plan expires five years from the date of its approval unless construction has commenced on particular approved phases. But what if the landowner does not perform as it is represented in the master plan? Here again the Ordinance provides a ready answer: in the event that a developer fails to comply with an approved master plan regarding particular phases, the town is permitted to amend the phasing plan or to revoke approval of the master plan. This provision affords the town considerable leverage in "persuading" an owner to meet its undertakings.

Categories of Standards in the Planned Resort District Ordinance

Turning from the procedures to the standards applicable to planned resorts, the ordinance has a very detailed and comprehensive set of performance standards, each of which must be met. All master plans must be consistent with the joint town and county 1994 Comprehensive Plan. Although a resort's master plan should in general comply with standards of the town's land development regulations, alternative standards might be approved due to unique circumstances and community objectives. Each master plan must include a statement of the reasons for the proposed resort expansion and also a "design theme" for the development. A master plan must also contain a site plan illustrating where the proposed development will occur and also specification of dimensional limitations consistent with the design theme (e.g., densities, floor area ratios, and setbacks). Additionally, the master plan must address several specific elements: design, transportation, capital improvements, land use, phasing, character, and, as an option, community services.

Regarding *design,* the theme should normally emphasize outdoor recreational activities. Additionally, it should "create a sense of place" by incorporating natural features and aspects of the area's cultural heritage into the construction. The scale and character of the development should be compatible with the existing environment and exhibit visual continuity. Concerning building design, the approach should be an appropriate reflection of those current conditions that the Comprehensive Plan had discussed as being essential to preserve: community architectural character, pedestrian orientation, nearby nature, appropriate building materials and colors, and consistency with community cultural and aesthetic values. The bulk and scale of the construction should be compatible with the natural environment and nearby structures.

The design element portion of the master plan must also include criteria and locations regarding signage and exterior lighting (which should be low intensity and shielded). Spaces and structures should generally be oriented to provide scenic views. Natural resources on the site should be integrated into the design by preserving and incorporating such features as rock outcroppings and water bodies. The site design should include careful planning for pathways and pedestrian facilities to encourage their safe use and decrease the need for motorized transportation. The circulation plan should take into account the natural terrain and landscape, as well as afford maximum preservation of such features as wooded areas. Landscaping should be consistent with the overall thematic design and incorporate existing vegetation, especially if it provides habitat for wildlife.

Regarding *transportation,* the master plan must include approaches for limiting undesirable effects of vehicular traffic and providing an "optimum mix" of walkways, automobile facilities, and the like. This must be accompanied by a traffic impact analysis and methods for managing travel behavior of tourists and resort employees to minimize vehicular trips. The master plan must also identify and analyze parking and loading facilities.

An impact analysis is also required in connection with the *capital improvements* element, covering such facilities and services as transportation, water, wastewater treatment, waste management, utilities, storm water, and snow storage. The impact analysis, for example, must examine existing maximum daily peak capacity and current daily peak demand, with analysis of how those data will be affected by the proposed new development in the planned resort. The applicant must also state how it will phase in the needed capital improvements.

One of the most important components in the master plan standards is the *land-use* element. Land uses must be identified and be consistent with the design theme and resort "character" objectives. The ordinance includes a number of permitted uses such as residential, recreational (e.g., skiing), and special events (e.g., dance festivals and live theater if compatible with the resort)—all of which are seen as auxiliary uses to the resort itself. There are a number of identified uses that are prohibited, such as "regional-serving commercial uses" unless they are related to the resort itself, as well as commercial amusement uses that "undermine the natural and outdoor character" of the area.

One of the very interesting set of performance standards in the land-use element relates to the purpose of the resort expansion and its impact on the community character. First, the "overall amount of development" in the town of Jackson/Teton County should not undermine the "community character (as set forth in the Comprehensive Plan and the governmental land development regulations)." Second, infrastructure required by the resort expansion should not exceed the infrastructure capacity that can be appropriately introduced without undermining community character goals. Finally, a master plan for resort expansion should encourage resort visitors to stay within the confines of the resort so as to minimize vehicle trips.

The master plan must include also a *phasing* element that establishes the "logical sequences" of development of built amenities and public service expansions in relationship to the construction of resort uses. As an example, if a phase of construction involves expansion of units within a particular location, then "open space dedications, amenities, and required performances that mitigate the impacts of the resort" must be developed at the same time and in the proper proportions. When approving a master plan, the town must include a process for monitoring the performance of the various phases as set forth in the master plan, and if the town deems that a particular phase has not been performed properly, then it can withhold approval of future Final Development Plans pending full compliance as to that previous phase.

Probably the most interesting and elusive element required to be included in a master plan is the *character* element. The ordinance addresses "character" in terms of the single resort regulated by the ordinance, Snow King. It lists a number of "factors and resort characteristics" that are intended to be used in evaluating the character and design of all future Snow King expansions. The ordinance describes Snow King as a main convention and conference facility and a "unique, resort-oriented urban commercial node serving both visitors and residents." There are nine identified "factors and characteristics" of Snow King, including its creation of a sense of arrival, its pathways that also provide connections to the Jackson Hole pathway system, and the high quality pedestrian streetscape that connects to the Jackson Town Square.

The ordinance imposes several capacity maximums to maintain Snow King's character: as to lodging capacity, no more than 2,460 guests; as to size, no more than 28,000 square feet of conference facility meeting rooms and no more than 800 and 90,000 square feet of built structures on the whole parcel (with some exclusions). Land uses are generally limited to those needed by guests of the resort and local residents as opposed to those land uses that would attract patrons from the region as a whole. There is a detailed set of requirements for landscaped surface area (generally a minimum of 0.25 landscape surface ratio) in order to create attractive streetscapes, constitute high quality urban design, and invite pedestrian access through the use of a "porous edge" to the resort.

A master plan must also include an *environmental analysis* as to potential visual impacts in keeping with a separate ordinance governing a Scenic Resources Overlay District. The environmental analysis must also address likely impacts on wildlife and methods to mitigate any adverse impacts.

Closing Comments

The Jackson Resort District Ordinance is noteworthy because of the extensive interrelationships with the previously adopted Comprehensive Plan, the excellent scope of its coverage, and the quality of its internal detail. The 1994 town and county Comprehensive Plan set the stage for the regulatory Planned Resort District Ordinance by approaching tourism growth from the perspective of the community character desired by the citizens. The town selected a targeted regulatory approach to address special problems that expansion of an already very large resort could pose for the community.

The ordinance has a great deal of built-in flexibility, nicely meeting one of the purposes set forth in the earlier Comprehensive Plan of avoiding rigidity of regulation. The procedural elements of the program are well crafted: a resort master plan must address and solve important impact issues in order to be approved; after approval, the plan must be filed in the land records, at which point it becomes legally binding on even future owners of the resort. The standards themselves are broad in scope, covering the major categories of impact. At the same time, they provide a great deal of specificity, thus guiding the resort owner, the public, and governmental officials, even as to the important but often elusive concept of "community character."

Most communities apply performance standards in response to applications for permission to develop land according to the underlying zoning. Permission is granted after careful study of how the proposed development meets established performance standards and consideration of revisions that could mitigate any negative impacts that are expected from the development. In an unusual and complex approach adopted for Lake Tahoe in the American Southwest, every individual parcel of land is assessed for its environmental suitability for development on the basis of objective performance standards. All parcels are then ranked in order of suitability. It is these rankings that are the basis for future development approval.

Case Study: Lake Tahoe, Nevada and California

A specially created two-state political entity hired environmental experts to undertake a detailed parcel-by-parcel study of land around a famous recreational lake to determine the environmental carrying capacity of each parcel for development.

Lake Tahoe, known as the "Lake of the Sky," is famous for its captivating beauty and clear water. (See Photo 4-4.) Bounded by the Sierra Nevada Mountains to the west and the Carson range to the east, it is the largest alpine lake in the world. Located at the border of California and Nevada, portions of the lake's large basin lie within the jurisdiction of four different counties in the two states. (See Map 4-6.)

Few found their way to the Tahoe Basin until 1859, when mining activities in Nevada started to boom. From the late 1800s through the mid-1900s, Lake Tahoe became a favorite

Photo 4-4 Boating on Lake Tahoe, Nevada and California (Courtesy of Lake Tahoe Visitors Authority)

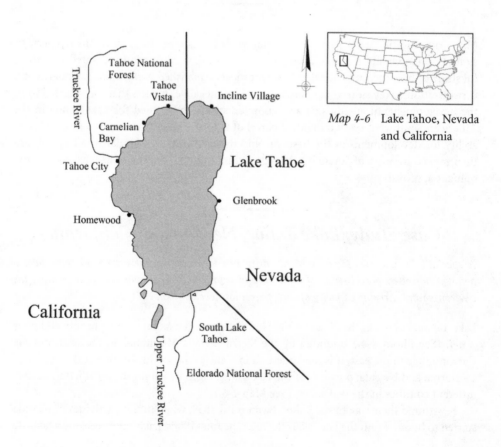

Map 4-6 Lake Tahoe, Nevada and California

spot for wealthy vacationers. Rapid development in the area did not begin until after World War II, when the lake's scenery, outdoor activities, and gambling drew greater numbers of tourists. Population centers quickly developed and by the mid-1950s, the ski industry had transformed Lake Tahoe into a major tourist destination.

The transformation of Lake Tahoe has for some time included luxury second homes, but the most recent building activity in that submarket has been extraordinary. In the town of Incline Village (known to some as "Income Village"), billionaires have been creating retreats worthy of kings. One financier purchased and then demolished seven homes in order to build an 8,000 square-foot mansion. One large private estate was recently sold for a record $50 million. And as property values increase, long-time residents find property tax bills skyrocketing.

Environmental Fragility of Lake Tahoe

Lake Tahoe's primary attraction is its crystalline waters. Nutrients, contaminants, and sediment resulting from rain and mountain runoffs are naturally absorbed by "stream environment zones" (SEZs) throughout the basin. By absorbing these potentially polluting elements, the SEZs protect the lake from increased nutrient concentrations, which would result in higher algae production, which would reduce the level of oxygen in the water, which would, in turn, cloud the remarkably clear and high quality waters of the lake.

SEZs are characterized by the presence of meadows, marshes, watercourses, drainage ways, and flood plains that provide surface water conveyance from upland areas into Lake Tahoe and its tributaries. Vegetation strips generally run parallel to the stream course. As well as providing water purification and scenic enjoyment, the SEZs sustain a wide diversity of plant species that are vital to the support of the wildlife habitat throughout the Tahoe Basin.

Despite the general health of Lake Tahoe, there have been numerous signs of deterioration. The most obvious is visual: visitors can no longer see clearly to the depths that were previously visible. Of the 205,250 acres that comprise the basin, almost 18,000 are in SEZs. Of this total, 2,466 acres have been built on or disturbed in some manner. Fewer than 1,483 acres of the developed SEZs are likely to be restored. Once the soil and vegetation have been disturbed, the SEZs cannot retain nutrients, sediment, and contaminants as they have for years. Instead, the potent reserve nutrients and sediment that have built up in the SEZs run off during and after rainfalls, clouding the pristine waters of the lake. The lake's aging process is being accelerated. Scientists estimate it would take Lake Tahoe 700 years to fill itself, the only self-cleansing measure available once it is contaminated.

Citizens and public officials in California and Nevada recognized in the late 1960s that development of the land surrounding the Tahoe Basin area was placing the lake—its stunning beauty, water quality, and wildlife—in jeopardy. Full protection of the SEZs was essential, and all future development needed to be coordinated and planned to ensure that the lake maintained its water quality level.

The Tahoe Regional Planning Agency

The effects of uncontrolled development began to materialize during the 1960s after the Lake Tahoe area experienced a rapid growth in population. Construction and landfill activities had damaged the basin slopes, causing erosion and water pollution. By this time, the clarity of the water was decreasing by over half a meter per year.

To address this emergency, the states of California and Nevada entered into the Tahoe Regional Planning Compact, through which they created a single interstate agency to correct the situation, the Tahoe Regional Planning Agency (TRPA). TRPA is not controlled by either of the two states, functioning more as a "political subdivision of the two states, comparable to a county or municipality." California and Nevada effectively contracted to delegate regulatory powers for lands located within the Tahoe Basin to the TRPA. The two states authorized TRPA to devise a plan to control development of all private land located within the boundaries set by the compact.

In the 1970s, TRPA developed a Land Capability Map and a General Plan Map based upon the physical capacity of the land to sustain development. This included identification and mapping of all SEZs within the area of TRPA's jurisdiction. In 1972, TRPA adopted a plan that controlled development, specifically on land most likely to significantly impact the lake, such as SEZs. Structural problems in the Compact itself limited the success of this early TRPA effort.

The condition of the lake continued to deteriorate during the 1970s. Water quality and clarity were rapidly declining, and the aging process was accelerating. In 1980, Congress approved an amendment to the 1969 Compact that expanded TRPA's power and required it to enact a plan that would curtail any development that "failed to contribute to attaining or maintaining specific environmental threshold carrying capacities." In that amendment, the term "environmental threshold carrying capacity" was defined as "an environmental standard necessary to maintain a significant scenic, recreational, educational, scientific or natural value of the region or to maintain public health and safety within the region. Such standards shall include but not be limited to standards for air quality, water quality, soil conservation, vegetation preservation and noise." Thus, environmental protection became the key standard for allowing private property development.

TRPA adopted a new regional plan in 1987, as well as a comprehensive Code of Ordinances, to implement the detailed terms of the plan. The plan evolved from several years of "Consensus Building Workshops," where representatives of often conflicting constituencies—conservation and property rights groups; federal, state, and local government; utilities and other businesses; and the general community—met to frame a mutually agreeable plan.

The 1987 Plan

The plan is an impressive document, both in its scale and its internal quality. One of its commendable features is the clear articulation of what it calls "development and implementation priorities," the steps by which the plan will meet its primary goal of improving Lake Tahoe's water quality by limiting residential, commercial, and tourist accommodation development in the Tahoe Basin. The first priority is to "direct all residential development first to those areas most suitable for development in accordance with environmental threshold carrying capacities and other considerations, such as infrastructure capacity and progress toward accomplishing water quality improvement programs." An "individual parcel evaluation system" identifies which areas are appropriate for development.

The second priority is to "manage the growth of development consistent with progress toward meeting environmental thresholds." Regulations impose strict numerical limitations on the total number of additional residential units over rolling periods of time and call for reviews every five years. The third priority is to "encourage consolidation of development through separate transfer of development and transfer of land coverage programs." The final priority is to "condition approvals for new development in the Tahoe

Region on positive improvements in off-site erosion and runoff control and air quality." Regulations require all public and private developments to include "complete offset" elements (or contribution to funds for that purpose) to mitigate all water quality, transportation, and air quality impacts brought on by that development.

The plan sets three major objectives regarding future residential development: (1) to limit the total amount of residential development that may occur in the Basin; (2) to control the pace of development by limiting the number of building permits issued each year; and (3) to limit the amount of impervious coverage resulting from permitted development (i.e., from structures, driveways, and parking areas). These limitations on future and existing development are offset by a Transfer of Development Rights program (this and other trade-off strategies are addressed in greater detail in the next section). The broad policy objective is to spread the burdens and benefits of limited development evenly and cluster residential development in optimal locations.

Individual Parcel Evaluation System

Under the TRPA ordinances, a property owner must secure three "rights" to be permitted to build a residential unit: (1) the right to build a residential unit upon an eligible parcel (a residential development right); (2) the right (a permit) to construct a residence during a specific calendar year (a residential allocation); and (3) the right to place "land coverage" on the parcel (the maximum percentage of impervious coverage allowed for that parcel). All three of these rights may be sold and transferred to other parcels according to the TRPA's transfer development program (TDR).

Though all property owners of vacant residential parcels (even those that include SEZs) automatically receive one "residential development right," the other two rights are determined by the Individual Parcel Evaluation System (IPES) on the basis of how well each individual parcel meets very specific and objective performance standards. Under the IPES, a group of experts evaluates each parcel using a standardized protocol and assigns it a rating number that reflects its suitability for development. If a parcel contains an SEZ, then only the land outside the SEZ is evaluated for development. A property owner who believes that the assigned rating is too low (i.e., the environmental threshold carrying capacity of the land is higher than judged by the team of experts) may request review by another "appeal panel" of experts. The seven environmental criteria upon which the evaluations are based are the relative erosion hazard, runoff potential, degree of difficulty to access the building site (i.e., excavation factors), water influence areas, condition of the watershed, ability of the land to revegetate, and need for water quality improvements in the vicinity of the parcel. Small bonus points can be granted if the landowner constructs off-site water quality improvements.

Following the numerical rating of vacant parcels, TRPA staff then ranks every such parcel in order of environmental suitability for development, thus creating a list running from the most suitable to the least suitable for each of the several county jurisdictions. Experts then refine the lists by establishing (the criteria are complex, but objective) a level on each list above which all properties are allowed to compete for "building allocations." (There are many highly complex provisions for alternative methods of competing for an allocation, such as transfers of development rights or allocations from other parcels.) Total allocations are limited by TRPA to approximately 300 per year for the entire Lake Tahoe area.

Only parcels with a certain minimum IPES score are potentially eligible for development. A parcel that is located entirely within an SEZ is always ineligible for residential development and is always given an IPES score of zero. With limited exceptions, the agency permits no "additional land coverage or other permanent land disturbance" on such a parcel. The 1987 Plan alleviates the impact of these development restrictions by granting property owners "bonus units" that may be sold to owners of parcels eligible for construction. SEZ owners also receive land coverage rights equal to a very modest one percent of the land.

In 1997, the United States Supreme Court held that an eighty-two-year-old landowner, on whose property a home could not be built, could sue TRPA for taking her land without just compensation under the U.S. Constitution. In December 1998, a trial began to decide whether her property and many other highly restricted parcels were in fact unconstitutionally barred from development.

Transfer of Development Rights Program

TRPA's TDR program[33] is an elaborate and highly detailed mechanism. Generally, it allows property owners (subject to many limitations and prior TRPA approval) to sell and transfer all three of the elements required to develop land: residential development rights, residential allocations, and land coverage rights. The following summary highlights a few of the many interesting aspects of the TDR regime.

If the transferring parcel is classified as "sensitive," transfers of rights are conditioned on a permanent ban on that transferring parcel's development. A property owner may transfer land coverage rights only to another parcel within the same "hydrologically related area" as the transferring parcel. (There are nine hydrologically related areas in the Lake Tahoe region.) The amount of coverage that can be transferred to a project is determined by the classification of the project and the land capability rating of the parcel. TRPA approves transfers of coverage when it approves a project on the receiving parcel.

Residential development rights may be transferred anywhere in the Tahoe region. Some projects, such as multiresidential projects like duplexes, apartments, and guesthouses, actually require transferred residential development rights. Parcels located in environmentally sensitive areas, including SEZs, may receive bonus residential development rights that can be transferred. Residential allocations may be transferred from a parcel with a low IPES score to a parcel with a high IPES anywhere in Lake Tahoe, as well.

Closing Comments

The Lake Tahoe performance standards approach integrates scientific evaluation based on carefully drawn standards with a procedural method for managing the location and pace of development with the goal of protecting fragile environmental resources. It is a well-crafted, sophisticated, and complex strategy that has its own limitations. One major drawback is the expense involved. The expert evaluation, the analysis of applications, the monitoring of the TDR program—all require highly qualified personnel. In addition, there are other costs of lake quality protection. Both California and Nevada assert that they cannot bear the very high cost of protection themselves. In late 1997, the federal government (with great fanfare including a presidential visit) pledged $50 million in additional funds to assist in meeting the $1 billion in erosion control and associated projects determined by TRPA to be essential to maintaining water quality. Some interested parties suggest that user fees be imposed on tourists, on the theory that they should bear some of the cost of protecting what they have come to visit.

A secondary issue relates to TRPA's strong emphasis on environmental protection at the cost of other important goals. Some have voiced concern that the strict limitations on development have prevented the area from meeting its moral and practical responsibilities to provide low- and moderate-cost housing. In December 1997, TRPA was at least temporarily satisfied with progress and withdrew its "threatened" moratorium on new subdivisions to induce local governments to permit and assist in funding a reasonable stock of low-cost housing projects.

Finally, the initial "parcel by parcel" environmental evaluation, rating, and ranking—the centerpiece of TRPA's performance standards strategy—is a lengthy and involved process that may well be beyond the resources, human as well as financial, of many other communities. What can be replicated, however, is an approach that incorporates clear and objective performance standards with a recognition that each parcel in an environmentally sensitive area may well be unique and should be evaluated individually for development potential.

Drawbacks of Performance Standards Strategies

Although performance standards strategies are options available to most communities eager to mandate a level of quality, they have their own limitations and constraints.[34] The first and most obvious is that they can control only future development or expansion of existing uses. They cannot address existing problems or alleviate the negative impacts of existing development. Other legal methods are required for this purpose (such as pollution cleanup laws to mitigate existing environmental degradation). Most often, communities must learn to live with past mistakes. Regardless of how offensive a development may be, if it complied with all applicable regulations at the time of construction, there may be few steps a disgruntled community can take. Early adoption of performance standards can help a community avoid this all too common situation.

A second limitation to performance standards strategies relates to the fact that to be effective, the regulations must be specific and detailed enough to secure the desired results. Communities must guard against a tendency toward excessive regulation, however. Performance standards can cover multiple aspects of development, but need not cover every aspect. Regulations that raise costs beyond a certain level may well scuttle development. Standards that are imposed on almost every component to ensure uniformity may stifle imaginative or creative development.

Communities should also remember that one of the greatest strengths of a performance standards strategy is the flexibility it affords. Decisions concerning density, design, buffers, open space, and other important aspects of development can be made on a parcel-by-parcel basis, taking into consideration the unique qualities of each site. If the performance standards are written too rigidly, applying the same requirements to each development, much of this flexibility can be lost.

At the same time, if the standards are too vague, instead of being flexible, a performance standards system becomes unpredictable. This can be particularly problematic for property owners who are unclear as to their development rights. In most situations, developers approach the government with detailed plans that the city, town, or county staff reviews in light of the adopted performance standards. There is often a great deal of discretion built into the system, so that the developer may not be sure of the siting of the development on the property, the permitted density, the dimensional aspects, the landscaping, and what mitigation actions may be required until the government acts on the application. The process of securing development approval is often lengthy, and because of the inability to predict precisely what will be required under a performance standards approach, it may be extremely difficult for a developer to predict the final cost of a project. This creates great uncertainty for a potential developer and can impose a high degree of financial risk. An imprecise performance standards system may discourage development by all but those with "deep pockets."

A related issue with performance standards approaches concerns staffing needs. As performance standards become more technical, based on scientific and engineering criteria, communities need personnel with the appropriate skills to draft, monitor, and enforce them.[35] Writing and enforcing a typical zoning enactment that involves a particular side-yard setback is vastly different from drafting and enforcing a performance standard that relates to wastewater treatment. Administration of some standards may well depend on the use of complex and often expensive instruments to measure compliance.

Additionally, restrictions that are meant to safeguard environmentally sensitive areas need to be continually reviewed and periodically revised to take into consideration new and sophisticated techniques that are available to mitigate negative impacts. Staff needs to keep abreast of the latest available information. The costs to the community for qualified employees and the latest equipment can be substantial, and may well be beyond the means of many.

Because performance standards strategies regulate so many different aspects of development, they impose a greater responsibility for implementation activities on the part of the government than many other approaches. Monitoring efforts may well last indefinitely when a particular performance standard regulates operational aspects of a new use that will continue to occur after the development is completed. (In general, see Chapter 2 for a discussion of the importance of monitoring the effectiveness of strategies.) For example, if there is a standard barring noise beyond a certain level (e.g., sixty decibels at the property line) at an outdoor concert stage, there must be trained and honest inspectors in place to ensure that the noise level is not exceeded as concerts actually occur. Once again, this is a personnel need that will be a cost to the community for the life of the development.

A final wrinkle of performance standards is what consultant Christopher Duerksen calls the "margin-of-error issue": What steps should a government take if performance standards are adopted, but then later turn out to be imprecise or to be insufficiently rigorous to control particular identified impacts. To address this possibility, Duerksen suggests that the enactments should be slightly more restrictive than current studies suggest are necessary, providing a "built-in cushion—a margin of error," and that there should be a proviso in the law that the government may in the future amend the standards if needed for the public good. This would allow the government to impose stricter standards on existing developments if the need should arise (in the case of excessive environmental degradation, for example). This would, however, again increase the financial risks for developers. In so doing, a community may make itself a less appealing location for any development.

Trade-off Strategies

The premise of trade-off strategies is that communities can protect some of those qualities that are most important to them if they offer developers appealing incentives. The *quid pro quo* is fairly straightforward: the community gets a measure of what it wants (to preserve open space or agricultural land, for example) in exchange for giving developers what they want (an opportunity for increased profits). Trade-off strategies are useful when a community either cannot or will not enact regulations that control development to the extent it wishes. When regulation alone is insufficient to achieve community goals, trade-off approaches may be successful. These are often methods of persuasion and encouragement, supported by that most compelling prospect: financial reward.

In the most ordinary (and oversimplified) development scenario, profits are tied to the number of units rented or sold. In the most common trade-off strategy, the developer is granted permission to increase the density of development in exchange for giving the community something it wants. The community of Coral Gables, Florida, wanted to preserve the architectural homogeneity of the city. It offered developers who would design their buildings in a Mediterranean style increased floor area ratios and additional building units. Known as "bonus" or "incentive" zoning, these approaches offer a developer an economically valuable benefit, such as increased density and/or intensity at some appropriate location on the parcel being developed, in exchange for voluntarily providing a previously specified amenity desired by the community (e.g., a certain number of affordable housing units, architectural conformity, or more open space, as in the Teton County, Wyoming, case study that follows).

Trade-off strategies are most often used to supplement mapping and zoning restrictions on land that is for one or more reasons "sensitive." This would include such diverse spots as scenically important parcels, fire or flood hazard areas, prime agricultural land, wetlands, and wildlife habitats. Unrestricted development on sensitive sites runs great risks of incurring undesirable impacts. However, limited development may not result in such problems. Trade-off strategies allow governments to promote important public policies relating to the use of land, without depriving landowners of legitimate interests in pursuing reasonable development.

Sometimes development restrictions on one portion of a site can be reasonably balanced by increasing the allowable density or intensity of development on another portion of that site. Assume, for example, that a developer owns a six-acre parcel, where the underlying zoning regulations allow two dwelling units per acre, which would permit twelve units to be constructed in total. However, a two-acre portion of that parcel is the nesting site of a rare species of bird, and the local government has prohibited any development there. To offset this total ban on development, the government has also adopted special rules that allow four dwelling units to be built on the remaining acres of that parcel in addition to the units otherwise permitted to be built there.

In essence, the community allows the developer to transfer the right to develop four dwelling units from the restricted site to other land. The total number of permitted units remains the same, but their location and density is changed. In the United States, such systems is sometimes called "density transfer" or "clustering" programs. They are often included as elements of a flexible zoning technique known as "planned development," under which the governmental body reviews design and engineering proposals within a regulatory framework of discretionary permitting and fewer rigid rules than under more conventional land-use ordinances.

Still another system of trade-offs involves a considerably more complex approach: restricting development on a site but permitting the rights to develop to be severed from the restricted land and sold or used elsewhere. Known as "transfer of development rights" or "TDR," these systems have been used by urban centers and rural counties to further a variety of public policies: to protect environmentally sensitive areas, to promote the preservation of open spaces and views, to preserve agricultural lands, to avoid suburban sprawl, and to preserve historic landmarks. The Lake Tahoe case study earlier in this chapter includes a brief discussion of a transfer program used in conjunction with an elaborate and complex performance standards system, while the Santa Fe case study refers to a transfer program developed to supplement the underlying mapping and zoning scheme.

TDR programs can vary considerably depending upon the conditions of the area and choices made by the government enacting the program. The system can be voluntary or mandatory; it may involve transfers of precisely the same development rights that have been restricted or may transfer greater development rights; and it may or may not include the establishment of a special TDR "bank" for depositing, buying, and selling the rights. The one common element in all TDR programs is the concept of creating "sending" sites, whose restricted development rights have been measured in some fashion, and creating "receiving" sites, where the development rights can be used to increase otherwise allowable development. TDR programs generally maintain the same development potential of a community but reallocate the density of permitted development throughout the community in order to promote certain community goals.

In Monterey County, California, there is a 60-mile scenic corridor along the famous Highway 1 that runs along the edge of the rugged Pacific coastline through "Big Sur." Each year tens of thousands of visitors from throughout the world drive that scenic and dramatic route with its panorama of rugged hills, steep cliffs, and ocean waves. The area is justifiably renowned for offering some of America's most spectacular vistas. To preserve the views, the county enacted a "viewshed" protection program that prohibits development that could be seen from Highway 1, but allows a "double credit" to be used on other property not within that viewshed. If a single home could not be built because of the restrictions, then two homes could be constructed elsewhere after a transfer of the development "credit." The sending land would be burdened by a legally enforceable easement allowing only open space uses such as agriculture and "passive recreation."

In another successful TDR program, Montgomery County, Maryland,[36] has approved the transfer and sale of more than 5,000 development rights. In that county, severe development pressures and spreading suburban growth from nearby Washington, D.C., threatened to undermine the ability of the community to preserve agricultural and open space land. In response to that ever-worsening situation and after extensive consultation with experts and citizens, the county created a 110,000-acre "agricultural reserve" by reducing allowable building density from one dwelling unit per 5 acres to one per 25 acres (commonly known as "downzoning"). At the same time, the county created one TDR for each five acres of land in the agricultural reserve area, which could be transferred and sold for use on parcels outside of the reserve.

The approach of establishing a set number of development rights per acre was rejected in an innovative program in the Santa Monica Mountains of California. There, properties deemed more suitable for development than others in a coastal area were allocated more TDRs than other, less appropriate parcels. The TDRs varied downward from one to fewer per acre. Interestingly, a private conservation group administers the program[37] on behalf of a governmental agency, the California Coastal Commission.

One of the rationales often cited for TDR programs is that of equity. When a community wishes to preserve open space or scenic vistas, for example, it is because the community as a whole benefits from enjoyment of those elements. But regulations that severely restrict development in those areas are limiting the ability of the affected landowners to benefit economically from the development or sale of their land. Farmland may be worth ten times more to the developer of condominiums than it is to another farmer. In essence, the effect of such restrictions on development is that a small number of landowners bear the economic burden of providing benefits accruing to the entire community. A TDR mechanism allows the community to further its goals, while still affording the affected landowners the right to develop land.

While many TDR programs are based on legal restrictions on the right to develop land (e.g., the Big Sur example described earlier), many others are voluntary programs. In these instances, the program must be designed not only with equity in mind, but also with the recognition that the incentives must be sufficiently appealing to landowners to induce them to participate. In the Pinelands area of New Jersey, a voluntary TDR program was designed to preserve biologically rich rural land from the seemingly inexorable spread of suburbia as more and more New Yorkers left that city in search of affordable housing. In this program, which designated both sending and receiving areas, the number of development rights granted to a landowner participating in the program depended on the degree of environmental sensitivity or agricultural importance of the land. The program has been successful and has generated little opposition. Although it was not targeted directly at impacts of tourism growth, it is a strategy that could well be used by other communities facing the loss of sensitive areas to tourism development.

One benefit of a voluntary program like the Pinelands is that it normally generates less resistance than a mandatory program. The Lake Tahoe TDR program has faced any number of court challenges. Almost all TDR programs, however, are complex and administratively challenging. Frequently they involve the creation of a TDR bank to facilitate transfers, an element that some commentators regard as essential to the long-range success of a TDR program. Trade-off strategies that provide for density transfers on the same site are much simpler to manage and, in some circumstances, can still work to preserve open space and a rural character.

Case Study: Teton County, Wyoming

A rural county experiencing very strong growth in second home development has adopted a comprehensive plan and enacted open space preservation regulations that afford a trade-off of increased development density where strict open space requirements are imposed.

We have already discussed how the town of Jackson has coped with aspects of its strong tourism growth by use of a comprehensive plan and a Planned Resort District (p. 87). That town is located within a larger governmental jurisdiction called Teton County, which has experienced similar pressures. (See Map 4-7.) The county collaborated with the town in developing and adopting in 1994 a joint Comprehensive Plan; the county also adopted very similar rules to regulate planned resorts within its jurisdiction. There is one major difference between the town of Jackson and Teton County: the county has a great deal of existing open space, in the forms of ranchland, corridors of rivers and streams, woodlands, buttes, and open meadows. Citizens and governmental officials have long been very protective of those open spaces and the values they embody.

The 1994 joint Town/County Comprehensive Plan included an entire chapter on the "community character" of the planning area. It identified as a key aspect of community character "lands which have essentially no built environment directly associated with them . . . a significant portion (of which is) privately owned." The plan also established as one of its "fundamental objectives" to preserve rural character: " . . . to allow development, but to make sure that new development is consistent with rural character. Primarily, rural character is defined by large amounts of open space in relationship to the floor area

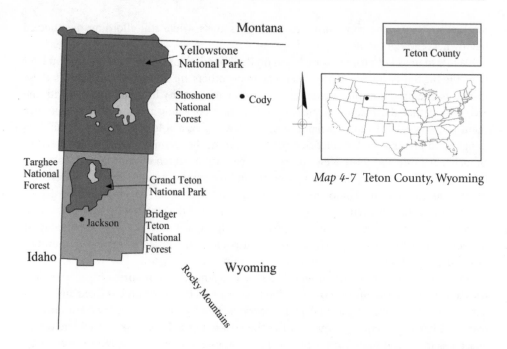

Map 4-7 Teton County, Wyoming

and volume of structures. Therefore, preserving a rural character requires that very large amounts of open space be set aside as development occurs. Open space also results in the preservation of natural resources, wildlife habitat, and scenic vistas, if the regulations are structured to protect these attributes." The trade-off approach embodied in Teton County's open space ordinance admirably fulfills that ambitious set of goals.

Density Transfers

Under its land development regulations, Teton County allows increased density in "exchange for" greater open space requirements. In almost all cases, such increase in allowable density would result in substantial economic benefit to developers who would be able to build and sell more units per acre of land, more than economically offsetting the impact of the unproductive open space.

As described in a "table of dimensional limitations," the regulations increase the ratio of required open space to the total acreage of the parcel to be developed, but at the same time increase the maximum permitted density. Developers have some limited discretion as to how dense a project to build, depending on a choice about the balance between density and open space. For example, if a developer elected to set aside 50 percent of the land for open space, a density of 0.057 dwelling units per acre (or two dwelling units per 35 acres) would be allowed. (Recall that Teton County is part of the "wide open spaces" of the American West.)

If the developer chose an alternative option and agreed to set aside 70 percent of the land for open space, a greater density would be allowed. Under this option, 0.171 dwelling units per acre (six dwelling units per 35 acres) would be allowed. The greatest density of 0.257, or nine dwelling units per 35 acres, is afforded developers who agree to set aside 85 percent of the land for open space. Thus, the regulations confer a substantial economic benefit in exchange for a significant increase in the amount of open space. These are very high incentives for preservation.

Open Space Standards

A trade-off of this sort would not be justified as a matter of public policy unless it furthered important public interests. In this case, the regulations recite findings and purposes that easily satisfy that standard because they identify the sense of openness as the predominant quality of the county that needs to be retained:

> Open space is critical to Teton County because it enhances the community's character, economic stability, property values, tourism and the quality of life for residents and visitors. The location, designs and use of open space affects the effectiveness of open space to enhance the community's attributes.

> These (regulations) provide landowners with a variety of development options for their property. (The dimensional table) offers several options that permit increased development density or intensity in return for the preservation of open space that contributes to community goals as set forth in the (Comprehensive Plan).

> The purpose of this (portion of the ordinance) is to establish standards for the open space that is preserved in exchange for increased development density or intensity, and to establish the process by which the design of the open space receives equal attention as the design of the development area.

The Teton County regulations are very sensitively tailored both substantively and procedurally concerning open space standards. The ordinance enumerates in order of priority the six types of open space that the county will accept for a density trade-off. These "areas of public benefit" are wildlife habitat and migration corridors; scenic vistas and natural skylines as viewed from public roads; waterbodies and their floodplains, plus wetlands; agricultural areas; certain public pathways; and public parks and accesses to public lands.

To minimize subjectivity when determining whether certain land qualifies as an "area of public benefit," the regulations also provide a list of sources to be used to identify such areas on property. These include the county "community issues" maps; natural resource and scenic resource overlay district maps; 100-year floodplains on Federal Emergency Management Agency maps; relevant sections of the Land Development Regulations; and an environmental analysis of the property.

The ordinance requires an "open space plan" to be created by the developer and approved by the county. The substantive rules cover several key aspects of open space preservation: (a) the preserved open space should be configured so as to preserve all or most of that land's "areas of public benefit"; (b) additional open space should be configured to expand protection of the "areas of public benefit" or to expand existing open space; and (c) the open space shall continue to be owned by the landowner but is subject to legally binding restriction documents recorded in the county land records that limit its uses to a very few activities and built elements.

The ordinance sets forth with commendable clarity the permissible uses to which open space may be put. No use may conflict with or diminish the public benefit that exists on the land. "For example, if the open space protects a designated wildlife habitat area, the uses and activities permitted on open space lands shall be consistent with protecting and maintaining the habitat value of the property."[38] In the rural district, all open space must remain in agricultural use or in a natural state. In public parks, less than half the open space may be developed to accommodate park uses. A few ancillary structures are permitted if they are consistent with the public benefit on the property: fences and non-residential structures for agricultural use, cross-country ski trails, and wildlife habitat improvements.

Closing Comments

Among the many desirable features of the Teton County ordinance is the special targeting of open space as a preservation goal. The county recognizes that not all open space provides equal benefit to the public and therefore sets qualitative standards for determining which type of open space will be accepted for a density trade-off.

By affording meaningful and well-drafted economic incentives to developers in the form of density bonuses, the regulations allow landowners to make rational judgments on whether to configure the site plan with additional open space and thus have more dwelling units to market. At the same time, by choosing a mechanism that is voluntary in nature, the county is relying on the marketplace for the success of its open space preservation approach. The question is whether buyers will prefer to live in closer proximity to neighbors in order to have larger vistas of open space in the distance; or whether they would prefer to have greater space between themselves and their neighbors; and what they will be willing to pay for their chosen option. Few developers will provide more open space unless there is some economic incentive to do so.

Constraints of Trade-off Strategies

Trade-off strategies can be very effective ways for communities to restrict development in sensitive areas without limiting the overall development potential of the community or severely curtailing the development rights (and related profits) of certain landowners. They can also encourage developers to provide amenities that the community believes it cannot otherwise secure. They can be used to promote a variety of community goals, from providing additional affordable housing to protecting scenic views.

The major drawback to many trade-off schemes is their voluntary nature. Developers may find that the financial benefits that result from an increased floor area ratio and reduced setbacks, for example, are not worth the extra costs of architectural and engineering plans and construction materials needed to conform with a town's preferred design (e.g., Coral Gables). The farmer of a significant area of agricultural land, who wishes to retire and move to a gentler climate, may find it economically prudent to sell that land to a developer, rather than take the lesser price offered by the county for the development rights. Communities that institute voluntary trade-off programs should be very careful to monitor their success, and their cost, so that if they are not achieving the desired results, the community can quickly modify them to try to solve their weaknesses (or consider different strategic approaches).

A second liability of many trade-off strategies is the increase in density in other, less sensitive, areas. In Teton County, where incentives allow only up to nine dwelling units per 35 acres, overcrowding may not be an issue. But for many communities, the number of development rights that may be transferred from open space or agricultural land to areas within an already fairly developed community may have a significant impact. Communities need to plan ahead and to envision what their community may look like in the future. Presumably, areas are zoned at a certain density level for reasons of public policy. When those density levels are changed, in order to promote other public policies, communities need to recognize that they are making a trade-off of their own. It may well be a viable decision, but it should be one that is carefully considered.

A final potential drawback relates to cost. In some instances, it is the government that purchases the development rights from the landowner (following authorization by the elected legislators or by the voters in a referendum) for placement in a bank for sale to another developer. The expectation is that eventually other developers will purchase those development rights and the cost to the community will be repaid. Nonetheless, it is the government that bears the up front purchase costs, as well as the expenses associated with operation and maintenance of the bank, and administration of the program. Depending upon the resources of the community, this can be an expensive method for preserving land (although much less expensive than a Purchase of Development Rights Program, where the government purchases and holds in perpetuity the development rights of land identified for inclusion in the program).

Final Observations

The case studies have shown that whether tourism development is in its infancy, well-established, or rapidly expanding, a destination community can fashion an appropriate quality control strategy to protect the shared assets it values most highly from unwanted impacts and to promote those aspects of development desired for the future.

Districting techniques are most appropriate to protect areas that are of particular significance to a community from harmful encroachments and to separate potentially incompatible uses. Used as a planning tool, mapping can identify locations for future government action (e.g., prioritizing areas for capital expenditures for infrastructure) or identifying sites where future private action will or will not be permitted (e.g., which areas will be designated for phased growth or which sites have environmental constraints to development).

Performance standards, in combination with mapping and zoning techniques, can address quality concerns relating to site and design aspects of development. They can also be a highly effective mechanism in providing protection to environmentally sensitive parcels, allowing distinctions between contiguous parcels, and even among different sections of a single parcel, when the topographic and environmental features of land change significantly in relatively short distances. By regulating aspects of design, performance standards approaches can also ensure that permitted development will meet a host of community expectations.

Finally, communities can use trade-off strategies to secure desired amenities that they either cannot mandate (because of legal impediments) or opt not to require (because of political or cultural considerations). When a community wishes to restrict development severely—usually on environmentally sensitive, open space, or agricultural land—it may decide to create a system for the transfer (or purchase) of development rights. These programs are often costly and complicated to administer, but they have helped various communities preserve valued land from unwanted development.

The case studies also provide numerous examples of how quality control strategies can operate at national, regional, and local levels to further a broad array of public policies. However, when there are multiple levels of government active in growth management, there can be diverse goals, separate planning bodies, conflicting regulations, questions of jurisdictional authority, and issues of autonomy. The case studies suggest that destination communities carefully consider how the "nested systems" discussed in Chapter 3, might affect their own autonomy and flexibility in designing their strategy.

For example, Indonesia's approach of directing the location of tourism growth is aimed principally at fostering economic equity: the national government wants to extend the economic advantages of tourism development to the less prosperous communities throughout the country. This goal has clear ramifications for each of the islands and local communities as well, since national funds are now committed to providing infrastructure and facility improvements for the eastern portions of the country so that they will be able to support increased tourism. (However, whether the 1998 economic and political upheaval will merely delay implementation of the tourism plan or completely scuttle it is as yet unknown.) The fact that the national plan also includes identification of appropriate tourist markets for each zone will also determine to some extent the type of tourism development that is likely to occur at the local level.

New Zealand's Resource Management Act, on the other hand, has a goal of promoting sustainable management of the country's natural and physical resources. Here, the national government sets the public policy and adopts the law, which is then implemented at the regional and local level by Regional Councils and District Councils. Unlike Indonesia, where the national government retains planning and administrative control, all three levels of governmental hierarchy are involved and have a degree of decision-making authority in New Zealand. The three levels are not, however, equal partners: local and regional plans must conform to the national Resource Management Act.

Santa Fe is an interesting example of a strategy that is designed to operate at multiple levels to further a variety of public policies. At the smallest scale, Santa Fe's draft strategy includes an innovative element—neighborhood planning. Local residents design guidelines for future development in their own neighborhood. To address issues at a slightly broader scale, clusters of neighborhoods work together to develop community area plans. These very localized plans then guide city officials in making decisions concerning future development. At the next level, the draft plan identifies a variety of regulatory techniques to manage growth within the entire city and provides forums for community participation.

Moving beyond the municipal borders to address issues of regional growth and its impacts on natural resources, Santa Fe no longer has the same measure of control or autonomy. The county, the Extraterritorial Zone Commission, and various other federal, state, and Native American bodies all have jurisdiction over portions of land in the immediate vicinity of the city. Santa Fe faces a particularly complex nested system in which governing rules may change from section to section, making it far more difficult to develop a comprehensive growth management strategy.

In addition to the need to consider the hierarchies of management systems within which a community operates, the case studies also suggest that established destination communities need to coordinate their planning efforts on a regional level when their tourism growth has impacts beyond their municipal borders. Park City and the towns of Jackson, Lake Tahoe, and Santa Fe have all entered into joint planning agreements. There is a realization in each situation that the impacts of tourism growth are not contained by jurisdictional boundaries and that cooperative efforts are necessary to protect all the parties from the potential negative impacts of growth and to protect their shared assets.

Many of the elements of a successful shared asset management regime that we identified and discussed in Chapter 2 are particularly relevant in regional contexts: carefully defining the boundaries of the extended planning area; identifying the legitimate players; creating an inclusive planning and decision-making process that will be perceived as fair by the players; and developing a strategy with enough broad-based support that the players will feel they can rely on its permanence. Planning area boundaries may need to be reconsidered as tourism grows and newly affected parties must be included in the planning process.

It is also more difficult to build consensus in a regional context where multiple and diverse constituencies have different concerns and objectives. There may be distrust around the issue of annexation, perceptions of power imbalances, and little history of collaboration. There may be conflicting goals and standards among bodies with competing missions and different degrees of decision-making authority. Particular efforts need to be made to promote participation from representatives of all affected parties if any final strategy is to enjoy the degree of support necessary for long-term success.

Another element found in many of the case studies is the inclusion of a market-based mechanism to further public policy objectives. Park City, Teton County, and Santa Fe all offer density bonuses to developers for voluntarily providing certain amenities valuable to the community. The assumption is that developers will be willing to provide the desired amenity in exchange for the chance of increased profits. The community receives the amenity at no financial cost (beyond the burdens attached to increased density) and without mandating its provision, by relying on the incentives of the marketplace. Of course, when quality control strategies rely on voluntary actions, there is no guarantee that developers will find the incentive sufficiently attractive to provide the amenity (since the marketplace is remarkably changeable)—an aspect that reduces the efficiency of the mechanism.

Another element of some of these growth management strategies is a requirement for impact assessment on the part of a developer. New Zealand, Lake Tahoe, and the town of Jackson all include impact assessment in their development approval process. This does not have to be limited to environmental impacts alone but can include a broad array of impacts relating to the shared assets that the community wishes to protect. While there is a potential that a community could impose so many impact assessment requirements that the cost and complexity would deter all but the most experienced and financially sound developers, regulations that are carefully framed to reflect local conditions and concerns can serve as a guide for developers as they draw their plans. This process can result in reasonable financial projections for the developer, appropriate mitigation measures for acceptable impacts on the community, and projects that are sustainable over the long term.

A final lesson from the case studies is a cautionary one. Santa Fe, Park City, Jackson, and Lake Tahoe are all sophisticated areas with significant financial resources. In the United States, the primary source for local government funding is property tax; thriving commercial centers and expensive real estate translate into a strong tax base. Planning and environmental studies can be very expensive: the professional evaluation of Lake Tahoe's stream environment zones; the analysis of Park City's slopes and ridges; the transportation planners, urban design consultants, fiscal consultants, and civil engineers who were hired by Santa Fe—all of these were paid for by public bodies. Because these plans are also complicated to administer and enforce (remember Lake Tahoe's parcel-by-parcel approach and Park City's alternative regulations depending upon the degree of a slope), the costs continue. Every destination community needs to keep in mind its own financial resources, as well as its other public obligations, to fashion a quality control strategy that is financially sustainable and equitable.

In addition, it should be noted that a number of the case studies in the following two chapters also include strong quality control elements, although we have classified them under quantity management or location enhancement. Bermuda and Times Square are two examples. This illustrates the fact that the division of quality–quantity–location is simply one emphasis and that these categories are not mutually exclusive.

5

Quantity Management Strategies

When tourism growth escalates, a superabundance of visitors can destroy the very qualities of a destination that first attracted tourists and residents alike. The Greek island of Santorini, often described as the lost Atlantis, is a stunning sight, with its white stuccoed houses and domed churches hugging the black volcanic rocks rising from the Aegean. Twenty years ago it was a jewel among the Cyclades, and tourists weathered long ferry rides to ride donkeys up the steep path from the dock to the town to enjoy the spectacular views and village ambiance. Now the narrow lanes are clogged with tourists, Americans serve as waiters in the "authentic" tavernas, there is a constant clamor of motorscooters, disco music reverberates through much of the night, and guidebooks warn of the congestion and inflated prices.

Bodrum, on the southwest corner of the Turkish coast, suffered the same fate. Once known as Halicarnassus, home of one of the seven wonders of the ancient world, this quiet fishing village had a beautiful setting and peaceful charm that attracted international as well as Turkish tourists. Then it became the neon "hot spot" for Istanbul's twenty-some-thing crowd. Within a few years, Bodrum was a traffic nightmare, with delivery trucks, taxis, rental cars, donkeys, and wagons jockeying for space on the narrow lanes. The main street is now jammed with T-shirt shops and fast food stalls. The harbor is lined with restaurants, their electrical wires strung haphazardly across the streets, and their lights flickering on and off all evening. At the top of the hill overlooking the old fortress, a once pleasant small hotel is now the multi-level Halicarnassus Disco, blaring music over the town every night until four or five in the morning.

Neither Santorini nor Bodrum had planned to have its tourism take this course. Massive growth in a short period of time can cause seemingly irreversible changes in a destination community and can be difficult to address quickly and thoughtfully. Successful destination communities should not wait until faced with an emergency to consider the potentially negative impacts of growth. Even those communities that are first embarking on tourism development should carefully consider the expected impacts of growth to ensure that it is consistent with what the community envisions.

"Please Come . . . but Not Too Many . . . and Not Too Often"

There is no magic number that identifies the optimal quantity of tourists for a destination. It depends upon multiple variables that relate to the particular characteristics of the site itself, the host community, the tourist activities, and the visitors. At the Lescaux caves in southern France, it was discovered that the mere breathing of tourists in the caves was destroying the delicate paintings. Even one tourist was deemed to be too many. Visitors now can see remarkable reproductions in a museum, but only researchers can go into the caves themselves.

On the other hand, New York's Times Square and Nathan Road in Hong Kong thrive on throngs of tourists and locals. The profusion of people is an inherent part of their vitality and appeal. Careless snorkelers have done extensive damage to the coral reef at Turtle Bay in the waters of St. John's in the U.S. Virgin Islands. The same number of swimmers at Cannes or Coney Island have a negligible effect. Traffic that would hardly be noticed in Boston will clog the narrow streets of medieval European cities. Hyde Park and the Serpentine in London can pleasantly accommodate a large number of visitors strolling the paths and boating on the water. But transfer that same number of people across town to the smaller Regent's Park, and it will feel overcrowded.

Host communities often have a far greater tolerance for a multitude of culturally comparable tourists than for smaller numbers of culturally distinct visitors. In the United States, groups of Hell's Angels arriving on their motorcycles are rarely greeted with the same enthusiasm as middle-class families. In Moslem countries, a few bikini clad young women sunbathing on the beach are perceived as having a far greater negative impact than bus loads of more "appropriately" garbed visitors. In Hawaii, visitors from Asia are prized more highly than those from the United States mainland for a different reason: they spend more in the local economy.

How many tourists is too many tourists also depends on when they visit. The Cairngorms, a granite mountain range, are Scotland's main ski area. The climate of the windswept summits is so severe that only arctic-alpine flora can survive. There are no roads for cars and the weather can change suddenly and treacherously, but adventurous hill walkers make the climb for the magnificent panorama visible from the peaks. In winter, the snow protects the vegetation. But when the snow cover is melted, the fragile lichens are easily killed by hikers tramping on them. Yet it is the first ten or twenty or fifty walkers who cause the major destruction. The fragile flora has been effectively eradicated, and only sturdier vegetation can survive the cold and the boots. The next hundred hikers cause little degradation.

Conversely, the first mountain climbers in Annapurna, Nepal, didn't make much of an impact on the environment. But when numbers increased and trekking around the lower reaches of Mt. Everest became popular, the problems of soil erosion, litter, and waste disposal grew. Even the high camps near the summit are now covered with discarded tent stakes and empty oxygen canisters. It was the cumulative effect that caused the degradation in this instance. Similarly, the slopes of sacred Mt. Fuji in Japan are now strewn with litter, and a foul stench rises from the wastes of the mountainside toilets that have been emptied down the slopes.

Sometimes the issue of quantity is seasonal. The U.S. Forest Service is considering reducing the number of people allowed to raft on the Salmon River in Idaho. Congestion in the high season of July and August is so great that it is interfering with visitors' "wilderness experience." Tourists in Florence during the summer months may not even be able to glimpse Botticelli's famous *Primavera* over the shoulders of the crowds, while a November visitor might find only two or three companions in contemplation of the painting. Cities that host Olympic events prepare for years for the tourist onslaught, which will consume their community for a period of weeks, never again to be repeated.

Sometimes "when" there are too many tourists is as narrow as a particular time of day. The streets in Windermere in England's Lake District become clogged every morning and late afternoon during the summer, as day-trippers arrive and leave. A ten-minute drive through the attractive town becomes a bumper to bumper crawl that frustrates both tourists and residents. Tourists who visit St. Paul's Cathedral or Notre Dame on a Sunday morning are intruding upon the worshipers and their religious service, while a Thursday afternoon visitor may disturb no one. The lovely but small rose garden in Christchurch, New Zealand, is a charming spot to meander and literally smell the roses. But when a tour bus unloads forty-five passengers who descend on the garden *en masse,* the pleasures of scent and color and shape are overwhelmed. The aesthetics of the garden are ruined until the tour group leaves, as suddenly as it arrived.

How Many Is Too Many?

Destination communities do not have intrinsic use levels that are clear and immutable. The mythical "perfect" number of visitors can never be established; there are simply too many variables that form part of the equation. What communities desire is not a fixed number of tourists, but certain benefits and minimal burdens will flow from their tourism development. What communities need are strategies to control and manage the rate, intensity, and type of their tourism growth so that its impacts are conducive to those conditions the community desires.

Carrying Capacity Analysis

Carrying capacity analysis has been a mainstay of tourism planning relating to issues of quantity since the 1970s. The subject of much scholarly debate and little consensus, it has spawned numerous articles and books as well as a prodigious number of definitions.[1] The concept originated in the field of wildlife management, where it related to the maximum number of animals that could graze on a piece of land without destroying either the existing food supply or the ability of the soil to bear future crops. In the 1960s, the notion of carrying capacity was applied to outdoor recreation management. Here it involved an analysis of how many people could use a particular recreation site before its special qualities, and the pleasure of the recreational experience, were destroyed.

As the carrying capacity concept was adapted to areas experiencing expanded tourism development, it generally focused on the ability of a setting to sustain tourism growth within the environmental and physical constraints of the site. Studies centered on such tangible issues as whether the water supply, sewage treatment system, roads, and other infrastructure could support increased numbers of tourists and whether the natural environment could survive such growth. Although the carrying capacity concept never implied that the optimal number of tourists for a destination could be identified, an implicit component was the notion that limited resources could not support unlimited growth and that communities could establish some "threshold" limitation on the number of visitors they could sustain without undue damage.

While this approach was helping communities wrestle with quantity issues by providing an analysis of elements that are essentially quantifiable (environmental impacts, adequacy of existing infrastructure, public health implications, etc.), there was a recognition that there were other important elements much less amenable to measurement: the relationships between hosts and visitors, the visitors' experience, the perceptions of residents toward tourists, and the impacts of tourism on the quality of life of the community. These elements not only are more subjective, but they also vary from individual to individual and over time. Because they are dependent upon so many changing circumstances, there is much less clarity concerning cause and effect.

And if one cannot precisely identify the cause of a negative impact, how can one devise a technique to mitigate that impact? If a community cannot provide potable water to more than 6,000 people and there are 5,000 residents, then there is a clear rationale for limiting the number of visitors to the community to no more than 1,000 a day (at least for the time being). But if members of a community can psychologically accommodate 1,500 visitors each day who speak their language and whose behavior is similar to their own, yet cannot tolerate smaller numbers of "foreigners" whose clothing, eating habits, and attitudes are different, then the "cause" of the perceived negative impact is not quantity alone and simply limiting the number of tourists will not necessarily bring about the desired results. As carrying capacity analysis was broadening to include an examination of the social impacts of tourism, there was growing agreement that the level of use was but one factor among many that needed to be considered, and that other techniques were needed to mitigate unwanted impacts not caused solely by the number of tourists.

THE "LIMITS OF ACCEPTABLE CHANGE" APPROACH

One of the new approaches that reflected these changes in the concept of carrying capacity is referred to as the Limits of Acceptable Change (LAC).[2] Once again, the setting was outdoor recreation areas that were seeing increased usage, and the impetus was the need by managers for a strategy to deal with the problem of a limited supply and growing demand. The major shift in the LAC framework is from the earlier emphasis on "how much use an area can tolerate" to "the *conditions desired* in the area." This is a significant change: first, the threshold of acceptable use is reduced from the ultimate amount of use that can be borne by the environment to the degree of use that comports with future conditions desired for the area; and second, the power to determine effectively the amount of usage now belongs to whatever group defines the desired conditions. In most recreation areas, the determining group would be the visitors; but when the LAC approach is adapted to tourist destination situations, the host community could be the determining group.

The LAC system spells out nine sequential steps that should be taken to determine the limits of acceptable change. These include determining what social and resource conditions are desired for the setting; comparing the existing social and resource conditions with the desired conditions; identifying various alternatives for achieving the desired conditions; evaluating the costs and benefits of each alternative in terms of environmental impact and impacts upon visitors; implementing the chosen alternative; and monitoring to judge the effectiveness of the management actions.

A major component of the LAC approach is an insistence upon the use of measurable objectives, even when considering such subjective issues as social conditions. For hikers on wilderness trails, for example, solitude is one of the desired social factors. To see if this objective is being met, managers could measure the number of contacts on the trail, whether the contact was with a party or single person, and whether the contact was with another hiker or someone on horseback. Campsite solitude could be measured by the total area of unused ground in a camping area, the number of damaged trees in the campsite area, the number of other people camping within sight or sound, and the total number of sites. The LAC approach emphasizes measurable objectives as a means by which recreation park managers can determine whether specific actions are achieving the desired goals.

THE "VISITOR IMPACT MANAGEMENT" APPROACH

A second approach that builds on a carrying capacity framework is known as Visitor Impact Management (VIM).[3] The VIM approach focuses on determining precisely which factors result in exactly which elements in a broad range of impacts, and then developing management techniques tailored to mitigate any unwanted impacts. The VIM methodology starts with an identification of unacceptable impacts; identification of measurable indicators for each element contributing to these impacts; establishment of acceptable standards for each indicator; comparison of these standards with existing conditions to identify areas where acceptable standards are not being met; development of management techniques to address those areas where standards are not being met; and a continual monitoring process to ensure that the management strategies are alleviating the negative impacts.

Measurable indicators of social impacts include such elements as the means of transportation used by visitors, number of visitors each day, size of visitor groups, and amount of litter. Strategies to minimize negative visitor impacts include a wide array of nonregulatory options. By targeting specific types of tourists, a community could increase the number of overnight visitors, for example, who provide more economic benefit to the host community than day-trippers. Consistent and carefully coordinated marketing can increase the number of visitors from that targeted group. Traffic management techniques can often resolve problems of vehicular congestion and noise. Similarly, management of "people flows" can relieve overcrowding of popular sites and streets.

While neither LAC nor VIM was developed with tourist settings in mind, both systems have influenced much of the current thinking about quantity management in tourism destinations. Both consider the social impacts of tourism, although they stress the visitors' experience rather than that of the host community. Both insist on the identification of measurable objectives so that success in reducing unwanted impacts can be accurately assessed. Both build on a carrying capacity framework but seek techniques that are different from the imposition of numerical limitations. Both insist on the importance of continued monitoring to ensure that the management strategies are having the desired effects. Many of these elements are now commonly included in quantity management strategies in tourist destinations.

THE "SUSTAINABLE TOURISM" CONCEPT

A separate but related concept that has dominated much of the discussion in the past few years is that of sustainable tourism.[4] The principle of "sustainability" has had enormous worldwide influence, generating literally thousands of articles, reports, and books in a variety of disciplines. It is a concept that lies within a global framework, transcending not only local and regional, but national boundaries as well. It has broad implications that cover such disparate issues as international treaties, equitable distribution of resources among the developed and nondeveloped nations of the world, slash-and-burn agricultural practices, and acid rain.

The concept grew out of research concerning the rapidly escalating world population, industrial expansion, and the related growth in pollution. Many scholars concluded that continued development could result in unbearable pressure on the planet's limited resources. By the mid-1980s, the concept of sustainable development was entering the general vocabulary.

In 1987, the World Commission on Environment and Development met to address the growing threats to the environment stemming from industrial practices. Its immensely influential Brundtland Report, appropriately titled *Our Common Future,* provided the often quoted definition of sustainable development as "development that meets the needs of the present without compromising the ability of future generations to meet their own needs." This was supplemented by a list of fourteen components that were part of the understanding of sustainable development. These generally related to environmental protection, economic growth, and issues of equitable access to and distribution of resources.

In 1992, the United Nations Conference on the Environment and Development was held in Rio de Janeiro. This controversial and well-attended meeting attempted to develop agreements among countries and private companies to protect the global environment, limit harmful industrial and development practices, and adopt methods of sustainable development. Although the conference met with only qualified success, it did once again place the issues at center stage, where they remain today.

Following the U.N. Conference, the World Travel and Tourism Council, the World Tourism Organization, and the Earth Council adopted what is known as the "Agenda 21 for the Travel and Tourism Industry," which adapts the concept of sustainable development to tourism. Sustainable tourism is presented as a wise business practice. If development destroys the resources that attract tourists to a destination, tourism cannot be sustained there. For the tourism industry to continue to prosper, it needs to ensure a balance between growth and the capacity to sustain growth. The Agenda 21 report emphasizes appropriate planning to ensure that tourism development will avoid "environmental and cultural degradation." The report further suggests that in sensitive or protected areas, local governments require a full environmental impact assessment before tourist development or prohibit any further development. Finally, it proposes that local or regional authorities should assess the "capacity" of a destination's land, water, energy, infrastructure, ecosystem health and biodiversity, and culture to sustain tourism.[5]

Preservation Rules Strategies

There are some places that are almost universally agreed to be deserving of special protection. They may be environmentally sensitive areas—beautiful barrier reefs, wilderness areas, rainforests—that most of us dream of some day visiting. They may be sites of historic significance—Stonehenge, the Easter Islands, Machu Picu—that we first heard of in school. Perhaps they are culturally important to our human history—the Pyramids, the Parthenon, the Taj Mahal. Or perhaps they are special only to a relatively small group of cognoscenti—the bay that first attracted settlers to a community, the mountain that has religious significance to a particular group. Whatever the reason for their importance, if they are in danger of losing their special qualities from excessive use, they merit protection.

Since the greatest threats to special places are posed by inappropriate uses, the most common technique to preserve these places is the establishment of special zoning districts (discussed in the previous chapter), supported by supplemental controls such as permitting systems and stringent use limitations. Very rarely does preservation necessitate a total prohibition on access. Sometimes restrictions are imposed in the interest of public safety—volcanoes come to mind, or hiking trails that are prone to avalanches in the wintertime. More often, regulations impose a gradation of restrictions that relate to the fragility of the environment, whether natural or built, and the value placed on potentially conflicting uses, the most common of which is tourism. As visitor pressures grow, so do the threats that numbers pose to special places. Quantity management strategies may need to be developed for the first time or modified to cope with changing circumstances.

Case Study: Great Barrier Reef Marine Park, Australia

A legally enforceable management plan complements existing zoning plans to protect the national marine park from cumulative tourism impacts.

One of the most ecologically sensitive tourist attractions in the world is the Great Barrier Reef Marine Park, located in the remote northeast portion of Australia. This is also the world's largest coral reef and protected marine park, covering over 350,000 square kilometers of marine land located on the continental shelf. Separated from the mainland by a shallow lagoon 161 kilometers wide, the park extends 2,000 kilometers along the Queensland coast. There are more than 2,900 individual reefs in the park, as well as hundreds of species of coral, birds, and fish.

Growth in Tourism Activities

Not surprisingly, when the tourist attraction is a barrier reef, the principal tourism activities are conducted in or on the water. The scope of these activities is extremely broad. In the words of Great Barrier Reef Marine Park Authority manager Carol Honchin:

> Commercial tourism use of the marine park is represented by a diverse range of operations ranging from vessel-based day-trip tourist operations encompassing small yachts and power boats carrying less than 15 people at a time to vessels of greater than 35 meters with up to 450 passengers; extended vessel-based tourist operations—involving vessels undertaking extended trips throughout the reef with overnight stays usually in a number of different locations; aircraft based tourist operations—involving the use of conventional aircraft, seaplanes, helicopters; structure-based tourist operations—involving the use of structures such as tourist pontoons, permanently moored at a reef; and resort and other shore based tourist operations.[6]

Visitor numbers have grown dramatically from approximately 150,000 annual visitor days in the early 1980s to an estimated 1.5 million annual visitor days in 1995. Technological change has generated some of this dramatic growth. Floating hotels, for example, have recently been constructed on top of the reefs themselves and very large catamarans now are available for visitor use. Continued growth of 10 percent per year is expected at least until the year 2000.

Two particular areas of the park have lately generated more than 90 percent of all the tourist visits: the Cairns Planning Area and the Whitsunday Planning Area. This concentration of tourist activity could easily become unmanageable; the total number of permits that have already been granted for tourism programs in the park is much higher than the number of permits actually being used, producing what the park managers refer to as "latent capacity." In the Cairns and Whitsunday areas alone, if all currently effective permits were fully used, then tourism would increase by a factor of five.

This dramatic tourism growth—both real and potential—has created widespread concern about the impacts of tourism activities on at least four important aspects of the park. Manager Honchin refers to them as Nature Conservation Values, Presentation Values, Use Values, and Marine Park Management Aspects. The principal conservation concerns relate to the coral damage and bird breeding disruptions produced by heavy visitor use, especially in Cairns and Whitsunday. The Presentation Values concern relates to the status of the park as a UNESCO World Heritage Area:[7] park managers have a responsibility to preserve undeveloped areas so that visitors can experience and behold the wilderness aspect of the park, a goal that is threatened by heavy tourism use. The use values relate to the effects of increased tourism activities on local users of the marine park other than tourists—commercial fishers and indigenous peoples, both of whom to some extent feel crowded out from areas they previously used. From the perspective of marine park management, the threat comes from the "latent capacity" condition and the need to focus limited management resources on those areas where management tools can be most efficiently used.

Earlier Regulatory Approach

Prior to 1995, the regulatory system was almost exclusively reliant upon a zoning and permitting regime. This legal structure was created and enforced by the Great Barrier Reef Marine Park Authority, established by an Australian federal statute (The Great Barrier Reef Marine Park Act of 1975). That statute empowered the Authority to manage development within the park and to ensure that it was appropriately protected. In the words of the Authority, the primary goal was "to provide for the protection, wise use, understanding and enjoyment of the Great Barrier Reef in perpetuity through the development and care of the Great Barrier Reef Marine Park."

The entire area of the Marine Park was subject to a series of zoning plans (with accompanying maps), one of which provides an illustrative example of how the zoning operated. The heavily visited Cairns area was designated as a distinct section in 1981 and became subject to special zoning rules. (See Map 5-1.) A 1992 version of those rules identifies six principal zones: general use, habitat protection, conservation park, buffer, national park, and preservation. Additionally, there is a "no structures subzone," which functions as an overlay zone, whose purpose is to ensure that certain areas of the park remain in "a natural state, largely unaltered by human works." There are also six "designated areas" that further restrict use of the Cairns section. The "fisheries experimental area," for example, provides special areas for scientific research into the effects of fishing on the living natural resources of the park; while the "seasonal closure area" protects areas of particular importance to animals in the park from human intrusion during limited time periods. For each of these designated areas, there are additional restrictions on who may enter and use the area, as well as special permit requirements. Finally, there are complex overlay rules and zonal subdivisions that fine tune the permissible uses.

Commercial tourism operations are allowed in most areas of the park, provided that businesses obtain a permit in advance, generally subject to specific conditions applicable to those uses. Applicants must satisfy the Authority that "no unacceptable environmental impacts will occur as a result of the use of the area."

Tourism coordinator Allan Williams noted[8] that use of the zoning and permitting process was effective in evaluating individual projects with particularly identifiable impacts and also in areas where the overall levels of uses were relatively low. On the other hand, the zoning process was inadequate in several other respects. First, it "had proved to be poorly suited to consideration of the cumulative impacts of many operations, each of which individually has relatively minor impacts." Second, a great deal of management time was required for *ad hoc* evaluation of individual permit applications. Third, there was an unpredictability about the zoning-based permitting process because of the statutory appeals mechanisms. Finally, the zoning process failed to address the fact that similar impacts might occur from different uses; the zoning plan allowed some uses to operate as of right without permits while it required other uses with similar impacts to have permits.

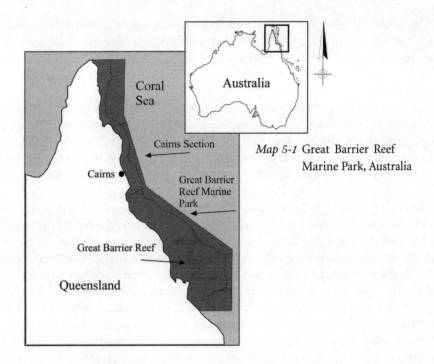

Coral
Sea

Australia

Cairns Section

Map 5-1 Great Barrier Reef
Marine Park, Australia

Cairns

Great Barrier
Reef Marine
Park

Great Barrier Reef

Queensland

"Plan of Management" System

In 1995, amendments to the Great Barrier Reef Marine Park Act made significant changes to this regulatory scheme. First, management plans for areas of the park, which had been merely advisory documents, became statutorily enforceable. Second, amendments established statutory policy governing the granting of permits. Instead of granting individually determined and conditioned permits, the act set a limited number of standard categories for which one could be granted a permit. "This approach is more equitable, predictable and . . . generally means that while some issues are subject to tighter regulation, there is also scope for less stringent regulation and more flexibility in other matters."[9]

The Plan of Management is designed to complement the zoning plan. It may restrict some activities that otherwise would be permitted under the zoning plan, but it may not expand on the uses allowed under the zoning plan. Various park regulations, the zoning plan, and the Plan of Management together make up the legally enforceable tools for regulating the marine park. These mechanisms are themselves supplemented by other nonlegal methods, such as widespread use of responsible environmental practices and cooperative working relationships between the private and public sectors.

The Plan of Management for Cairns

The prototype Plan of Management for the heavily visited Cairns Planning Area was promulgated in 1997. The purpose of the plan is to protect and preserve the "values of the area": coral reefs and associated biota; aquatic animal and plant life; terrestrial fauna and flora in, or adjacent to, the area, including seabirds; scenic integrity; and aspects of the area's culture and heritage. By "scenic integrity" the plan means the combination of attractive islands, cays, fringing reefs, and surrounding waters that draw visitors from around the world. "Cultural and heritage values" refer to the historic relationship of indigenous people to the area's marine environment. They have conducted traditional subsistence activities in the waters for years and have specific sites within the park that are of cultural significance to them.

The Plan of Management is concerned with the existing uses in the Cairns area. Although the plan lists traditional hunting, fishing, and collecting, commercial fishing, and general recreation as existing uses, the first essential use it identifies is tourism. Although the Cairns section represents only 6 percent of the entire marine park area, it accounts for more than 60 percent of total visitor days within the park, making it the most intensely used location within this World Heritage Area.

The plan candidly enunciates its belief that "effectively managed, tourism is a desirable use of the marine park when it promotes awareness and understanding of the Great Barrier Reef Marine Park, and if the effects of its use are environmentally acceptable." Recognizing potential negative impacts from tourism use, the plan clearly identifies six "key concerns for the area" resulting from tourism use: pressures on the natural environment, especially coral damage; pressures on cultural and heritage values; conflicts of use and range of opportunities, particularly the issue of displacement of traditional users of the marine park; the potential for significant increases in tourism based upon the number of existing unused permits; decline in certain marine mammal populations; and disturbance of roosting and nesting birds. A variety of regulatory mechanisms addresses each of these concerns.

Permit Limits

The principal management technique to control tourist numbers is a system of permits. Although existing permits for most tourism operators will be grandfathered into the system, others must obtain a new permit for operation and then contact the authority to book a place in a specified area. Four different types of permits allow limited degrees of access to various areas of Cairns: access no more than 50 days a year; access for 365 days a year but not to any individual locations for more than 50 days a year; access to nonsensitive locations for more than 50 days per year; and finally, access to a sensitive location for more than 50 days a year.

"Usage" Settings

Another useful tool in the Plan of Management is a limitation on the size of groups and vessels at particular locations, described in the plan as "usage settings on the basis of acceptable impact." Individual reefs are categorized as being suitable for different types and levels of use. Vessels visiting "low use" reefs are limited to a maximum of 5 persons per vessel including crew and a maximum vessel length of 20 meters. Vessels at the "moderate use" reefs may include a maximum number of 60 persons including crew and have a maximum length of less than 35 meters if anchoring. There is no limit on the number of people at "intensive use" reefs, but vessels are limited to 35 meters if anchoring. Larger vessels may anchor only in "general use zones" or a few otherwise identified reefs. The criteria used for assigning these "use settings" were "existing values for a location, existing use of a location, zoning and implications of use allowed under the zoning plan, and characteristics of the reef location, such as size of reef, coral, cover and anchoring opportunities."

Sensitive Locations

Even stricter limitations flow from the identification of "sensitive locations" on the basis of special environmental and cultural attributes. Sensitive locations generally have been allo-

cated a "low use setting" and have additional limitations on the number of tourist operations (e.g., the number of vessels anchoring) that are permitted to visit on a particular day,
based upon "booking" for that day. However, some existing tourist operations on those
"sensitive locations" may well be permitted to continue at the current level and type after
being studied by authority staff and following negotiations. Exemptions are made based on
group size, frequency, and vessel size.

Limits on Moorings and Pontoons

Another regulatory provision of the Plan of Management involves limiting the number of
moorings and pontoons within the overall Cairns area. Generally, the criteria for determining these limitations relate to the usage setting of particular locations. By way of example, in the "offshore Port Douglas sector," there is a reef called "Opal Reef" where twelve private moorings are permitted, whereas only one private mooring is allowed in "Agincourt
#2 Reef." How to allocate these limited mooring or pontoon permits, which used to be han-
dled on a "first come, first serve" basis, has yet to be determined. One approach being considered is to advertise for private mooring applications, giving preference to particular
types of permits and to operators who presently hold mooring permits at other locations.

How the Restrictions Promote Values

In an especially well-crafted portion of the Plan of Management, the authority discusses
how the various new restrictions promote the goals of the plan. Prohibiting anchoring by
any vessel on coral within a conservation park zone, a buffer zone or a national park zone,
while still maintaining access, protects the "coral conservation value." Limiting growth of
regular use in specific inshore coastal areas will protect marine mammal populations and
preserve aquatic life. Prohibiting the use of loudspeakers and sirens, restricting the permitted speed of powerboats, and prohibiting airplanes from flying within a bird breeding area
will limit noisy activities that interfere with the seabirds' breeding. Four management
methods promote "scenic integrity": having some areas free of infrastructure; limiting the
number of moorings and pontoons at most reefs; limiting the places large vessels can
anchor; and limiting vessel size to 20 meters at some locations. Restrictions on the number
of moorings and pontoons at locations of cultural significance to indigenous people will
prevent further impairment of cultural values.

Closing Comments

For a period of 20 years, the regulatory system that protected the Great Barrier Marine Park
relied on a regulatory system that combined zoning controls and a permitting mechanism.
While the regime generally worked well, as tourist activities in the park increased the sustainability of the system was increasingly in doubt for three reasons. First, although the permitting system provided a mechanism for evaluating individual projects with clearly identifiable impacts, it could not address the issue of cumulative impacts. Second, since some
negative impacts resulted from uses that were allowed as of right under the zoning plan,
the permitting system provided no mechanism for mitigating these impacts. Third, anyone
denied a permit on the basis of a negative impact could appeal that decision, arguing that
the denial was unfair since permitted uses created the same negative impact. This inherent
flaw meant that the strongest mechanism to control unwanted impacts, the denial of a permit, was undermined by the probability of a successful appeal.

The revisions to the regulatory system, intended to address these problems as well as
the impacts resulting from tourism growth, are a fine example of adaptive management

responding to changing circumstances (discussed in more detail in Chapter 2). Amendments to the statute creating the Park Authority established a limited number of use categories for which one could be granted a permit, taking into consideration cumulative as well as individual impacts. Clearer standards in the regulations also promote equity in the granting of permits. The Plan of Management approach also includes a variety of restrictions to limit use in sensitive areas of the park, each one of which has specific objectives that relate to the goals of the plan. However, disputes among users have surfaced and are likely to continue. One example occurred in mid-1998, when a recreational fishing group complained that charter boats filled with tourists would "monopolize" key mooring areas. The Park Authority rejected the group's claim that its members were being "excluded by stealth," stating that the special moorings would be few in number and environmentally sensitive.

The Cairns prototype Plan of Management, together with the zoning regulations and permitting mechanisms, form a complementary combination of techniques designed to protect the clearly identified "values" for the Cairns area of the marine park while providing visitor access. It is important to remember, however, that there are external factors that may well be affecting the marine park. The reef has been suffering from the invasion of exotic species and the decline of coral populations for reasons as yet unknown. Until there is a greater understanding of the causes of these changes, there is little that can be done to minimize their impact on the quality of the park. Depending upon the nature of the cause, it may require international or even global attention and be well beyond the scope of any local management strategy.

While the Great Barrier Reef Marine Park has been in existence for more than 20 years, its primary challenge has remained the same: to balance protection of the coral reef environment with increasing tourist pressures. Although there have always been other uses in the area, the vast numbers have been associated with tourism. This is not always the case. Sometimes special places need protection from the cumulative impacts of a variety of equally prominent uses: commercial, recreational, and tourist. The challenge in these cases is to develop a strategy that will allow all these competing uses to operate while still providing adequate protective measures to a sensitive environment.

Case Study: The Saguenay-St. Lawrence Marine Park, Quebec, Canada

National and provincial governments jointly establish a marine park to develop and protect a fragile marine environment through the use of zoning.

North and east of Quebec City, Canada, the Saguenay-St. Lawrence Marine Park encompasses an area of approximately 1,100 square kilometers. (See Photo 5-1.) The park stretches from the bed of the Saguenay River at Cap à l'Est on the west, to include the western half of the St. Lawrence Estuary from Gros Cap à l'Aigle upstream to Les Escoumins downstream. (See Map 5-2.) The estuary is characterized by numerous small islands, a coast of steep cliffs, and long sand bars. Running generally in a southwesterly direction from the Atlantic Ocean, the estuary provides an abundant food supply for large mammals;

Photo 5-1 The Saguenay-St. Lawrence Marine Park, Quebec (Courtesy of the marine park)

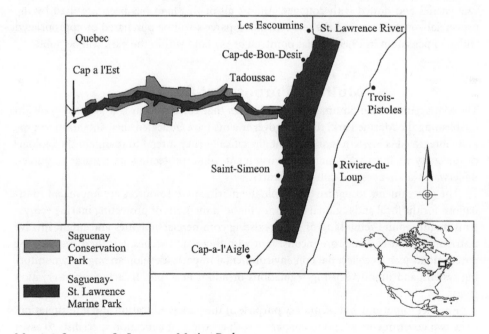

Map 5-2 Saguenay-St. Lawrence Marine Park

each year from June to October, the waters attracts blue, fin, minke, and beluga whales, as well as an occasional humpback or sperm whale. The Saguenay River flows into the Saguenay Fjord, an ancient valley carved by glaciers and lined with rugged cliffs, an unusual formation in southern Canada. At the confluence of the fjord and the estuary, there is a powerful interaction of St. Lawrence tides with water currents of the fjord, producing swirling waters and nourishing more than 300 species.

Creation of the Marine Park

In 1990, the governments of Canada and the province of Quebec agreed to establish the Marine Park to conserve this exceptional marine environment. They held public hearings in late 1990 and 18 months later established a board to advise the governments on general outlines of the proposed park. In spring 1993, the two governments announced the park boundaries and two months later conducted public hearings respecting the over-all proposals. By October 1995, a management plan had been agreed upon and a diverse Coordinating Committee conducted its initial meetings. Then on June 5, 1997, the province of Quebec passed a statute, providing a legal basis for establishment and regula-tion of the park with the goals of "protecting the environment, the flora and fauna and the exceptional natural resources of a representative portion of the Saguenay River and the St. Lawrence Estuary, while encouraging its use for educational, recreational, and scientific purposes." A very similar statute was passed by the House of Commons of Canada in the summer of 1998. Both the Quebec enactment and the Canadian statute were required in order for the joint management and regulation of the Marine Park.

Originally there were a number of parcels of land along the shore lines owned by pri-vate parties and dotted with cottages. Almost all of this land has been acquired by the provincial government, and the few remaining parcels will be purchased or appropriated with compensation in 1999. At that point, all of the land within the park will be public.

Multiple Purposes of the Park

The Management Plan Summary of 1995 notes that conservation is a primary goal: "in establishing the Marine Park, the two governments have indicated their intention to pro-mote integrated ecosystem management. Specifically, they intend to maintain the biologi-cal diversity of the park's marine environment while protecting its natural resources, underwater landscapes and cultural features."

The governments recognize that while the marine park resources are important foun-dations for the local and regional economy, modern methods of protecting marine ecosys-tems might require rethinking of some existing commercial activities and might involve restricting new uses if they are inconsistent with those approaches. For these reasons, the governments plan to collect data on environmental impacts, develop an ongoing monitor-ing system, and modify existing regulations or adopt new ones to achieve conservation goals.

Another important, but secondary purpose of the park is education and interpretation. "The two governments intend to cooperate with a variety of education specialists to assist visitors in discovering, understanding and appreciating the many facets of the Marine Park, notably the reasons for establishing it, the extrinsic value of its features and the need for conservation." Strategically located interpretation and observation centers offer educa-tional materials, while a number of particularly significant sites have been selected as examples of the relationships between people and the marine environment. The principal activity centers in the park each has its own theme: Rivière-du-Loup is "an archipelago full of life and history," while Baie-Éternité is "a unique fjord at the heart of a kingdom."

The educational goals are closely allied with recreational goals. Each of the activity centers is part of a network that forms a land and marine tourist circuit. Visitors can learn about the major ecosystems of the park and also be directed to hiking trails, beaches, wilderness camping sites, scuba diving, or cross country skiing opportunities. "Discovery Areas" on the periphery of the park encourage tourists' independent activities, while Reception and Orientation Centers at each entry point of the park provide information on recreational and educational activities.

A final goal is to conduct scientific research to improve understanding of the park's ecosystem and to promote effective management of various activities conducted in the marine park. To achieve these goals, the two governments are establishing partnership relationships with outside organizations such as universities and research institutions. These organizations can provide information that will guide park administrators in their conservation and education efforts.

The Districting System within the Marine Park

The key management tool to accomplish the purposes of the Marine Park (especially the conservation goals) is districting according to uses. In the words of the 1995 Management Plan Summary, "the purpose of planning human use of the Marine Park is to rationally organize activities compatible with the protection of the park's marine environment, through management practices addressing ecological, environmental, social, cultural and ethical concerns."

The Quebec statute establishing and regulating the park identifies four districts from most restrictive to least restrictive: comprehensive preservation, specific protection, general protection, and general use districts. Additionally, the statute contemplates that the government will adopt regulations for each district defining its boundaries and characteristics, listing permitted uses, setting the terms and conditions for use, as well as the time limits and conditions for undertaking activities in each district.

The government may adopt regulations closing particular districts to the public and restricting or prohibiting activities in the park generally or in particular district. Particular times of the year might govern when there are such closures, restrictions, or prohibitions. Regulations may also be described in a vertical dimension, identifying the part of the "water column" or "seabed" that is being regulated. Although the statute itself is silent on this point, an official Quebec publication states that "all forms of exploration, utilization and exploitation of resources for mining or energy production purposes are prohibited within the park, as is the passage of oil, gas or power transmission lines." Finally, regulations may limit the number of permits for specific activities within the park.

A separate Discussion Paper, dated February 1997, was prepared concerning control of whale-watching activities in the park. The primary issue related to the enormous growth of this popular tourism activity (a more than tenfold increase from 600 annual excursions in 1988 to nearly 7,000 in 1993) and its impacts on the park. Commercial whale watching is a significant factor in the local economies, grossing nearly Canadian $7 million from ticket sales alone in 1995. More than 50 boats operate within a very small area, ferrying Canadian and international tourists to viewing sites.

However, in the words of Claude Filion, Director of the Marine Park "no framework exists to properly manage these activities, which have grown exponentially over the last few years. Furthermore, based on experience it is clear that the existing (regulations) which stipulate that disturbing marine mammals is prohibited . . . (are) inadequate to protect the whales."[10]

There are a variety of concerns related to whale watching. Crowds of boats can result in increased whale injuries, collisions with whales, disturbances during the breeding season, and eventually a diminishing number of whales. Secondary concerns relate to the safety of seagoers in congested shipping lanes and the mounting dissatisfaction among visitors, whose experiences are diminished by traffic and tourist numbers. There are, however, no legal mechanisms yet in place for controlling the expansion of the whale-watching industry or even properly managing it.

The Discussion Paper did not recommend specific measures but did recommend "guiding principles." These included providing increased protection of marine mammals; fostering the preservation of ecosystems through integrated management; offering a public education program to enhance understanding of ecosystems; guaranteeing an excellent tourist product and superior park experience; complying with public safety standards; and promoting sustainable development principles.

Regional Cooperation

The governments of Quebec and Canada agreed early in their discussions that the Marine Park should be characterized by "harmonious integration into the region." The overall purpose in this respect was "to encourage local governments and community groups to integrate projects and activities compatible with the Marine Park's objectives into its program." To foster long-term cooperation among municipalities surrounding the Marine Park, non-governmental organizations, and businesses, and to encourage the development of tourism facilities consistent with the park conservation purposes, the governments established a Coordinating Committee.

This Coordinating Committee is composed of nine members, one nominated by each of the municipalities bordering the park, a representative of the indigenous community, a scientist, an environmentalist, and two members selected by the Federal Department of Canadian Heritage and the Quebec Ministry of the Environment. In the words of park director Claude Filion, "these different groups have learned to work together toward the fulfillment of the park's objectives described in the Management Plan. The Coordinating Committee has recently adopted an action plan (identifying) precise goals to attain for next spring (of 1998)."[11]

Closing Comments

The joint efforts of the national and provincial governments to establish and manage this significant Marine Park are still in the early stages of development. The success of the use districting approach along with supplemental mechanisms to protect the ecosystem and adequately control activities within the park is as yet unknown. There is a long history of mixed uses that potentially conflict with preservation goals as well as with each other. As each use increases, the pressures on the environment multiply exponentially. The challenge is to develop regulations and management techniques that will protect the ecosystem in a heavily trafficked transportation corridor and a highly popular tourist destination, where various water-related activities provide a major source of local income.

A further challenge is to maintain the cooperative attitude that the various players have thus far practiced. As restrictions are implemented, there may well be changes in the allocation of the economic benefits of tourism. As the impacts of the new management system are felt, it may well be more difficult to sustain the support of the varied players.

Both the Great Barrier Reef and the Saguenay-St. Lawrence regions have had years of experience dealing with tourism. Many of the challenges they face come from a recent surge in the numbers of visitors coming to their waters. Not all tourist destinations have the benefit of long familiarity with the impacts of tourism nor a lengthy amount of time to plan for them. Tourist destinations can now be created in areas that had been tourist wastelands (Disneyworld is a prime example); and areas that were off the beaten path a few years ago can suddenly become tourist meccas. Mayan ruins that were buried under hundreds of years of jungle growth have been rediscovered by archaeologists and now have tourists clambering over their crumbling stones. The Antarctic used to be a subject of interest for only the most dedicated and adventurous scientists. Now tourists who've been everywhere and done everything can pay their way to this ultimately special place, creating unknown impacts on that forbidding environment.

As tourism spreads, more and more special places are vulnerable to pressures that didn't exist just a few short years ago. The challenge is to frame an approach that will protect what is fragile in their settings, while still creating opportunities for tourist development and economic expansion.

Case Study: Cancun-Tulum Corridor, Mexico

Municipal, state, and national governments cooperate to try to protect land and marine environments along a rapidly developing 100-mile tourism corridor through use of zoning and mapping.

Located on the Caribbean coast of the state of Quintana Roo on the Yucatan Peninsula, Cancun was the first master-planned tourism center in Mexico. Created in the 1970s by the governmental tourism development entity FONATUR from undeveloped land, Cancun is one of Mexico's most well-known and visited resort areas. Private development by almost every major international hotel chain over the decades has generated thousands of overnight beds for the 2.5 million visitors from throughout the world who are attracted to the long, sandy beaches, warm year-round climate and broad range of facilities. (See the discussion of Cancun as a classic example of a concentration strategy, p. 228.)

The dramatic economic success of Cancun has, not surprisingly, triggered powerful interest in extending tourism projects to currently sparsely developed beach land to the south. (See Map 5-3.) Travel essayist Terry Pindell's 1995 drive along the corridor south of Cancun convinced him that this was "where the development drama is still being playing out." In the fishing town of Puerto Morelos, he stayed at a small beachfront hotel around which "(p)roperties recently have been bought by outfits that put towers in Cancun. . . . Bulldozers are pushing sand around, and the road (to his hotel) is muddied by their activity."[12]

Many of the beachfront properties south of Cancun are controlled by small owners (sometimes expatriates from the United States or Canada), who operate bungalow facilities

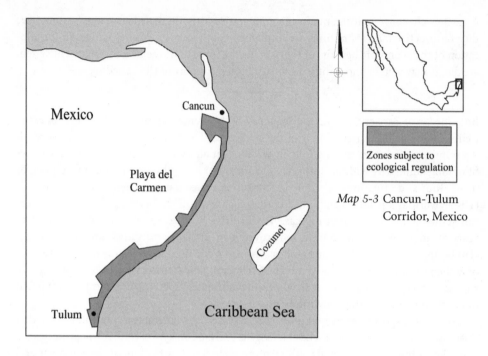

Map 5-3 Cancun-Tulum
        Corridor, Mexico

for budget travelers. Some contend that Mexican businessmen are now eyeing their parcels as sites for lucrative, more upscale accommodations (as well as gambling casinos and marinas) to capitalize on the popularity and excellent transportation access of the area. Land values have risen dramatically, from $2 to $80 per square meter, for some beach sites south of Cancun.[13]

Development of the Tourism Corridor

About 100 miles south of Cancun, on a steep cliff overlooking the Caribbean is the Mayan ruin Tulum. In great contrast to the party atmosphere of much of newly created Cancun, Tulum is haunting and mysterious, with intricate carvings of gods and sacrifices and stone buildings of unknown use, given such beguiling names as "Temple of the Wind."

A single, poorly paved north–south road currently services the corridor between Cancun and Tulum. Soon Highway 307, presently under construction, will provide an easy and rapid route along the entire corridor, connecting now remote regions with the large international airport just outside Cancun. This key transportation linkage is among the important factors prompting rapid tourism development in the area, a process that is expected to increase over time.

Much of the corridor is already being transformed. Playa del Carmen, located about 40 miles south of Cancun, has an ideal setting, sheltered from high waves, with largely empty beaches of powdered sand. A few years ago this once tranquil town was known primarily as a ferry stop for nearby Cozumel Island, popular with scuba divers and snorkelers. As growth began, the town boasted small beach cabanas made from native palapas, beachfront bars with strolling Mayan musicians, and a quaint pedestrian shopping street. As a 1995 visitor described it, "In Playa the Mexican penchant for passionate fun, which is such a rich vein to the tourist industry, thrives without being forced or formulated. The place has been discovered, but it is not yet Cancun."[14]

Now new resorts, hotels, and restaurants are sprouting throughout "Playacar," as the locals refer to the town. Very popular with Europeans (especially from France and Germany), Playa del Carmen is now a cruise ship stop as well as home to new four- and five-star hotels. Companies that own and operate resorts in such well-known sun-and-sand Mexican locations as Manzanillo and Puerto Vallarta are now moving into the Playacar area as well.

Summarizing the transformation of Playa del Carmen, *London Sunday Times* travel writer Mark Ottaway wrote in late 1996: "Such have been Mexico's political and economic uncertainties, however, that investors have, until now, felt safer over on Cozumel or the virtual island of Cancun's hotel zone. Suddenly, for no apparent reason, Carmen is airborne. Property prices have gone up by 400 percent in a year. It has eclipsed Cozumel for the fun crowd . . . (and) has become the sort of freewheeling good-value place with rooms to rent, snack stalls, bars, and restaurants that one associated more with the Med and Southeast Asia than with the Caribbean."[15]

The Cancun-Tulum Corridor, called by some the "Yucatan Sandbox," already includes many built tourist attractions of varying quality. Every day hundreds of tourists from Cancun take buses to visit the Xcaret theme park, an aquatic zoo with underground rivers and caverns for snorkelers and for forms of family enjoyment, accurately billing itself as an "eco-archeological park." Another popular commercial operation is the Xel-Ha facility along the coast, characterized by its natural lagoon system, restaurants, deck chairs, and tour buses from Cancun. By contrast, 16 miles south of Playacar is the little used but naturally beautiful Paamul Beach on a crescent shaped lagoon. Development again appears south of Paamul Beach at Puerto Aventuras with its overbuilt 900 acres of hotels, condominiums, and marinas.

Given the rapid development of the Cancun-Tulum Corridor, it is not surprising that industry representatives believe that the boom will continue. Cesar Bistrain Tanus, president of an international resort company based in Mexico, was quoted in mid-1997 as predicting that the corridor will have more than 48,000 hotel rooms by the year 2000. Travel essayist Pindell also predicts rapid change: "The return trip to Puerto Morelos again convinces us that someday this entire coast will be developed; it is such a natural. We turn off the highway (north toward Cancun) to check out several of the little beach hideaways. . . . Each fulfills a vision of 'the perfect little beach paradise'—at least for the moment. It's heartening to know that they still exist at all. It's sobering to imagine what may march down this coast from Cancun."[16]

The 1994 Ecological Regulations for the Cancun-Tulum Corridor

Anticipating tourist development along the 100-mile corridor, government planners and officials from a number of departments and jurisdictions adopted a set of ecological regulations in 1994. The intention of this "Ecological Ordering Plan" is to mitigate many of the otherwise potentially harmful effects of the corridor's growth. The plan involved cooperation and decision making at three governmental levels: national, state, and municipal. It also reflected the concurrence of a number of departments. At the national level, coordination involved the offices of Social Development, Ecological Planning, Urban Development, Natural Resource Use, and Federal Land Use. Participating departments from the state of Quintana Roo were Environment and Land Regulation, Touristic Development, and an agency known as "FIDEICARIBE." Three separate municipalities lie along the corridor, and each was involved in promulgating the plan.

The regulations are grounded on a mapping technique that divides the corridor into 46 separate land zones and 28 individual marine zones. Each of these is assigned one of four major use designations. "Actual usage" zones permit varying degrees of urban development or industrial use. "Conservation" zones may permit small rural or tourism development and are designed to protect wildlife. "Protected" zones limit uses to those that are compatible with existing ecosystems. Finally, "restoration" zones aim to restore the natural state of the land.

In addition to these use designations, each of these land and marine zones is subject to a number of specified environmental regulatory "criteria," from as few as one to as many as 29. There are additional mapped areas, which act as "overlay zones" to protect such natural assets as tortoises, crocodiles, manatee, primates, and reefs. Specific reefs, for example, may have few restrictions on their use, may be limited to educational use only, or may have absolute restrictions on their use.

The number of various restrictions and ecological criteria that can apply to relatively small land and marine areas allows for very tailored regulation. For example, zone T-30, which lies inland from the beach area in Playa del Carmen, is mapped for "actual usage" that permits urban development with a density of 300 persons per hectare and is subject to just a few ecological criteria (one prohibits drainage of wetlands or interruption of water flow). By contrast, zone T-31, which lies just south of T-30 on the coastline and is also mapped for "actual usage," has a limit of 50 rooms per hectare; while zone T-32, abutting T-31 to the east and also lying on the coast, can build only ten rooms per hectare. Both of these last zones are subject to 25 separate restrictions, including prohibitions on use of nearby cenotes (wells that are used by surrounding communities), a maximum height limitation to the level of surrounding vegetation, and the requirement of a buffer zone between the tourist area and the nearby protected area.

The area just west of the Tulum archaeological zone is a "conservation" zone whose development is limited to 15 rooms per hectare. Additionally, there are 27 ecological criteria that apply, ranging from the requirement for a water treatment system for any tourist area, maintenance of the natural vegetation, and construction that conforms to the surrounding terrain. An illustrative example of a site zoned for "restoration" is a very large inland area, also near Playa del Carmen. Here the criteria permit human uses provided that they will not inhibit recovery of the land to its natural state, while they bar human settlements on deteriorated ecosystems.

The 28 marine zones are all designed either to protect or to restore the area so mapped. The Bay of Chemuyil, for example, is a "protected" zone where applicable criteria limit uses to "scientific and contemplative" activities in compliance with a separate governmental control decree; there may be no fishing, boat docking, or waste disposal. The offshore reef area known as Chak-Helal, west of Playa del Carmen, is a marine restoration zone. Here, any use that will prevent a return to the natural state is prohibited, and all restoration activity must support the existing ecosystem.

Closing Comments

The zoning system attempts to tailor regulations to the specific needs of each mapped area to a remarkable degree. Development is more restricted in environmentally sensitive areas and much of the ecosystem is protected from what is deemed inappropriate uses. The regulatory system has preceded much of the projected tourism growth, and much of the area has yet to be developed. While this offers the opportunity to shape future growth, it also suggests that there will be a great deal of opposition to the restrictions by those wishing to reap the economic benefits of development.

This zoning approach has serious limitations that could stymie its effectiveness. Because it treats relatively small areas differently, applying vastly different restrictions to abutting spaces, it is open to the argument that criteria were inappropriately applied. "My parcel is like the one to the east that permits twice as much development without worrying about the vegetation." There is a great need for data and analysis that clearly identify expected impacts from development in each zone to support the restrictions. There is also the question as to whether the various zones are large enough to protect the environment as they are designed to. The restrictions also need to take into consideration the cumulative effects of development (an issue that the Great Barrier Reef Plan of Management approach is trying to address). Finally, because there are enormous economic incentives to develop tourism facilities, the regulations will succeed only if there is adequate and universal enforcement.

Zoning systems have been used to protect the environmentally sensitive areas of the Great Barrier Reef and are being adopted in an attempt to protect the Saguenay-St. Lawrence Marine Park and the Cancun-Tulum Corridor from the escalating impacts of tourism development. In each case, regulations limit the amount of development and use in designated areas. Another technique that can be used functionally removes permission to develop the land at all: the purchase of development rights. This very expensive mechanism is often used to protect prime agricultural land from the pressures of residential development, whether tourist related or not.

Case Study: Peninsula Township, Michigan

Following combined government, nongovernmental organization and citizen involvement in research, planning, community education programs and an active campaign, Peninsula Township passed a referendum permitting the purchase of development rights to save agricultural land and open space and control the rapid development of seasonal homes.

The Old Mission Peninsula is a narrow spit of land jutting from the northwest edge of lower Michigan into Grand Traverse Bay. (See Map 5-4.) Just 17 miles long and 2.5 miles wide, the peninsula has had a history of agriculture since the days when Native Americans grew corn and squash on the land. European settlers moved to the area in 1839, harvested timber from the forests, and soon most of the gently rolling terrain was being farmed. The first cherry orchard was planted in 1852, and red tart cherries became the dominant crop of the peninsula. The week-long National Cherry Festival still attracts thousands of tourists each July.

The long shoreline and mild (for Michigan) climate of the peninsula have long attracted summer visitors. Church groups from Chicago and Cincinnati created their own summer resorts in the late 1800s, and before long wealthy residents from large midwestern cities followed their lead, building summer homes along the bay. Relationships between

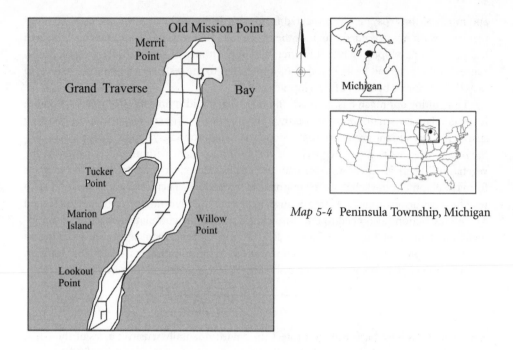

Map 5-4 Peninsula Township, Michigan

local farmers and summer visitors were mutually beneficial: resort guests provided a market for the farmers' produce, while the farmers supplied fresh fruits and vegetables for tourists' consumption.

Then between 1950 and 1990, the population of Peninsula Township more than doubled from 1,531 to 4,340. Declining farm incomes and a growing market for second homes that resulted in escalating land values, produced a dramatic increase in the sale of farmland. Second homes were often rented out to multiple tenants over the summer, and seasonal tourism pressures grew. The cordial relations between farmers and visitors and some new permanent residents as well became strained when residential areas abutted agricultural zones, with the smells and noises inherent in farm practices. The community felt that its heritage as a farm community was imperiled by the nature and extent of new residential development and wanted to protect its agricultural land and prevent what it saw as "urban sprawl."

Early Attempts to Control Growth

Peninsula Township established its first Planning and Zoning Commission in 1968 and passed its first comprehensive zoning ordinance in response to citizen concern about uncontrolled growth. The major regulatory technique used by the ordinance was a minimum lot size requirement of five acres per dwelling unit on agricultural land. While this succeeded in keeping population density on farmland relatively low, it did not affect other trends. Second homes continued to be built along the shoreline, and year-round residences increased as well. Open space and recreational land were being lost. Much of the prize farmland was sold, especially land on rising slopes that afforded panoramic views of the bay.

A second attempt at control was made with the 1975 Comprehensive Plan. The five-acre minimum remained in effect, and although fewer variances from the plan were allowed, the development trends continued. Public concern steadily grew, often in response to specific development proposals. Local advocacy groups sprang up, candidates opposed to further development were elected to township offices, but new construction continued to encroach on farmland. Peninsula Township needed additional mechanisms to protect agricultural land and direct second-home and permanent residential development to areas that would be most appropriate for residential use.

Research and Planning Efforts

One of the first steps the township took was to secure funding from public and private sources for needed expertise. It then sought out professional help to gather data about the peninsula, create comprehensive maps with both physical and cultural features, develop a computer geographic information system, and provide information about farmland conservation easements. At the same time these research efforts were underway, the township was seeking to learn what the residents thought the government should be focusing on. The three issues that were identified as of greatest concern were (1) the size and breadth of the increase in second-home development; (2) the loss of agricultural land; and (3) the increasing population in the township. The residents wanted the township to retain its farmland, protect its scenic views, and control new residential developments.

Simultaneously, the Planning and Zoning Commission was working on revising the Comprehensive Land Use Plan. Citizen-based study groups identified conservation easements (a technique permitted under Michigan law) as a tool to consider for preservation of farmland and open spaces. These are permanent restrictions on land that bar future development. Other groups that studied the fiscal consequences of development concluded that residential development, particularly sprawling development, often did not generate sufficient tax revenues to pay for the cost of additional community services, while agricultural use normally created more tax revenue than the services it needed cost.

With all the information it had gathered, the township now focused on a combination of increased zoning controls and a conservation easement purchase program, permitted under Michigan law, as the best strategy to achieve its goals. The next steps were to flesh out what such a program would look like and to secure community support for it.

The Purchase of Development Rights Plan

The purchase of development rights (PDR) is a voluntary program used in any number of states in the United States to protect agricultural land from development pressure. In essence, the owner of property gives up rights to develop the land in return for payment for the value of those development rights. In practical terms, the fair market value of the farm property is determined, usually by an appraisal; from this number is subtracted the fair market value of the same property subject to the terms of a conservation easement (i.e., the property without the ability to be developed); the remaining number represents the value of the development rights given up by the owner through the conservation easement. This is, generally, the amount of compensation due to the property owner from the government or a conservation organization for its purchase of the development rights.

PDR programs have any number of benefits. Since conservation easements remain with the land, even in the case of a sale, the agricultural land is protected virtually in perpetuity. At the same time, since the landowner retains all rights to the property other than the right to develop it, farming operations are not compromised. Additionally, because payment is made for the development rights, "cash poor and land rich" farmers are able to access funds without selling off their land. Finally, communities can establish their own criteria for a

PDR program, ensuring that local priorities direct which parcels' development rights will be purchased.

There are also any number of drawbacks to a PDR scheme. Since the program is entirely voluntary, owners of the most desirable agricultural land may opt not to participate but to sell their land to the highest bidder and retire with a comfortable nest egg. Unless combined with other comprehensive zoning techniques, PDR programs can result in scattered patterns of development, with farms and residential development abutting each other, exacerbating problems and conflicts between sometimes incompatible uses.

Similarly, while PDRs may protect agricultural land, those techniques alone do not halt the expansion of second-home and tourist development, with the concomitant change in the social fabric of a community. Finally, PDR programs are expensive and communities usually need to be willing to tax themselves for the privilege of conserving farmland.

Peninsula Township attempted to address these potential problems in drafting their PDR program. The Township determined that it would need sufficient funds to purchase some 3,000 acres of farmland to ensure a large block of preserved land as opposed to a piecemeal approach of scattered parcels. It also felt that agriculture would not remain viable on the Peninsula unless a sizeable amount of land was protected. At the same time, the community wanted to preserve scenic views on the peninsula. Therefore, the township developed criteria for selection as part of the PDR program which would address each of these issues. The Comprehensive Plan also limited development in an "agricultural preserve area," established new regulations safeguarding scenic views, and identified residential districts where future development would be permitted.

The other significant issue was how to afford to pay for the program. The township decided that the best plan was to have a referendum vote for a property tax increase. In order for such a referendum to pass, the township needed to convince the voters that the PDR program would achieve its goals and be worth the cost of increased taxes. Three months before the referendum was to be voted on, various groups working together as the "Concerned Citizens in Support of PDR" launched a well-coordinated campaign to garner support.

Community Campaign

Over three years of effort had gone into the process of developing the PDR strategy. During that time, various members of the community had participated in one way or another, with the result that many people were already committed to the PDR approach. A group of citizens banded together as "Concerned Citizens in Support of PDR" and launched a comprehensive community-wide campaign to both share information and persuade voters to support the PDR strategy. The campaign's success relied in part on the ability of its organizers to develop techniques tailored to the local community (see generally the discussion of "Let the Players Make the Rules" and "Localize Rules" in Chapter 2).

A community education effort with the motto "Preserve Our Heritage" began with an article in the local newspaper explaining the PDR plan and listing the current supporters. This was followed by mailings to every Peninsula Township resident, addressing particular aspects of the program and identifying farmers who supported the program. Campaign organizers established relationships with newspaper reporters and other media representatives, providing information on an ongoing basis. A series of letters to the editor were written on carefully chosen topics, with the bulk of letters going out the week before the vote.

Township officials met with the editorial board of one newspaper to respond to concerns about the PDR plan and to explain the program in more detail. Newspaper advertising focused on listing the names of supporters of the PDR program and on visuals that contrasted productive farmland with farmland in the midst of development. Compelling photographic ads ran the night before the vote. Campaign organizers decided against buying the more expensive radio and television advertising. However, some radio news programs addressed the issue in-depth, and a special contribution covered the cost of limited television advertising during the final week before the vote.

The campaign included another very effective, but labor-intensive method of persuasion: personal contact. Volunteers went door-to-door on densely populated streets and through some subdivisions with information packets, and the Township Supervisor spent hours in local coffee shops talking with farmers and gaining their support for the program. In an effort to secure more visible endorsement of farmers for the program, a statement of support was taken "tractor-to-tractor" and garnered the signatures of 57 percent of the farming community. Volunteers also went to see young people working in fast-food restaurants, talking with them about the PDR and its positive effect on the environment. They enlisted their help to share the information with other young people.

Three well-publicized public meetings provided addition forums for public education, with a slide show, a video produced by a local citizens' advocacy group on how the PDR program would affect residents of Peninsula Township, presentations by local experts, and a question and answer period. Materials available for distribution to all audience members included copies of the video, sample ballots, reprints of newspaper articles, maps of the agricultural preservation zone, and copies of the PRD ordinance. Postcards introducing the PDR were also given to audience members so that they could write short notes of endorsement and drop them in friends' and neighbors' mailboxes. There was also a list of supporters of the PDR plan for audience members to sign onto.

Approximately 300 copies of the video that was shown at the public meetings were distributed throughout the peninsula; others were available at the local library and grocery store for borrowing. The video included discussions by four local residents, one of whom was a senior member of the farm community. All discussed their reasons for supporting the PDR program. Finally, the American Farmland Trust (AFT) suggested that the most persuasive tool would be a demonstration project involving real farms. With the support of the campaign organizers and the township, the AFT worked with the regional land conservancy group to identify some working farms whose owners might agree to sell their development rights and to secure options to purchase those rights.

Three options were signed before the referendum vote with respected members of the community, and the details of the agreements were made public: the highly visible location of the farms, the appraisal approach, the price paid per acre, and the conservation easement terms. The demonstration project was credited with convincing many voters that farmers were willing and even eager to participate in the PDR program.

The referendum in the summer of 1994 permitting a property tax increase to provide for purchase of development rights to approximately 2,000 acres of agricultural land was passed by a vote of 1,208 to 1,081.

Closing Comments

Peninsula Township had broad-based community involvement from the beginning in the planning, development, and adoption of a strategy to achieve the three goals established by the citizens: to preserve agricultural land, to protect scenic views, and to direct second home and permanent development to areas most appropriate for residential use. Whether the PDR program, in conjunction with other provisions of the zoning ordinance, will achieve its long-term goals is still not clear. Conservation easements have protected about 20 percent of the agricultural land on the Peninsula from development; farmers have applied to sell development rights on an additional 14 percent, leaving 57 percent of the agricultural land as yet unprotected. Residential development is being channeled away from agricultural areas, but second-home development and the pressures of seasonal tourism continue, as does the loss of some farmland.

The close vote on the referendum suggests that there may not be widespread support for the program. If farmers cannot feel assured that the PDR approach will continue, they may be less likely to participate in the program and permanently lose the development rights to their property. They may choose instead to wait, to see what the future holds, and perhaps to sell their land to the highest bidder. Unless an appreciable number of farm owners in Peninsula Township decide to participate in the PDR program, its chance at success will be severely compromised.

Potential Pitfalls of Preservation Strategies

Preservation strategies can, as these case studies have shown, be adapted to a variety of circumstances. Combining zoning controls with other techniques, they can address many of the expected impacts from tourism growth. It is important, however, to recognize that the restrictions themselves may have significant impacts. For example, there are often unanticipated social impacts, particularly when the affected parties have not been involved in the process. When Kenya established protections for some of its national parks, it imposed restrictions on the use of land for grazing. However, the nomadic Masai people, whose economy is based on cattle and sheep, traditionally used much of that land for grazing their herds. The restrictions essentially outlawed a traditional and cultural way of life. Similar problems have been posed when preservation zones have restricted traditional hunting and fishing rights of native peoples.

Such restrictions have a significant economic as well as social impact when the activities are not recreational, but are essential for subsistence. Less severe restrictions may also have economic effects. Limitations on commercial activities may well impinge upon the ability of the local community to maintain a healthy economic base. There has been an ongoing debate in the United States about the degree of protection that public lands should be afforded. If logging, mining, and cattle grazing are prohibited on public lands, what will happen to the jobs that sustain many small towns in the West?

Preservation zones can also have unexpected impacts on surrounding areas. Uses that are restricted or prohibited in a protected area may locate just outside its boundaries. Gatlinburg, Tennessee, is a gateway to the Great Smoky Mountains National Park.[17] The past few decades have transformed the town into a massive commercial hub. It is now filled with fast-food franchises, motels, factory outlet stores, theme parks, and amusement centers. Businesses serving residents have been displaced by those catering to the tourists who visit the park. Most Gatlinburg residents now work in low-paying, seasonal jobs in a community that bears little resemblance to what it used to be.

Similar to the possibility of having unexpected impacts is the possibility of not achieving the hoped for impact. Unless vary carefully crafted and based on accurate data, preservation zones may be too narrow in scale to achieve the desired results. A two-mile wide marine protection area where fishing is prohibited may not have any significant effect on preventing depletion of the fish population if everyone simply fishes three miles out from shore.

Comparable problems may occur if zoning does not take into consideration regional issues. Agricultural pesticide use in outlying areas can have an enormous impact on the ecological system within a protected zone. Sometimes there are relevant factors that are well beyond the range of the protected area. Animal migration patterns are a prime example. Special regulations can limit activities where birds breed and turtles lay their eggs, but they cannot protect those animals when they leave the site.

A final concern is not unique to preservation strategies. Regulations, no matter how well designed, can succeed only if they are enforced. Egyptian laws prohibit any alteration to the coast along a portion of the Red Sea bordered by delicate coral reefs. Nonetheless, hotel developers hurrying to build enough rooms to accommodate the tourists who've been frightened away from Cairo and Luxor are apparently excavating lagoons and breaking up reefs with impunity. In Cyprus, environmental groups accused a government Minister of voting to relax zoning restrictions to permit the construction of a 352-bed hotel on an untouched nature reserve. By their very nature, special places are more fragile and susceptible to damage than other places; that is why we must accept such stringent restrictions on their use, and why enforcement is of such particular importance.

Growth Limitation Strategies

While some special places need strict preservation rules to protect their irreplaceable resources, there are many more distinctive but hardly unique locations that still need a measure of protection from the impacts of tourist numbers. The strongest available controls for places not requiring preservation rules—the second tier of protective strategies, as it were—are growth limitation regulations. When a destination determines that it *cannot* support any growth beyond a certain identified range, it may impose regulations that effectively limit growth to what it has determined to be its maximum sustainable level. The basis for such a strict limitation is often the *incapacity* of the destination to support additional growth in conjunction with its *inability* to remove whatever obstacles there are to sustaining further growth.

How to determine the point at which a community's resources are so constrained that it cannot support any additional growth usually involves an analysis of the environmental and physical carrying capacity of a site, because these are basically quantifiable. The important point for destination communities to remember is that in order for a strict limit on growth to be accepted (at least under U.S. law), there must be a reasonable correlation between carrying capacity limitations and any numerical limit that is imposed.

Destination communities may need to explore whether there are any measures that can be taken to increase the carrying capacity. If the limitation is tied to an inadequate water supply, perhaps a new desalinization plant can be built to increase the water supply; or if the roads cannot support any additional traffic, perhaps the government can finance a public bus system to alleviate congestion. When there are affordable technological solutions to constraints on growth, there may be no need for a restriction as severe as mandated growth limitation.

In some cases, management techniques may alleviate many of the negative impacts caused by the number of tourists so that growth limitations are not needed. Heidelburg, Germany, has kept certain "hidden" attractions popular with local residents out of guide books and off tourist maps. Martha's Vineyard in Massachusetts has no signs directing visitors down the unmarked dirt roads to locally popular "public" beaches.

At Westminster Abbey, more than 16,000 people would crowd into the church on a single summer day, noisily overwhelming its spaces. To safeguard the sense of the sacred, the Abbey initiated a series of management steps that it dubbed "Recovering the Calm." These measures reduced the number of tourists by a third and the noise levels by half. The Abbey now charges admission fees and reroutes visitors so that they don't intrude on worshipers.

Oxford has suffered numerous negative impacts from the visitors to its ivy-clad towers of academe.[18] There is crowding on the sidewalks and congestion on the streets, increased litter, noise, and wear and tear on its venerable stones. Christchurch, one of the smallest and most frequently visited colleges, faced serious capacity issues, which it was able largely to resolve by using a variety of management methods. First, it initiated an entrance fee for tourist visitors, while still permitting business visitors, local residents, and college alumni in free. It enforced strict limits on the number of people who would be admitted at one time, monitored congestion at "pressure points" within the college, and halted admissions until the congestion dissolved.

Westminster Abbey and Christchurch, however, are both examples of supremely contained and small sites. Tools that can manage a single building cannot necessarily resolve carrying capacity issues of a larger destination. Honolulu instituted various management techniques to control the number of visitors to Hanauma Bay Nature Park, one of Hawaii's most popular attractions.[19] It restricted access to the park by hiring parking attendants to turn vehicles away when the 300 legal parking spaces were filled; prohibited tour buses from discharging passengers in the Park; and closed the park on Wednesday mornings. Unfortunately, resourceful visitors found ways to circumvent the rules. Some people arrived at the park on mopeds; many more took to using the city bus, which was still permitted entry to the park; others parked their cars in nearby residential areas and walked to the park; and tour bus operators contracted with private taxis to carry their passengers the short distance from a convenient drop-off spot to the park. Visitor numbers dropped, but the management tools did not achieve the success that was originally anticipated.

Suitable Sites for Growth Limitations

Growth limitation strategies are most easily applied to areas with unchangeable borders: islands, sites with clearly defined geographic boundaries like mountains or rivers, contained ecosystems, national parks. In locations like these, it is far easier to determine the environmental and physical capacity of the site to support increased usage. First, the area to be studied for relevant data is sharply defined. Second, inherent in the location itself are certain limits to growth: the borders cannot be extended to accommodate ever-expanding numbers of people. Third, the physical separateness of the location means that there are fewer external factors to consider. The fact that a regional government is going to finance a new sewer system on the mainland will not solve the waste disposal problem of an island. Fourth, the geographic location may limit otherwise possible solutions. Increased means of access, for example, is a common method for relieving congestion on a single entry corridor. While there may be a multiplicity of affordable ways for a small city to increase access, there may be none that are even technically feasible for a valley surrounded by mountains.

Even in these well-defined areas, there are sometimes ways to increase the carrying capacity. In such instances, limitations on growth could be amended at a later date. The island of Nantucket, Massachusetts, is one of the most popular summer resorts in the U.S. It has for years been experiencing salt water intrusion into its water supply. In 1989 it undertook a comprehensive study to determine the carrying capacity of the island in terms of its water supply and water quality limitations. The study included an analysis of the demand, assuming a total build-out of the island. Based on the findings, Nantucket is developing land-use and zoning regulations to protect areas identified as critical water resource areas and limiting growth throughout the island. Should there be technological advances that allow it to increase its quality water supply in an economical manner, then it could choose to modify the growth limitations so that the number of people on the island could increase to its new carrying capacity level.

Growth Limitation Mechanisms

Successful growth limitation strategies involve a combination of techniques. First, of course, are regulations limiting the number of tourists, usually by limiting the number of overnight accommodations available to them. There often are additional limitations as well, sometimes on the number of parking spaces or ships that may dock. Management tools—particularly methods of traffic management—are often used as supplemental measures to support the overall strategy. Economic and social carrying capacity and visitor satisfaction capacity are often important components, even if they do not form the basis for the supply–demand explanation of the limitations on growth. They do shape the strategy though, because complementary techniques can be included to address their impacts.

Case Study: Sanibel Island, Florida

This barrier island connected to the southwest coast of the Florida mainland by a causeway bridge limits the number and intensity of dwelling units to prevent exceeding the ability of the island both to evacuate residents and visitors in the event of a hurricane and to sustain the natural environment.

Sanibel is a 12-mile-long, crescent-shaped barrier island in the Gulf of Mexico off the southwest coast of Florida near Fort Myers. (See Map 5-5.) Half of the 12,000-acre island is devoted to conservation. Much of that land is the federally owned and managed J.N. ("Ding") Darling National Wildlife Refuge; most of the remainder is owned by the Sanibel-Captiva Conservation Foundation. Sanibel is a haven for roseate spoonbills, great blue herons, egrets, anhingas, and migratory birds. Its interior freshwater wetlands are home to alligators, while its beaches are covered with a myriad of seashells.

The island is located in a coastal floodplain, in an area prone to tropical cyclones and hurricanes. Storm tides create serious risks of flooding for the low-lying island. In fact, a devastating 1926 hurricane inundated the entire island with salt water, destroying all farming activities and changing the character of Sanibel to this day. Most of the farmers were financially ruined and left the island; many of the residents who remained turned to providing services to winter visitors and tourists.

Sanibel recovered slowly from the effects of the 1926 hurricane. Its very small population, reported to be a mere 100 in 1944, increased gradually through the 1950s, largely because of the island's reputation for low-keyed tourism and particularly for collecting shells on the Gulf Coast beach. (See Photo 5-2.) Then in 1963, the causeway bridge connecting Sanibel to the Florida mainland was built, and opened the island to much easier automobile access. A development boom occurred, unrestricted by sensitive zoning regulation, and suddenly long stretches of the Gulf of Mexico beaches were lined with massive

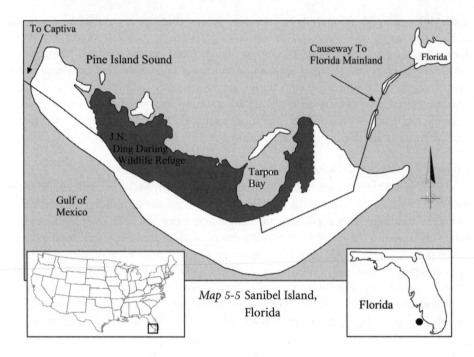

Map 5-5 Sanibel Island,
Florida

condominiums and hotels, while fragile interior wetlands were sporting golf courses and man-made lakes. The population soared to nearly 3,000 permanent residents and 12,000 seasonal residents.

The Original 1976 Sanibel Plan

Citizens of Sanibel have for 25 years been concerned about sensitive management of population growth and land-use changes. Before Sanibel incorporated as a municipality in 1974 with legal authority to regulate its own land uses, the governing development standards were set by the county in which the island was located, and which had statutory power of zoning and subdivision controls. At that time, the county standards were extremely permissive and would have allowed roughly 30,000 residential units to be built on the island with almost no measures to avoid environmental degradation. The total resident population could have ballooned to 70,000.

In the face of rapid development following the opening of the causeway, the newly incorporated city hired consultants in a variety of disciplines to assist it in creating a legally binding comprehensive land use plan and associated development standards. At the time of its preparation, the Sanibel Plan was the leading example of applying the methodologies of various disciplines to provide factual information upon which to base land use regulations. Three of the major concerns with the rapid growth of tourism were the ability of the island to handle hurricane risks to life, beaches, and buildings; the ability of the natural resources of the barrier island to tolerate increased human activity; and the ability of the infrastructure to provide adequate water supplies and sewage treatment for increased development. Meteorologists provided the latest information on forecasting major storms, indicating how much time the island would have from the initial forecast until landfall contact; traffic engineers studied how many cars would be able to leave the island in what period of time, and offered ways to improve traffic flow; construction engineers recommended revised building standards to increase the ability of new construction to withstand storm damage; environmentalists studied the impacts of growth on the fragile ecosystem of the barrier island; other experts analyzed Sanibel's capacity to provide potable water and adequate wastewater treatment and its ability to expand utility services.

Based on these studies and analyses, the 1976 Sanibel Plan and the planning guidelines later adopted in the 1980s embodied a carrying capacity strategy to guide future development. A key element of that first plan was the limitation of dwelling units to 7,800, a mere 26 percent of those that would have been allowed under county regulations. Not surprisingly, many landowners and developers objected to the strictures of the plan and, on a number of legal theories, sued the city in attempts to bar it from enforcing some or all of the new regulations. As a result of plan amendments and the results of such lawsuits (and settlements of some of the litigation), the 7,800 unit figure was increased between 1976 and 1989 to 9,000 units.

The 1997 Plan

The state of Florida planning statutes contemplate continual review and modification of comprehensive plans as conditions change. Sanibel amended its plan in 1989 and then in the mid-1990s, the city retained consultants to guide it in a thorough evaluation and appraisal of that plan. As part of that process, citizens engaged in an elaborate program of responses to questionnaires, public workshops, and other community consultative efforts, which culminated in a Vision Statement, adopted by the City Council as official policy in 1997. This Vision Statement summarized Sanibel's situation as of 1997:

> The specter of rampant development has diminished as the community has matured. Nevertheless, unwanted changes are occurring; visitation increases as new "attractions" are developed; beaches and refuge areas are being stressed by overuse; traffic congestion is turning to gridlock; and formerly "green" scenic corridors are becoming urbanized and commercialized. These and other conditions and trends cause residents to realize that, unless protected, their island's historic and cherished way of life is in jeopardy.[20]

The Vision Statement confirms policies and goals implicit in the 1976 plan and the 1989 revision and endorses three concepts to guide future decision making. First, "Sanibel is and shall remain a barrier island sanctuary" that strives for harmony between human uses and the island's natural and wildlife habitats. Second, "Sanibel is and shall remain a small town community" characterized by diversity, a casual style, development that emphasizes natural conditions and characteristics over human intrusions, a rural character, and a sense of responsible stewardship of the land for present and future generations.

Finally, "the Sanibel community recognizes that its attractiveness to visitors is due to the island's quality as sanctuary and community" and will welcome tourists who share those values, but resist "attractions and activities that compromise these qualities." The Vision Statement goes on to relate these concepts: "This . . . statement of the community's vision of its future is a hierarchy: one in which the dominant principle is Sanibel's sanctuary quality. Sanibel shall be developed as a community only to the extent to which it retains and embraces this quality of sanctuary. Sanibel will serve as attraction only to the extent to which it retains its desired qualities as sanctuary and community."[21]

Photo 5-2 Beach at Sanibel Island, Florida

Carrying Capacity Analysis

The strategy embodied in the 1976 Sanibel Plan was so thoughtfully and carefully crafted that there have been no abrupt revisions or changes in direction in either the 1989 plan amendment or the 1997 plan. Both these documents adjust the regulatory techniques to reflect current circumstances and up-to-date data, but both reaffirm that the key to shaping a variety of limitations to development is a carrying capacity analysis: "The use of land and buildings in the City of Sanibel should be determined by the capacity of natural and human-made environments to accommodate such uses without hazard to the health, safety and welfare of the citizens and visitors to the city. The Sanibel Plan provides that the type and intensity of future land uses permitted will be determined by the capacity of the City to accommodate further development in an orderly manner with minimum negative impact." The plans approach such varied issues as emergency evacuation, environmental protection, infrastructure, and identification of residential and commercial zoning districts from the framework of a carrying capacity analysis.

Evacuation

Sanibel's only evacuation route is over the causeway bridge connecting the island to the mainland of Florida. Sanibel has one main thoroughfare running the length of the island from the causeway and linking Sanibel to Captiva, another barrier island to the northwest. Because of the threat of hurricanes and the possible inundating of the entire island, any evacuation plan must provide for all the people on both Captiva and Sanibel islands to get off before disaster strikes.

As of 1995, there were an estimated 9,400 dwelling units on the two islands. The "functional population" (the total number of residents and overnight tourists) that would need to be evacuated was estimated to be 16,000 at the beginning of the hurricane season in June and as high as 17,300 in November. Only 5,700 of these were Sanibel residents. If all the rental units were occupied, the numbers would be even higher. The number of vehicles to be used for evacuation was estimated between 6,850 and 8,000. In addition to the functional population, there were also approximately 13,000 day-trippers visiting the island via the causeway each day during the peak hurricane season.

Since the 1976 plan, the evacuation plan has been based on a variety of studies projecting how many people could be evacuated in what length of time, as well as projections of how much warning the city would have before a hurricane struck. One key element of each plan has been the limitation on the number of dwelling units that could be built, in order to limit the *number* of people on the island to an amount that could be safely evacuated. The *location* of residential units has also been controlled in an effort to limit the density of development. Since island roads are limited and everyone must secure access to the one main thoroughfare in order to get to the causeway bridge, development is directed to areas where access will not create gridlock. Also, development is directed away from coastal areas subject to storm surges.

Sanibel has decided *not* to widen its roads to provide increased capacity for hurricane evacuation. This is largely through concern that easing the evacuation process would itself create an impetus for additional development on the grounds that more people could safely be evacuated in an emergency. This would, in turn, lead to additional pressures on the limited resources of the island, make further demands on infrastructure, and, by increasing the number of people who would need to be evacuated, destroy the benefit of any road-widening.

Instead, the island has chosen to focus additional efforts on traffic management. Depending on the type of storm, its intensity, direction, and the projected evacuation time, both lanes of the evacuation route and the causeway (itself low-lying and prone to inundation) will be converted to outgoing lanes. Additionally, within 48 hours of a projected landfall of a hurricane, Sanibel can restrict all vehicular access to the island.

A further complicating issue is that once over the causeway, virtually all Sanibel and Captiva evacuees will follow the single main road going north. Unfortunately, this is also the evacuation route that will be used by thousands of people who live in the low-lying coastal areas of the mainland. Development along that evacuation corridor has grown to the extent that traffic can be congested during the peak season, even without the threat of a hurricane. Sanibel recognizes the need to work with surrounding communities to ensure that the capacity of that mainland evacuation route to handle both mainland and island residents is not reduced through further growth.

Sanibel has also strengthened building standard requirements, so that new construction must meet hurricane resistant standards. Since the 1976 plan, construction has been prohibited beyond the federally delineated flood control line running parallel to the Gulf of Mexico (the Coastal Construction Control Line). Additionally, all structures must be elevated above or floodproofed to the height of the 100-year storm's projected wave length. These measures should minimize damage in case of hurricanes and may allow some people to remain safely on the island in case of less severe storms. They will not, however, save anyone from the need to evacuate in case of a truly devastating hurricane.

Finally, Sanibel has improved a variety of secondary measures: its public notification program, use of volunteers, tide gauges, improved storm drainage along the evacuation route, and a tree management program to lessen the risk that a tree could fall across the sole evacuation route during a storm.

Conservation and Environmental Protection

The carrying capacity approach is also used with regard to Sanibel's environmental, natural, and scenic resources. With its commitment to being a barrier island sanctuary, Sanibel has strong measures protecting its special ecology. Approximately half the island is already located within conservation areas. However, much of the remaining land is environmentally sensitive: mangrove swamps, wetlands, beaches, and areas with rare vegetation. To control development in these areas, the 1997 plan divides all the island into six ecological zones, the parameters and locations of which were determined by scientific criteria.

The list of permitted uses for each zone is based on the determination of what type of human activity the area can tolerate. Thus, there is a Gulf Beach Zone where no buildings are allowed seaward of the Coastal Construction Control Line. In the Upland Wetlands Zone permitted uses are conservation, passive recreation, public facilities, agriculture, and low intensity residential (single family detached plus duplex and limited multifamily in designated areas). The Mangrove Zone has a low tolerance for any alteration by humans and is also dependent upon regulation of activities in adjacent zones. Here, only conservation, passive recreation, and very low intensity residential uses are permitted.

Development Intensity

The Sanibel Plan is particularly noteworthy for its thoughtful treatment of development intensity, again based primarily upon the concept of carrying capacity. As noted previously, the carrying capacity analysis—with special reference to hurricane evacuation needs, natural resources protection, and municipal services, such as water and sewer services—produced a maximum number of dwelling units of about 9,000 with the assumption of an average of 2.2 persons per dwelling unit. The analysis recognizes, however, that the total may need to be adjusted. "If dwelling units are kept to within (the stated) range, the water consumption and sewage generation can probably be handled in a manner consistent with the public health, safety, and welfare, based upon present knowledge. *Further data could, of course, indicate a need to reduce or the ability to increase these limits.*" (Emphasis added.)

The 1997 version of the Sanibel Plan mirrors the basic approach taken 20 years earlier in the 1976 plan with respect to allocating densities of residential development within the island, so as to spread out the allowable additional units to suitable sites, based for the most part upon availability of city services and the relative environmental fragility of those sites. A series of 36 Development Intensity Maps for use during the planning period 1995–2015 identify every parcel as within a particular density designation. There are 16 such designations, plus one for "open space" (i.e., no dwelling units). The least intensive designation is one unit per 33 acres and the most intensive, slightly more than five units per acre, with finely drawn levels in between.

Commercial Development

The concept of carrying capacity also informs another aspect of the Sanibel Plan: commercial development. Here the regulations are not dependent upon scientific studies to determine a physical carrying capacity, but rather relate to the social carrying capacity.

Sanibel has long been resistant to extensive commercial development, in order to preserve its residential character. The 1997 plan describes the concern this way: "The city desires to maintain a balance between the residential and resort (tourist) segments of the community, so that Sanibel remains an attractive and desirable residential community. It is apparent that the commercial developer views Sanibel as primarily a nonresident commercial market. And, left unregulated, this trend can be expected to continue to the point that Sanibel could become a destination shopping area, contrary to public desires."[22]

To address this concern, the plan reduces the potential supply of retail space "consistent with reasonable demand considerations." Applicants for centers with more than 12,000 square feet of retail space will need to demonstrate that there would be no adverse economic or other consequence from the development. Additionally, the Plan proposes that land use regulations provide incentives and disincentives to guide all future commercial development into clusters, particularly in outlying areas, to avoid a commercial strip and to provide commercial uses that would primarily serve residents' needs.

Existing resorts present their own set of concerns. These are generally large condominium structures built prior to the 1976 plan and are often located close to the water at high density levels. Over time, they have become resort hotels with short-term rentals. The restaurants at these resorts depend heavily on nonguest patronage, thus taking on the character of a public restaurant intruding upon the scenic beauty of the beach. In the future, such uses as restaurants will be more tightly limited in type and scope so as to be merely ancillary to the resort guests' own needs. Additionally, resort housing uses will be permitted only in the Resort Housing District.

Another challenge is to ensure that future commercial uses are "compatible with the Sanibel Plan's objectives for scenic preservation and maintenance of the character of the community." The Community Design Plan that is yet to be developed can address such diverse elements as size, exterior materials, architectural design, and vegetation buffers to ensure compatibility with neighboring structures. Adaptive design regulations can require that buildings adapt to the island's climate to minimize use of utilities; for example, orienting buildings to maximize natural ventilation and increasing shade by enlarging the size of overhangs.

Closing Comments

Sanibel has been a pioneer in using a carrying capacity analysis to manage tourism growth. The 1976 plan relied on meteorology, environmental analysis, studies of water quality, statistical models, and other sophisticated research for the information upon which to base its land use regulations limiting development. More than twenty years later, the situation has evolved. There has been more growth on Sanibel, Captiva, and the Florida mainland area. There have also been advances in our ability to forecast hurricanes and other potentially devastating storms.

The Sanibel community has, however, reaffirmed the concepts and approaches of the 1976 plan. They agreed upon a Vision Statement to guide all future planning decisions and adopted a plan based upon current analyses and scientific studies that apply the strategy of the earlier plan. There has been a commendable degree of continuity that has benefited residents, developers, and tourists alike. Sanibel is an extraordinarily fragile barrier island that needs adequate protection. The plan will need continued monitoring and evaluating to ensure that it continues to provide that protection and achieves the goals the community has outlined.

Sanibel remains, after 25 years, the premier example of a successful growth limitation strategy. It has enjoyed the economic benefits of tourism, protected its sensitive environment, and maintained the casual character that it values. It severely limited its growth potential and has steadfastly maintained that its essence as "sanctuary" and "community" are more important than its tourism.

Sanibel also has large areas that are preserved from all forms of development and all but the least intrusive human use. The locations and intensity of permitted tourism facilities are restricted to other areas, based on the environmental and physical carrying capacity of the island. Another long-standing tourist destination, Bermuda, has imposed growth restrictions because of a different type of carrying capacity issue: virtually all the land is already developed and the small amount of remaining open space needs to be protected.

Case Study: Bermuda

This long-popular tourist destination promotes preservation of its unique built and natural ambiance by use of principles of sustainable development and special controls on additional accommodations, time-share developments, cruise ships, and charter air flights.

The Bermuda Islands, located in the North Atlantic Ocean, 650 miles east of North Carolina, form a self-governing dependency of Great Britain. Only about 20 of the 150 or so small islands are inhabited, and the sole island of touristic importance is also called Bermuda. It is 14 miles long, with a narrow, highly irregular shape, curving around numerous bays and sheltered harbors. (See Map 5-6.) Its mild climate, warm waters, golf courses (more acreage per square mile devoted to golf than anywhere in the world; see Photo 5-3), recreational opportunities, architecture, restaurants, and entertainment have long attracted visitors and residents. The island is largely developed, with very little remaining open space and the third highest population density in the world. Population of all the islands was 62,000 in 1995 and is expected to grow to 66,000 by the year 2000. Bermudans enjoy a very

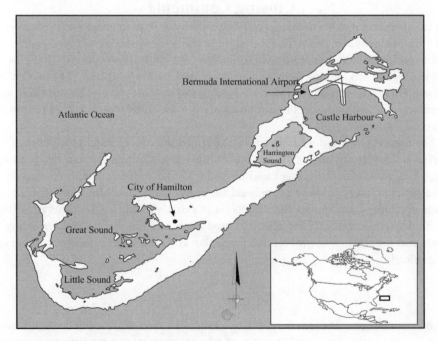

Map 5-6 Bermuda

Photo 5-3 Golf St. Georges, Bermuda (Courtesy of Bermuda Government Department of Information Services)

high standard of living, no national debt, no income tax, and very low unemployment, as well as an economy resting on two pillars: tourism and international service businesses.

Tourism in Bermuda

For many years, Bermuda has enjoyed robust tourism. Its regulatory efforts have primarily been aimed at the dual goals of maintaining rather than increasing the number of tourists and enhancing the quality experience it offers its visitors to ensure that high-income tourists from North America and Europe continue to visit. Bermuda's marketing has long focused on these tourists in its effort to attract what it regards as an optimum number of 550,000 arrivals per year. Accommodations range from very large, elaborate resort hotels to small cottages and housekeeping arrangements, with a total of 79 government licensed accommodations for six or more guests. This licensing program began in 1969, reflecting a long-standing policy of limiting the number of hotel beds to a number that reasonably balances with demand and ensuring that the facilities are well built and maintained.

The Bermuda Plan 1991

In 1991, the government of Bermuda adopted Bermuda Plan 1991, designed to be consistent with the United Nations' emphasis on "sustainable development" and the need to balance social and economic benefits with limitations on the negative impacts of development on the environment. The plan is intended to promote environmental management as opposed to being development oriented. To that end, it states three broad policy goals: to conserve open space and promote a high-quality environment; to provide sufficient development potential to meet community needs; and to encourage more efficient use and development of land. This reflects a long-range perspective and the need for community involvement at the earliest opportunity to determine "community need."

To achieve its conservation goals, the plan proposes restricting new building in certain areas in order to establish and protect a green belt around the entire island. Additionally, the plan calls for discouragement of tourist-related development on the coastline and on other islands in order to preserve their visual importance and unique environmental qualities. From the perspective of Bermuda's built heritage, the plan calls for the listing of significant architectural and historic structures and strict legislation governing demolition of or alteration to the external appearance of any listed building. The plan is aimed at preserving important structures characterized by a "Bermuda" look: pastel exterior walls built of coral stone with white roof and trim.

Concerning the second broad goal of addressing community needs, the plan notes that as of its enactment date, there were more than 2,000 vacant lots on Bermuda. This indicates that land had been subdivided beyond the island's housing needs. Approval of future applications for subdivision of large tracts of open space will require both a determination of the need for additional housing and careful attention to the physical characteristics of the parcels.

As to the third goal of encouraging efficient use of land, the plan notes that tourism is the largest generator of foreign currency, household income, employment, and public sector revenue in Bermuda's economy. Maintaining that level of contribution will require maintaining the image, character, and quality of the island. The plan emphasizes the upgrading of existing facilities, rather than the development of new ones. Additionally, any new development of future hotels should be limited to small cottage-type operations of not more than 50 rooms per development. The plan proposes that an optimum operating level is about 10,000 bed spaces, sufficient to accommodate the average 567,000 visitors per year.

The Bermuda Plan 1991 is implemented by a two-tier zoning method using maps that separately identify environmental constraints and developmental opportunities. Underlying maps represent parcels and their relationship to conservation goals; the overlying or second-tier maps illustrate the permissible development zoning.

The Bermuda Plan 1992 Planning Statement

Supplementing the 1991 plan is a shorter document entitled "The Bermuda Plan 1992 Planning Statement." One of its objectives is to provide for the regulated development and upgrading of tourism facilities consistent with the operation of a successful tourism industry. The 1992 plan incorporates a flexible system that allows the Development Applications Board some measure of discretion in acting on development applications. This appointed board may consider the proposed site plan, the character and appearance of the development, the proposed setbacks, and, most importantly, the potential effect of the development on the environment pursuant to an environmental analysis approach.

The board is also empowered to approve applications for small guest houses, provided that it is satisfied that the location provides reasonable access to public transportation, is served by an adequate paved road, and is harmless to the environment and neighborhood residential ambiance. All guest houses must be constructed to a high standard, with appropriate amenities and open spaces, be well landscaped, and provide screened outdoor facilities. These small guest houses may locate in residential zoning districts.

The plan also establishes Tourism Development Zones. Regulations for this zone provide for orderly development, expansion, and upgrading of tourist facilities; ensure that design is compatible with a "Bermuda" image; enhance the overall quality of hotels and cottage colonies on the island; and prevent the overdevelopment of sites, allowing only those developments whose scale and density are compatible with site characteristics. Additionally, the plan empowers the Development Applications Board to determine that a particular site is of such importance to the future of Bermudan tourism, that *only* tourist accommodations will be permitted on that site. Significantly, the board has *plenary* discretion to establish development regulations and planning details.

Hotel Phasing Policy

Bermuda has had a Hotel Phasing Policy in place since 1970 with the goal of ensuring that the supply of hotel beds on the island does not exceed the demand by visitors. The original policy established a general moratorium on the construction of new hotels in order to maintain an optimum number of bed-spaces of approximately 10,000. Additionally, it prohibited existing licensed hotels from increasing their number of beds. Exceptions to these limitations may be granted by Cabinet decision "in exceptional circumstances." In the case of existing hotels that wish to expand, permission is usually tied to an agreement to do extensive upgrading.

The Hotel Phasing Policy is amended and adopted every five years or so. The current policy covering the period 1993–1998 created what is known as a "bed bank." When a hotel closes down, the number of its beds[23] go out of circulation and are placed in a bed bank for eventual reallocation to existing hotels wanting to expand, or to new developments approved by the government. There are specific criteria that existing hotels must meet before applications are approved for even a very modest number of new beds, including a consistent record of high standards, high annual occupancy levels, ability to provide necessary additional support services for the expansion, and appropriate financing.

Another paragraph of the Hotel Phasing Policy document lists criteria for applications to convert existing housing units into tourist accommodations. For example, the property must have some on-site recreational facilities such as a swimming pool or sun terrace.

Finally, the policy states the general intention of the Minister of Tourism "to continue to raise the licensing standards to ensure that all licensed properties attain the highest possible standards of safety, maintenance, and operations, in keeping with Bermuda's reputation as a quality resort destination." The Minister furthermore gives notice that "[he] will not renew the operating licenses of properties whose standards of safety, maintenance and/or operations have been found to be consistently low over the past several years."

Hotel Construction Approval

There is a great deal of intergovernmental review of any hotel proposal in Bermuda. For that reason, the 1996 "Informal Guide for Hotel Developers Interested in Bermuda" highly recommends local legal guidance together with plenty of time, patience, and understanding. Prospective hotel developers are expected, first, to confer with a staff of the Department of Tourism. The Minister of Tourism then makes an initial decision whether to permit the application to proceed. If the preliminary decision is favorable, then a detailed proposal document must be submitted to a technical governmental committee including a representative from each concerned governmental ministry. Following that review, the Minister of Tourism presents the proposal to the entire Bermuda Cabinet of Ministers for a preliminary decision. The developer may then submit detailed plans to the Department of

Planning and other governmental agencies. The Development Applications Board makes the final decision to grant or deny approval. Technically, the Minister of Environment has the power to grant an appeal from a decision of the Development Applications Board, but such appeals are rarely granted. The informal Guide for Hotel Developers candidly warns applicants that "if this is a project that might arouse public interest, now may be the time to approach relevant community leaders. Any negative feedback from the public may result in loss of government (political) support."

Prospective hotel developers are advised to address a number of "issues of concern in Bermuda" in developing proposals. These include the following:

- potential impact on limited local labor resources;
- effect on open space on an island which is already overdeveloped;
- sensitivity to environmental needs;
- compliance with such technical aspects as appropriate sewage disposal, ridgeline preservation, appearance, and building height;
- effect on existing public and private transportation system where Bermuda traffic density has reached a saturation point;
- housing and transportation for any foreign workers;
- effect on Bermuda's immigration policy if any foreign workers are needed to operate the proposed development;
- compliance with Bermuda Incorporation and Foreign Exchange Rules; and
- recognition that the labor movement in Bermuda is strong and often confrontational.

Application approval rests, in part, upon a developer's response to these issues.

Time-Share Controls

In 1981, three time-sharing projects existed on Bermuda; as of 1996, only two remained. Because of various perceived difficulties with that form of tourism development, the government passed very strict rules and also instituted a moratorium on any additional time-sharing projects. The state provides for licensing and control of marketing, operation, and management of time-share developments. Transfer of time-share licenses, including the fees and conditions of transfer, is also covered by the statute, as are required inspections and similar matters. There are a number of sanctions for operating a time-share without license: a possible $5,000-per-day fine, or imprisonment not exceeding one year, or both. The statute also includes a number of technical requirements for time-share developments, such as the inclusion of nondisturbance clauses, provisions for revocation of purchase contract, and the plan of payment for the time-share interest.

Cruise-Ship Policy

Concerned that Bermuda was becoming overcrowded, the government reduced the number of cruise-ship arrivals in 1990. The number of passengers per day is limited to 6,000 during the high season of May 1 through October 31 of each year. The Minister of Tourism may issue any number of cruise-ship permits, providing the 6,000 passengers-per-day limit is not exceeded. The Minister first issues permits to those ships under contract with the government, and each permit is subject to an annual fee. Thereafter, the Minister may issue permits to ships not under contract provided that they are in accordance with policy guidelines.

There were several reasons for limiting the number of cruise-ship arrivals. First, it limited the daily influx of tourists crowding onto the streets. Second, since cruise-ship passengers do not spend the night in Bermuda accommodations and often do not eat in Bermuda restaurants, the policy ensured more comfortable daytime space for those tourists who provided more economic benefit to the community. Third, limiting the number of passengers perpetuates Bermuda's reputation as one of the premier cruise destinations in the world. Finally, because of limited resources, allowing a maximum of 6,000 passengers per day offers an exceptional vacation experience to all tourists without producing undue strain on Bermuda's "delicate infrastructure."

In another, later cruise-ship policy, the government recognized that many cruise passengers felt they were not getting full value for the cost of their shore excursions. Bermuda is now making excursion contracting and pricing a more open process in the sense of full disclosure. The policy calls for greater dissemination of information about site-seeing trips and recreational activities in Bermuda, as well as more information on places to shop.

In what is presumably an effort to provide economic benefit to local musicians and entertainers, Bermuda has established a commission headed by an independent chairman and consisting of musicians and entertainers, to promote Bermudan entertainment on-shore. At the same time, the government is prohibiting entertainment on-board ship while in port, other than music for dancing.

The cruise-ship policy also increases the fee the cruise operator is assessed for each passenger. To rationalize this increase, the government points out that Bermuda is considered a preferred destination by the majority of the cruise line's target-market customers. Additionally, the contract for serving the island on a regular basis protects those lines from competition, which is very valuable, considering the particular attractiveness of the Bermuda market. Finally, cruise-ship passengers contribute relatively low levels of revenue compared to other travelers and industries on the island.

Charter Flight Policy

Bermuda also tightly controls the number of air charters arriving on the island. This is designed, in large part, to avoid mass-market tourism in an effort to maintain and upgrade the image of a high-quality destination. Additionally, Bermuda has limited facilities for the handling of all civil aircraft; seasonal and peak traffic already saturates the airport, and charter flying is regarded as sufficiently irregular that it creates particular management problems.

To address the problems associated with air charter arrivals, the government requires that air travel organizers obtain a permit; they must satisfy the government that they are financially sound, with an appropriate operational background. Interestingly, plans for all advertising and promotional material must be submitted to the government, presumably so that it can monitor the image being created. In order to ensure compliance with the various requirements imposed upon charter operators, the government may require the provision of a bond "for the due performance of the conditions of these rules for the accommodation of persons and the operation of the aircraft."

Closing Comments

Bermuda has long been in the enviable position of having an established and healthy tourism industry. The challenges facing Bermuda have been to maintain the number of tourists and the quality that has made it such a popular destination. For almost thirty years Bermuda has followed policies aimed at limiting its tourist numbers to what it perceives as the "optimal" amount and at enhancing its tourist product to ensure that it attracts the higher-income visitor. It has developed a network of stringent regulatory mechanisms to achieve these ends. Techniques to limit growth include moratoria on hotel and time-share development, "bed bank" provisions, and cruise-ship controls. Zoning tools protect open space and identify areas where there are environmental constraints to further development. Various design controls and intensity regulations ensure development compatible with the "Bermuda style" so attractive to tourists. Licensing regulations give the government wide latitude to ensure that high standards are maintained by tourist facilities. Charter flight regulations limit mass-market access to the island, while government involvement ensures that the high-income North American and European markets are targeted.

The relatively small size of Bermuda, its economic and social stability, and its generally positive attitude toward tourism have all contributed to the success of its regulatory approach. One aspect of particular interest is Bermuda's continued monitoring of what is generally considered a successful tourism program. Reevaluation and revision of plans and policies have reflected changing values (the concern for "sustainable development" and environmental protection) while retaining those elements that form the basis of Bermuda's appeal.

Few places have limited their growth as strictly as Sanibel and Bermuda. It is much more common for tourism numbers at popular destinations to steadily increase until their impacts suddenly seem intolerable. Existing mechanisms have proved insufficient to protect the site from excessive growth. At this point, it is not just the *environmental* and *physical* carrying capacity that is endangered, but also the ability of the site to provide a *quality* visitor experience. At this point, destinations face the difficult and time-consuming task of developing equitable and politically acceptable mechanisms to reduce the existing level of usage. Yosemite National Park in California is in the midst of just such a process, drafting carefully planned alternative solutions that are then submitted to public comment, revised, resubmitted, and revised again.

Case Study: Yosemite National Park, California—A Plan in Progress

A draft National Park Implementation Plan proposes severe restrictions on automobile use within Yosemite Park because the current number of vehicles grossly exceeds the park's carrying capacity.

Yosemite National Park is one of the jewels of the U.S. national park system. Just 150 miles east of San Francisco, it is a place of stunning beauty. (See Map 5-7.) Yosemite Valley, carved by glaciers and following the path of the Merced River, is over nine miles long, but just one-half to one mile wide. Its sheer, nearly vertical walls rise dramatically from the valley floor, climbing as high as 4,000 feet. Lying in the midst of the Sierra Nevada Mountains, the park features breathtaking cascades, rocky cliffs, alpine meadows, polished granite domes, sequoia groves, and a subtle pastel light that has captivated painters and tourists alike.

The area was granted to the state of California by an act of Congress in 1864 to be held

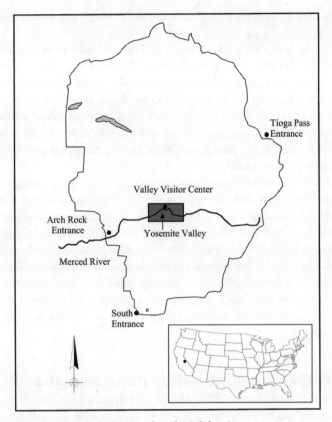

Map 5-7 Yosemite National Park, California

"for public use, resort and recreation . . . for all time." It was decreed a national park in 1890, and then in 1906 was transferred to the Federal Government for administration by the Secretary of the Interior. Yosemite's history is an attempt to meet its two main goals: to preserve the natural splendors of the park and to make those splendors available to the public for "enjoyment, education, and recreation."

Over the years, despite well-intentioned efforts to preserve and protect the natural environment, decisions were made permitting extensive man-made development. By 1980, there were more than 1,000 homes, garages, stores, lodging facilities, and restaurants in the Yosemite Valley. Even more significantly, there were 30 miles of roadway along the valley floor, which accommodated some one million cars, trucks, and buses each year. The beautiful valley was clearly congested.

1980 General Management Plan

The 1980 General Management Plan for Yosemite National Park was designed to serve as a comprehensive guide for the future of the park for the next ten years. The plan had five goals for park management: to reclaim priceless natural beauty; to markedly reduce traffic congestion; to allow natural processes to prevail; to reduce crowding; and to promote visitor understanding and enjoyment. The plan identified the increasing automobile traffic as "the single greatest threat to enjoyment of the natural and scenic qualities of Yosemite." The related overcrowding of the park greatly interfered with visitor enjoyment and threatened "park values."

To deal with "the noise, the smell, the glare and the environmental degradation caused by thousands of vehicles," the plan proposed the eventual removal of *all* automobiles from Yosemite Valley. Recommended interim steps to limit cars within the park included removing more than 1,000 parking spaces and restricting access at certain entry points to the park. An information system would be established at park entrances and when a predetermined daily carrying capacity for automobiles was reached, access would be restricted to the east end of the valley. At the same time, shuttle bus service would provide access to the valley from various parking areas.

To deal with visitor overcrowding, the plan proposed limiting the number of overnight accommodations, campsites, and day parking spaces. When capacity was filled, access to the park would be restricted. The number of overnight accommodations was to be reduced, as were the number of parking spaces. The overnight carrying capacity of the developed area of the park (not including areas accessible to backpackers) was determined by adding up the number of overnight accommodations and campsites. The day use carrying capacity was based on the number of parking spaces plus the number of day visitors who entered the park on tour buses. The plan recognized the very real threat that congestion, both of cars and visitors, was causing to the park; but its carrying capacity analysis was far from sophisticated.

Draft 1997 Yosemite Valley Implementation Plan

Despite the laudable goals of the 1980 General Management Plan, overuse of Yosemite National Park continued and worsened. By 1997, almost double the number of visitors in 1980 were annually arriving at Yosemite, more than four million in all. Most arrived in automobiles, and at peak times there were over 6,000 automobiles in the park. Traffic was still the greatest threat to visitors' enjoyment of the park. Once again, officials responsible for Yosemite opined that "the visitor experience should be dominated by the majesty of the valley without the distraction of traffic and parking. A more appropriate balance should be restored to the valley so that nature's wonders are not over shadowed by the intrusions of the modern world."[24]

The Draft 1997 Implementation Plan clearly identifies various adverse impacts from the traffic congestion: stress on the natural resources (for example, air quality); compromised visitor safety; a diminished visitor experience; and reduced efficiency and reliability of the shuttle bus service. Attempts to reduce the volume of cars by reducing the number of parking spaces had resulted in people parking their cars in illegal locations, causing additional negative impacts on the natural resources. The draft plan presents four alternative approaches for achieving the goals of the 1980 plan, including reduction of traffic congestion in the park, and analyzes each in terms of its impacts.

Proposals to Address Traffic Congestion

The alternative favored by park planners (Alternative #2) proposes the development of a regional transportation system by the year 2001, buttressed by National Park Service actions within Yosemite itself. Regulations would restrict vehicular access at the east end of the valley to overnight visitors with reservations either at a lodge or a campground; their vehicles would be parked upon entry and could not be moved until the visitors departed. This alternative also includes a number of circulation changes; closes certain parking facilities and roads, converting them instead to bicycle and pedestrian pathways; and eliminates 2,300 parking spaces for day-use vehicles from the developed areas in Yosemite Valley.

To significantly reduce the number of cars entering the park, this alternative proposes construction of an orientation/transfer facility three miles west of Yosemite Village (the largest developed area within the park). This new facility would be the point of entry for Yosemite Valley visitors, who would park here and then take a shuttle bus, walk, or ride a bicycle into the valley itself. Shuttle buses would run to the Yosemite Village Visitor Center, trailheads, picnic spots, and other sites.

Assuming the successful construction of the planned regional transportation system, day visitors would arrive at the entry point by bus and there would be no need for parking spaces for them. If, however, a regional system is not established by the year 2001, then this alternative proposes constructing 1,800 parking spaces for day-use vehicles, 120 spaces for backpackers with permits, and a staging area for 20 tour buses. As regional alternatives develop, day-use parking spaces could be reduced and perhaps eliminated entirely. The draft plan recommends periodic review and assessment of the state of the regional transportation system to determine whether the number of parking spaces can be reduced.

Impact Analysis of Transportation Recommendations

The draft plan carefully analyzes the expected impacts, both positive and negative, of each of its four alternatives upon three general categories: the natural environment, the cultural resources (a broad classification that includes everything from Native American sites to visitor education and recreation), and socioeconomic conditions. In each area, it relies on studies and data compiled by various sources. It also outlines the analytic bases it uses in making its comparisons among the four alternatives.

Impacts on the Natural Environment

Noise is the principal negative impact from excessive vehicular activity in Yosemite park. In many locations, the background noise is almost constant, easily drowning out the sound of waterfalls, rivers, and wind. At peak periods, certain popular drives have more than 6,000 vehicle passes a day, and more than 600 per hour. During late afternoon and early evening, as many as 720 cars exit the park on one road. Additionally, the high number of vehicles requires extensive road and parking facilities throughout the valley, which extends the noise problem "to nearly every attraction and vista and along every major meadow, which negatively affects the visitor experience."

The draft plan includes data concerning the decibel levels of various vehicles, at different sites, at different times. Planners estimate that the proposed Alternative #2 would considerably lessen the noise problem: what vehicle noise there was would be from shuttle buses operating on regular schedules, moving between service facilities and attractions. The number of vehicles would change dramatically, dropping by a projected 70 percent at the popular Four Mile trailhead. Additionally, all visitors would arrive at very popular park attractions by shuttle buses rather than automobiles or motor coaches, greatly reducing vehicular sound. How much noise is created by the shuttle buses will depend in large part on the type used (electric, compressed natural gas, diesel). Finally, the reduction in overall number of vehicles will also mean a reduced need for roads and parking sites. For those portions of the roads and parking facilities that would be converted exclusively to bicycle and walking trails, quiet would prevail.

The draft plan also includes an analysis of the impacts of Alternative #2 on water quality in the park. The recommended removal of three bridges would significantly reduce flow constriction in the Merced River and the resulting erosion-related contamination of the water. Removal and relocation of campgrounds and secondary structures would minimize the impacts of human activity on the water quality, and removal of related stables would eliminate an existing source of water pollution.

The reduction in the flow constriction of the Merced River, combined with restoration of areas in the floodplain and the relocation of certain campsites and campgrounds, would allow a much more natural flow of the river throughout the east end of the valley. By restoring the natural flow to the river, and creating the Mercer River management zone, currently fragmented natural habitats would be reconnected into larger biotic communities. Previous water table levels and subsurface water flows would be restored, as would soil contours, all of which would provide an improved habitat for riparian, meadow, and aquatic communities. Campgrounds would be relocated to far less sensitive areas, where their impact upon the environment would be less serious.

The impact of Alternative #2 on wildlife is more mixed. The increase in meadow, riparian, and mixed conifer habitats in the east end of the valley would support increased numbers of wildlife species that use these habitats. However, new development at the west end of the valley would affect some previously undisturbed areas, thus creating a new opportunity for negative impacts on wildlife.

In terms of air quality, Alternative #2 would have a generally beneficial effect by reducing emissions by limiting automobile use and relying instead on shuttle buses. The draft plan includes comparative emission levels for buses using various fuels and recommends that electric buses be purchased because of their low emission levels as existing buses need to be replaced. The plan does recognize that sources outside the park continue to have the greatest impact on the air quality, and that a regional transit system would result in the greatest reduction of pollutants.

Impacts on Cultural Resources

In the broad area of recreation impact, the draft plan predicts a number of positive effects from the elimination of independent auto touring. Relaxation would be more possible, with a reduction of noise, crowding, and visual distractions. Fewer vehicles should result in reduced levels of pollution and noise, thus enhancing the attractiveness of biking, walking, and sitting. Walking and bicycling safety is generally likely to improve as well. It would be easier for hikers and campers to reach trailheads via the shuttle buses, without having to find places to park privately owned vehicles. Vehicular touring of the valley would be on shuttle buses, making interpretation opportunities available and enhancing both visitors' safety and their ability to concentrate on the sites themselves without worrying about traffic hazards. Bicycle touring would become much improved with a larger number of vehicle-free bike paths. Because of improved air quality and fewer vehicles, photographic opportunities would be enhanced.

Needless to say, there are a number of potentially negative impacts as well, particularly in the area of inconvenience: waiting for shuttle buses; inability to spontaneously stop at an appealing site; the necessity to tour in groups; transporting equipment such as picnic gear on shuttle buses; or lugging a purchase around all day instead of locking it in the trunk of your car. Increased numbers of bicycles might make some paths less safe for hikers and may cause some resource degradation. On balance however, the draft plan finds that the cumulative effects of the automobile restrictions are highly positive:

> Interpretive services would be more central and integral to movements about the valley, since they would be linked to the in-valley transportation network. The reduction in automobiles in Yosemite Valley would greatly improve the quality of the visitor experience and recreational environment. The visitor experience would be more dominated by the valley and available opportunities than by the frustration of dealing with traffic and finding a parking space. Some resource protection and transportation measures would reduce visitor freedom and discretion.[25]

Impacts on Socioeconomic Conditions

The draft plan expects that construction and related work proposed under Alternative #2, most of which is based on the transportation recommendations, would cost approximately $43.7 million for construction and project administration over a period of five years. The plan estimates that this would create 261 full-time equivalent jobs locally. Since the plan expects that these jobs could be filled by individuals currently residing in the area, there should be a drop of 1.1 percent in total unemployment in the affected region. This would then result in a personal income gain by local area residents of about $38.5 million over the five-year construction period.

Closing Comments

The 1997 draft plan sets out four various alternatives for future action to achieve park goals. Each alternative is spelled out in detail, is supported with maps, and is analyzed broadly for both its positive and negative impacts on a broad range of resources, including: air quality, water quality, vegetation, wildlife, archaeological sites, American Indian traditional cultural properties, historic districts, cultural landscapes, visitor use and interpretation, and recreation. The greatest problem facing Yosemite is traffic congestion, and all four alternatives agree that the carrying capacity of the park has been exceeded: in terms of the physical, environmental, visual, and social/psychological effect of the sheer number of vehicles entering the park.

Underscoring the importance of the Yosemite effort, Secretary of the Interior Bruce Babbit, in December 1998, personally announced that the new plan would be formally presented to the public in May 1999. Thomas Kiernan, president of the National Parks and Conservation Association, noted at Secretary Babbit's announcement that the transportation element was the most important means of accomplishing the vision of the 1980 General Management Plan.

Alternative #2, which is the one favored by the planners, proposes the eventual elimination of all cars for day use in Yosemite Park and the creation of alternative transportation systems. It is a bold proposal in a country long dedicated to private automobiles rather than bicycles, buses, or mass transit systems. In the first four months following release of the draft plan, the Park Service received over 4,000 sets of public comments on the various alternatives. This high level of public interest reflects not only the popularity of Yosemite, but also the American love affair with the family car. Whatever plan is finally adopted, following an additional period for revision and further public comment, park officials will face the daunting challenge of convincing the public that the restrictions are in truth necessary.

Both Bermuda and Sanibel have been in the comfortable position of enjoying healthy tourism to the benefit of both the destination community and the visitors. Theirs is the situation that most communities dependent upon tourism aspire to. In some cases, however, communities find there have been unexpected impacts from tourism development and may feel that tourism's costs are outweighing its benefits. The original optimistic projections for tourism growth may not match the destination's actual ability comfortably to sustain that degree of growth. Communities then face the challenge of revising expectations, developing new plans to confront the realities of the situation, and garnering support for difficult decisions.

Case Study: Bonaire, Netherlands Antilles—A Plan in Progress

A strategic plan recommends placing limitations on the number of new accommodations based upon the social, environmental, and physical carrying capacity of this popular island.

Bonaire is a popular tourist destination in the Dutch Caribbean, lying east of Aruba and Curacao and 40 miles north of Venezuela. (See Map 5-8.) Only 24 miles long, narrow, and flat, the island[26] has a semi-desert landscape studded with rock formations and salt flats. Iguanas and cacti share the island with colonies of flamingoes. Long known for the diverse life supported by innumerable reefs, Bonaire is the premiere Caribbean destination for snorkelers and scuba divers. Its waters have been legally protected since 1979 and remain the primary attraction of the island. Until recently, tourism numbers on Bonaire varied little year by year. Then between 1986 and 1995, the number of visitors grew from 25,000 to 59,000 arrivals. There was a 10 percent increase in 1996, producing 65,000 arrivals. At the

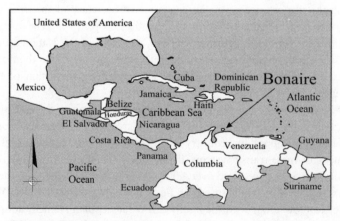

Map 5-8 Bonaire

same time, Bonaire experienced a dramatic surge in immigration numbers. Suddenly, the island was changing.

Previous Planning Initiatives

Over the years Bonaire was the subject of a number of tourism and related plans, generally prepared by consultants and funded by such organizations as the European Community. Implementation, however, has been uneven. Prior to 1997 the principal study, known as the Pourier Report, identified tourism as Bonaire's principal economic activity; proposed that efforts should focus on developing specific tourist markets rather than "mass tourism;" and suggested that no more than 1,600 accommodation units be permitted on the island, even if that limitation involved renegotiating existing, but as yet unexecuted, permits. The report was unanimously adopted by Bonaire's legislative body and became the "National Tourism Policy." This policy included a number of very specific elements that were never implemented, such as a moratorium on all new hotel and other tourist accommodation development beginning in the first quarter of 1994 and a five-year ban on all coastal zone development.

Current Tourism Conditions in Bonaire

A thoughtful 1997 Tourism Strategic Plan prepared by British consultants,[27] and not yet formally adopted, calculated that existing building permits could increase the 1996 total of 1,200 accommodation units to 1,600 units by the year 2000. The consultants—after interviewing numerous Bonaireans and taking into account a body of socioeconomic data developed by other professionals—concluded that the island was near its "social carrying capacity." Bonaireans faced an inadequate housing supply (especially affordable housing), increased rents, inflation, and pressures on schools and infrastructure because of high immigration rates. There was a widespread sense that the Bonairean identity was being weakened by the steady "expansion of the population through immigration, fueled in large measure by the expanding tourism sector and associated construction activity." The consensus was that tourism should be limited because of its negative social impacts.

Aside from the issue of social carrying capacity, the study indicated that demand for tourism was insufficient to *absorb* the 1,621 units estimated to be the year 2000 total of new plus existing accommodations. Despite growing tourism numbers, 1997 saw the very low yearly occupancy rate of 50 percent, well below the 1993 Caribbean average of approximately 70 percent. This indicated an excess of accommodation units, which was likely to worsen over time. From both a demand and also a supply perspective, the study reached the "inescapable findings" that two policies should be initiated: first, a reduction in permissible additions to the number of accommodation units; and second, a reevaluation of the unbuilt but approved projects to further restrict capacity.

The study also identified a public health carrying capacity issue arising from the lack of modern, safe sewage treatment infrastructure. Bonaire has no sewage system but rather relies on cesspools or septic tanks on individual properties. This creates a serious risk to the reef system from leakage. Additionally, because septic tanks provide only a first level treatment, the wastewater emptied into the sea through the porous limestone carries with it pathogenic bacteria that create a serious health risk for persons swimming in the water, frequently generate smells, and attract vermin.

The 1997 strategic plan identifies some short-term strategies to alleviate this situation, such as requiring the installation of individual treatment plants by hotels as a condition of receiving permit approval. However, in the long run a modern sewage system is essential. The strategic plan proposes that sewage be targeted for funding priority before *any* other infrastructure projects, such as expansion of the airport, to protect the public health and protect the environment.

Proposed Restrictions on Increases in Accommodation Capacity

The principal policy proposed by the consultants in the 1997 strategic plan was to restrict new building. This would involve limiting the rate of growth in accommodation units, capping overall growth to remain within social carrying capacity, targeting the type of growth desired to enhance opportunity for all citizens, encouraging the upgrading of existing hotels rather than attracting large new developments, and encouraging apartment developments that would provide additional housing for the resident population.

The Tourism Strategic Plan calls for "an integrated package of measures to bring greater control to the expansion of existing accommodations, and to match this with likely levels of demand." Specifically, it would bar expansion beyond 1,600 units and promote gradual increases of 50 to 70 units per year; additionally there would be increased focus on upgrading existing developments. The strategy does not endorse the imposition of a moratorium because it would inappropriately increase the value of existing but unexecuted permits and encourage developers to step up their permitted projects prior to permit expiration dates.

Instead of a moratorium, the strategy proposes that existing permits be reevaluated and relicensed. To implement this idea, existing permit holders would be required to resubmit a business plan with bank guarantees within a set period; noncompliance would result in permits automatically lapsing. An independent committee would evaluate all resubmitted projects, which would also be subject to a public hearing. The committee can attach various conditions to the permits it approves, such as infrastructure contribution (e.g., an on-site sewage treatment plant and affordable housing for staff). New development must comply with certain Coastal Development Guidelines with respect to such elements as sewage disposal, stormwater, building standards, landscaping, and the requirement for an environmental impact assessment using the European Union approaches.

The strategic plan also recommends a number of criteria for granting permission to build new developments and to expand existing ones. Condominium developments, for example, should not be approved unless used to provide additional rental housing. Activities not tied to scuba diving are to be encouraged to diversify the Bonaire tourist product and to protect the marine environment. Small hotels that are locally owned and managed, designed in a Bonairean style and aimed at specific submarkets of tourists, will increase local economic benefits while attracting new markets. Additionally, there should be continued efforts to eliminate hotel development projects that have received permits but have never been built (called "ghost" hotel projects). The strategic plan also recommends two other specific sets of actions: detailed plans and programs for encouraging energy and water conservation consistent with the ecotourism image being promoted in Bonairean publicity and improving the room tax collection system.

One of the most important elements of the strategic plan calls for a clear expression of present and future governmental support for the various policies designed principally to limit accommodation growth. To that end, it recommends that because the control mea-

.sures constitute a national issue, the policy should be ratified by the island legislative body as well as by the Executive Council.

Closing Comments

The 1997 strategic plan is a thorough approach to tourism management, that incorporates a variety of techniques to control future growth. It also includes such diverse elements as design guidelines, landscaping requirements, changes in the tax structure, measures to protect the Bonaire Marine Park, work permit fees, and education and training initiatives for the Bonaire labor force. It has not, however, been formally adopted either in whole or in part. The restrictions on development, particularly the reevaluation of existing permits, could meet with resistance, since it is possible that the holders of previously valid permits might seek financial compensation from the government.

The infrastructure needs are of prime importance, particularly the need for a safe sewage treatment system. This has significant implications for the environment, the public health, and the economy (in terms of both the cost of researching and building an adequate system and the potential impact upon tourism growth). Infrastructure contributions may be required of new developments, but until Bonaire has an adequate sewage treatment system in place, sustainable development is impossible.

Liabilities of Growth Limitation Approaches

Growth limitation strategies, implemented by zoning regulations, management tools, and a variety of other mechanisms can provide long-term solutions for destinations needing to balance limited resources with unlimited tourist growth. As the case studies show, they are best suited to areas that are clearly delineated, whose environmental and physical carrying capacity can be researched and to some extent measured, and where less restrictive mechanisms are not available to solve the problems associated with increased numbers of tourists.

This means that for many communities, it is hard to justify the imposition of growth limitations. If there is more developable land that is not environmentally sensitive, or if there are no physical constraints to providing additional utilities or roads, then it is probably wiser to use other strategies. If traffic management tools can cope with congestion and associated pollution problems, then that is a far less intrusive solution than the imposition of severe growth limitations. When there is relatively easy access to a destination, growth limitations may not even be practicable. Limiting accommodation beds will not affect the number of day visitors. Although Christchurch college was able to install turnstiles at its doorways to control the flow of visitors and to halt all entry when congestion dictated, no one has suggested that the city of Oxford try the same techniques.

Another liability to the growth limitation approach is its expense—not a insignificant factor. Research into environmental and physical carrying capacity issues requires specialists, usually in a variety of fields. Sanibel and Yosemite both hired multiple consultants to prepare the studies they relied on. Developing feasibility studies, researching potential solutions, and determining their financial ramifications also costs money. When a growth limitation strategy is the best approach, the economic investment may well be worth the long-term benefits. But every dollar or dinar spent on carrying capacity studies will mean funds not available for other uses. Without grants from international sources, many destinations simply cannot afford properly to prepare a growth limitation strategy.

An additional consideration for communities considering a growth limitation strategy is the effect that a limited supply will have on tourist demand. Traditionally, limited supplies increase costs; and higher prices narrow the number of potential consumers. Bermuda has long appealed to the high-income traveler and continues to target this segment of the tourist market. The government and tourism industry agree that limiting access to Bermuda increases its appeal for this preferred type of visitor. Sanibel may enjoy its casual ambiance and low-keyed lifestyle, but condominium rentals are far from cheap. Gourmet food shops, beach-wear boutiques, and seafood restaurants all cater to high-end tourists with more disposable income than that of many of the locals. There are social and economic impacts that result from a tourist market that is concentrated in this fashion. For Bermuda, they have not been negative. For other communities, they might be. Any community considering a growth limitation strategy should take into account the implications of a limited supply and include techniques to manage whatever negative impacts it expects.

Incremental Growth Strategies

As we have seen, preservation rules can protect truly special places. Growth limitations can control increasing tourism that threatens to outpace the capacity of limited resources to sustain that growth. For most communities, such tough measures are not needed. There may be environmentally significant features that contribute to the appeal of a destination—a trout-filled river or a beautiful view of the mountains—but there are environmental controls and visual access regulations that can protect them. There may be pressures put upon a destination's infrastructure and environment by visitors, but not to such an extent that additional growth is literally insupportable and threatening to create a public health or environmental hazard.

The much more common situation is that as tourist numbers grow, the destination community feels that the burdens imposed by tourism are becoming increasingly more onerous. The community finds itself changing, often in unsettling or unpredicted ways, and its tolerance of visitor use diminishes. The host community is losing its ability to absorb tourism growth without damage to its quality of life. The destination needs a strategy to control and manage tourism growth so that those aspects that the community values are not lost.

Community Character Analysis

Incremental growth approaches often combine a community-based perspective with carrying capacity analyses. Tourism numbers may have resulted in some environmental degradation. Increased visitor usage may require expensive infrastructure improvements that the community is unwilling to make. There may have been unexpected economic impacts from tourism development; perhaps the cost-of-living in the community has risen dramatically without a similar rise in wages. Tourists may now outnumber locals, and fancy resorts or large vacation homes may have displaced bungalows and old-timers. The environmental, physical, economic, aesthetic, and social carrying capacity may all be showing signs of stress; but there may not be a single one that has in fact reached its limit of tolerance. Taken together, however, they indicate that the ability of the community to absorb tourism growth is rapidly diminishing.

Carrying capacity analyses have usually been based on determining the greatest degree of tourism use that a destination can support. A *community character* analysis approaches the issue from a different perspective, beginning with a determination of what kind of place the community wishes to be. What are the special characteristics that describe the desired community? This includes everything from the demographic composition to architectural style and public facilities. Decisions concerning tourism (as well as other types of activity) are then made on the basis of what type and degree of growth would contribute to this vision.

For example, if a community decides it wishes to retain its rural and agricultural character above all else, then perhaps it will develop a program to preserve prime agricultural land and limit the size and density of condominium rentals that may be developed in other, less desirable areas. If a community wants to retain its small residential neighborhoods with convenient shopping areas, then it may not permit any tourism development in neighborhood business districts. If the population demographics have changed significantly over the years because of tourism growth, the community may wish to restrict growth and devise techniques to encourage a return to the previous social blend. Tourism will not be permitted to grow until it reaches the community's "saturation point." Rather, its growth will be controlled so that tourism will be both sustainable and compatible with the community's desired future.

Incremental Growth Techniques

The most common strategy used to achieve this objective is the imposition of incremental growth restrictions combined with a variety of other techniques. The same mechanisms that are used in growth limitation strategies may be applied for short periods of time. For example, communities often restrict the number of overnight accommodations for tourists that can be developed each year, to ensure that the rate of growth does not outstrip the social carrying capacity of the destination. Or they may impose a short-term moratorium on tourism development, until a package of complementary regulations can be adopted. Zoning can identify those locations where growth will be allowed or prohibited, ensuring that tourism will not interfere with other desired uses in the community. Agricultural and open space areas can be protected from development. Impact fees are often tied to development permits to ensure that at least a portion of the cost of infrastructure required by any new development will be paid for by that development. Design and architectural standards can ensure that new development will blend with the characteristic appearance of the community. Management systems can alleviate some of the negative impacts of tourism growth without the imposition of restrictive regulations.

One of the great strengths of incremental growth restrictions is that they are an adaptable technique. Implicit in an incremental growth control strategy is the recognition of change. Growth is paced with the expectation that the community will be able to support the increased level of tourism without being overwhelmed by it. There is a search for a balance between community tolerance and tourism growth, between the host community's quality of life and the visitors' quality experience. Each year the balance shifts slightly. Each year, the community is different somehow from what it was the year before. Incremental growth restrictions assume such change and can be adapted to changing circumstances.

Because these techniques are not meant to be immutable, incremental growth restrictions require a high degree of ongoing monitoring to ensure that the degree of tourism growth remains compatible with community desires. For this reason, they are also strategies well designed for coping with unexpected negative impacts. Branson, Missouri, has seen a marked increase in crime since it became a country music Mecca. Cyprus has suffered from gang activity that is blamed at least in part on the influx of foreign tourist wealth. Many communities that are originally ambivalent to the intrusion of foreign cultures become openly hostile. The sooner such negative impacts are identified, the better the chances that tourism growth can be managed in such a way to mitigate those impacts.

Suitable Sites for Incremental Growth Restrictions

Unlike preservation rules and growth limitations, incremental growth restrictions can be used by a variety of destinations. Long-established and well-developed tourism destinations, like Provincetown, Massachusetts, at the tip of Cape Cod, can use these strategies to ensure that any additional growth is congruent with what the community wants for its future. Established in the seventeenth century, Provincetown is now a well-known artists' colony that attracts hordes of summer tourists from the Boston area. It recently undertook a community character analysis that it has used as the basis of developing land use categories and decisions about future permitted use. The desired future character of the community also determines such elements as scale and design of buildings, density and intensity levels, protection of scenic vistas, and the provision of various public facilities.

Growth management strategies can also be used in the very early stages of tourism development by communities that are concerned about their ability to predict and cope with the changes that may result from tourism growth. There are potential approaches for almost any community experiencing a degree of pressure from tourism growth. By slowing the pace of development, incremental growth restrictions can be a very helpful tool to safeguard a community from being overwhelmed by the impacts of sudden growth.

Case Study: Whistler, British Columbia, Canada

A world-class tourist destination continues its process of community participation in monitoring the impacts of development and adapting its growth management strategies to fit a changing environment.

The face of tourism changed for Whistler when, in 1965, the highway connecting the small mountain community to Vancouver was completed and the area's first ski lift was constructed. The permanent population of 250 had offered cabins and small lodges to the occasional fisherman or trapper who visited the lakes at the base of the Coast Mountains. By 1996, the resident population had grown to 7,400, and Whistler had become a world-class, year-round destination resort offering 37,000 beds to the 1.5 million tourists who visit each year. (See Map 5-9.) Despite the rapid pace of change, Whistler has managed its growth, protected its environment (see Photo 5-4), and addressed the needs of both the resident and tourist communities to a remarkable degree.

Background

In 1975, following local lobbying efforts that grew out of concern over tourism pressure and the potential problems of uncontrolled growth, the provincial government passed the "Resort municipality of Whistler Act." This Act officially incorporated Whistler, provided the municipality with provincial support, placed no limit on its borrowing power, and gave it the authority to establish regulatory controls governing tourism development. Whistler has adopted Comprehensive Development Plans and four Official Community Plans (OCPs) since its incorporation, all with the active participation of the community. (In Chapter 2, we described how the community was and continues to be involved in planning

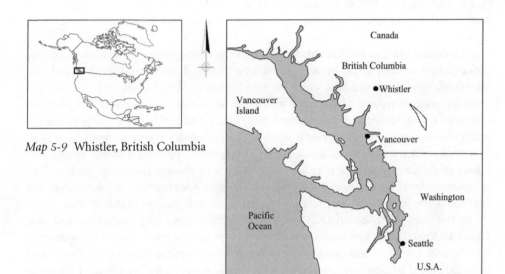

Map 5-9 Whistler, British Columbia

Photo 5-4 Blackcomb Mountain and Alta Lake, as seen from Rainbow Park, Whistler, British Columbia (Courtesy of Chris Laing, Planning Development, Resort Municipality of Whistler)

Whistler's tourism management strategy.) All four of the plans focus on growth management mechanisms. "The quality of the natural environment, the calibre of the resort experience, and the livability of the community are all dependent on the management of growth and development: how much, what type, in what locations and over what time period."[28]

The earliest plan, in an effort to curtail sprawling development throughout the valley, concentrated development in an undeveloped landfill between Whistler and the Blackcomb mountains (an area which became known as Whistler Village) and placed a general moratorium on development in most other areas of the municipality. The plan also addressed the social needs of the resident community[29] and included a village center on publicly owned property to provide a sense of community for the municipality as well as to centralize the resort facilities. The Whistler Village Land Company, a wholly owned subsidiary of the municipality, was created to develop and manage the village center. (This company suffered from a variety of problems, became bankrupt in the recession of the 1980s, and was replaced by the provincial government with a crown corporation.)

By the time of the second OCP in 1982, ski facilities were fully operational and over Canadian $200 million had been invested in development projects. This OCP maintained the controlled development focus of the earlier plan. It restricted the total number of bed units that could be developed to 45,000, tying development to the capacities of the available infrastructure (essentially the water and sewer facilities). The plan also included an evaluation procedure for new accommodation proposals based on site performance standards, environmental impact analysis, and capacity analysis. While the emphasis remained on controlling development and protecting the environment, there was a new objective included in the plan: "To provide for an adequate supply of affordable housing for permanent residents and employees."

By the time of the next plan, Whistler was an established ski resort and the focus shifted to efforts to develop the area as a summer recreational attraction. The 1989 OCP approved an additional 7,500 bed units provided that they enhanced the viability of the resort as a four-season destination. Most of these were associated with projects that also included golf or tennis facilities. Convention facilities that could attract visitors year round were also encouraged. The OCP also placed a yearly limit on the number of other bed units that could be developed.

The 1994 OCP maintained the overall 52,500 bed-unit limit. It made no significant changes to the planned pace and location of development, which generally still reflected the vision that shaped the original 1976 plan. It did, however, introduce additional regulatory and monitoring systems. It improved the process for community participation, expanded the information base through a comprehensive monitoring program, and strengthened various regulatory mechanisms.

Regulatory Mechanisms

The municipality's integrated package of regulations is based on the goals of developing Whistler into a successful, high calibre resort destination, providing a high quality of life for the residents, and protecting the natural environment that is the main attraction for both visitors and residents. To achieve these goals, Whistler has used a variety of mechanisms, which have been refined over the years according to the stage of tourist development and the needs of the community.

Growth Management

The thrust of Whistler's approach is not to curtail development but to manage its growth to the long-term benefit of the resort and the community. The municipality has restricted the pace of development by limiting the specific number of bed units that could be developed, on the basis of the capacity of the existing water and sewer infrastructure. This approach does not result in a rigid limit to future building, but it is flexible and amenable to change. First, the OCP is reviewed every five years and the impacts of the existing development on the community and resort are analyzed to determine what level of future growth is appropriate. The cap on bed units has been, and can be in the future, amended in each plan. Second, water and sewer facilities could presumably be improved to allow additional development. Third, every plan has included mechanisms (such as plan amendments, rezonings, and zoning trade-offs) that permit exceptions to the restrictions on development.

A complementary strategy employed by Whistler was to concentrate development in the generally compact area of Whistler Village, in order to minimize sprawl and to create a center of activity for both residents and visitors. This approach, which involved a moratorium on development of almost all other land in the municipality, at first encountered a fair measure of resistance from some local landowners. The municipality then offered various zoning trade-offs, allowing landowners to develop land within the village area in compensation for the moratorium placed on development of other land.

When the resort had reached a level of success as a ski destination, the municipality determined that the next goal would be development as a four-season resort. In order to attract year-round visitors, Whistler needed additional amenities, such as tennis courts, golf courses, swimming pools, and parks, which it could not afford to develop on its own. It therefore increased the number of bed units that could be developed but tied development permission to the provision of amenities that the resort and the community required.

Environmental Protection

Although environmental objectives have been part of Whistler's management strategy from its inception, they became much more thorough following the 1994 OCP. The municipality now conducts an environmental inventory, which is the basis for identification of environmentally sensitive lands that should not be developed, and of areas that have various constraints to development. All applications for any form of development must include an initial environmental impact review, with more detailed assessments required of more sensitive lands. All visually or environmentally sensitive lands are also required to receive additional development permits, which may impose such requirements as tree preservation, buffered setbacks, and landscape design elements. Development of land above 730 meters is restricted because of negative impact upon both the environment and the scenic views. General environmental regulations provide protection for conservation areas and special habitats. For all major projects, Whistler requires the developer to pay for the cost of environmental monitoring of all construction activities.

Aesthetic Controls

Design controls have ensured that development projects adapt to the local landscape and address the needs of residents as well as tourists, particularly in Whistler Village. Streets, for example, must frame important viewscapes; solar access and view corridors are maintained at important locations; most parking for the pedestrian village must be underground; covered walkways are mandated for certain areas; resident services are located in the more conveniently accessed areas, while tourist services are closer to the ski lifts; there are required elements of architectural style and only certain materials, finishes, and colors are permitted. Prior to the development of Whistler Village, which was created on an empty landfill, strict design controls were adopted. In addition, every single parcel had specific design guidelines approved for it, including such items as the permitted size of the building, required elements of the architectural style, materials to be used, and landscaping.

Community Amenities

The improvement of facilities for the residents, not just the tourists, has been a constant goal of the municipality. Much of its development approval process has included various trade-off provisions. Whistler received land for two wetland parks, approval for residents to play on golf and tennis facilities, and cash contributions for park construction in exchange for increasing the number of bed units that could be developed. Employers are now required to provide employee housing, or funds for that purpose, in order to receive development approval. The municipality imposed impact fees on new developments, which, when combined with taxes from the expanded tax base, financed the building of a recreation center with an ice arena and a swimming pool, a library, and medical facilities. A capital expenditure plan identifies infrastructure, community facility, and land requirements for the next 20 years, most of which is expected to be financed by this same combination of impact fees and taxes.

Closing Comments

The Whistler approach has resulted in a highly successful mountain resort destination where both residents and tourists express great satisfaction with the quality of their experience. The growth control mechanisms have ensured visually attractive development within relatively compact areas, protected the natural beauty and environment, and provided for resident as well as tourist amenities. The impact on the surrounding region is to some degree less benign. Whistler's growth management measures have resulted in the dispersal of some development to less closely regulated areas. Only a high degree of regional planning and coordination can avoid the potential negative impacts of displacement.

Whistler has also included an unusually thoughtful process for ensuring opportunities for diverse constituencies to participate in the planning, implementation, and monitoring of the tourism growth strategy over the 20-plus years of the municipality's history. The Community and Resort Monitoring Program solicits feedback from both community members and visitors on a variety of issues, summarizes the responses, develops statistical information about various aspects of the destination community, updates and adds to the information base, undertakes new studies and initiatives in response to community priorities, analyzes the information, reviews results of the monitoring program in terms of past findings, trends and standards, and provides all the information to every member of the community. The goal is to "provide the information that allows the community to measure how it is changing and, more importantly, to predict how it will change in the future if there is additional population growth, development, and visitation."[30] It is a fine example of how the *process* affects the *substance* of a strategy, and how an informed citizenry has responded to changes over time.

Like Whistler, Aspen, Colorado, is a famous ski resort that has, for more than 20 years, been incorporating growth management strategies into its plans. It also, like Whistler, has a strong community participation component to its planning approach, which has evolved over the years to adapt to changing circumstances.

Case Study: Aspen, Colorado

The resort community of Aspen redesigned its growth management strategy, grounding it on a community character analysis, to respond to changing priorities and unexpected impacts from second-home development.

The city of Aspen, nestled in a valley of the Elk Mountains near the highest point in Colorado (see Photo 5-5), was first developed in the silver boom of the late nineteenth century. After growing to a population high of 11,000 during those glory days, the town dwindled to just 705 during the Depression. Then in 1947, Aspen had a rebirth as a ski destination. It saw swift and steady growth during the 1960s, and by the early 1970s, the community was talking of the need for controlling future growth in order to maintain the quality of life for both residents and visitors. In 1972, a Goals Task Force composed largely of Aspen citizens began meeting to address ways to deal with the burgeoning development. Their work led to the adoption of Aspen's first growth management plan, permitted under Colorado law.

Photo 5-5 Wildflowers on Independence Pass, Aspen, Colorado (Courtesy of ACRA Burnham/Arndt)

The 1976 Growth Management Policy Plan

The 1976 Growth Management Policy Plan (GMPP) had two goals: to preserve the environment and the quality of life for both residents and visitors and to achieve a development balance between the economic needs and the fiscal capabilities of the community. To achieve these goals, the plan outlined three separate policies: a growth rate policy, a community development program policy, and a community services policy.

Growth Rate Policy

The growth rate policy established an annual limit of 3.47 percent for new developments. In addition to the overall limit, the plan specified residential, commercial, and lodge development quotas. Further regulations governed the location of permitted new development and its timing. Later amendments to the GMPP established an elaborate point system for determining which development applications would be approved. Specified numbers of points were given for various elements in the broad categories of design, energy efficiency, infrastructure provision, employee housing provision, and transportation impact.

Community Development Program Policy

The community development program policy was designed to balance the needs of residents and tourists. It established priorities concerning the type and location of ski area developments and directed new development into Aspen and the adjacent resort of Snowmass, where there was already adequate infrastructure to service expansion. To encourage building of additional affordable employee housing, such units were initially exempt from the quota limit and the number competition system for development approval.

Community Services Policy

Finally, the community services policy was aimed at providing certain infrastructure elements, such as transportation, water and sewer services, in response to rather than *prior to* growth. The community felt that growth should pay for itself, rather than impose additional burdens on the residents. Therefore, development permits included impact fees, special assessments, and various other conditions to cover the initial costs of these types of capital improvements.

Evaluation of the GMPP

Since the GMPP was a growth management mechanism, there was a need to monitor and evaluate growth as it occurred. Aspen, with the help of consultants, studied such items as population growth, visitor numbers, development permits, and various environmental indicators. Generally, the community was pleased with the shape of development and the way the GMPP was managing growth.

But by the early 1990s, four interrelated changes had occurred in Aspen, which the 1976 GMPP had not foreseen. First, seasonal or second-home ownership had increased until it represented almost 30 percent of all residential units. Second, the rising cost of housing had driven many people who worked in Aspen to seek housing elsewhere in the region. As late as 1983, about two-thirds of Aspen's workforce lived in the city; by 1990, that number had dropped to one-third.[31] Third, businesses serving tourists were displacing those serving locals. Finally, new second-home residences were often quite large and seen as out-of-scale with existing residential development.

Many in the Aspen community believed these changes were having negative impacts on the quality of life in Aspen. Fifteen years after the GMPP was passed, conditions in the community had changed and community priorities had changed. The market alone was incapable of either preventing the changes or minimizing their impacts on the Aspen community. It was clear that the community needed to revise the way it was managing growth to address the new problems it was now facing. In July 1991, the Aspen City Council and Pitkin County Commissioners met to set up a cooperative process for developing a new Aspen Area Community Plan. The officials appointed five citizen committees to evaluate alternatives and develop action plans covering major areas of concern to the community. After more than two years of study, community meetings, surveys, interviews, citizen committees, and the participation of an estimated 400 individuals, Aspen adopted a new plan in 1993.

The 1993 Aspen Area Community Plan and Its Community Character Analysis

The 1993 Aspen Area Community Plan (AACP) represents a philosophical as well as practical shift from the earlier plan. During the more than two years of discussion, a consensus emerged that although tourism is the "economic force of the community," the "spirit that is Aspen draws its vitality from a unique patchwork of miners, entrepreneurs, ranchers, artists, intellectuals, sports-minded people, free spirits, and visionaries."[32] The diversity of Aspen's population was identified as the most important element of the Aspen community. As greater numbers of working people were forced to move out of their town, Aspen's vitality was being "seriously diluted." Aspen's "unique spirit" was in "danger of eroding into a bland and irrelevant society lacking its former character" by the shift in population demographics. People wanted the "funkiness" back in their community; they didn't want a community made up only of upper income tourists and wealthier residents.

To ensure that future growth and development would support this vision of the Aspen community, the AACP grounded its policies on a "community character analysis." This analysis began with an identification of those elements that give Aspen its desired character. These may include existing physical attributes, heritage, social factors, and those features that contribute to the ever elusive "quality of life" that the community values. For Aspen, its "architectural and cultural heritage" as a small mining town was just as important as its present function as a resort town. The small scale of buildings, the pedestrian-oriented streetscape, the scenic vistas, the natural setting, and the diversity of population were all elements that the community identified as important to them, and which they wanted to preserve. This "community character" would be the determining factor for future land use decisions. Every detail of the planning and regulatory program—covering such issues as siting, scale, intensity, use, and design—would take into consideration the identity and spirit the community wanted for Aspen.

Growth Management Plan

The most important changes between the AACP and the earlier 1976 plan were in the area of growth control. First, noting that both natural and built resources were nearing their limit and recognizing that Aspen's growth had a regional impact, the AACP projected a peak population of 30,000 for the combined city of Aspen and its metropolitan area. Next, it reduced the permitted annual growth rate from 3.47 percent to 2 percent for new development. This meant that no more than 84 new units would be permitted each year. These were to be divided by the annual quota system into 24 lodge (tourist) units, 7 free market residential units, and 53 affordable housing units. A simple review process was to be developed for affordable housing that would enable it to be developed more quickly.

The greatest revision came in relation to the point system that was used to determine which applications for development would be approved. The 1976 system was largely quantitative and included points for providing infrastructure. The new system removed many of these items (water supply, sewage disposal, transit, storm drainage, recreation facilities, fire protection, and school systems) from the scoring list, although there were still minimum threshold standards for proposals to meet concerning infrastructure provision. In place of this carrying capacity analysis, the new plan included analysis of the consistency of a proposed development with community goals (i.e., a community character analysis). Applications would now be scored on compatibility with the goals of the AACP, the relation of the proposal to the need to revitalize the permanent resident community, the documented community need for the proposed use, the economic and environmental sustainability of the proposal, the quality of the design, and the transportation innovations.

Other aspects of the growth management plan were designed to address the overriding community concern with the need for affordable housing. All new residential subdivisions that would compete for development permits under the new quota and point system were mandated to provide a minimum of 60 percent affordable housing. The plan also gave high priority to on-site housing within the commercial core; increased the percentage of allowable floor area that could be used in commercial buildings for on-site affordable housing; and set up a timetable for studying incentives that could be used to encourage commercial uses serving local needs. The growth management plan was addressing just those elements that had changed since the 1976 plan and that the community felt had negatively affected the quality of life in Aspen.

Housing Plan

The AACP housing plan reflected the consensus that there was a "critical mass" of local residents that was necessary to sustain a sense of community and that Aspen began to lose that critical mass when more and more workers started moving from Aspen around 1987. The desirable critical mass translated into the AACP goal that 60 percent of the workforce should live in Aspen, in housing compatible with the scale and character of the community.

To achieve this, the housing plan proposed, among other items, development in specified locations of 650 new affordable housing units (see Map 5-10); the creation of a housing advisory panel to propose creative approaches and new initiatives such as mortgage assistance, tax incentives, and buy-downs; zoning revisions to permit more on-site affordable housing for in-town sites; and creation of a housing mortgage pool with local financial institutions.

Transportation Plan

The goal of this plan was to provide an integrated transportation system that would address the needs of residents, visitors, and commuters, as well as reduce congestion and pollution. Much of the impetus for this plan was based on the increased commuter traffic (and parking) caused by the displacement of a large portion of Aspen's resident workforce into other outlying communities.

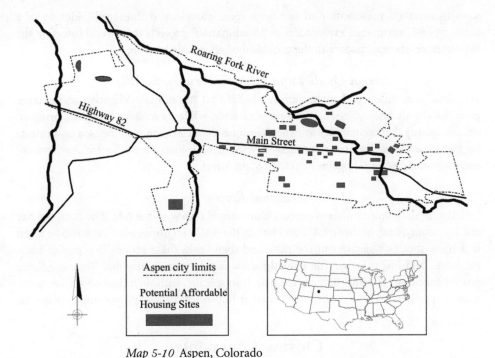

Map 5-10 Aspen, Colorado

The plan identified five goals, most of them with a regional focus. There was a clear recognition that the community did not have the financial resources to implement all the required components of the desired transportation system at once, and that there would need to be ongoing community education efforts to ensure that "the hard choices" would be made.

Commercial/Retail Plan

The underlying thrust of this plan was the belief that "people should be able to shop in the community where they live." High rentals for office and retail space were driving local business people and local services out of town, and they were being replaced by tourist-oriented businesses. The challenge was to find ways to provide affordable office space for local businesses.

The plan proposed numerous financial and zoning incentives for local businesses; zoning changes that would permit only businesses serving local needs in certain zoning districts; and creation of a neighborhood office zone district. Small lodges, as opposed to large resort complexes, were seen as promoting the sense of scale and feel that the community wished for Aspen and attracting visitors who would enjoy the small town experience of Aspen. These tourists would find an appeal in small, local shops as opposed to expensive, up-scale boutiques. To help achieve this shift, the plan proposed that Aspen should along with small lodge owners market itself as "Aspen, the Community" as opposed to "Aspen, the Glitzy Resort."

Open Space/Recreation and Environment Plan

This plan addressed preservation and enhancement of the natural beauty of the area for the enjoyment of all parties. It included numerous environmentally oriented projects and measures to maintain preservation of key open space parcels; it discouraged widening of a highway; and encouraged exploration of "combination" projects that would integrate the maintenance of open space with the provision of affordable housing.

Design Quality and Historic Preservation Plan

This final plan reflected the community's belief that Aspen's late-Victorian architecture gives the city its historic essence and sense of scale, while its modern buildings bring an eclectic quality that contributes to Aspen's unique character. The plan focused on protecting historic architecture from removal by development or insensitive adjacent development and encouraging eclectic businesses along Main Street.

Annual Review

Included in the implementation process is an annual review of the AACP by both the city and the county. Each of the five Action Plans in the AACP identifies what steps will be taken to achieve specific objectives of the plan, and then ranks these actions in terms of high, moderate, and low priority. The annual review is meant to ensure that items are being accomplished on schedule. Because the plan is so specific, with such clear objectives, community members can effectively judge whether implementation is proceeding as planned.

Closing Comments

Aspen adopted its first growth management plan in response to the high degree of development that accompanied the city's evolution as a popular ski resort. It was a carefully crafted plan that addressed the most pressing needs of the growing community. Fifteen years later, the community recognized that there had been unexpected changes both in the way development had progressed and in the way the community had grown. The original plan was no longer meeting the needs of the changing community or mitigating what the community saw as the negative impacts of development.

With a high degree of public participation, the Aspen community agreed upon a vision for its future and revised its growth management strategy to address issues from the new perspective of "community character analysis," rather than a carrying capacity analysis. It stressed the importance of tying development approval to consistency with community goals. Those goals now put the provision of affordable housing ahead of resort development, an increase in the number of permanent residents ahead of seasonal or second-home residents, and encouragement of businesses serving local needs ahead of commercial uses catering to tourists.

The five-year AACP is a clear reflection of community preferences, with a recognition that growth management strategies need to be reviewed often and revised to adapt to changing conditions. The provisions for annual review of the AACP by both city and county to ensure that items are being accomplished on schedule is a practical way for the community to monitor implementation. This also fosters a sense of confidence in the efficacy of the management strategy and its permanence.

There is, however, no formal monitoring process in place to make certain that the goals of the plan are being achieved. Real estate prices in Aspen continue to soar with the influx of second-home owners, and many homes sell in the multiple millions of dollars. The average sale price of a house in Aspen was over $1.8 million in 1995.[33] (The maximum income level for subsidized housing is so high that some lawyers and engineers qualify for assistance.) Growth in the Aspen area has been so significant that areas beyond Pitkin County are now experiencing second-home and residential growth. Despite its affordable housing program, much of Aspen's workforce is now being forced by the high cost of real estate to live in communities even farther afield in outlying areas of Eagle County. Nevertheless, there are promising signs. Although the targets for affordable housing have not yet been met, progress is being made. Public schools in Aspen are operating at capacity for the first time since the 1970s, indicating an influx of families.

Whether Aspen will be able to recover the "funky" mix that the community wants, though, is not clear. The plan is a worthwhile attempt to achieve community goals, and the community needs to continue to monitor its successes and failures and to realize it will again need revisions, as the community and the pace of development change once again.

Both Whistler and Aspen are well-known resort communities with financial resources stemming from their tourist base and a sophisticated city staff capable of implementing a Community and Resort Monitoring System (in the case of Whistler) or a community character analysis (in the case of Aspen). Both destinations have had over 20 years experience with quantity management strategies. Door County, Wisconsin, is a rural area whose significant tourism growth didn't begin until about the time Whistler and Aspen imposed their first growth control ordinances. The county includes any number of small villages, most of which have had almost no zoning controls in place. Despite its contrasts with Whistler and Aspen, Door County is employing a variety of similar techniques to control its growth in order to preserve its special characteristics.

Case Study: Door County, Wisconsin

An organization composed of representatives of local businesses calls for growth control initiatives to limit development and preserve rural amenities in this Midwest county.

Door County, in northeastern Wisconsin, is a peninsula that extends 80 miles from the town of Green Bay into Lake Michigan. (See Map 5-11.) Along its extensive shoreline, there are sandy beaches on the east and high bluffs overlooking Green Bay on the west. Most of the interior is rural, with cherry and apple orchards and dairy farms. North of the town of Sturgeon Bay (which divides "north" and "south" Door County), less than 3 percent of the land is developed. The tranquil scenery, meandering country roads, forests, walking and biking trails, small villages, and arts and crafts galleries combine to give Door County its quaint charm.

Tourism in Door County

Within driving distance of Chicago and several large cities in Wisconsin, Door County has been a popular weekend, vacation, and second-home destination for decades. Its fame began in the early 1970s when *National Geographic* magazine featured Door County as "A Kingdom So Delicious." Since then, its appeal has continued unabated and Door County is now Wisconsin's primary tourist magnet, attracting two million visitors each year. The historic inns, small guesthouses, and beach cottages scattered throughout the peninsula have been joined by resort hotels and large condominium developments. These condominiums are usually purchased by owners who plan to vacation in their unit for only a few weeks

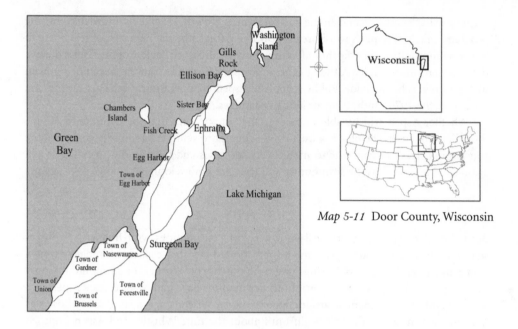

Map 5-11 Door County, Wisconsin

each year, and then rent it out for the rest of the season. As a local county newspaper described it, north Door County was in the midst of a "condo craze."

A Galvanizing Event: Construction of an 80-Unit Condominium Project

One particular project symbolized to many concerned citizens the erosion of Door County's scenic charm by unbridled development. Completed in the late summer of 1996, the "Eames Farm Condominiums" was an 80-unit development, built on the high limestone bluff above Egg Harbor on the west coast of Door County (see Photo 5-6). Sited at the highest point on the bluff and enjoying a commanding vista across Green Bay, the development dominated the landscape. The position of the buildings along the ridgeline, combined with their white exterior siding and bright green roofs, made the condominiums so glaringly obvious that they commanded attention not only from the village below, but also from boats many miles out on the Bay. The *Milwaukee Journal Sentinel* newspaper quoted the developer as agreeing with hindsight that "a less conspicuous color scheme" might have been preferable. He also pointed out the ironic fact that approximately 300 trees were planted throughout what had been a cherry orchard; eventually those trees would be large enough to partially screen the development. Undaunted by the criticism of his bluff units, however, the developer announced plans to build ten more condominium units and 90 single family homes on the same parcel.

Regulatory Pattern

One of the reasons condominiums took root so quickly in the agricultural land of Door County in the early 1990s is that, for the most part, there were few regulatory controls. Most of the towns south of Sturgeon Bay had no zoning beyond countywide restrictions on development within 1,000 feet of the shoreline. The 14 towns and villages of north Door

Photo 5-6 Egg Harbor with Eames Condominium development on the bluff, Door County, Wisconsin (Reprinted with permission of the *Green Bay Press-Gazette*)

County had some zoning mechanisms in place, but usually not comprehensive zoning ordinances. In areas outside the jurisdiction of established towns, there is now a Door County zoning plan adopted in 1995 after more than ten years of very acrimonious debate. This county plan calls for development in clusters within already established towns and villages in order to preserve undeveloped rural areas. This would intensify development in contained locations, avoid sprawl, and result in clear legal and visual boundaries between "urban" and "rural" areas. However, it is up to individual communities whether or not to adopt local zoning ordinances with the tools to implement the county plan.

The Chamber of Commerce Growth Control Recommendations

The 700-member Door County Chamber of Commerce, a private organization composed of representatives of local businesses, had for a year expressed its concern about whether the tourism boom in the county could be sustained. Then, in June 1995 it sponsored a two-day conference on sustainable tourism, which included a panel of experts, together with representatives of the business, tourism, environmental, agricultural, and property-owning communities. To the disappointment of the Chamber organizers, no developers and only a few government officials attended.

As a result of that conference, the Chamber members began to consider growth control mechanisms to avoid the overdevelopment it saw in comparable areas. Cape Cod, Massachusetts, was reported to have one-third of its land developed, a percentage the Chamber believed inappropriate for Door County. "Suburban sprawl" was a common description of the threat of continued uncontrolled development. A further issue related to groundwater, unprotected by the peninsula's cracked limestone foundation. Northern Door County did not have water and sewer systems in place to keep up with the growth of condominium developments.

In August 1996 (in the midst of the controversy over the Eames Farm Condominiums development), the Chamber of Commerce Board of Directors adopted a resolution outlining a number of pressing concerns generated by rapid growth in tourism. The primary problem they identified was the negative impact of growth on the character of Door County:

> As Door County business owners and residents, we are united in our desire to protect the quality of life in Door County. We also are convinced that while tourism is the economic engine that makes the Door County lifestyle possible, the forces of uncontrolled growth and development threaten our collective investment. . . . The Door County Chamber of Commerce is a business organization and, as such, recognizes that our local economy requires growth. However, the Chamber realizes that abandoning the future of our Peninsula to unchecked development will quickly ruin the essence of what makes our Peninsula such a special place for both residents and visitors. The time for action is now, while the county still retains its charm, not after the ravages of uncontrolled and irresponsible development make us another last best place.

The resolution continues with particular recommendations for government action.

This was a significant step for a Chamber of Commerce to take; business groups are often more likely to oppose additional governmental regulation and planning than to propose it. The Chamber resolution encourages the 14 towns and villages of north Door County to consider a wide range of growth control approaches, recognizing that uniformity throughout the entire county would not be either possible or desirable. In order to allow local governments to consider such alternatives, the resolution calls for all villages, townships, and the county itself to enact moratoria on any proposed new building projects (whether or not condominium hotel projects). The resolution then proposes that local governments:

1. Adopt comprehensive zoning ordinances in all municipalities;
2. Restrict the use of sewage holding tanks in new large-scale developments and direct large-scale projects to locations where sewer systems already exist;
3. Adopt ordinances requiring building projects to be "in scale" with surroundings—to include lot coverage, height, and architectural guides;
4. Adopt ordinances that limit the ratio of impervious surfaces to pervious surfaces and encourage on-site green space;
5. Implement impact fee requirements on all new developments;
6. Consider the use of purchase of development rights and similar programs to protect scenic resources; and
7. Pursue affordable housing programs to ensure that there is a workforce living in Door County to adequately service its commercial activities.

These actions taken together would combine zoning restrictions, infrastructure needs, design and intensity regulations, rural and agricultural land preservation programs, and housing initiatives in a comprehensive approach to control growth in Door County.

Responses to the Chamber of Commerce proposals were broad-based and immediate, reflecting a widespread concern with the impacts of growth. A resolution of support came from the village of Ephraim, which described itself as "a leader in attempting to balance growth and development by the use of innovative zoning and the creation of an historic district . . . (engaged) in discussions regarding the implementation of an impact fee ordinance which will assist in the funding of necessary future services."

The Door Property Owners, Inc., issued a press release, endorsing the Chamber's call for a moratorium and encouraged wide-ranging "round table discussions" among citizens, businesses, and other groups. "We want consensus about the growth plans in our communities. If only a few write the development plans and zoning ordinances and choose the new tools to guide our growth, there will be no political will to enforce the regulations. And without enforcement we have no rudder to steer the new developments."

Not all reactions were so supportive, of course. Some felt the concern with preserving the rural character of the county was misplaced. As one local entrepreneur put it, "(p)eople come to Door County to shop. The other stuff is secondary. . . ." Some business people were concerned that the participants in the process were not properly reflecting business interests. They wanted to ensure that "the thousands of workers, the millions of dollars of investment, and economic impact they represented be properly and positively involved in any decisions concerning Door County's future development."

The Mayor of Sturgeon Bay in south Door County indicated that his community was concerned with the creation of jobs and was looking for "new business and business expansion." Government officials there were pleased with the development of a 147-room condominium-hotel complex with convention facilities. In effect, Sturgeon Bay declined the invitation to become involved in any regional planning effort to control growth on Door County and caused a *de facto* redrawing of the boundaries of the planning area.

A property owners group emphasized the importance of impact fee programs to help fund the infrastructure made necessary by any new development. "Those who profit most directly from development must help pay the community costs of their developments. The spin-off costs of development are considerable. For example, the Town and Village of Egg Harbor are considering the purchase of a half-million dollar aerial ladder truck to protect the new developments in Egg Harbor."

In the summer of 1997, the village of Egg Harbor, the site of the controversial Eames Farm Condominiums, enacted a one-year moratorium in order to allow time for updating the village's comprehensive plan. In late September 1997, the Door County Chamber of Commerce reissued its call for all villages and towns to impose moratoria on all new development until zoning and land-use tools to control growth were in place. The Chamber wanted to continue the "Future Search" process until "(w)ell attended community meetings involving stakeholders from all walks of life have been held and agreement reached on priority issues . . . (and) builders, business and property owners, environmentalists, farmers and government officials have found common ground for action."

Communities were responding to the call for restrictions on growth. In addition to the village of Egg Harbor's moratorium, Liberty Grove adopted an impact fee ordinance, the village of Ephraim established an affordable housing task force, and five south Door County townships were meeting to consider adopting consistent zoning ordinances. The county recently adopted a purchase of development rights program using tax dollars, and many local businesses are now contributing to a "green fund" to enable the Land Trust and The Nature Conservancy to buy land for open space, especially along garishly developed commercial strips.

Closing Comments

Aside from these new initiatives, whose success is as yet unknown, Door County does not have comprehensive mechanisms in place to control the growth of condominiums and mitigate the impacts of steadily increasing tourism. It appears, however, to have a strong community consensus that the issue is of immediate and significant concern because uncontrolled growth is destroying the special qualities that people love about Door County: its open space, rural character, and quaint charm. The leadership role played by the business community in seeking government planning and restrictions is unusual but seemingly effective. Whether the various villages, towns, and the county itself will cooperate to develop a coordinated and consistent program remains to be seen.

Whistler, Aspen, and Door County are already facing differing degrees of tourism pressure and unwanted impacts stemming from visitor numbers. Incremental growth restrictions are a way for them to pace the growth they can reasonably expect. The situation is somewhat different for relatively young destination communities entering the tourism fray. Community character analyses and carrying capacity issues may seem far from the concerns of Bermuda or Aspen wannabes, but they should be considered from the start. New hotels that dump their waste into the water because there is no sewage treatment facility, restaurants that rely on an inadequate electrical supply for their refrigeration, buildings that are constructed on dunes to capture the perfect view, visitors who throw their litter on the streets and paths because there is no garbage collection system—all create serious problems. Incremental growth restrictions should be imposed at the onset of a tourism program so that the community can safeguard itself from being damaged by unknown impacts.

Case Study: Ambergris Caye, Belize

This Central American country focuses on expanding tourism in keeping with the general character of the island to achieve desired economic benefits and considers multiple techniques to control the pace of growth.

Ambergris Caye is the largest of the more than 200 islands off the coast of Belize, just south of Mexico's Yucatan Peninsula. (See Map 5-12.) It has a varied history as a Mayan trading center, a hideout for English pirates in the seventeenth century, an asylum for refugees fleeing from civil war in Mexico in the eighteenth century, a prosperous fishing community in the early days of this century, and recently as a budding tourist destination. Just a half-mile off the barrier reef, Ambergris Caye has clear, warm, turquoise waters; colorful tropical fish; and spectacular scuba diving and snorkeling sites. Tourists discovered its potential in the early 1960s, but their numbers began to grow only in the 1980s. Ambergris Caye's main town, San Pedro, still has unpaved streets of sand (see Photo 5-7), but now it also has barefoot tourists, golf carts for tourists to rent for driving on the island roads, gift shops selling local and Guatemalan handicrafts, several hotels, bars, restaurants, and two discos.

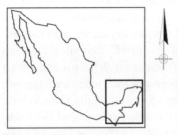

Map 5-12 Ambergris Caye, Belize

Gulf of Mexico

Mexico

Caribbean Sea

Belize

Ambergris
Caye

Guatemala

Honduras

Pacific Ocean

El Salvador

Photo 5-7 Sand street scene, San Pedro, Ambergris Caye, Belize (Courtesy of Karen Lauer, Ivory Isle Travel, Kennelworth, Illinois)

The Master Plan for Ambergris Caye

The World Tourist Organization, under the auspices of the United Nations Development Program, prepared a Master Plan for Ambergris Caye in the late 1980s at the request of the Belize government. Covering the period of 1988 to 2005, the primary objective of the plan is "to provide opportunities for the further expansion of tourism in keeping with the general character, environment, and the unspoiled nature of the island." Tourism is seen as a source of economic benefit: it will create new job opportunities for Belizeans and attract foreign currency to the island. However, the plan recognizes that unfettered tourism growth may have negative consequences on the carrying capacities of the Caye as well: excessive rates of immigration, environmental degradation, overburdening of the infrastructure, and unacceptable social strain upon the community. The Master Plan adopts a combination of limitations on the quantity of tourist development with recommendations for infrastructure improvements, incremental growth controls, and zoning techniques to adjust tourism growth to the capacity of the Caye to absorb that growth.

The plan was never formally adopted with a statute, but "Interim Development Control" was triggered under the terms of the Belize Housing and Town Planning Act. This meant that the Caye was declared a "Planning Scheme," a designation that signifies that plans are under development and therefore the Planning Committee has the authority to regulate development by requiring it to meet *proposed* plan elements.[34]

Tourist Accommodation Limits

The plan proposes strict limits on the numbers of new tourist beds that can be developed each year through 2005. The maximum rate of 120 new beds per year, which the plan allocates largely to hotel rooms, reflects the development rate experienced in Ambergris Caye just prior to the drafting of the plan. The rate was unchanged in order to ensure tourism expansion in a form similar to what had already proved successful: hotels of not more than 60 rooms, suited in size to the character of the Caye. In fact, many of the hotels on Ambergris Caye have no more than four rooms. This limitation would also protect the community from abrupt increases in tourist numbers, which could have negative impacts on the environment and social fabric of the Caye. Tourism growth would be limited to an amount that Ambergris Caye could comfortably sustain.[35]

Infrastructure Requirements

Even this very limited amount of growth is conditioned upon increased sources of potable water. At the time the plan was developed, there was an insufficient supply of water to meet existing demands. Additionally, the inadequate groundwater supply, which was restricted in the dry season, suffered from saltwater intrusion and was to some degree polluted. The plan proposes a deep drilling feasibility project to test for additional potable water to the west of the island.[36] The plan is clear that *any* additional development would necessitate either an alternative source of water, a desalination plant, or other technological solutions. Other infrastructure needs were not so compelling. The airport is well located—it abuts San Pedro town—and is adequate for quite a number of years. The only adjustments that needed to be made were in the interests of safety—for example, a safety zone between the end of the runway and San Pedro town, and a fence to keep animals, pedestrians, and vehicles away from the airstrip. Since the plan was developed, the gravel airstrip has been paved and a small fence now separates the airstrip from the south end of the town.

Although there was a proposal for a new road, the plan does not consider it a pressing need. In fact, the four hotels it would serve objected to it: they were accessible by sea and wished to retain the special ambiance their seclusion conferred. Recognizing that at some point the road would be needed by the community, the plan recommends reserving land for its construction at the furthest reasonable point from the beach to protect the depth of sites along the waterfront for future hotel development.

Electrical service runs less than six miles north and three miles south of San Pedro; the rest of the 28-mile long Caye runs on generators or does without. Nevertheless, electrical needs are deemed so far less significant to increased development than are water supply issues, that the plan does not even directly address them.

Zoning Controls

The plan establishes various use districts throughout the Caye to protect areas with special qualities. The entire north section of the island is to be maintained as a Natural Reserve, with only trails for walking and tracks to provide public access to the beaches. Three Conservation Areas are created, with even greater restrictions on use. These zones protect offshore reefs, a turtle hatchery site, and the shore and swamp adjoining a marine reserve.

The plan also designates five Special Coordinated Development Areas (SCDAs). These are the areas identified for future tourism and residential growth, where all development must be planned comprehensively and jointly by owners and the planning authorities.

Within these SCDAs, limited growth is to be permitted on the east coast. Here, the plan provides for the development of three resorts,[37] each consisting of a number of beach front hotels (at the maximum number of rooms permitted under the tourist accommodation limitations) with an equal number of tourist rental apartments. Each resort would also be permitted to have a small commercial center with shops, a restaurant, and an entertainment facility. A number of lots would be available for local workers and families, where they could build houses. The three resorts would be separated by undeveloped areas with natural vegetation. This same concept controls future development on a portion of the west coast. There, nuclear resorts would be built behind bays with long beaches. Smaller bays would be left undeveloped to provide buffer zones between resorts.

The plan concentrates growth in two areas: San Pedro town and the center of the island. Two as yet undeveloped areas of San Pedro town to the north and south are zoned for a mix of holiday condominiums, subdivisions for vacation and retirement homes, hotels, and general residential development for local workers and their families. The current town—only three streets running north and south, crossed by six streets running east and west—will become the town center as San Pedro expands, providing commercial services for both residents and tourists and permitting high density hotel development. Density levels decline as one moves away from the town center, and only low density tourist establishments may be located along the beach front to the south of town. The farther northern and southern suburbs are zoned primarily for general residential and will be protected from the incursion of tourist uses. One paved road will travel north and south, with three car parks on the edge of the town center. This should allow the town center road to remain unpaved, an important element of San Pedro's charm and character.

The center of the island is identified as the location for a future settlement on the assumption that San Pedro will eventually reach its physical population carrying capacity. At that time, the center of the island will be developed for general residential use.

Economic Impacts

The plan projects that, given the limited increase in tourism beds it allows, visitor numbers are likely to increase from approximately 10,000 in 1988 to between 69,000 and 89,000 in 2005, with an estimated visitor expenditure in 2005 of US $37 million. The growth in tourism should create approximately 4,000 new jobs, about 80 percent of which could be filled by Belizeans. Even with substantial leakage of tourist revenues out of Belize, the amount that would remain in the country would make a significant contribution to the economy.

However, maintaining this projected level of employment of Belize citizens will require job training, tighter immigration controls, and providing the services on Ambergris Caye that will attract people to live there. This will involve creating new affordable sites for housing, providing loans to build houses, and building new schools for an expanded local population. A new clinic is currently needed, as is a commercial center to serve residents. All of this will cost money and take time, which is another reason to ensure that tourist development does not grow at a rate faster than the plan permits.

An additional economic impact of tourism was already being felt at the time of drafting of the plan. Because there was virtually no control over land use and development, and because tourism was already a growth industry on the island, non-Belizeans were buying land for retirement or vacation homes or for speculation. This had two unfortunate impacts: the cost of land was rising steeply, with the result that native Belizeans could no longer afford to buy land on which to build their homes; and as the market value of land rose, so did real estate taxes. Belize citizens were thus paying higher taxes based on increased land values created by foreign investment.

Urban Design Guidelines

One of the objectives of the plan is to maintain the character of the urban and rural environment of the Caye. Density restrictions provide some protection from insensitive development. In addition, building height is restricted to two stories throughout the island, with two exceptions. In these tourist-oriented locations, three-story height is permitted on a maximum of 60 percent of the site. On much of the land designated for tourist development, buildings are required to conform to traditional designs and be finished in white-painted wood siding with open verandas and low-pitched roofs. In other locations, more flexibility is accorded designs, but the emphasis remains on using materials that are "in harmony with the tropical environment and Belizean architectural idioms."[38]

Implementation

When the plan was drafted by the World Tourism Organization, it identified six "Action Priorities" for a successful program to control tourism growth on Ambergris Caye. The first was formal adoption of the plan. (This has not been accomplished, but the guidelines are otherwise enforced.) The second was to establish an Ambergris Caye Planning Authority, composed of representatives of relevant government bodies. (This occurred in 1990; the ten-member group must include five private citizens.) The third step was for the Planning Authority to create a technical group to undertake the professional work necessary for implementation: a senior planner, an assistant planner, and a building technician. These experts would be responsible for monitoring development, initiating enforcement action when necessary, modifying the plan in the face of changing circumstances, and evaluating proposals for development and making recommendations to the Planning Authority for approval or disapproval.

The fourth priority was for Belize to have various tests done to determine the availability of potable water on the Caye and, if inadequate for the planned development, to identify alternative water sources and the costs. Ambergris Caye also needed a water supply distribution network. This was an essential step, because the viability of any tourism growth rests on an adequate water supply.

Fifth, Belize needed a feasibility study, designs, and cost projections for improvement of the airstrip. And finally, the government needed to introduce restrictions on the sale of Belize land to aliens and to amend tax laws so that real estate taxes could be levied at differential rates for Belize citizens and aliens.

Closing Comments

Since the drafting of the Master Plan, Ambergris Caye has seen relatively slow but steady tourism growth. The combination of tourist accommodation limitations, infrastructure tie-ins, zoning controls, and design guides seem to be directing growth as the Belizeans want it. The profile of the island is still low, with two- to three-story buildings lined with wide verandas shaded by palm trees. The casual mood remains, and tourists interested in duty-free shopping and elegant dining are rarely seen strolling down San Pedro's sandy streets. There are more small hotels being built, there are more condominium units rented out for vacations, and time-shares overlooking the beach are available. But the growth is generally within the boundaries established by the plan.

There have been some unexpected negative impacts. Much of the new construction is being built by Americans, with material from the U.S., creating not only issues of economic "leakage" but also continuing problems with land values. There is also a new private school, attended largely by the children of Americans, which creates at the very least the appearance of a "segregated" school system and a division between native Belizeans and immigrants.

Belizeans themselves are divided over the amount of tourism growth they want. There is, as an example, an old Shell Oil airstrip on the north end of the island that some want to turn into an international airport; others want it to remain as it is now—a largely forgotten strip of land in a beautiful part of the Caye near a marine reserve and a beach devoted to turtles. Some tourist offerings also seem to clash with the laid-back atmosphere appreciated by most residents. One example is the recent introductions of an underwater "K-10 Hydro Speeder," a vehicle resembling both a jet fighter and a motorcycle that performs corkscrew turns above the reef.

In an effort to generate income without imposing additional tax burdens on the local residents, the government has recently imposed high landing fees at the airport, so that flying to Ambergris Caye is a relatively costly endeavor. It also imposed a hefty 15% V.A.T. Whether these taxes caused the slight drop in tourist numbers in 1997 and whether they will change the market that has been so stable is hard to say. The long-term effects of Hurricane Mitch, which destroyed most of the Caye's piers and "over water" dive shops, are also unknown.

A further financial issue is whether Belize, if it fully implemented the WTO plan, would ever be able to recoup its investment costs. The casual tourism that Ambergris Caye attracts may never provide sufficient economic benefits to outweigh the costs of proper research and studies to solve the water supply problems, a water distribution network, an improved airport, and needed technical staff (to say nothing of schools, housing, and medical facilities), and thus fail the standards for efficiency (as we discussed that term in Chapter 2).

Impediments to Incremental Growth Strategies

The very aspects of an incremental growth strategy that are its greatest strengths also produce the greatest impediments to its success. The analysis of social and cultural impacts and community character that underlies the approach may lead to the most sustainable tourism, but it is a time-consuming process that requires the participation of a significant segment of the community and the willingness to arrive at a consensus. Additionally, the social carrying capacity of a community relies on innumerable variable factors. Defining regulations and choosing management tools that will mitigate impacts that are construed to be negative on the basis of subjective attitudes of diverse individuals is a complex project. Issues of architectural style, scenic views, and affordable housing are the easier part of community character to address.

Adaptability to change and indeed the very assumption of change that is built into the concept of incremental growth restrictions both assume an ongoing system of monitoring to ensure that the desired conditions in the community are being achieved. If they are not, then the techniques need to be modified. Once again, this demands a high degree of commitment. The community must have the political will and organizational ability to implement, enforce, monitor, and revise the various elements that make up its incremental growth strategy. The human and financial resources to do what is necessary may be beyond the means of many but the most successful destination communities.

Final Observations

When popularity threatens to destroy those aspects of a tourist destination that make it attractive to both hosts and visitors, quantity management strategies can protect and preserve its special shared assets. As the case studies have shown, communities can establish a network of mechanisms, each of which addresses a separate aspect of the overall strategy. The techniques available will vary from place to place, but most successful quantity management strategies generally include a combination of legal regulations (e.g., zoning regulations, stringent use restrictions, moratoria on development, permitting systems, land acquisition programs), economic policies (e.g., tax credits, preferential tax assessments for open space or agricultural land, impact fees), and management tools (e.g., usage settings, traffic management systems).

As we discussed in Chapter 2, successful strategies should reflect community norms and reflect local goals and conditions. Many of the quantity management case studies provide excellent examples of how destination communities translate the often intangible aspects of "community character" into public policy and then devise a management strategy to fulfill those policy objectives. Peninsula Township wanted to preserve its heritage as a farm community: the *public policy* became preservation of agricultural land and the prevention of urban sprawl; the *strategy* to achieve this included the purchase of development rights program, regulations protecting scenic views, and restrictions on the location of residential development.

Sanibel wanted to remain a "sanctuary" and also to preserve its casual, small town ambiance. The public policy that embodied these goals was the limiting of the use of land and buildings to the capacity of the natural and built environments to accommodate those uses without undue negative impacts. The strategy included restrictions on development based on a carrying capacity analysis (particularly in regard to evacuation in case of a hurricane and impact upon the special ecology of the island), restrictions on commercial development, and a variety of traffic management techniques. Aspen wanted to return to a simpler, less "glitzy" atmosphere, which translated into a policy of increasing the availability of affordable housing; this led to changes in the point system used for development approvals, requirements for a percentage of affordable housing for new subdivisions, and a simpler review process for affordable housing applications. Moving from the lofty language of "visions" and "community character" to practical, specific measures that will achieve those elusive qualities can be difficult. These case studies indicate that, with time and care, it can be done.

Even in situations where future land-use decisions are being made on the basis of consistency with the desired community character, the case studies show that few jurisdictions are immune to *regional* influences. In Chapter 4, we addressed regionalism in the context of impacts caused by the growth of a popular tourist destination, often involving the desire of that destination to expand its borders (as was the case with Santa Fe and Park City). Communities that have chosen quantity management strategies have usually rejected expansion as a mechanism to accommodate increased numbers. The focus, instead, is on balancing the number of visitors with the ability of the community to sustain them.

Nevertheless, this approach also has regional implications. In some instances, the growth that is restricted within the destination community is merely displaced to the immediately surrounding area. This has been true to some extent for both Aspen and Whistler. In other situations, the efficacy of the strategy is compromised by changes beyond the borders of the destination community. Sanibel's evacuation plan depends on citizen access to the single road heading north from Fort Myers. If that road is clogged with people from the Florida mainland, Sanibel residents will not be able to get out of the path of a hurricane quickly enough. Similarly, Yosemite's plans to reduce traffic within the park will minimize negative impacts on the air quality. But the major source of pollutants comes from vehicular emissions outside the boundaries of the park. Until a regional transportation system has been established, Yosemite's efforts to improve air quality will have minimal overall effect.

The case studies suggest that whenever a community considers a quantity management approach, it should take into account the possible impacts its plans could have on the surrounding region, as well as the degree to which its plans rely on actions of its neighbors, and develop cooperative and coordinated planning approaches with the players within the boundaries of the extended planning area.

The case studies also indicate the special relevance of monitoring to the success of quantity management strategies. Issues of quality are largely (though not entirely) under the control of a destination community. When it comes to the *numbers* of tourists who choose to visit a particular destination, there are a multitude of factors beyond the control of the hosts. The number of day-trippers may suddenly surge when there are major improvements to a state highway system that provides access to the community, creating unexpected congestion on the streets and overburdening the facilities during the day. Strong economic growth in one area of the globe may result in a flood of tourists from countries that have never been part of the destination's traditional market, with unforeseen social impacts on the community. Increased demands on a regional water supply may deplete reserves that the destination community relied upon to serve tourist needs, so that it can no longer sustain even its existing level of visitors.

Because it is so difficult to predict tourist numbers, destination communities need constantly to monitor their strategies to see if they are still adequately mitigating negative impacts, or whether circumstances have changed to such a degree that the overall approach needs to be revised or the techniques modified.

Sanibel, Bermuda, Whistler, and Aspen are all established and successful destination communities. Each has had a tourism management strategy in place for over 20 years. Yet each has recently revised its approach because, in the words of the Sanibel plan, "unwanted changes are occurring." Each adjusted aspects of both the goals and the implementation techniques of its strategy to respond to changed conditions that were related to tourism growth, in order better to mitigate unwanted impacts and maximize desired benefits.

The case studies suggest another reason for communities adopting a quantity management strategy to continually be involved in monitoring and reviewing their chosen techniques: the relevance of new information. Additional sources of governmental revenue may make it possible to provide needed infrastructure for additional growth. Technological advances may offer solutions to the environmental problems that originally necessitated the quantity management strategy; conversely, new scientific data may suggest the need for more stringent regulation.

The plan for managing the Cairns area of the Great Barrier Reef Marine Park reflects new thinking about the impacts of human activity on its special environments. This plan imposes tighter regulations on the granting of permits and shifts the basis for determining what activity will be permitted to expected impacts from merely the type of use. The Saguenay-St. Lawrence Marine Park regulations are growing out of recent realizations that many of the commercial uses in the waters of the park are having negative impacts on that unique environment. Researchers are also investigating whether placing time limits on some uses and closing some environmentally sensitive locations at different times of the year will give them adequate protection, so that more stringent restrictions will not be needed.

Finally, the case studies suggest that destination communities should consider including a marketing strategy in their overall approach. Some degree of quantity management can result directly from marketing to those targeted groups that the destination desires. The Bermuda government has long been an active participant in tourism marketing. While many other destinations may not be open to this level of governmental involvement, it has resulted in a uniform message to a defined group of tourists. Bonaire, on the other hand, wishes to expand its tourist base and so is aggressively marketing itself to new groups. Marketing can go hand in hand with other quantity management tools to promote sustainable tourism that is in the long-term best interests of the host community, the visitors, and the tourism industry.

6

Location Enhancement Strategies

When a destination community has enjoyed the various benefits of tourism development, thoughts often, and understandably, turn to encouraging future growth in order to secure even greater benefits. "Bigger" is seen by many to be "better" and, by some, as necessary for survival in a global economy, where many destinations are competitors for tourism revenues. Countries and cultures from all parts of the world are venturing into tourism development. Traditional healers in a South African village have discussed highlighting their district as a cultural tourism destination. At least one cattleman in western New Mexico in the United States has plans to offer "ecotours" to visitors wishing to see the Mexican gray wolves that have recently been released in the area (and that prey on his cattle). The Saudi Arabian government is officially interested in attracting only domestic tourism. However, the US $1.6 billion Durrat Al-Arus, which is designed and operates in keeping with the conservative religious attitudes of most Saudis, is hoping to broaden its beach clientele to include some of the two million religious pilgrims who visit the holy city of Mecca each year.

Despite the widespread (and often unjustified) presumption that tourism can be an economic panacea, there are certain caveats that destination communities should not forget. As we discussed in Chapter 1, all tourism development brings with it a variety of impacts, some of which will inevitably be negative and some of which may well be unexpected. The canyon country that surrounds Moab, Utah, in the southwest United States is known as a "landscape of extremes," with deep gorges, sheer cliffs, strange rock formations, and rivers with dangerous rapids.[1] Familiar to many as the background in advertisements for Marlboro cigarettes and the Jeep Wrangler, it has lured thousands dreaming of adventure in the legendary American West. In 1997, Moab drew 1.5 million visitors who bought $2,500 mountain bikes, went whitewater rafting and rock climbing, worked as "guest cowhands" on ranches, and tried sky-diving.

Unfortunately, the harsh environment is tougher than many innocent tourists realize, and Moab now averages 145 search and rescue missions a year. Volunteers have had to undergo special training to develop the skills to rescue people trapped in vertical positions on sheer mountain faces and to find lost mountain bikers in the dark of night. During a 42-day period in 1997, 43 people needed to be rescued after having been thrown from rafts on the whitewater. Taxpayers are tiring of the increased, and unforeseen, costs of rescuing foolhardy visitors.

Before any increase in the level of tourism development, communities should carefully evaluate potential impacts and adopt mitigation measures. The fact that a destination community has been able to support the existing level of tourism without unacceptable negative consequences does not mean that additional tourism will be benign.

An increase in the number of tourists or a change in the type of attraction may also mean that the destination is no longer attractive to the types of tourists who have been visiting. Families tend not to choose beach vacations at spots known for marijuana smoking; and hard-rock concerts rarely attract opera goers. One cannot be all things to all people, and destination communities cannot reasonably appeal to every niche market.

One serious risk of growth is the possible overreliance, at the local, regional, or national level, on tourism. Tourists can be remarkably fickle, and the tourist hot spot of one year can quickly become passé. Tourism is also a global phenomenon these days, with innumerable contributing factors outside the influence of the destination community. The Asian monetary crisis of 1997–1998, for example, had immediate effects on New Zealand's tourism: overnight stays in the central hub of Queenstown were down almost 90 percent during the height of its summer season. In fact, so few Koreans were traveling to New Zealand, normally that country's largest market, that Air New Zealand canceled all flights to and from Korea.

It's not just foreign economies that are beyond the control of destination communities. Portola is a rural mountain town of about 2,500 in California, near Lake Davis. When logging and railroad jobs started disappearing in the 1950s, Portola transformed itself into a tourist destination for fishermen and campers attracted by the lake. By the mid-1990s, tourism accounted for almost half of the county's economy. But in the fall of 1997, the California Department of Fish and Game poisoned Lake Davis in an attempt to kill the northern pike that had invaded the Lake and threatened the trout population and salmon fisheries. Unfortunately, residue from the poisonous chemicals did not evaporate as experts expected, and as of the time of writing, no one can precisely foretell when they might. Meanwhile, tourism has plummeted and many of the small-time entrepreneurs are going out of business. As one local official put it, "Very few people are drawn to lakes that have been poisoned."[2] Communities need to consider diversification, as do businesses and investors; it is risky to rely solely on tourism as a source of income, and the greater the reliance on tourism, the more important it becomes to appeal to a broader market.

Despite these caveats, tourism growth can be highly beneficial when it is managed carefully. Every community can discover ways to enhance the assets that make it a special place, and thus attract more visitors. There are various strategies that communities can adopt and implement to enhance and enlarge their tourism. For some, it will mean expanding their attractions or making them available to even more tourists; for others, the best approach may be to divert additional tourists to an entirely separate location, while still others may choose to concentrate tourism within a confined area. For communities just starting on tourism development, it will mean identifying a "product" and attracting a whole new market. All of these strategies have been successful in a variety of settings, and all have been used on local, regional, and national scales.

Expansion Strategies

Most successful tourist destinations have, consciously or not, adopted an expansion strategy to some degree. Cafés are allowed to push out onto the sidewalks so that they can serve more people; additional buses or ferries are scheduled for heavily traveled tourist routes; museums stay open longer hours; hiking trails and bicycle paths are lengthened and improved. Over the years, communities adapt to accommodate more visitors.

Samuel Johnson in his 1775 travel classic, *A Journal to the Western Islands of Scotland,* devotes large portions of his account to the quiet glory of Loch Ness. Still a "honeypot" in the Highlands, the lake now attracts busloads of tourists hoping for a glimmer of the legendary Loch Ness monster. In the 1920s, the novelist and traveler D. H. Lawrence wrote evocatively of the sea and shoreline in *Sea and Sardinia;* today's cruise ships sail over much of that territory, and certainly disembark more passengers than in Lawrence's day. Tourism growth in the past was often a slow and steady process, allowing communities gradually to adjust to changes. In our quickly evolving world, this is rarely an option. Once a community has decided to pursue the benefits of increased tourism, conscious planning for expansion is the wisest course.

Temporal and Physical Elements of Expansion

The first logical step to an expansion strategy is to identify those assets of the community that attract tourists. This is usually a simple matter on the superficial level. Crete's shorelines and historical seacoast towns have always been primary attractions on that island. But looking with more depth at those two assets makes it possible to identify other, though less obvious, advantages. The northern seacoast town of Chania, for example, itself has many local cultural and artistic elements. The squares and gardens have a quiet charm even in high season. A lovely Turkish fountain, fourteenth-century ramparts and Venetian walls, a ruined fort, a pleasant harbor with an ancient plane tree, and the town's buildings are historically interesting relics from Crete's past. A May dance festival celebrates the Battle of Crete. These are among the key existing shared assets of Chania, and each has the potential for being enhanced to attract even more visitors.

The next step is to decide which assets to enhance and how to extend their use. Expansion strategies can involve both *temporal* and *physical* elements. Festivals, for example, can be extended for a longer season, thus attracting more tourists and generating more income over time without the negative impacts of increased crowds. The Shakespeare Festival in Stratford, Ontario, now runs from May to November, performing plays by Moilère, Beckett, and Tennessee Williams, as well as the Bard of Avon. Performances at Ravinia, the summer home of the Chicago Symphony Orchestra, now begin in June with jazz and end in September with ballet. The Salzburg Festival still highlights Mozart but now presents everything from Wagner operas to contemporary plays.

Temporal expansions can also be used in an effort to extend tourism beyond a single high season, thus generating a steadier stream of income for the community. Ski destinations may decide to market themselves to attract outdoor enthusiasts in the off-season. Aspen, Colorado, promotes the summertime pleasures of "mountains to climb, rivers to plunge, elusive trout to uncover, balloons to soar." Jackson Hole, Wyoming, offers convention facilities between the winter skiing and summer hiking seasons. Special events can also become a way to extend tourism in a shoulder season. Natchez, Mississippi, offers a springtime tour of many of its private antebellum mansions. Washington, D.C., attracts even greater crowds (especially from Asia) when the cherry blossoms bloom each spring. The Mardi Gras parade in New Orleans and Carnival in Rio de Janeiro have turned the beginning of the Christian Lenten season into a tourist high season.

Physical enhancements are perhaps the most common way of expanding tourism. Communities often improve their infrastructure both to attract more tourists and to allow the community to handle increased numbers of tourists. This might include upgrading utility services (e.g., providing more reliable electricity along the road leading to Manuel Antonio National Park outside Quepos, Costa Rica); cleaning up unsanitary and unsightly conditions (e.g., removing garbage along the roadsides of the Pacific coast tourism strip in northern Baja, Mexico); or modernizing transport (e.g., constructing a modern subway system in Hong Kong, allowing visitors and others to get quickly and safely around the island).

Other improvements can enhance and enlarge tourism attractions so that a community's appeal is expanded. The former royal capital of Luang Prabang, Laos, is physically expanding its offerings in a number of ways: restoring many of its dazzling Buddhist temples; refurbishing the Royal Palace and opening it at regularly scheduled hours; constructing a new, traditionally designed, international airport terminal; and renovating old, dilapidated buildings. All these efforts are in the hope of tripling the number of yearly visitors to one million by the year 2000. The town of Kinsale in Ireland has won numerous national and international awards for consistent efforts at improving its presentation of buildings, approach roads, gardens, and other amenities, while enlarging the attractive portions of the city through limitations on mobile caterers and late night, "stag weekend" (premarriage) carousing in pubs. On Cyprus, a commercial entity purchased and restored traditional homes that were scheduled for demolition, converting them into attractive tourist rental units. Another company, Excursion Alternatives, is encouraging preservation and expansion of local architecture and crafts. The town council on the Greek island of Mykonos has embarked on an extensive improvement program to maintain its competitive position and its distinctive in-town character that relies so heavily on its white houses with bright blue shutters and windmills along the harbor. In Latin America, many cities and towns are rehabilitating structures and entire neighborhoods. In Salvador de Bahia, once the capital of Portuguese Brazil, such efforts have resulted in extending the average stay of tourists by one day and have created 15,500 new jobs to service visitors to the port district of that city.

All these measures enhance the quality of the destinations, thus creating "added value" that tourists will presumably be willing to support with greater expenditures, longer stays, return visits, and word-of-mouth "advertising" to friends at home. Conversely, *not* improving the existing product can have serious negative repercussions. Many visitors fail to return to the Costa Brava on the Mediterranean coast of Spain or the western shores of Corfu in Greece because of perceived and real failures of communities and tourism operators to improve the substandard and declining quality of much of the development there.

Physical expansion can also involve literally enlarging the area of the attraction. The San Diego Zoo is building new habitats, and the Chicago Botanic Garden is designing special landscapes, on undeveloped land surrounding their existing exhibits. Potential tourist attractions that are within easy traveling distance can be developed and marketed to extend a destination's appeal. Tourists visiting Paris often take a day-trip to see Versailles, and visitors to Beijing go to a nearby section of the Great Wall of China. The same "bundling approach" can work well for other destinations. It not only serves to extend the average length of stay of visitors, thus increasing the economic impact of the visit, but it also helps to distribute the economic benefits more broadly, allowing more citizens to share in the income generated by increased tourism.

Case Study: Oaxaca Valleys, Mexico

A broad upgrading program, including a new corridor plan, calls for expansion of tourism opportunities in the colonial city of Oaxaca and in nearby villages.

For many years a successful cultural tourism destination, the central Mexican colonial capital city of Oaxaca, Mexico, and a few of the towns and villages nearby are now the subject of an innovative tourism corridor plan. One of the primary goals of that 1994 corridor plan is to improve the economic condition of the indigenous Indian and culturally Hispanic population in one of the poorest states in Mexico. By expanding tourist opportunities, planners hope to increase the number and length of stay of tourist visits and spread the economic benefits to a wider population. An associated initiative of rehabilitating large, but deteriorated, colonial structures in the city itself will help preserve a rich cultural and architectural heritage.

The Oaxacan Appeal

The state of Oaxaca (of which the city of Oaxaca is the capital) is located approximately 300 miles southeast of Mexico City. It extends a vast distance between the Pacific coast on the west across into the Sierra Madre mountains. There are over 16 different ethnic groups, speaking more than 90 different languages and dialects. Culturally distinct groups live in different valleys, separated from each other by mountains as well as language, developing their own crafts and traditions.

Erosion and deforestation characterize much of the state of Oaxaca including the environs of the city of Oaxaca and its surrounding villages. Coupled with population increases, this environmental degradation has undermined the general standard of living of the population, which often lacks basic water, education, and other amenities.

There are a number of significant tourist magnets close to the capital city. Only six miles away (through an area characterized by scattered shacks and serious environmental degradation) is the large and impressive ruin of Monte Alban, a Zapotec complex dating from 350 to 750 A.D. The Regional Museum in the city of Oaxaca, located in the sixteenth-century Santo Domingo Monastery, includes such treasures as gold necklaces and carved jaguar bones from the Monte Alban tombs. Other pre-Columbian ruins (Mitla, Dianzu, Lambityeco, Yagul, and Zaachila) lie within 25 miles of the city.

The city of Oaxaca itself is colonial, exhibiting a rich Spanish heritage from the 1500s. The more than 450,000 annual visitors (29 percent of whom are international, generally from Europe and the U.S.A.) are attracted by the small plazas, Dominican churches and convents, baroque monuments, and Spanish colonial architecture. A delightful town square (the *zócalo*), boasting a wrought iron gazebo and surrounded by delicately flowered trees, is a popular congregating spot for both tourists and local families. During the day there are local crafts for sale, while in the evenings band concerts, festival dances, and other cultural events entertain the crowds. A few streets have been turned into pedestrian areas, where shops offer tourists quality crafts from nearby villages; a lively, outdoor Saturday market on the edge of the city attracts locals as well as residents, and vendors hawk everything from handmade hammocks and delicately embroidered dresses to plastic shoes and nails.

Government Involvement Prior to the 1994 Tourism Plan

Most of the early governmental involvement relating to tourism uses in the city of Oaxaca and its surrounding areas was related to historic preservation. A federal preservation statute was enacted in the 1970s, tightly regulating construction style, materials, and other aspects of development in the historic areas of the city. By way of example, the statute mandates that architectural integrity be maintained even though a structure might undergo a change of use (such as conversion of a home into a commercial entity).

The government, especially through its tourism development authority FONATUR, has been quite active in encouraging high-quality hotel accommodations. Three center city structures in three different price categories were extensively renovated with FONATUR funds. The government has also converted several streets near the Regional Museum and the Church of Santo Domingo into pedestrian malls to promote shopping and strolling. Craft sale sites on side streets and nearby small plazas complement the attractive shops in renovated homes.

Prior to 1994, the government undertook some small-scale activities to improve the accessibility and attractiveness of local craft markets in nearby towns and villages. The government constructed new access roads from the principal highways to the centers of several "craft villages," such as Teotitlan, prominent for its weavings. At the terminus of the Teotitlan road, the government also built a modern, although simple, brick building with adjacent facilities to permit a wide range of small, local stalls. There was also partial government funding of a pottery sales center near the village entrance of Atzompa, whose residents produced a distinctive style of green glaze pottery. The famous village of Arrazola, well known for its carved and painted fantastical animals, received governmental funding to help build a similar, small craft sales store in the center of that village. At the same time, many other towns and villages suffering from extreme poverty failed to receive any financial support. Funds were directed primarily to villages known for a particular craft that appealed to tourists, and within easy driving distance of Oaxaca, in an effort to bring economic benefits to the village as a whole. It was a relatively successful, though limited effort.

Tourism Situation in Oaxaca and the Central Valleys

Tourism is one of the largest sources of employment and economic benefit within the city of Oaxaca and its central valleys. In 1994, there were about 460,000 annual visitors to the area. Presently there are about 160 hotels and 4,600 rooms, most of which are operated by small entrepreneurs. These overnight accommodations are complemented by 400 or so restaurants, travel agencies, auto rental outlets, and other service enterprises. The government estimates that 8,200 persons work in the tourist industry, accounting for 5 percent of the total population in the city plus its environs and 12 percent of the jobs in the city itself; and that about 20,000 indirect jobs result from tourism activities. It predicts a 5 percent annual growth rate for the years 1995–2000 and 4 percent thereafter. Given the substantial base and the growth projections, it is not surprising that the government regards the tourism industry as having the potential to create many new jobs and future economic stability.

Opportunities for Tourism Development

Government planners in 1994 identified a number of opportunities to improve the economic benefits of tourism: increasing the number of visitors and the amount of money they spend, extending the visitor seasons, and achieving higher hotel occupancy rates. There were a number of positive factors supporting efforts to meet these goals: the general worldwide increase in international tourism; a strong international demand for authentic cultural experiences; the construction of a new superhighway between Mexico City and Oaxaca; more convenient international and national airline flights; the diversity of tourists' interests that could well mean more visitors who would stay longer; the expansion of Pacific coast beach facilities, where tourists could combine in one vacation the cultural experiences of the interior with the sun-and-sand attractions of the beach; and finally the possibility of rehabilitating and changing the uses of many historic buildings so as to expand opportunities within the city of Oaxaca itself.

Constraints to Tourism Development

The 1994 evaluation also identified a number of situational weaknesses and dangers. The most serious of the dangers was the inadequate attention to the maintenance of environmental quality. Population increases and human settlements had intruded inappropriately on the environment. Consequences included unappealing visual impacts, degradation of drinking water, and similar undesirable impacts. The evaluators believed that this destruction of the natural environment was especially unfortunate in areas around the principal tourist sites such as Monte Alban and Mitla, where deterioration was identified as both highly noticeable and difficult to correct.

Another significant problem was that the sides of the roads and highways connecting the city of Oaxaca with the three principal valleys were cluttered with unattractive, muddled development of mixed uses, including warehouses, industrial complexes, living quarters, and commercial complexes. Additionally, the planners identified congestion and noise problems in the historic center of the city itself, caused by the very large number of visitors who gathered daily and nightly in the central square and also by vehicular traffic. The planners believed that improving the *zócalo* ambiance would require both promoting other places for tourists to gather within the historic center and improving traffic routing and transportation systems. The traffic problem was expected to worsen because the new superhighway from Mexico City would encourage residents of the capital and its visitors to use private vehicles to travel to Oaxaca, thus generating even more congestion in the center city, which already had grossly inadequate parking facilities.

The 1994 Plan

In 1994, the government planners identified a number of broad goals and specific objectives for a comprehensive plan of action with respect to tourism for the city of Oaxaca and the three central valleys.

The five goals were (1) to demonstrate to the traveling public that the city and valleys are high-quality tourist sites, because of their cultural history, natural beauty, and hospitality; (2) to increase potential travelers' awareness of the diversity of tourist attractions in the area; (3) to increase employment by developing increased locations and economic activities of interest to tourists, diversifying them broadly within the towns and city; (4) to improve the natural beauty of the area; and (5) to improve infrastructure and transportation systems in particular corridors and toward newly identified tourism sites.

The objectives, believed by the planners to be achievable by 2005, were (1) to increase, in constant pesos value, total tourism revenues from 292 million pesos in 1995 to 515 million pesos; (2) to increase (again in constant pesos) daily spending from 330 pesos per tourist to 378 pesos; (3) to increase the number of visitors from the current 461,000 to 703,000; (4) to increase the number of rooms available from 4,633 to 5,600, primarily in the three-star and above categories; (5) to achieve a minimum average hotel occupancy rate of 60 percent; and (6) to increase the number of tourism sector jobs from 8,203 to 9,450.

The 1994 comprehensive tourism plan then identified eight "programs" for meeting the previously listed goals and objectives. Six of these ambitious programs are beyond the scope of this case study but should be identified briefly: promotion programs, tourist infor-

mation program, increase in tourism promotion personnel program, environmental rehabilitation program, infrastructure and tourism investment program, and convention cen-
ters/exposition development program. Two of the eight programs are particularly significant for our purposes: the creation of three tourism corridors and the expansion of
historical ambiance in the central city of Oaxaca.

Touristic Corridor Program

The government identified three valleys for special treatment as separate tourist corridors:
the valley of the Tlacoulula (encompassing 11 towns and villages), the valley of Ocotlan
(including eight towns and villages), and the valley of Etla (with seven towns and villages).
(See Map 6-1.) Each of the three corridors is designed to offer a visitor the opportunity to
experience cultural variety. The corridor construction activities are designed to improve
the ecological amenities and also to encourage and offer opportunity to local artisans to
demonstrate their traditional crafts and way of life. Each of the corridors will include
archeological, cultural, and natural attractions. The planning, implementation, and infrastructure improvements will be coordinated by the State Commission for Planning for the
Development of Oaxaca (COPLADE) with extensive collaboration by local communities as
well as persons and entities in the tourism industry.

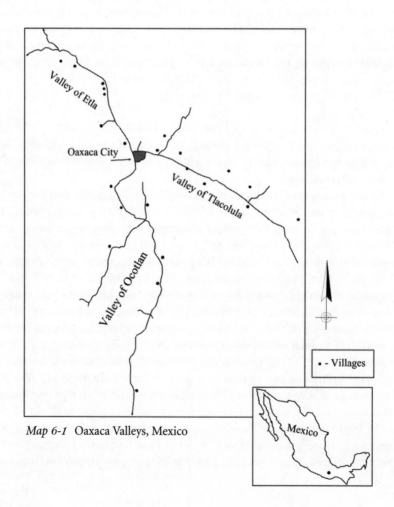

Map 6-1 Oaxaca Valleys, Mexico

In each of these three corridors, there will be extensive infrastructure improvements: creation of sidewalks and possibly bicycle paths; design and construction of paved sight-seeing access roads to allow visitors to conveniently enter towns and villages; improved and additional signage, especially in the urban sections of the roads; construction of tourism booths and service center areas along highways; and creation of "look-out posts" for observing particular archeological and other sites. Additionally, there will be new zoning controls regulating the parcels that front the roads and highways.

In populated areas within the central valleys, there will be general civic improvements that will also have tourist impacts. Examples include increased vegetation, better street lighting, improvements in traffic patterns, rehabilitation of existing tourism attractions, creation of new support elements such as restaurants, hotels and parking lots, road paving, improvements in drainage waterways and drinking water, and development of an overall plan of urban development for the area to guide future human settlements.

Program for the City of Oaxaca

Another of the eight programs announced by planners and officials in 1994 calls for urban improvements within the historical center of the city itself. This program has several elements, two of which are especially noteworthy. First, the center city program contemplates a new circuit of sidewalks, patterned generally after the successful pedestrian malls in other historic centers of the world. This would involve enlarging existing sidewalks as well as redirecting pedestrian flows to make it easier for visitors to appreciate architectural and other city qualities and also to facilitate shopping. The design of the sidewalk circuit was developed so as to encompass a large number of interesting public areas.

As of April 1998, only four additional blocks of streets have been repaved for pedestrian use, but that work has been important because it allows the city to integrate a closed circuit between the *zócalo* and the church of Santo Domingo, which is the most culturally significant area of the city. That area is now ready for closure from traffic, but that has not fully occurred. According to Sr. Martin Ruiz Camino, the creative Minister of Tourism Development of the state of Oaxaca: "The City Council of (the city of) Oaxaca has been closing it little by little to traffic so the community can get used to it but attempts with merchants have not been very successful."[3]

The second, but more complex, element of the central city improvement program is the identification and rehabilitation of architecturally significant abandoned houses. There were 110 such houses listed as of 1994, usually in fair exterior condition but in serious disrepair on the inside. Most were very large and thus had considerable economic potential, especially 48 of the structures that are located on the new sidewalk circuit. Rehabilitating these abandoned houses was recognized as a complex task, acquiring some governmental funding together with agreements with property owners and appealing economic incentives. Planners identified several of these buildings as potential new homes, available after rehabilitation to meet the goals of expanding available beds within Oaxaca generally. Still other buildings could potentially be rehabilitated into restaurants, bars, and perhaps nightclubs.

Closing Comments

The city of Oaxaca and many of its surrounding towns have for many years enjoyed the benefits of tourism, including a fine record of repeat visitors. Government assistance has been one important factor in this primarily cultural tourism base. The plans for infrastructure improvements are ambitious, but necessary, if the corridor plan is to succeed. After all, few visitors choose to drive even moderate distances on very poor roads or dirt tracks to visit a village, no matter how appealing its crafts might be. And rental car companies might well bar their cars on especially problematic roads. Bus routes and dependable public vehicles are currently an inadequate means for visits outside of the city.

Regarding the conservation of abandoned houses in the city and creation of pedestrian circuits, government planners have targeted opportunities that have worked well in other settings throughout the world and, if adequate funding is provided, should be successful in Oaxaca as well.

Initial efforts to improve access to villages and provide financial and technical assistance for construction of central markets have already brought increased numbers of tourists to many of the most famous craft villages. As always, however, there are some unexpected impacts from the new flow of tourists. The Day of the Dead is a popular Mexican holiday that has for years been drawing tourists to the city of Oaxaca. Many villages celebrate the event with elaborate costumes, music and dances, and parades. Soon, however, tour buses from one of Oaxaca's five-star hotels will be carrying guests to watch the festivities in the small village of San Agustín. Residents are ambivalent about turning their traditional fiesta into a commercial event. "And the whole question of where to draw the line between allowing tourism and preserving the sanctity of their private village world is a very big deal."[4]

The state of Oaxaca, Mexico, shares many similarities with the Southern Lakes district of New Zealand. Both have a single popular destination city where the vast majority of tourists congregate. Both are attempting to expand tourism to outlying areas in order to increase the economic benefits of tourism and to distribute those benefits to a broader number of citizens. Both have a mountainous terrain that places constraints on travel. There is one major distinction between the two: while Oaxaca is in the midst of implementing its expansion strategy, New Zealand is still in the planning process. It has developed a series of draft strategies to achieve its goals but has not yet garnered the public support necessary to adopt and implement them.

Case Study: Southern Lakes Region, New Zealand—A Plan in Progress

This UNESCO World Heritage Area developed a multifaceted strategy to expand its nature-based tourism products to increase economic benefits and reduce seasonality.

One of New Zealand's most heavily visited tourist areas is the Southern Lakes region in the southwestern portion of the South Island. (See Map 6-2.) Many of the one million yearly tourists who visit the area are attracted by the Fiordland National Park, a UNESCO World Heritage Site. Almost all of the 500,000 annual visitors to the park are highly concentrated in a very narrow corridor, from Doubtful Sound on the coast eastward to the town of Te Anau and northward to Milford Sound.

In the Southern Lakes region, tourism is a major economic force, accounting for two-thirds of the employment in the area. Reflecting the significance of the industry, a Southern

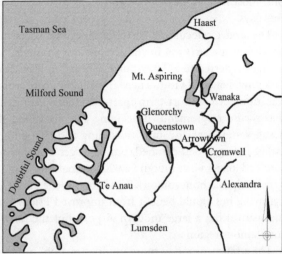

Map 6-2 Southern Lakes,
New Zealand

Lakes Tourism Strategy Steering Group, composed of representatives of the New Zealand Tourism Board and various district councils, came together to develop a strategic plan for the future of tourism in the area. In June 1997, the group published a comprehensive draft tourism strategy document and submitted it for extensive public comment. A final strategy document, dated February 1998, establishes five goals to guide future decisions concerning tourism development in the Southern Lakes Region:

1. to ensure environmental quality in the Southern Lakes is safeguarded or enhanced;
2. to ensure tourism development is supported by local communities;
3. to enhance the economic benefits of tourism to the Southern Lakes;
4. to encourage the benefits from tourism to be spread throughout the entire region; and
5. to ensure product meets or exceeds visitor expectations.[5]

In an effort to meet those goals, the strategy document identifies a number of objectives, two of which are of special interest. The first is to increase the average length of stay, which would then trigger visits to additional regional destinations. The second is to increase the range of tourist offerings to ensure that the needs of visitors are met and that the Southern Lakes Region remains competitive with other destinations. The tourism strategy proposes a number of strategies to bring this about.

Strategy to Increase Length of Stay

The primary strategy aimed at encouraging longer stays is to expand attractions beyond the central town of Queenstown, the largest town in the area, which attracts the vast majority of all overnight tourists in the Southern Lakes region. Located on the shore of a very deep lake and backed by the appropriately named mountains (The Remarkables), the town resembles a Swiss or Italian mountain lake resort hub. Upscale shops and restaurants abound, as do such day-tripping activities as a 1912 steamboat cruise, as well as more contemporary pursuits such as hang-gliding and bungee jumping. Queenstown offers five-star hotels with dramatic water and mountain views, as well as a variety of other accommodations, most notably elegant bed and breakfasts. The typical stay is Queenstown in two or three days.

The strategy document correctly notes that opportunities to enhance the quality and quantity of longer stays in the region—for example, with five- to ten-day self-catering packages (referred to as "stay-put vacations" in New Zealand)—will require international marketing. Potential visitors need information concerning the amenities available for such a vacation, such as short-term apartment rental listings in Queenstown and elsewhere. The strategy also recommends developing and marketing allied elements, such as rental car packages and local discounts for dining and shopping. The existing honeymooner sub-market is largely self-planned, but packages oriented to that group could well produce more and longer visits (about 22,000 international visitors presently state that the purpose of their trip is a honeymoon). The luxury lodge and "elegant" bed-and-breakfast product is growing but would benefit from improved Friday through Sunday air transportation. Queenstown has a large modern airport, but the same is not true in other areas of the mountainous region.

The strategy proposes more "multiattraction" products that would appeal to the family market (especially from Asia). With more things for families to do, and with more potential overnight accommodations that would permit families to move from place to place, stays could lengthen. One popular family attraction is a "jet boat" trip along the very shallow Dart River north of Queenstown. The experience begins with a one-hour scenic bus ride along the newly paved road along Lake Wakatipu from Queenstown to the small hamlet of Glenorchy. Along the way, the driver discusses geological, cultural, and social aspects of the route. The second element of the attraction is a three-hour jet boat ride of approximately 100 kilometers in a wilderness setting with high mountains on both sides. This activity is locally controversial because the boats have considerable power and some noise. On the other hand, the Department of Conservation has licensed only one company to offer such a service and has limited the number of boats allowed on the river at any one time. Animals on the riverbank seemed unfazed by the boats or their noise. Despite its appeal, this will presumably not develop into an activity for mass tourism because of the combination of governmental restrictions and its relatively high cost (US $105 per person in late 1997).

The strategy document also proposes an increased emphasis on improving and expanding special subject "trails." These suggested routes—some day-trips and some longer itineraries—are individually planned and created to expose visitors to local crafts, heritage, wine, or other regionally interesting attributes. The strategy also recommends improvements to and added information on nature trails in the countryside. There are many excellent day hikes (as well as overnight tramps) from such locations as Queenstown and Te Anau, but there is limited international information about those opportunities. Most tourists learn about them when arriving at a visitor center or a store selling hiking or camping gear. These initiatives could increase the average length of stay once visitors are aware of the variety and number of such opportunities in the area.

Finally, the strategy document mentions developing new products for specific markets: stays on local farms for Japanese school excursions (which generally involve 100–300 students) and lakeside health spas and resorts for Asian women.

Strategy to Reduce Seasonality

The primary strategy to reduce seasonality is to develop products to increase demand during the low winter and autumn season. Skiing is an attraction that currently draws thousands of visitors during the New Zealand winter. Its appeal could be expanded by offering regional ski passes to all sites in the area, creating a "super-ski" region. Promoting other snow-based activities, such as tobogganing and sleigh rides, could also expand the market. The Southern Lakes region already stages autumn and winter festivals and special events (an annual Bunny Shoot, for example), but they have never been actively marketed outside the country itself. Finally, the strategy suggests developing specialized niche attractions like food and wine tours, mountain biking, hunting vacations, and agricultural tourism. Conference-based programs and education trips for "seniors" offer another opportunity for low season activities.

Strategy to Increase Heritage-Based Tourism

A third promising approach to expanding visits is to create new products to differentiate the Southern Lakes region from other areas of New Zealand. One promising avenue is the development of regional heritage activities. The culture of the indigenous Maori—their legends, history, religion, and crafts—have considerable tourist appeal. The high-quality Waitangi National Reserve in the Bay of Islands area of the North Island and the vastly more commercial New Zealand Maori Arts and Crafts Institute (incorporating a religious Thermal Reserve) in Rotorua on the South Island are both popular tourist destinations. Although the commentary on both the Doubtful Sound and Milford Sound cruises mention that the Maori used to travel to the fiords to seek out jade for their carvings, there is little other information on the Maori in the Southern Lakes region. The strategy document wisely notes the importance of cultural sensitivity if the Maori heritage is used as the basis of new tourist attractions.

Another potential for development is to capitalize on the gold mining history of the Southern Lakes Region. This has already proven to be attractive to tourists. The restored Chinese Goldfield settlement in Arrowtown, a half hour-drive from Queenstown, is a popular day trip. The 17 sites along a pathway illustrate through restoration and interpretive plaques the lives of some of the 1,200 Chinese who arrived there in 1889 to rework gold claims abandoned by their previous owners. The restorations include such places as a store, huts, an outhouse, and an opium den. A small museum in the immaculate and pleasant town has nineteenth-century artifacts, pictures of the miners, and a history of the town. This superior 1988 project was a collaboration of the Department of Tourism and the Department of Conservation.

Strategy to Increase Nature-Based Tourism

Another strategy is to market the region as a nature tourism focal point, with the towns of Te Anau and Glenorchy as particularly promising overnight locations because of their positions on the edge of the World Heritage Area (Fiordland National Park). As explained in more detail in the following case study on Milford Sound, Te Anau is the gateway (via the scenic 119-kilometer Milford Road World Heritage Highway) to the world famous Milford Sound on the coast. The road includes a number of spectacular viewing locations, picnic and camping sites, trailheads for nine day-hiking trails, and an interpreted self-guided trail for the less adventurous but curious visitor. Also discussed in that case study is Glenorchy, as of the time of writing a tiny hamlet but likely to be quickly developed because of the recently paved, scenic road from Queenstown. At least that is the hope of horseman Bill Macmillan, who anticipates that most of the new visitors will be neophytes in horsemanship, interested in trying a ride in the rural setting. Certainly rapid tourism growth is the plan of Minister of Tourism Murray McCully, who was selected to dedicate the new road. Minister McCully was ebullient in dedicating the new 47-kilometer road: "The road opens up new tourism opportunities for Glenorchy and the whole Lakes District. This road is tourism-creating, wealth-creating, and employment-creating." That may well be true. But at least one local farmer, John Hasselman, is concerned that maintaining community character should be a high priority as the impacts of the road paving become more evident.

The nature-based tourism focus of the New Zealand tourism leaders and officials led to the conferring of the 1996 Supreme Tourism Award for the well-designed Doubtful Sound tour. This day-long activity begins in Te Anau with a short but scenic bus trip to the eastern tip of Lake Manapouri, a clear glacial lake dotted with islands. A boat takes riders across the lake where they transfer to another bus and travel over Wilmot Pass on a road carved over a two-year period in the rain forest wilderness, with a view of Doubtful Sound below. Once at the Sound, the visitors board another boat for a 40-kilometer cruise of the remote and majestic sound (ten times larger than the more visited Milford Sound), with glimpses of bottlenose dolphins, fur seals, and sometimes rare penguins. The return trip follows the same path, with an added two-kilometer trip by bus down a tunnel to visit a power station deep within a mountain. The overall quality of the experience is high and well deserving of the national award, with excellent and extensive interpretation of the natural features, flora, and fauna.

Closing Comments

The region's strategy to expand tourism opportunities is commendably broad. It consists of a number of objectives—reducing seasonality, encouraging longer overnight stays, improving heritage-based tourism, and increasing nature-based tourism—that are mutually complementary and include very specific steps for implementation. This is much more than lofty goal setting; it guides citizens and others in practical ways.

Implementation of the strategy, however, is a complicated matter because of the cooperation and coordination it requires. The marketing elements require that independent promotion groups throughout the Southern Lakes area work together to promote the entire region as a destination in its own right. Necessary infrastructure improvements and environmental management rely upon the cooperative efforts of regional councils and the national Department of Conservation. The strategy document itself states that "(t)he broad range of issues associated with tourism development in the Southern Lakes means that implementation of the strategy is dependent upon the involvement of a number of groups and agencies,"[6] including district and regional councils, community boards, Maori tribes, regional conservation boards, fish and game councils, the national transit authority, tourism organizations, local associations, health services, tourism businesses, and local communities. As Chapter 2 suggests, securing broad-based support and consensus from such diverse constituencies, with differing goals and often representing different levels of government authority, can be a challenging process.

The Southern Lakes region strategy is broadly directed to expanding tourism for the economic benefit of the entire region. One element of that plan involves strategies for coping with the single instance of tourism that is too intensive: the congestion at Milford Sound. The original draft plan proposed three separate solutions; each one was an expansion approach with both temporal and physical elements. Although carefully thought-out, each alternative involved controversial elements and had significant drawbacks. The Milford Sound Strategy is a excellent example of the practical difficulties of building consensus for any complicated option from distinct constituencies.

Case Study: Milford Sound, New Zealand—A Plan in Progress

Current tourist numbers approach the limit of both the physical carrying capacity of Milford Sound and the visitors' satisfaction capacity. New means of access are being considered to alleviate midday congestion and overcrowding at this popular tourist attraction.

One of New Zealand's most well-known international attractions is under considerable pressure because of its very popularity. Milford Sound is a fiord, opening into the Tasman Sea on the west coast of the South Island's mountainous Fiordland National Park, a UNESCO World Heritage Area. It is spectacularly beautiful, surrounded by perennially snow-capped peaks, with hundreds of waterfalls cascading down its steep cliffs, seals resting on its rocky outcroppings, and bottlenose dolphins playing in its pristine waters. Tourists are drawn to this remote and rugged site to encounter the majesty of nature in a cloistered setting.

The Road to Milford Sound

Access to such beauty does not come easily. The four-day, strenuous hike along the 54-kilometer Milford Track, across mountains and through glaciated valleys in a temperate rainforest (the source of those awe inspiring waterfalls), is one way to approach Milford Sound. The priciest passage is by small plane, over the often foggy mountains. Most of the 300,000 tourists who visit every year, however, opt for a lengthy day-trip. For the vast majority of visitors, the 12-hour excursion begins in Queenstown, 300 kilometers away. Motor coaches (see Photo 6-1) carry their passengers south and west along the aptly named Remarkable Mountains and across valleys filled with sheep and deer, to the small town of Te Anau. Here the buses pick up more passengers for the remaining 120-kilometer ride along the Milford Road World Heritage Highway. This scenic route follows the shore of Lake Te Anau, then snakes up and down through the Eglinton and Hollyford Valleys, passes through a mountain tunnel, and finally arrives at Milford Sound, resting beneath the towering Mitre Peak.

The national Conservation Department has devoted extensive recreational funding and staffing resources to improving the Milford Road. It now provides camping facilities, picnic areas, trailheads, a self-guided interpretive walk, and scenic viewing areas. Plans for the future include additional and expanded interpretation facilities, more self-guided walks and an audiotape that interprets important features along the road. While it may be true that "(t)he journey along the road is spectacular and adds value to the Milford Sound experience," it is also true that few tourists in rental cars are willing to tackle the often challenging drive on the narrow, winding road, subject to landslides, washouts, and, in winter months, avalanches.

Once they've arrived at their destination, the motor coaches discharge their passengers, who board one of the charter boats that offer 1.5-hour cruises, with commentary, along the Sound. Scenery is the biggest draw in Milford Sound, but there is a fairly recent underwa-

Photo 6-1 Overland tour bus to Milford Sound, New Zealand

ter observatory as well. At the end of this part of the excursion, the tourists reboard their busses and retrace their journey of the morning.

Midday Congestion at Milford Sound

Milford Sound has attracted so many visitors that there is a growing disparity between visitor expectations and the tourist experience. The lure of Milford Sound is the vision of awesome and untouched natural splendor. For the vast majority of visitors, however, the first sight is a large parking lot full of tour buses, followed by a view of the Sound obscured by the crowds of tourists filing onto a row of boats lining the wharf. The psychological and visual effects of the sheer number of tourists detract from the Milford Sound experience.

This growing "disconnect" between expectations and reality is of no minor concern. The Southern Lakes region attracts around one million visitors annually, and Milford Sound is its most famous attraction. Tourism supports approximately 75 percent of the jobs in the region and is vital to the economic health of the local communities. To address the issue of how to manage the volume of tourists at Milford Sound—and more generally the issue of sustainable growth of tourism in the entire Southern Lakes area—the New Zealand Tourism Board joined with representatives of various district councils to devise a tourism strategy.

The Southern Lakes Tourism Strategy Steering Group in its 1998 Tourism Strategy document (see the preceding Southern Lakes region case study) identified the essential problem at Milford Sound in terms of the physical and psychological carrying capacity phenomena addressed in detail in Chapter 5. Because most tourists take day-trips from a considerable distance, "visitor facilities are now reaching full capacity during peak midday periods over the summer months, in particular around the wharf area." At the height of the season, there are on an average 60 tour buses discharging 45 people each for the early afternoon cruise; eight or nine boats are needed to carry the 2,700 tourists around the Sound. Motor coach numbers have been as high as 97, pouring more than 4,000 visitors onto the waters in a single midday. The facilities cannot physically accommodate any more people at the same time; nor can the visitors experience the magic of Milford Sound with any more congestion.

Travel from Queenstown is likely to remain the route to Milford Sound for most tourists. The unusual and rugged topography of the fiordland precludes extensive overnight accommodations anywhere near the Sound; furthermore, National Park regulations sensibly and strictly limit construction within its borders in order to protect the environment. The topography and rainforest climate also severely limit air access, so that increased air service to the Sound is not feasible. Even if it were, aircraft noise would itself interfere with the visitor experience. Te Anau offers a variety of pleasant but modest accommodations, and tourists who stay overnight there can take an earlier bus to Milford Sound and arrive in time for a longer and much less crowded 2.5-hour morning cruise. Te Anau, however, is geared largely to the backpacker crowd, with its access to any number of long hiking trails. While appealing in its own right, it doesn't boast the range of restaurants, shops, and varied tourist excursions that make Queenstown so popular.

Proposed Solutions: New Access

With Queenstown likely to remain the starting point for almost all visits to Milford Sound, the question becomes how to alleviate the enormous midday congestion. The earlier 1997 Tourism Strategy draft document proposed the creation of alternative road or rail access. A new, more direct route would limit the driving time to the Sound, allowing visits to be spread out over the entire day and also improving the visitor experience. Improved access would also have a number of collateral benefits. It would increase the potential number of tourists who could visit Milford Sound, thus increasing carrying capacity without major on-site developments; spread the economic benefits of tourism to new areas because of a revised route; benefit travelers in terms of lower fuel costs, shorter driving time, and increased driving safety; facilitate the targeted marketing of the World Heritage Area as an essential travel destination for visitors to New Zealand; and provide conservation education opportunities along the new access routes.

The strategy draft document proposes three alternative access routes. (See Map 6-3.) The Greenstone Road would run from Queenstown to link up with the Milford Road about 20 kilometers from the Sound. This would be the shortest and least expensive option, using the existing road north from Queenstown to Glenorchy, and then building a new road running west through the Greenstone Valley. This would be the most direct route and the alternative with the fewest engineering difficulties. However, about eight kilometers of the proposed route runs through pristine forest inside the Fiordland National Park; it would interfere with one of the popular trails, the Greenstone Valley Walk; and finally, the proposed road passes through land promised to a Maori tribe under a treaty.

The second alternative is the Riverstone Monorail. In this option, the tourist would cross Lake Wakatipu from Queenstown to the southwest shore, then take a monorail south and west across the mountains via Mavora Lake, to link up with the Milford Road approximately 30 kilometers north of Te Anau for a coach ride the rest of the way. This privately funded project would have the least environmental impact but would not offer travelers the independence and flexibility that a road would.

The final alternative is the Haast-Hollyford Road, the only route that does not include Queenstown. This road would run from Haast, on the west coast of the South Island, in a southern direction approximately 160 kilometers, linking up with the Milford Road for the final 20 kilometers or so of the trip to Milford Sound. The route is much longer and more expensive than the other two options but is relatively straightforward from an engineering

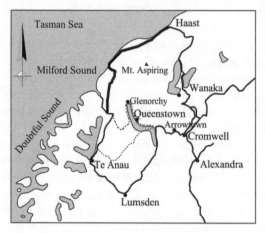

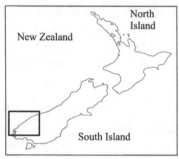

Map 6-3 Milford Sound, New Zealand

standpoint. It would offer an entirely new route into the Southern Lakes District for visitors. Its major drawbacks are that because of the remoteness of the area and its extreme winter weather, construction could be difficult. Additionally, the entire route is within a World Heritage Area, and one-third is within the Fiordland National Park, both of which are subject to strict conservation and environmental regulations. It would also interfere with the Hollyford Track, even more well known than the Greenstone Valley Walk.

All three alternatives have their supporters and opponents. The Greenstone Road would forever change Glenorchy; this small hamlet of 170 people, with 30 children in the local school, would suddenly have thousands of tourists driving through each summer day. Some residents are eager for the economic possibilities such a transformation would offer; others don't want to see their quiet community change. The road from Queenstown was just paved in 1997, and for the first time rental cars, and their tourist drivers, were able to drive to Glenorchy. That change was itself controversial; the road to Milford Sound would be much more so.

When the Steering Committee sought public comments on their proposed Plan, they received over 150 comments from the Te Anau community alone. Every one of the alternatives under discussion bypasses Te Anau. Currently, almost all visitors to Milford Sound include Te Anau in their itinerary. Trackers start their journey there; every rental or private car and tour bus passes through; even those who fly in by plane usually depart by bus following the cruise. While some of the residents who retired to Te Anau may not mind the loss of the tour bus crowds, everyone who works in or owns a guest house, motel, T-shirt shop, or restaurant must be concerned about the effects of any new route. Many of the comments from the Te Anau community opposed any faster access to Milford Sound and instead supported the encouragement of a more relaxed visit to the Sound with a longer length of stay and an overnight in Te Anau.

Regional Planning Recommendation

The final 1998 Tourism Strategy document, heeding the breadth and depth of comments the draft proposals had received, does not make a recommendation concerning how to relieve the congestion at Milford Sound. Instead, it states that:

> Options for dealing with these issues, whether they include the further development of facilities, improvements to access or maintaining the status quo, will need to be considered and debated in detail by the stakeholders in Milford Sound. In terms of improvement to access, submissions to the draft Strategy revealed rejection of the Greenstone Road proposal but divided opinion on the Riverstone Monorail and Haast Hollyford Road proposals. Therefore, access options will need to be considered further. Attention should also be given to the role of the Milford Sound Development Authority as there is likely to be implications for the future management of infrastructure at Milford Sound.[7]

What the final strategy *did* recommend was consultation among all the constituencies interested in Milford Sound and a coordinated planning approach:

> That the regional and district councils within the Southern Lakes and the Department of Conservation, liaise with the Milford Sound Development Authority, other private sector operators at Milford Sound, Fiordland Promotion Association, other RTO's (Regional Tourism Organizations), Transit NA, the New Zealand Tourist Board, Ngai Tahu (a Maori tribe) and any other interested stakeholders to establish the parameters of and the process for formulating a strategic development plan for Milford Sound. The plan should identify the future vision for Milford Sound, the necessary actions to address issues such as capacity and access and the impacts they have on visitor experience at Milford Sound, and determine how those actions are to be implemented.[8]

Closing Comments

The long-term viability of Milford Sound as a tourist destination is of economic significance both to the Southern Lakes region and to New Zealand as a whole. It is one of the main reasons that 54 percent of all visitors to New Zealand go to the Southern Lakes. But its very popularity is creating problems that diminish the visitor's enjoyment of its spectacular beauty. Additionally, the existing infrastructure at the Sound cannot accommodate any more visitors at midday. The integrity of the Sound, and its tourist appeal, could be lost without thoughtful attention toward coping with the present threats to its environmental and visual qualities.

Although there is widespread agreement among local residents and businesses that providing an additional access route to Milford Sound is a far better solution to the midday congestion than imposing limits on the number of visitors, building consensus to support any alternative will be challenging. One of the three proposals put forward in the draft strategy is no longer being considered because of objections from various affected constituencies. Each of the remaining two alternatives would bring economic benefits to a different community, and each would have clear negative impacts on a separate environmentally sensitive area.

There are, of course, additional impacts that might result from all three alternatives. It is notoriously difficult to predict how changes will affect tourist behavior. It may be that creating easier access will simply result in many more tourists visiting Milford Sound, creating the same congestion problems spread throughout the day and increasing the environmental impact on the Sound. Or a new road or monorail system might destroy the very sense of remoteness that is an important element in Milford Sound's appeal.

Getting people to agree on the difficult choices may be a more complex and time consuming process than construction of a new road or monorail. The Strategy recommends a reasonable, but time-intensive approach: first, to develop a process that includes all "stakeholders"; then, to build consensus on the vision for the future of Milford Sound; and only after that, to develop a plan to address the problems of Milford Sound.

Limits to Expansion Strategies

Not all destinations can take advantage of expansion as a solution to tourism pressures. Environmentally fragile locations that need the protection of strict preservation rules are not good candidates for spatial expansion; nor are communities that are experiencing carrying capacity problems. In most situations, however, strategies that focus on how to make a community more attractive to tourists are viable mechanisms.

Expansion approaches often seem among the "easiest" strategies for communities to implement. Legal regulatory systems are often already in place (relevant zoning and taxing codes, for example). Developing more of the same or enhancing what already exists does not necessarily require any new legal enactments. Scheduling additional performances at a summer festival, extending the hours of a museum, opening more ethnic restaurants, marketing a hotel complex to business groups or an empty dormitory to the successful senior citizens' program called "Elderhostel"—these may require economic analysis and promotional efforts, but they do not require either complex regulatory supports or government funding.

A major problem of expansion strategies is this very ease. Individual business owners can often make unilateral decisions about their own private enterprises without considering the cumulative effect on the community. The owner of a town's largest hotel may want to attract guests in the off-season; restaurant owners may also want more year-round customers. But many people in the community, whose businesses do not cater to tourists, may yearn for the end of the season, when the tourists leave and the community returns to its "private" life. When there is no need for governmental involvement, there may be no impetus for a broad-based community discussion about whether tourism growth is desired.

Even when a community largely agrees that the benefits of tourism outweigh its burdens, the ease of some expansion strategies can be deceptive. Without the time required to adopt regulatory mechanisms or to secure government financing, efforts to enhance tourism resources and target new markets can quickly take on a life of their own, before the community has had time to reflect adequately on what the *impacts* of such expansion might be. Growth in tourism can change the dynamics of tourism in multiple ways. Communities need to consider carefully the diverse impacts increased tourism might have, how they might mitigate the negative impacts, and whether the benefits will still outweigh the burdens. This can be a difficult task to accomplish when there are no regulatory constraints on expansion.

Dispersal Strategies

When popular tourist destinations are threatened with overcrowding—as well as the aesthetic and environmental degradation and the general decline in the quality of life for residents that often accompany an overabundance of tourists—they are not interested in attracting more visitors. Their primary concern is usually managing their existing number of tourists (in general, see Chapter 5). Another approach that can sometimes avert the need for restrictive quantity control measures is a dispersal strategy: diverting tourists from a destination that is experiencing tourist pressures to another attraction.

A Classic Dispersal Model: Languedoc-Roussillon, France

In many ways, the prototype of tourism dispersal strategies is a well-known and well-studied French effort.[9] This successful regional dispersal program began in the 1960s, when several levels of the French government began planning to develop the southern Mediterranean coasts of the Languedoc-Roussillon region as tourist destinations. (See Map 6-4.) The program has been examined at different stages: in 1971 by Ann Louise Strong,[10] in 1978 by Fred Bosselman,[11] and in 1992 by Mary Klemm.[12] This account of the "grandfather" of dispersal strategies draws heavily from those studies.

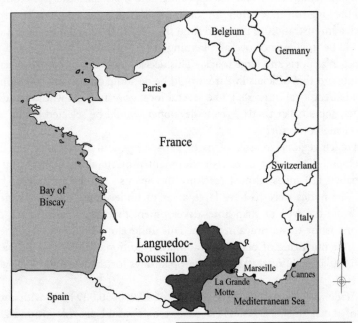

Map 6-4 Languedoc-Roussillon, France

The vast French regional undertaking had a number of goals, one of which was to attract tourists who might otherwise add to the overcrowding of the Riviera, the long coast of the Mediterranean including such famed locations as Cannes, Nice, and St. Tropez. Despite overbuilding on the Riviera, at the time when the plans were begun, France was in general far behind the growth rates of "sun and sea" destinations in Spain and Italy (25 percent in those two countries, but only 2 percent in France).

The area selected for new development was an underpopulated and insect-infested marshland west of Marseilles. Among the geographical advantages of the region were the technical feasibility of draining and filling the marshes, the availability of good crop land behind the marshes that could be used to grow food for tens of thousands of visitors, and the presence of medieval ruins which could become even more attractive tourism sites as supplements to "sun and sand." The chairman of the initial stages of the project recalled vividly the challenges of transforming this most difficult area: "When in January 1963, in a helicopter . . . I surveyed for the first time all that wasteland of swamps and shores infested with shanties and tents with no sanitary facilities whatsoever, I was dumbfounded. I thought momentarily that we never could clean up all that."[13]

In those early days, there were no tourist towns in the area, and planners soon recognized that private capital would be grossly inadequate to fund necessary infrastructure simultaneously. But not to do so would have produced piecemeal development that would have been both unattractive and less appealing to tourists, and thus less economically successful in the long run. The better approach would be for governments at various levels of the French administration to plan and fund much of the work. Thus, the national government would be in charge of overall planning, land purchases, drainage, and major infrastructure such as ports and large roads. (This decision was highly controversial, because of local resentment that officials in Paris would be deciding important development matters that would affect local interests.) The several local governments would handle sewer systems, water, and smaller roads. Private developers would be selected by the local governments to create new resorts.

The French regional master plans of 1964, 1969, and 1972 called for five nodes of new development and two large redevelopment projects along a very long coastline of approximately 120 miles, almost reaching the Spanish border and linked by an inland highway. The nodes were to have large areas of undeveloped land separating them, in order to avoid the type of strip hotel development that characterizes such densely built destinations as the Costa Brava in Spain. This undeveloped land was designed to be natural areas for nurturing of plants and animals. Additionally, there would be an approximately 10,000-acre national park with new plantings for shade, wind blockage, and scenic beauty.

Each node was to have a huge resort hub of 40,000–50,000 beds, with ancillary development of much smaller sites. These new resorts would provide around 250,000 beds, while expansion of existing hotel complexes would offer 150,000 additional beds. Australian tourism professor Douglas Pearce[14] accurately emphasizes the unusually high degree of governmental involvement in this very large-scale program, including major commitments of time and money in planning, implementation, and infrastructure construction. Early sketch plans called for a motor expressway with interchanges for access via primary roads to each resort node. Additionally, there would be "tourist roads" generally parallel to the coast and also leading back to the interior.

In 1961 and 1962, the government undertook secret land purchases of about 3,000 acres of land, in part to establish market values for much larger future purchases and con-demnations.

The resort area called La Grande Motte was one of the first two visitor nodes to be developed, and it is a useful example of how development progressed. The node as planned was to include about 1,700 acres of land (divided among sites for hotels, cottages, and campsites) and approximately 8,000 acres of lakes. Private developers were invited to pur-chase land at fixed prices that depended upon the use to which the parcels were to be put. A nearby pine forest of about 400 acres was acquired as part of the project. By 1974, La Grande Motte had about 31,000 beds and was 2,000 acres in size with man-made sand beaches. Most of the many hotels and apartment houses were designed as pyramids. The ambiance is far different from the mosquito-ridden marshes that previously characterized the area; now it has "a high-rise, city-like atmosphere, which attracts a high-style interna-tional yachting crowd. The boutiques boast Paris originals rather than local handicrafts."[15]

British lecturer Mary Klemm notes the enormous impact of the government's planning and its *f* 1.3 billion investment between 1964 and 1989. From a mere 30,000 visitors in the 1960s, the numbers grew to five million tourists in 1990; 88 percent of these were domes-tic tourists, generally of a "mass, middle market" character. Total bed capacity had risen by that year to approximately 1.3 million. Job creation was equally impressive: 50,000–60,000 permanent and 20,000 seasonal slots. Tourism is now the source of more than 10 percent of the region's total income, the highest percentage anywhere in France. Additional impacts include triggering a boom of second-home construction: by 1990, Languedoc-Roussillon had 2.25 million second homes, almost all owned by French citizens, the highest ratio of second homes to total lodgings in France.

It is ironic that the region now seems to suffer from what the 1960s planning sought to remedy—overcrowding at high season. This explains recent governmental efforts to dis-perse once more, this time with heavy emphasis on the interior portions of the region, mar-keting the cultural and sporting opportunities available in areas with "considerable differ-ences in character and tradition."

Dispersal to Relieve Overcrowding

The Languedoc-Roussillon prototype was so successful that many other communities have used a comparable dispersal technique to lure tourists from one individual site to others within a destination community or from one community to another within a larger region. The state of Hawaii encouraged the development of separate, self-contained resorts in var-ious parts of the island of Oahu to divert visitors from the overcrowded Waikiki Beach in Honolulu. In Mallorca, the walled city of Alcúdia was developed as an alternative tourist site to relieve pressure on the beaches and to attract tourists at the off-season. Greece is jus-tifiably proud of its very small, but high quality, "traditional settlements" program that is attracting tourists away from its crowded beaches to areas rarely visited ten years ago. Under this program, the government purchases and restores small buildings that are reflec-tive of the architecture and history of an area. It then arranges with local residents to oper-ate them as overnight tourist accommodations. This program now attracts visitors to stay in a renovated tower in the tiny village of Vathia in the Mani, small homes on the cliffs of Santorini, and villages in the northern mainland.

On a smaller scale, Oxford, England, is considering a variety of dispersal techniques to mitigate the problems of overcrowding within the city. A recent Oxford Visitor Study iden-tified a number of serious problems, most of which related to concentration and congestion of large numbers of visitors in the central portion of that famous university location. These included traffic and human congestion, noise, vehicle fumes, and litter. The study recommended several "strategic shifts" including "more dispersal of visitors, attractions and impacts, by season and location" and "more spreading of the benefits between the various groups involved (e.g., higher priority for local people)."[16]

Of course, avoiding overcrowding at popular "honeypot" sites by use of a dispersal strategy requires the active cooperation of visitors themselves. Communities are in no position to compel compliance with their designs for diversion to newly created or upgraded locations. The most obvious method to encourage voluntary spreading of tourism is through marketing: accurately depicting the benefits of new destinations to potential visitors. Marketing, however, has its own limitations. The official marketing of the Languedoc-Roussillon coast stressed "the planners' conception of varied but functionally interrelated resort clusters . . . set in rural support zones providing informal folklore and natural environmental attractions. The spatial behavior patterns of visitors and their perceptions of the region, however, largely ignore these characteristics."[17] Instead of responding to the appeals of the official marketers, most tourists apparently view their experience in the region in very limited "spatial" terms; they spend their entire vacation at a single resort, without venturing beyond that hub to other centers or to the interior where the planners are eager to lure them.

Dispersal to Spread the Benefits of Tourism

Another purpose of a dispersal strategy is to spread economic benefits to residents of areas to which the tourism is diverted. The Languedoc initiatives, for example, brought significant increases in job numbers and income to the residents of France's southwestern coast. One element of this goal is simple fairness: why should all of the benefits remain forever with individuals and businesses that happen to be located where tourism is currently focused. On a political level, when voters outside existing tourism destinations learn of the economic benefits enjoyed by others, they can exert political pressure to "share the wealth" through a dispersal technique. In some instances, certain cultural or religious groups may perceive inequality in the sharing of such benefits, thus triggering special sensitivities and as well as vocal, organized pressures.

Tourism also has important sociocultural impacts on both host and guests. Sociologists specializing in tourism have for decades been generating articles and books on this very broad subject. Much of the literature in the field addresses such distinctively negative impacts as child prostitution in Thailand and the loss of interest in traditional pursuits upon exposure to "vacationers' values." There are positive impacts as well, however, and dispersal strategies enable more communities to experience direct interaction between tourists and locals.

Learning about a different culture is one important reason that many tourists select particular destinations; few travel to India or Morocco to revive themselves through quiet relaxation. The same learning can occur in the reverse direction—hosts learning from, and being enriched by, contact with guests. One portion of an interesting 1990s study conducted by a United Nations agency established that residents of the Caribbean island of St. Lucia favored spreading of tourism throughout the island and did not support spatial concentration in the two existing enclaves, one on the west coast near the capital city, and the other on the south near a large town. The sampling showed that 71 percent of the respondents rejected concentration, citing such reasons as the need to spread economic benefits (25 percent), diversity of scenery that tourists should be exposed to (47 percent), and dangers of overcrowding in the two existing enclave areas (25 percent). Most impressive was the degree to which St. Lucian citizens felt positive about increased interaction with visitors. An overwhelming 85 percent of the respondents wanted tourists to have increased exposure to island life. There were a number of reasons given for that welcoming attitude: 35 percent cited a likely increase in mutual understanding, 28 percent referred to cultural experience, and 9 percent pointed to improving the rate of return of visitors. The sampled hosts felt by an 80 percent or higher rate that visitors should attend community celebrations and churches, and visit places of entertainment, beaches, and supermarkets. Not surprisingly, few residents felt that tourists should visit local "rum shops."[18]

Dispersal strategies can be adapted to a variety of settings. The following three case studies present starkly contrasting settings: the first is a historic city in England, where the dispersal occurs to relieve congestion within a relatively small area; the second is an archipelago country in the Indian Ocean, where tourism is dispersed over a multitude of small islands with the objective of limiting negative social impacts; the third is an island of New Zealand where the goal of the dispersal strategy is to spread the economic benefits of tourism development.

Case Study: Canterbury, England

A dispersal strategy has been introduced at an urban World Heritage site in Canterbury, England, to relieve the problems caused by congestion and overcrowding.

Canterbury's heritage, stretching back to the days of Roman occupation, is the focus of its longstanding attraction for tourists. The Saxons named the city "Cantwarabyrig," and in 597 St. Augustine arrived and shortly thereafter founded a cathedral. Construction of the present cathedral was begun in 1071 on the same site and finished in 1498. Archbishop Thomas à Becket was murdered in the cathedral in 1170, after which it began a long and prominent history as a site of religious pilgrimage, as so vividly depicted in Chaucer's classic *Canterbury Tales*.

Faced in 1994 with widespread local concerns over negative impacts resulting from the ever-increasing numbers of visitors to the small World Heritage Site, a newly created entity forged a program to diversify tourist attractions. Three years later the program succeeded in spreading the visitor pressures among a number of sites and mitigating the worst of the impacts.

Citizens' Concern with Intensive Tourism

During the mid-1980s, local council planning documents focused on how to deal with a substantial increase in visitor numbers. The primary technique, called "Park and Ride in Canterbury" (PARC), involved severely limiting vehicle access and encouraging use of pedestrian trails. This successful initiative was insufficient to cope with the growing numbers of visitors, however, and in the 1990s many citizens demanded additional measures. The citizens' concern was not misplaced: in 1993, an estimated 2,250,000 tourists visited Canterbury, which represented a very high ratio of 55 tourists to every resident.[19] Venice was burdened by twice that ratio, but Canterbury's 55:1 ratio was higher than those of many other "historic cities" in Europe (Salzburg 36:1 in 1992; Bruges, Belgium 23:1 in 1990; Oxford 12:1 in 1991; and Florence 10:1 in 1991). Moreover, since 1975 the numbers of visitors were increasing by an estimated 50,000 each year. Tourism, which had provided a major source of the city's economy since the twelfth century, had reached—in the eyes of many citizens—crisis proportions.

These very high tourist numbers created a particularly acute problem because visits were concentrated in a small area only one kilometer in diameter, in the center of which was the cathedral, which itself was surrounded by narrow streets, clogged with tourists. Although 1,900,000 people visited the cathedral in 1995, many fewer had ventured beyond that circumscribed area to see the city's other attractions. Only 129,000 visitors had gone to the museums, and a mere 13,000 had entered St. Augustine's Abbey (see Photo 6-2). Compounding the congestion were problems associated with the high use of excursion buses from London and continental Europe (parking, noise, pollution, and aesthetic harm). Canterbury is the closest English cathedral city to the mainland, and since the opening of the Chunnel it attracts large numbers of schoolchildren on school sponsored trips.

The Canterbury City Centre Initiative

Against that backdrop, a not-for-profit entity composed of community organizations, known as the Canterbury City Centre Initiative (CCCI), was created in October 1994. CCCI includes several leading businesses, the City Council, the Chamber of Commerce, local colleges, and countywide governments and bodies as constituent "partners." Its broad mission is "to identify and respond to the needs of residents and visitors; to stimulate the prosperity of the business community; to add value to the experience of visiting Canterbury; and to preserve the character of the city."

Photo 6-2 St. Augustine's Abbey, Canterbury (Courtesy of Canterbury City Council, in conjunction with Canterbury City Centre Initiative)

CCCI developed and implemented "practical solutions to key visitor and destination management issues not tackled by other organizations." According to City Visitor Manager Rita Skinner, the major need was for a mechanism for "moving people away from the honeypot of the Cathedral and around the city." The solution CCCI developed was a dispersal strategy based on upgrading and linking subsidiary sites to the Cathedral and to each other.

Dispersal Strategy

This dispersal strategy was largely in place by mid-1997, with several supplemental ideas still in development. The key element of the strategy is to upgrade the other two portions of the UNESCO World Heritage Site (St. Augustine's Abbey and St. Martin's Church, the oldest church in England in continuous use) and to link them to the Cathedral by a newly created historical trail, known as "Queen Bertha's Walk." (See Map 6-5.) Named after a Saxon queen who was a worshiping Christian at St. Martin's Church and who greeted St. Augustine when he arrived at the city in 597, the walk also includes twelve additional points of interest and fourteen explanatory bronze plaques installed in the new sidewalk. Visitor brochures note that the Queen might "possibly have taken" the new walk while going from the Cathedral to St. Martin's Church.

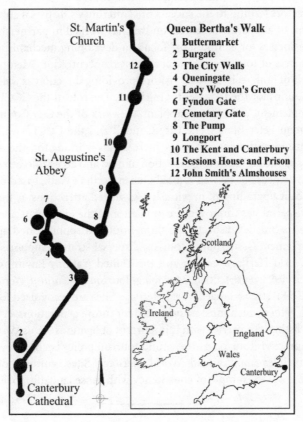

Map 6-5 Queen Bertha's Walk, Canterbury, England

After the cathedral, the most important attractions on the walk are the abbey and the church. A new museum, interpretation center, landscaping, and audio tour were added to the abbey in early 1997, financed by English lottery funds. The Abbey Museum includes many important and interesting artifacts that previously could not be suitably shown and had been in storage unseen by visitors. Lottery funds were also used to upgrade the grave-yard around St. Martin's Church and to create new paths and a terrace for viewing the cathedral and the city as a whole. The subsidiary sites along Queen Bertha's Walk are suf-ficiently interesting to spread out the tourists both spatially and temporally. They include, for example, the buttermarket (where produce was sold), the burgate (around which are buildings once used as inns serving pilgrims), the fourteenth- and fifteenth-century city walls, the pump (a water source given by the then owner of the abbey), and the sessions house/prison.

In addition to creation and upgrading of sites along Queen Bertha's Walk, authorities undertook extensive renovations to the impressive Canterbury Castle, which had previ-ously been closed to the public and was thus a new attraction. The castle improvements include safety and access elements, together with interpretive placards and landscaping. Rita Skinner regards those improvements as "phase one of a more ambitious plan for the site as a whole," for which the CCCI will probably seek additional lottery funding.

Closing Comments

There are two factors leading to the success of Canterbury's dispersal strategy. The first is the establishment of a separate organization that has worked in partnership with citizens, officials, and businesses for a "rifle shot" focus on developing mechanisms for mitigating the negative impacts of tourist congestion and overconcentration. Members of the CCCI address the needs of both residents and visitors, providing direction as well as financial and in-kind contributions for the City Centre Initiative. The role of the CCCI from the outset has been to complement, rather than supplant, the work of the City Council. In the words of CCCI Chairman Peter Brett, "The City Council and the CCCI have built up a good working relationship, and other bodies are increasingly working together to great effect."

The second significant factor is the creation of new, and accessible, attractions to appeal to visitors to the cathedral. The well-crafted Queen Bertha's Walk, based on the identifica-tion and significant upgrading of previously less visited attractions, is the cornerstone of the program. Dispersal has improved the ambiance of the area for residents and tourists alike. Viewed in its broadest aspects, the thoughtful and sophisticated approach used to develop and implement Canterbury's tourism dispersal strategy supports ideas shared by the UNESCO World Heritage Centre and the United Nations Environmental Program (UNEP). In their 1993 report titled *Managing Tourism in Natural World Heritage Sites,* UNESCO and UNEP stressed that "World Heritage Sites are recognized for their universal and outstanding values which must be protected for future generations. . . . The prestige of World Heritage listing also carries with it important obligations . . . as World Heritage list-ings can attract more visitors to an area, sound tourism policy becomes even more impor-tant. These principles apply to all World Heritage Sites, cultural or natural." The Canterbury case is a fine example of consistency with those laudable goals.

Canterbury's dispersal strategy focuses on enticing the growing number of tourists to nearby attractions to alleviate congestion that was concentrated in the area of the cathedral.

The approach mitigated the most negative impacts of tourism on the community, while enhancing the visitors' experience. The next case study provides a contrasting use of a dispersal strategy. It involves a much larger area, a nationally adopted strategy, hosts and visitors from different cultures, and tourist development of a very specific type: the single island "sun-and-sand" resort.

Case Study: The Republic of Maldives

A multi-island nation has called for dispersal of future tourism development among numerous atolls to achieve the economic benefits of tourism and to segregate residents from culturally distinct tourists.

The Republic of Maldives, for many years a British protectorate, became independent in 1965. Calling itself "a nation of islands," the Maldives is composed of a 500-mile-long string of 1,190 islands on 26 atoll formations in the Indian Ocean, some 400 miles south of the tip of India. (See Map 6-6.) The various islands, enclosed by coral reefs, boast white sand, clear lagoons with extensive and varied marine life, coconut palms, and over 2,500 hours of sunshine in the typical year. Only 199 of the islands are inhabited by a total of approximately 250,000 citizens.

Tourism Development on Uninhabited Islands

Although there are many hotels and guesthouses in the capital city of Male´, most visitors to the Maldives stay at a single resort island (see Photo 6-3). This concept is well described in a government pamphlet of general information. "A resort island is a world by itself. Developed on uninhabited islands, each island is just one hotel, exclusively maintained in

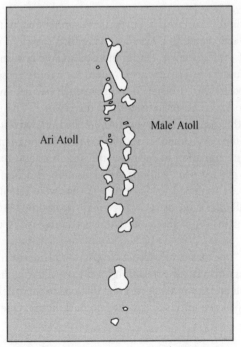

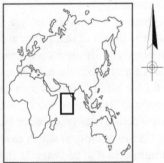

Map 6-6 Maldives

Photo 6-3 Aerial view of Bandos Island Resort and Kuda Bandos Island, Maldives (Courtesy of Mr. Mohamed Saeed, Deputy Minister of Tourism, Maldives)

pristine form and serviced for only a limited number of guests. . . . Just inside the vegetation line, well dispersed for maximum privacy along the beach in a typical resort island are small bungalow-style rooms where accommodation is provided. The rooms, though mostly shaded by trees, allow a clear view of the beach, the lagoon, and the horizon beyond. . . . Normally the hotel rates quoted are for full board—bed, breakfast, lunch and dinner included."

The pattern of allowing only a single resort on a particular uninhabited island is unusual. The details of that policy are articulated in a 1994 law regarding leasing of uninhabited islands for the development of tourist resorts. Under that statute, the government designates a particular uninhabited island owned by the government for a tourist resort. A public tender bidding process managed by the Minister of Tourism then occurs, and the "best proposal" is awarded the right to lease the entire island for the resort.[20] The maximum lease period is 21 years except in the case of a large resort where the initial investment exceeds US $10 million, in which case the government is authorized to lease the island for a maximum period of 35 years. At the termination of the lease, the buildings and fixtures are conveyed by the developer to the government without compensation and in a high standard of repair. Special provisions are designed to place resorts that were established prior to the 1994 statute, under generally the same lease arrangements regarding length of time and details of turnover at the conclusion of the lease. There are currently 74 resort islands.

The Maldives imposed the unusual "one island, one resort" restriction primarily to prevent tourism from impacting the conservative Islamic traditions of the population. Visitors arrive by plane on Male´ and almost all are promptly sped away by boat to their destination resorts, which they typically do not leave until the day they go back home. One local journalist captured the insular nature of the resort patterns: "Maldivians are still devoutly religious people, with strong family ties and they view the resorts as strange, un-Islamic places."[21]

Secondary reasons for the one island, one resort policy are to protect environmental resources and to produce an image of exclusivity. By law, once the government identifies an uninhabited island for resort development, it must simultaneously designate three other uninhabited islands for environmental conservation. Tourism Minister Ibrahim Zaki explains the rationale for the policy: "We are aware that our basic tourism product is totally dependent on our environment. We have hundreds of uninhabited islands suitable for resort development. But it is not numbers we are interested in, it is quality."[22] The limit of a single resort to each island simultaneously preserves much of its open space, protects three other islands from development, and promotes a sense of seclusion, which attracts visitors.

Success of Tourism

The tourism industry has been highly successful in the Maldives, attracting over 338,000 visitors in 1996. There are more than 10,000 bed spaces in the country, which could well double by 2005. Almost of all these existing beds are located in the "central region" of the Maldives, which are the two atolls of Male´ and Ari. There are only a small number of beds (769) in an area known as "nearby atolls" (the Ball, Lhaviyani, and Vaavu atolls) and only about 100 beds in the entire "southern region" (the atolls of Seenu and Gaafu Dhaalu). Thus, even though there is a dispersal of resorts to individual uninhabited islands, there is still a very high degree of concentration in the two central atolls.

Seasonal spread and occupancy rates on the Maldives are good. Tourism generated US $180 million in 1994, while foreign exchange earnings contributed 40 percent of the total governmental revenues through bed tax, lease rentals, and import duties. As measured by a percentage of gross domestic product, the tourism industry in 1996 contributed more than 20 percent. Growth in the industry is extremely strong, estimated at approximately 15 percent per year. The rate of growth has been dramatic: between 1991–1995 the average rate of growth essentially doubled that of the previous 15 years. In light of that growth and success, the consultants who prepared a "1996–2005 Tourism Master Plan" were certainly correct when they noted: "In the case of the Maldives, tourism has over the past decade been the principal engine of the national economy and as such deserves prime consideration (in the country master planning process)."

Tourism growth has not gone unmanaged in the Maldives. In 1983, the government adopted a ten-year tourism development plan, which included as a central element the direction of new tourism growth onto the atoll of Ari, which was thought to be a natural extension of preexisting tourism development on the atoll of Male´. Development continued apace, and by 1993, Ari atoll provided 25 percent of the total Maldivian bed spaces of 9,000, while almost all the others were located on the atoll of Male´. At that time, about 30 percent of all the resorts were concentrated on islands (selected, of course, by the government) within a 20-kilometer radius of the Hulule international airport and the capital of Male´.

This relatively centralized development pattern created population growth problems on Male´, characterized by planners as causing urban and environmental stress and lessening the social cohesion. In addition, the economic benefits of tourism were not being spread across the geographically large area of the Maldives as a whole. These considerations led the government in the mid-1990s to adopt a different approach: balanced growth with diversification to other regions.

Future Strategy of Decentralization

In the mid-1990s, a Tourism Master Plan, funded by the Commission of the European Communities and prepared by consultants, proposed a new policy, characterized by different emphases for three separate regions. In the "central region," the policy calls for a consolidation and upgrading of tourist facilities. In "the central region and beyond," the policy calls for expansion of tourism opportunities into nearby atolls. The third or "southern region" will be subject to much broader regional expansion and later operate as a gateway to "equitable development in other regions."

The Central Region

For the central region of the Male′ and Ari atolls, the plan calls for an intensification of development by encouraging the use of existing potential. An example would be to create an additional 1,200 bed spaces during the next ten years, representing approximately 50 percent to 60 percent of the existing, but unused, carrying capacity of those two atolls. Simultaneously, the plan calls for upgrading existing tourism infrastructure and other physical aspects of development. In deciding which tourism development proposals to accept, the plan suggests that the Ministry of Tourism give preference to projects that promote a "premium destination concept." The goal is to promote high-end tourism with a focus on ecotourism and to avoid mass market tourism (which is difficult in any event because of the high cost of travel to the Maldives for most visitors, the largest number of whom come from Germany and Italy).

The Central Region and Beyond

The proposals for the atolls beyond the central region and within a radius of 150 kilometers of the international airport would affect the atolls of Ball and Lhaviyani to the extreme north and Vaavu, Meemu, and Faafu at the extreme southern region. In the center portion of this identified region, the plan calls for high-activity, shorter-stay, and island-hopping activities. The outer rim would be characterized by "a traditional high quality 'paradise island' product" that would be a premium destination. Since the region in question is very large, the planners recognize the critical importance of improving transportation, including the probable need for a regional airstrip, appropriately characterized by the consultants as "major transport infrastructure provisions." The bed-space increase planned for this region over the period of 1996 to 2005 is ambitious: an additional 2,000 bed spaces, which would represent a greater average annual increase in rooms than that experienced collectively by the two atolls of Ari and Male′ over the longer period of 1977 to 1991. The consultants recognize that this very extensive growth would increase development pressures on Male′ itself, and thus require urban planning and other activities to avoid negative social, cultural, or economic impacts on the capital.

The Southern Region

The plan, recognizing that equitable expansion into other regions is appropriate, advised the government to focus resort development on the atoll of Addu (Seenu) and more particularly on the island of Vilingili. In order to create rapidly a critical mass of development necessary to support increased airport operations in this area, and also to maximize job creation, the plan calls for a density of 50 beds per hectare, which was deemed manageable given the physical characteristics of the locality. This density would be approximately *double* that on the prevailing resort islands in the atolls of Ari and Male´. The consultants calculated that at the conclusion of the southern region expansion, its tourism would generate approximately US $20 million per year; 25,000 visitors per year; and 3,000 jobs. Large-scale development on Vilingili Island would have an impact on several other elements of the plan, such as the economic feasibility of upgrading a regional airport at Gan, assuming that communications and harbor improvements were in place as well. The upgrading at Gan Airport would ultimately accommodate long-haul jets, and thus it would become the hub of the entire southern region.

The so-called "southern focus" element of the master plan complies with the "decentralization of economic development" strategy articulated in the earlier and more comprehensive National Development Plan. It would also slow down population migration to the island of Male´, which historically occurred because the national labor force for the tourism industry often came from the atoll of Addu in the southern region. Finally, the strategy would also effect a reduction of development growth in the central region by channeling growth to southern atolls, and thus allow increased opportunities in the central region for environmental protection measures.

Regional Airport Strategy Element

Another basic component of the regional expansion plan is to permit resort development on uninhabited islands that are very close to regional airports and to ban tourism development on all other uninhabited islands. This would essentially open up the atolls of Laamu and Haa Dhaalu and also the atolls of Raa and Gaaf Dhaalu for development. Only highly meritorious proposals should be permitted within those 20 kilometer areas.

Summary of Planned Growth

In the central region, currently planned expansions, coupled with hoped-for development pursuant to existing rights, would add an additional 2,000 beds. In the north and south expansion areas of the central region, approximately 3,500 beds could be developed during the planning period of 1996 to 2005, with perhaps 30 new resorts at a pace of two to three resorts per year. This would require identification of additional, appropriate uninhabited islands each year, with a concomitant designation of three times as many uninhabited islands for environmental conservation. In the southern region, 3,000 beds could be developed on Vilingili Island, with smaller increases on other islands and chains of islands. Assuming that the regional airport strategy is adopted, the consultants believe that the remote atolls in the southern region could be the location of a total of 250 beds in about four smaller resorts.

As of late 1998, 14 additional resorts were under construction for 1999 occupancy. The selected islands were surveyed to promote configurations and numbers of new beds consistent with each island's special characteristics. Presumably each of those new resorts will be required to adhere to the currently strict environmental protection guidelines imposed on existing resorts. These strictures relate to minimum beachfront per visitor (five meters) and availability of desalinization plants, incinerators, bottle crushers, and compactors.

Assuming that the "release of islands for development" plan is carried forward, it might be possible for the country to continue its dramatic 1985–1990 average gross domestic product growth of more than 10 percent per year. Such an expansion could help address the Asian Development Bank's concern that such a high growth rate will not be sustainable without increased tourism capacity (as well as without increasing the nation's fishing catch). However, in mid-1998 the government announced that it was reconsidering the initial decision to add 22,500 beds by the year 2005 because "we do not want to spoil our environment at the cost of tourism."

Closing Comments

The Maldives' one island, one resort plan used carefully drawn boundaries to limit tourism impacts. The plan was conceived primarily to insulate the local populations from tourists in order to protect residents from perceived negative impacts on their conservative morals and attitudes. This strategy was possible in part because of the local geography: a chain of islands can separate populations more easily than can a country in which internal transportation is more convenient.

The spillover effects of the policy included the establishment of resorts with a tone of exclusivity and under considerable public control, since the islands are owned and leased out by the government. The future application of the single island resort modality is also under strict governmental control, and more islands are being "released" to disperse tourism development to areas that have not as yet enjoyed its economic benefits. Plans include specific quantity goals in terms of numbers of beds, revenues, and jobs in each of the targeted regions and include identification of needed expansion of transportation infrastructure, especially airports needed for the dispersal effort.

Even such a carefully controlled program has had its own share of unexpected impacts. When the one island, one resort policy was instituted, the islands selected for tourism development were close to islands with major residential areas. Tourists could be rowed in small boats from the airport to the resort island. Most local people working in tourist facilities (almost all of whom were male) still went home every night. Few of the traditional patterns were changed.

As tourism development accelerated and spread to more distant islands, these patterns changed. People who chose to work in tourist facilities, which provided steady income and employment, were often separated from families because the travel from work to home was longer and most costly. Other times families moved closer to work, which broke up traditional living patterns. The social impacts have not been so serious as to undermine the effectiveness of the overall dispersal strategy, but they are of concern to a society that wishes to retain its traditional customs and values.

The dispersal strategy has also had environmental impacts that are just recently being addressed. Some popular dive sites have been designated as protected areas, and the government is considering establishing a Marine Park that would, presumably, limit uses that would have adverse effects on the marine ecology. Pending regulations would require major resort developments to carry out environmental impact assessments and submit them as part of the development application process. The government is also drafting more stringent performance standards that resorts would have to meet on water treatment, solid waste management, and energy efficiency.

Global warming may offer its own resolution to the problem of negative impacts. The average elevation of the Maldives is less than five feet above sea level, and the country has the distinction of being one of the first nations at risk of disappearing in the twenty-first century as the level of the sea rises. On a very practical level, these risks have created conditions that threaten the insurability of businesses. In late 1998, an insurance industry scientist remarked that because the Maldives, among other countries, is especially vulnerable to storms and rising sea levels, global warming could greatly affect tourism. This sense of vulnerability is shared by Foreign Minister Fathulla Jameel, who in 1998 asserted that because tourism and fishing could be "wiped out overnight," the United Nations should continue to list the Maldives as one of the world's poorest nations, rather than as a "developing" country, as the U.N. had proposed. The lesser designation would allow the Maldives to continue to enjoy a number of financial advantages, such as low interest loans and debt forgiveness.

Unlike Canterbury and the Maldives, Stewart Island in New Zealand is well off the ordinary tourist itinerary. While the island has a variety of natural attractions, it offers nothing spectacular to compete with Milford Sound in the Southern Lakes region. With fishing in decline, however, tourism is seen as a potential replacement source of income. The strategy for Stewart Island, largely developed by "outsiders" with community comment, is aimed at diverting some tourists from the popular South Island sites to spread the economic benefits of tourism more equitably throughout the country.

Case Study: Stewart Island, New Zealand

A small, underpopulated island with multiple natural attractions seeks to improve the scope and size of its tourism development to secure additional economic benefits.

Much smaller than New Zealand's other two principal islands, Stewart Island lies 30 kilometers south of the South Island across the Foveaux Strait. (See Map 6-7.) Its 1,700 square kilometers are largely undeveloped, with a rugged landscape. (See Photo 6-4.) The ecosystems on the island are rich in flora and fauna. There are numerous attractive bays and inlets on the eastern portion of the island, while the northwestern area boasts a broad sandy beach and dune system.

The climate is harsher than that of the rest of New Zealand. Winters are perceived by potential visitors as particularly inhospitable, while the summer months have fewer hours of sunlight and more rain than other, more heavily visited parts of the country. In fact, an official guide to Stewart Island candidly warns of "unpredictable weather," especially rain. The land ownership patterns of Stewart Island present important opportunities for sustainable touristic development. Approximately 90 percent of the land is public, administered by the Southland Conservancy of the New Zealand Department of Conservation. Of the 10 percent nonpublic land, 8 percent of the island is owned by a trust for the indigenous people (the Rakiura), and the remaining 2 percent is owned by private parties. Because so much of the island is public, there is both the political will and the legal power to ensure that tourism development proceeds without undue environmental harm. Indeed, a recent ten-year "Conservation Management Strategy" has been characterized accurately as a "cautious approach" to permitting the tourism industry to operate on the public land. The island has a tiny population of 360 full-time residents. As of the 1991 census, there were only 220 houses on Stewart Island, only 125 of which were permanently occupied. The population has been slowly declining, especially among the young who seek employ-

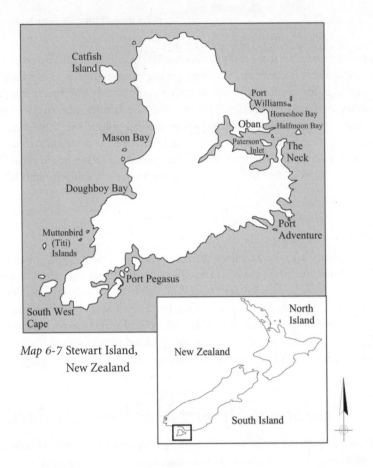

Map 6-7 Stewart Island,
New Zealand

Photo 6-4 Sunset on Stewart Island, New Zealand (Courtesy of Stewart Island Government, New Zealand)

ment elsewhere. For such a small population, it is surprising that there are more than 40 community groups and a wide variety of small businesses, as well as regular air and ferry service with more extensive schedules during the summer months.

There are two basic industries on the island: fishing and tourism. While fishing has historically been the major source of income for the residents of Stewart Island, it is now in a decline, primarily because of government restrictions designed to prevent undue depletion of fish. Tourism, long viewed as the junior and secondary industry, is now growing. As the June 1997 *Stewart Island Tourism Strategy* states hopefully that "(tourism) could well be the predominant source of revenue for the local economy in the foreseeable future."

Local leaders support an increased focus on tourism. E.J. Rooney, Chairman of the Island's Community Board, comments that "(t)he islanders are intrepid Southerners, quick to welcome visitors with hospitable warmth." In fact, Stewart Island was recently named the first New Zealand "Kiwi Host Island," in recognition of the successful training in being cordial to tourists received by many local operators.

Existing Scope of Tourism on Stewart Island

There are a number of varied attractions on the island, including ecotours, scenic tours, hunting, a tiny golf course, a community museum, day-hiking on some of the 245 kilometers of trails, long distance "tramping," and plants and wildlife (especially the large population of brown kiwi, which some believe makes the island the "premier kiwi-spotting location in New Zealand").

Each year there are approximately 24,000 visitors to Stewart Island; some 10,000 of whom are international tourists. There are overnight accommodations for about 300 people in various price ranges and offering various amenities, as well as a few cottages and Department of Conservation "huts" for hikers.

Of considerable concern to area planners and citizens is the fact that the visitor patterns are highly seasonal. Most attractions can be enjoyed only in good weather, which limits most visits to the summer months. This seasonality generates a "boom or bust" dilemma: capacity may be filled in the high season, while the winter months see widespread reductions of service levels and even shut-downs because of shrinking demand. This extreme seasonality results in a low level of business profitability, an unsteady income stream for workers in the tourism industry, and a natural reluctance of potential investors to allocate capital to the industry.

The estimated economic contribution of Stewart Island's tourism industry is NZ $8 million per year, which translates into NZ $21,000 per resident. Researcher Ellen Lim estimated in 1991 that every NZ $40,000 in New Zealand tourism revenues produced one full-time job. In the case of Stewart Island, tourism revenues would be equivalent to 202 positions, including both on- and off-island jobs. However, only about 67 on-island, full-time jobs are supported by tourism. This figure reflects the New Zealand Tourist Board's estimate of two tourism related jobs off-island for every on-island position, a division of benefits that is caused by the need for extensive off-island support services to back up on-island activities.

A New Strategy to Improve Tourism Opportunities

In 1998, the Southland District Council, the local territorial authority for Stewart Island, and the New Zealand Tourism Board formally recognized a plan for sustainable tourism development for Stewart Island tourism. Extensive interviews with many local residents and a public comment submission process had followed release of a first draft of the Stewart Island Tourism Strategy. Citizen opinions varied considerably, especially because many of the islanders fall within one of three lifestyle groups, each with different fundamental interests: fishermen, tourism operators, and those embracing an alternative culture on a small island. The final strategy document reflects many of the public comments.

Although the strategy has a number of interrelated elements, the principal thrust is to extend the visitor season and to encourage those visitors who do come to spend more per capita. The ambitious goal is to increase international tourism growth rates from 3 percent in 1997 to 8 percent in 2001 and domestic growth rates from 1.5 to 3 percent during the same period. This would produce an estimated total number of visitors in 2001 of 29,169 (a five-year increase of 5,169). The revenue goals are likewise ambitious and call for an increase of 42.5 percent from NZ $8.1 million to NZ $11.5 million by 2001. This would result in 29 additional on-island jobs. Researcher Ellen Lim calculates that, because of the "multiplier effect," the additional NZ $3.4 million in annual tourism revenues might well have a total direct and indirect economic benefit of NZ $8.36 million. "The tour operator spends part of his income in the restaurant which uses some of the money to pay the waitress who buys her groceries in a store," thus spreading the economic benefits to a greater number of people.

To achieve its goals, the strategy presents a number of components. Three of the most significant are the installation of a sewer system, better coordination among and interconnections within the island's tourism industry members, and use of targeted marketing strategies to attract more tourists.

Infrastructure Improvements

The strategy document recognizes that without prompt installation of the island's first modern sewage disposal system, the proposed comprehensive tourism measures will fail. The absence of a sewer system has had a number of very serious consequences. First, the individual systems (septic tanks, outfalls, or chemical toilets) were often substandard and were overloaded during rainy periods and also during the peak summer visitor season in the summer. The results were as predictable as unpleasant: sewage rising to the surface and producing foul odors throughout the populated area. Second, absence of adequate sewage treatment had a decidedly negative impact on visitor perceptions. New Zealand generally, and Stewart Island in particular, were noted for and marketed in terms of environmental sensitivity and standards. Upon arrival, however, visitors soon realized the incongruence between the "green" image and the reality of inadequate sewage disposal. Third, most overnight accommodations were able to offer only shared bathrooms, which limited the number of potential visitors, many of whom desire and expect greater privacy and convenience. Finally, the regional government had understandably been reluctant to issue Resource Consents to allow for upgradings and new construction, until a sewage system was on line to support such development. New Zealand Tourism Board official Sarah McLauchlan notes that some islanders fear that now that the sewer system is in place, Resource Consents will follow and one or more large resort hotels will be permitted to be built, to the detriment of the island's small-scale, slow-paced style.

Improved Coordination among Members of the Tourism Industry

Coordination among operators on Stewart Island is poor. Currently each performs marketing and reservation functions separately. Some measure of centralization (for example, providing better quality promotional materials and reservation staff for shared use) could decrease expenses and increase revenues. Another difficulty is the failure to coordinate schedules and activities, which too often produces a "disjointed experience" for visitors. Not only is this a negative feature for those affected tourists, but it results in a poor word-of-mouth promotion of the island. One example mentioned in the strategy document is an obvious need (not yet met because of the inflexible hours of operation of the principal restaurant) for food service facilities to be open at convenient hours to allow visitors to eat before taking scheduled sightseeing ferry trips. (A hungry traveler is not a happy one.) The community museum is also open for short and inconvenient hours for tourists; those hours could easily be coordinated to take account of tour and ferry schedules. Finally, there is no overall accommodation guide for the island, a clear need if the industry is to expand and operate efficiently.

Targeted Marketing Techniques

The strategy document proposes a "target marketing" approach to extend the visitor season to shoulder and winter months (summer months are at very high capacity usage already, and the most practical way to expand tourism during that portion of the year would be to increase capacity). The strategy is very clear about this approach: "Target marketing is identifying what potential visitors want and matching those needs with the island's competitive advantages. The main benefit of targeting markets is that by tightly relating the product to the market, development and advertising costs can be reduced and the productivity of the advertising increased." A number of tourist markets might find Stewart Island appealing if it adopts new approaches and expands it product. For example, one potential market is a purely domestic one that currently goes mainly to the "honey-pots" on the North and South Islands: those seeking a quiet weekend away from work pressures, who would probably respond well to a well-coordinated package of high-quality accommodations and all-inclusive meal service, together with such optional activities such as a bus tour, kiwi viewing, and a short trek. Another potential market are special interest groups of international as well as domestic tourists who could be attracted to the island if it developed such new attractions as a competition to hunt the prolific white-tailed deer, a volunteer program to create conservation projects or a "College for Senior Citizens" educational opportunity. Other promising markets are those needing group retreat facilities (e.g., school groups, conference tie-ins, and business training operations) and the growing "Nostalgia Tourism" market ("tourism to places where people spent time in their youth or to places that have facilities and/or an atmosphere that reminds them of experiences they had in their youth").

Closing Comments

The Stewart Island initiative is an integrated, multifaceted program designed to increase the size and scope of the existing nature-based offerings. It recognizes that attracting tourists from New Zealand's other popular destinations necessitates some "hard" infrastructure improvements and some "soft" efforts, in this case better coordination among tourism operators and specialized marketing techniques to communicate to disparate potential markets how the island's attributes fit the interests of those markets. It strongly recommends careful monitoring to ensure that in the future the carrying capacity of the small island is not exceeded.

Unfortunately, although the strategy includes measurable financial and employment goals, there seems to have been little analysis of the relation of the cost of providing necessary facilities and infrastructure to the hoped for economic benefits (i.e., whether this is an efficient way to spend public resources). Nor has the issue of whether the natural characteristics of the island could be sustained under more intensive tourism been adequately studied. Stewart Island supports a large number of rare species of flora and fauna as well as the brown kiwi. Its hiking trails wander through rainforests, wetlands, and along coastlines and are much more fragile than tracks on the South and North Islands. Despite the fact that one of the goals of the strategy is to safeguard the environment, there appear to be no data on what the expected impacts of additional human intrusion would be.

Although the strategy has been recognized by the local legislative council and the national Tourism Board, it has yet to be implemented as of the time of writing. While the planning process included public comment and the strategy reflects many of the concerns raised by Stewart Island residents, the degree of public support for the initiative is not yet clear. The strategy also relies heavily on voluntary efforts of the tourism businesses to follow environmentally responsible practices. Whether the Tourism Board and the local government will be able to build consensus among the different groups on the island and achieve a high degree of compliance with legally unenforced standards may well determine whether or not the strategy will succeed.

Potential Drawbacks to Dispersal Strategies

Dispersal strategies have worked well for Languedoc-Roussillon, Canterbury, and the Maldives. Nevertheless, no matter how many benefits tourism brings to a community or country, no matter how many salutary effects it produces, there can be negative consequences as well. When a community perceives tourism as having pernicious social, moral, or religious influences on the resident population, it may well decide to restrict tourism development as much as possible so that the feared harmful influences will be contained. Not every community wants to experience the kinds of changes that Corfu has undergone, where in 1989 an older woman, covered in the widow's traditional black dress and scarf, manned a ticket table on the beach for the "Ecstasy Disco," recently completed next to a white, domed shrine.

Reluctance to disperse tourism is certainly reflected in the 1983 First National Development Plan adopted by the South Pacific Island of Vanuatu. "(The) government will seek, through involvement in planning the development of the sector, to limit the impact of tourism on cultural and traditional lifestyles of the island communities. . . . The future development of tourism will occur mainly (in certain listed locations). Elsewhere it will be developed only after full consultation and agreement has been reached with the local people." A similar attitude is reflected in the 1981–1985 Development Plan for the island of Fiji. "The islands which constitute (the Eastern Division of three small islands) face specific problems and display very different needs. The social and cultural context of island life and the potential impact of tourism necessitate a more controlled approach to the development of any tourism facilities (here than is the case elsewhere on Fiji)."[23]

A second drawback to dispersal strategies relates to the fact that they are often instigated by communities trying to alleviate tourist pressures. One destination community is experiencing overcrowding because of the number of tourists and wishes to divert some of those visitors to another destination. A dispersal strategy clearly may meet that community's needs. The issue is whether it also meets the needs of the *receiving* community to which the tourists are being diverted. No tourism development is without possible negative impacts, and every community needs to consider carefully whether the benefits that tourism brings will outweigh its burdens. The fact that one destination wishes to adopt a dispersal strategy to alleviate negative impacts it is experiencing, is not sufficient reason for another community to embark on tourism development to accept the overflow. The strategy should prove beneficial to *all* the communities involved, and not simply solve one problem while creating another elsewhere.

Dispersal approaches are also frequently more costly to implement than other options. When development is spread out over a wide area, it usually requires significant improvements to infrastructure, as it does in Stewart Island. Roads need to be built, and often airports as well. Electrical lines, water pipes, and sewage treatment plants need to be put in place. Such upgradings may benefit various existing communities, but their upfront costs are substantial. Without special funding, many destinations may not be able to afford to implement a dispersal strategy.

There are also potential environmental drawbacks to dispersal strategies. Instead of having a single large airport hub with concentrated levels of noise and air pollution, for example, dispersal often results in multiple, smaller airports, each bringing a level of pollution to a new area. Each new airport and road covers more land with concrete, affecting water tables as well as aesthetics. Garbage disposal and sewage treatment facilities need to be up-to-date if they are to protect the environment where new development occurs. As development spreads, it may extend into areas that are more sensitive—prime agricultural land, wildlife habitats, or shorelines—that need protection rather than development.

Dispersal strategies, particularly when they are regional in scope, can have practical difficulties as well. The successful development of the Languedoc coast, which began before the Riviera was overwhelmed by crowds, took years of careful planning and phased implementation. Developing new tourist destinations takes skill, financial resources, and the cooperative efforts of government, businesses, and citizens. When dispersal strategies affect large areas, they are complex and often challenging to adopt and implement. They do not offer a "quick fix" to a crisis situation.

Dispersal strategies are also inherently chancy. For these approaches to be effective, tourists must opt to visit a new destination. Marketing can play a major role in making a strategy successful, but even the best advertising agency cannot predict all the vagaries that attach to tourism.

Concentration Strategies

In many ways the converse of the *dispersal* strategies, *concentration* strategies centralize tourism in particular locations and in some cases at particular times of the year. Even without efforts to encourage concentration, there is an inherent tendency for it to occur. Blockbuster attractions like the Acropolis in Athens, the Forbidden City in Beijing, and the Grand Canyon in Arizona draw large numbers of tourists, who may travel long distances essentially to see that one attraction and whatever else is interesting nearby. In the normal pattern, restaurants, souvenir shops, tourist accommodations, and auxiliary attractions develop in the immediate vicinity of a "honeypot" to take advantage of the heavy pedestrian and vehicular traffic. This promotes improvements to transportation and other infrastructure elements; soon more tourists visit, because the destination provides such a broad range of attractions and facilities, conveniently located. More visitors mean more opportunities for businesses to capitalize on an existing market, and the concentration pattern continues.

Concentration occurs naturally in other locations as well. On many islands, there are few attractions other than the beaches; in many mountainous regions, there are a limited number of things for the visitor to do beyond outdoor sports on the slopes. These types of tourist destinations are not only concentrated spatially, they are also concentrated temporally: beach vacations require sunshine and warmth, while ski trips need snow. Most of the tourist-oriented tavernas and accommodations on the Greek islands are closed by October or early November, because the beaches have no appeal in cold, wet weather. Ski slopes, whether in the U.S. Rockies or the Swiss Alps, are much less used during the summer months.

Any destination that is subject to major climactic shift is also prone to seasonal concentrations if the tourism occurs out-of-doors. Tourism drops dramatically in Bali during the rainy season. Many of the roads in Glacier National Park in Montana, U.S.A., don't even open until the snows melt, usually in June. And excursions to Ouarzazate and Zagora in the Moroccan Sahara are undertaken only by the bravest (or most foolhardy) visitor during the summer months. "Concentrations in both space and time . . . seem inherent to tourism."[24]

Quite aside from the natural tendencies that generate intensification of visitor uses, there are a number of reasons why a community might elect as a matter of public policy to take active steps to concentrate tourism.

A Classic Concentration Model: Cancun, Mexico

One of the world's best-known beach resorts began in 1969 as the first effort of a newly created Mexican governmental entity to increase the economic rewards of tourism and to improve the living standards of many of its poorest citizens. The 30-year story of Cancun's beginnings and development is a remarkable and important example of how governmental planning and implementation can produce economic benefit in a concentrated setting.[25]

Cancun is a barrier island in the Caribbean Sea, which is easily accessible to both U.S. and European tourists. (See Map 6-8.) The island is blessed by two beautiful and large lagoons on its landward side. There is a natural causeway permitting access for vehicles from the mainland. When first considered for resort development, few people lived on the 15-by-quarter mile island, in large part because of its lack of agricultural productivity, but the beach dunes spreading toward the blue Caribbean provided a perfect location for sun and sand resort activities. The weather for these popular pursuits could not be better: there are no extremes of temperature, the temperature averages 81 degrees Fahrenheit, and there are on average 243 cloudless and sunny days per year.

FONATUR, a tourism development arm of the Ministry of Tourism, was the lead governmental agency in the creation and management of Cancun. It procured a US $21.5 million financing from the Inter-American Development Bank for half of the costs of infrastructure designed to serve tourists, as well as residents (current and future) in a "service city" to be constructed on the mainland. The funding source was interested principally in assisting Mexicans who would live and work near the project site.

In acquiring and developing thousands of acres of land, FONATUR officials recognized that the undertaking was large and potentially problematic: "We took a great risk. (We learned, however that) we can do anything. We have gained a lot of credibility. We've gone to the moon."[26]

FONATUR was explicit when it chose to adopt a concentration model of tourism development. Guillermo Grimm, in the early 1970s a FONATUR vice president, identified the choices: "We had a choice of providing funds to improve existing resorts or to start new

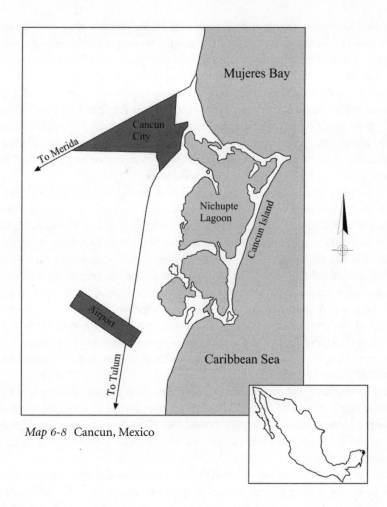

Map 6-8 Cancun, Mexico

resorts with integral master plans."[27] The decision was to try to avoid the haphazard and unsatisfactory private development patterns of the older and then overcrowded, polluted Acapulco on Mexico's Pacific Coast. In the course of doing so, the officials, according to Grimm, desired to provide local access for the first time to modern utilities, education, and a higher standard of living. Tourism development was to be the bridge to social betterment.

Infrastructure construction occurred first. This included a modern international airport, utilities, and roads for the long strip of land leading to the mainland and the service city. This was followed by private development of resort hotels and such ancillary facilities as a convention center, golf courses, shopping, tennis courts, and nightclubs. All private development was governed by a comprehensive master plan.

The master plan designated zones for hotel, commercial, urban, residential, and industrial uses, as well as strictures concerning density, height, bulk, lot coverage, setbacks, and parking. The plan afforded considerable flexibility regarding architectural design (not surprisingly, some structures are now widely criticized as lacking in design quality). Although the newly created municipal government had a number of implementation powers (e.g., issuing building permits and inspecting construction), the principal authority remained FONATUR, which retained authority to decide on all development proposals.

In the 30 years of Cancun's development, much has been accomplished. A prominent guidebook describes contemporary Cancun as "internationally renowned for its magnificent location, its luxurious tourist facilities and the incomparable beauty of its setting, with an exciting seascape of turquoise waters and coconut palms. . . . The daring, yet functional, Cancun architectural complex has fostered rapid development of shops offering imported goods, tourist services, and water sports."[28] One prominent travel writer well captured the ambiance of the island as of 1998: "From the moment it began beckoning to visitors less than 25 years ago, Cancun has been defined by contradictions. In a part of Mexico dominated by ancient Mayan temples, it was envisioned as a modern creation, all glass and concrete and steel. In an area surrounded by nature at its most raw and unspoiled in the form of beaches and jungle, it is a purely man-made place."[29]

Measured by tourist arrivals, the results are stunning: more than 2.5 million Mexican and foreign tourists visit every year; the growth rate from 1990 to 1996 was a very strong 9 percent per year. There are more than 75 daily arriving commercial flights, and a new terminal now assists in accommodating the charter flight arrivals, which represent about 60 percent of the all air arrivals.

From a small fishing village, Cancun is now a service city of roughly 300,000 residents. There are more than 22,000 hotel rooms (more than double the number originally contemplated in the master plan) in 122 often very large structures, with more hotel rooms under construction. The overall yearly hotel occupancy rate is approximately 80 percent. In 1994, a huge new convention and visitor center opened with 150,000 square feet of meeting space and a 6,500-person capacity. Almost a third of Mexico's very substantial tourism revenues originate at Cancun.

At the same time, the project has not been free from controversy. For one thing, many have been highly critical of FONATUR's lack of appropriate concern for the natural environment (e.g., mangroves and wildlife sanctuaries) in planning and implementing the program. Another category of criticism focuses on the ambiance of the highly concentrated developments.

Most of the 122 hotels are clustered along the boulevard that runs the length of the island, as are more than 200 restaurants and numerous stores and a few shopping malls. This atmosphere has prompted many visitors to compare the tone to U.S. tourism centers. Thus, a suburban Massachusetts woman noted that "Cancun is a lot more commercial that I thought it would be. If you want warm weather and don't want to put up with the hassles of being in another country, come to Cancun." Another visitor from rural New York commented that "It's what I thought it would be—Miami Beach."[30] Iowa travel writer Christine Riccelli recommended Cancun as an easy, safe way out of that rural state's harsh winter: ". . . there are things about Cancun—including the very things it's criticized for—that make it an appealing, quick winter getaway for Iowans. It's comfortable, clean, safe, and predictable, has great beaches and is, simply, a way to have a foreign vacation without experiencing the usual inconveniences of foreign travel. You don't have to figure out how to order dinner in Spanish or change dollars into pesos."[31]

Aside from the commercial nature of much of Cancun, the destination has recently been confronted with sometimes unruly U.S. college students thronging to the island during March "Spring Breaks." In part because of the low cost of packaged vacations, Cancun is now the most popular student destination during those weeks, when the average occupancy rate is an astonishing 97 percent, considerably more than the 70 percent otherwise expected. One popular Spring Break site is Daddy-O's Disco triplex, which during that period serves 11,000 drinks per night, often to students who have already had too much alcohol. Fortunately, the establishment arranges for a full-time ambulance with paramedics while this revelry is occurring.[32] To their credit, local officials and businesses have been encouraging the use of signed pledges of good conduct and obedience to local laws and an advertising campaign directed at the students called *Mi Casa Es Su Casa* (My house is your house). Hotel managers believe that the campaign has been "very successful" and should be repeated each year.[33]

Concentration to Preserve "Quieter" Areas Elsewhere

Although many residents of a community may be pleased to benefit directly or indirectly from tourism revenues, they frequently desire to live in neighborhoods that are not defined primarily by tourism. This is especially true in traditional settings where there is a distinct contrast between the social and cultural styles of tourism and local residents. This was well demonstrated in the town of Rethemnos, Crete, which was studied in the high tourism years of the late 1980s by ethnologist Michael Herzfeld.[34] He thoughtfully documents how the local population coped with tourism, a phenomenon that brought great economic progress for many but that also fostered a deep and widespread sense of suspicion and cultural unease.

In the "Old Town" section of Rethemnos, tourism uses came to overwhelm previous activities without any planning or control by governmental officials. Instead, the numbers of visitors prompted the private sector to expand and alter their goods and services to accommodate the tourists. This included adaptation of previous residential uses to commercial purposes, and the rental value of those Old Town locations soared. Local residents moved to quieter, new homes in the "New Town" outside the tourist areas. "Ties with the Old Town do not disappear; they just become more completely commercial. People understand the social consequences of the residential exodus."[35] This concentration of tourism uses in the Old Town was not necessarily unwelcome by those affected by it. "Those whose houses in the Old Town had been extensively refurbished by the historic conservation office could now turn a profit by converting them into tourist boardinghouses. They had, in effect, turned their homes into business premises and were therefore in a position to buy modern homes in the New Town for themselves."[36]

There is, of course, an element of choice at work here. Businesses are not forced to change from providing goods for residents to offering goods for tourists, although the economic incentives for such a shift are often powerful. Nor are local residents forced to move, unless rents increase to such a degree that they can no longer afford to live where tourism now abounds. In most situations, many local people choose to live in places with less congestion and noise (and fewer "different" people) and so move to areas where tourism is less concentrated. Alternatively, some people choose to remain in a tourism enclave. Owners of a late-night restaurant might prefer to live above their establishment rather than travel home late at night. Others might enjoy the lively atmosphere tourism often brings, or the convenience of proximity to shops, restaurants, and entertainment in a highly concentrated tourist setting.

Concentration to Reduce Infrastructure Costs

There is a large body of literature, especially in the field of land-use economics, demonstrating that the provision of human settlement services (for example, roads, water, sewer, fire, and police) is much more costly if settlements are spread out from central areas. Roads leading to a new settlement are expensive, whereas new accommodations in an already builtup area need no additional access routes. Providing sewage treatment to a distant point from the treatment plant involves great cost of extending pipes. Police protection is more costly and less efficient if cars must patrol areas with large distances between them. For these and related reasons, concentration is very often less fiscally costly than dispersion, because it avoids the "sprawl" syndrome.

Concentration to Prevent Perceived Social "Pollution"

Concentrated tourism can be viewed as a multifaceted phenomenon. Luxury tourist resorts are often "islands of affluence" where tourists are pampered and protected from the realities of life for the larger and much poorer country. In these types of situations "(a) tourist enclave then is not just a physical entity but also a social and economic structure."[37] Especially where governments are paternalistic in attempting to prevent social harm to the population, they might choose to adopt policies designed to keep tourists in very controlled settings, segregated from the general population. The Maldives, with a plethora of islands, chose to disperse tourism for this reason; the Indonesian government opted instead to concentrate tourism in a new luxury development at Nusa Dua on the Island of Bali.

Case Study: Nusa Dua, Bali, Indonesia

Following careful national planning and with extensive government involvement, a concentrated, self-contained resort complex of luxury hotels was developed on the island of Bali to serve as the center of tourism.

Bali is a justly famous island in the center section of the largest Islamic nation in the world, the archipelago of Indonesia. Its natural and cultural amenities have made it a tourism magnet since the 1930s, but its tourism exploded after the runway extension of its airport in 1969.

The island is small, just 5,620 square kilometers, with a population of approximately three million. The population is densely packed, leaving the extremely productive and fertile agricultural land for rice growing. Predictable monsoons, supplemented by successful irrigation practices, create reliable growing seasons. Beautiful sandy beaches and coral reefs contrast with the sometimes mountainous interior, offering different and visually rewarding sightseeing opportunities.

The Indonesian national government's policy regarding international tourism, known as "Pariwisata Buday," is grounded on promoting a type of cultural tourism. As described by the Director General of Tourism for Indonesia, Andi Mappi Sammeng, "(t)ourism development strategies are guided by the paramount goal of preserving and promoting local culture. In this way, . . . when the economic vitality generated by tourism is harnessed to real works that raise the standard of living of the population, the quality of its cultural productions also rises. And this in turn generates increased esteem for the culture—among both the local population and visitors alike—and sets a momentum of reciprocal reinforcement."

Bali is indeed blessed with a number of highly developed cultural elements important to tourism. Religious patterns are central to the lives of most Balinese and are also especially fascinating to visitors. The principal religion is a form of Hinduism (as opposed to the Islam practiced by 90 percent of the Indonesians generally), fused with animism, tantric Buddhism, and ancestor worship, a combination surely worthy of being called "vibrant and syncretic." Village and religious life are intertwined, because the Balinese believe that the gods are to be cared for communally. Each village has multiple temples, and families have their own temples as well. People regularly pay honor to the gods, particularly on the anniversary of each of the many temples. Visitors are often able to observe at least part of a religious ceremony, since temples are located in easily visible rice fields.[38]

Balinese music is also appealing to tourists. It is usually played on colorful gamelan—groups of percussion instruments of cymbals and gongs—together with flutes. Dances to the music are often performed by elaborately masked dancers or by shadow puppets.

The architecture of Bali, also of considerable interest to visitors, is usually composed of three elements: an entrance gate, a walled compound, and a pavilion (or several pavilions, open or closed), in which daily activities often occur in the warm outdoors. This appealing architectural pattern is common in homes, temples, and palaces.

1971 Master Plan

The seminal decision of the Indonesian government when it chose Bali as a high-growth tourism area was to extend the airport runway to accommodate international jet flights. That step had an enormous impact: between 1969 and 1975, air arrival tourists grew by an astonishing 27.5 percent per year, to 202,000; an additional 70,000 or so visitors arrived by sea in 1975. The boom had begun.

The government commissioned a Master Plan for tourism development, funded by the United Nations Development Program and executed by the World Bank. That plan, adopted as official policy in 1972, calculated that by 1985 there would be about 730,000 visitors, a huge number that was deemed to far exceed Bali's social carrying capacity. In fact, it was feared that such a high level of tourism would severely harm the culture that had developed over hundreds of years. Accordingly, the planners proposed a dual approach: a *concentration* strategy to encourage the construction of about 7,000 hotel rooms in one new location, Nusa Dua, and, at the same time, *expansions* of permits for tourism developments on the other island areas of Kuta and Sanur. According to the Bali Tourism Development Corporation (BTDC), the Sanur and Kuta areas were "tiny pockets of tourism . . . (that would be) allowed to develop spontaneously." Such spontaneous development was not without risks, and by 1993 the mood of Kuta was frenetic. Travel writer Bette Duke wrote that "(t)he beach town of Kuta has become a frat house for surfers, its traffic-jammed main street strung with banners advertising 'pub crawls.'"[39]

The principal recommendation of the 1971 Master Plan was extensive governmental involvement in a large pocket of new development. As characterized by the BTDC, "the centerpiece of the Plan (was) the creation of a huge, self-contained tourist resort complex geared to high international standards, from which tourists would visit specially designated sites around the island on excursion trips." There were multiple purposes of this concentration approach: first, to protect Balinese culture by attempting to minimize contact of tourists with residents in the interior of the island; second, to centralize the infrastructure construction and development guideline enforcement efforts; and finally, to spread economic benefit to residents and villages in the interior, where attractions could be viewed on a day-trip basis without perceived sociocultural harm that could come from overnight tourism.

The Selection and Development
of the Nusa Dua Peninsula

Nusa Dua in Balinese means "two islands," a suitable name for that arid peninsula of roughly hour-glass shape in southeastern Bali. (See Map 6-9 and Photo 6-5.) This site was chosen for resort concentration in Indonesia because of several advantages: proximity to the newly expanded international airport; isolation from most Balinese population centers and from other existing tourism developments; and proximity to a provincial center that could be enlarged into a "service town" for employees once electricity, sewage treatment, and road infrastructure improvements were completed. The site was also an excellent location for the contemplated beach-oriented resorts, with sandy soils, sunny conditions, and coral reefs to shelter the beach areas from the sometimes turbulent ocean. Additionally, there was a good natural harbor nearby, which could be improved to make it a marine port of entry as well as a departure site for water sports and day cruises. Finally, the agricultural value of the Nusa Dua peninsula was limited because of the sandy soil; only low-value coconut groves would need to be removed to permit the resort projects.

The quiet setting of Nusa Dua changed dramatically, but on a slower pace than was originally anticipated. Extensive infrastructure work preceded the buildings, and it was not until 1980 that the first hotel broke ground. That 450-unit facility was opened three years later. By 1991, seven other five-star hotels had opened. Then by 1994, the BTDC had leased out all 11 of the large parcels of land, and the room capacity of the then existing hotels amounted to 3,700. In response to a growing convention market, Nusa Dua expanded to include a large international convention center, which opened in 1991, with two associated hotel resorts and a meeting capacity of 2,500 persons.

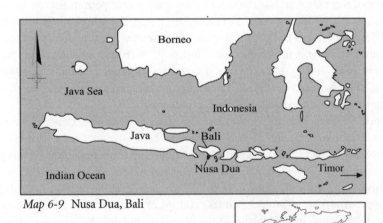

Map 6-9 Nusa Dua, Bali

Photo 6-5 Aerial view of Nusa Dua, Bali (Courtesy of Bali Tourism Development Corporation, Nusa Dua, Bali)

Governmental Tourism Development and Management Philosophy

Nusa Dua embodies one of Indonesia's principal tourism development philosophies. As explained by the Director General of Tourism, "(b)y its integrated design reflecting the architecture and traditional crafts of the island, it reaffirms the cultural character of the local population and provides a venue for the presentation of its arts." The BTDC, with plenary authority over the construction process, adopted a set of architectural design guidelines requiring such elements as open modular design and use of local building materials (e.g., terra cotta for roof tiles). An architectural board was created and empowered to review particular proposed designs to ensure consistency with established criteria. Building could not exceed a maximum density of 50 rooms per hectare, with a maximum building coverage of 30 percent of the lot. The BTDC also specified height limits (with a building height no higher than a coconut tree, or a maximum of 15 meters) and beach and building setbacks (about 25 meters).

The Nusa Dua concentration approach meets another stated government objective: "As a collaboration between government and the private sector, it encourages investment while permitting a coordinated development of infrastructures for the benefit of the local population as well." More specifically, the role of the BTDC from its creation in 1973 (soon after adoption of the 1971 Master Tourism Plan) has been to be the *single agency* to supervise the development and management of Nusa Dua. It negotiates with developers, pursues the necessary infrastructure installations, and in general acts as a permitting and enforcement authority before completion of construction. Additionally, it is responsible for maintaining the infrastructure and all landscaping, security systems, and transportation among the hotels. It also attempts to encourage strong relationships between hotel operators and nearby villages and operates an employment-training center.

Significantly, Nusa Dua is exclusively a "high-end," five-star resort enclave, reflecting another of the national government's goals: "As a tourist resort of international hotels and facilities of the highest quality, it sets the standard for future development in other regions of Indonesia." One good example of the type of development on Nusa Dua is Amanusa, one of three upscale resorts on Bali owned by the same company, Hong Kong's Aman resorts. A 15-minute drive from the international airport, Amanusa was completed in 1992. It has 35 detached pavilions, each of which has a sleeping/living section divided by a native stone wall from a very large bath and dressing area. Many of the pavilions have private pools, and all have a front garden and rear patio with an outdoor dining table.

The Four Seasons Resort, completed in 1993, has 147 private villas, pleasantly situated on a gentle hill overlooking the water. Constructed of traditional materials, the complex has extensive locally carved wood and stone.[40] Local citizens also play an important (and originally unsolicited) role in integrating the Four Seasons into Balinese religious and cultural traditions. When the hotel first opened, holy people would quietly appear on the grounds three times a day to prepare offerings to the gods. "Quickly, the hotel management realized the necessity of honoring local traditions, then the shamans, offering-givers and masseurs, the ritual dancers and those who play sacred music, as well as the cooks aware of the spiritual significance of the spices in each dish—became as indispensable as the doormen."[41]

Closing Comments

The Indonesian national government is understandably pleased with the Nusa Dua planning and implementation. The BTDC has apparently succeeded in its goals of developing a very high-end enclave, whose design reflects the artistic heritage of the island, and improving the infrastructure of nearby villages. However, international corporations own and operate the resorts, with inevitable issues of control and economic leakage. With the influx of large numbers of tourists, the demand on natural resources has dramatically increased, with a concomitant growth in disposal needs. Coastal erosion is a further problem.

It is also not clear whether traditional values have been protected. The Nusa Dua developments are all luxury resorts, affordable to only a small segment of the tourist market (it is sometimes referred to as the "Golden Ghetto"). Less affluent tourists, as well as those who prefer not to be isolated from Balinese society, still visit the island, and many stay in the old artists' colony of Ubud, now filled with the ubiquitous T-shirt shops and souvenir stalls.

Professor Geoffrey Wall and S. Dibnah note that as of 1996, there had been no systematic evaluation of the impacts of the impressive Nusa Dua developments. Nonetheless, the future may well bring additional use of concentration strategies in the country. The BTDC has engaged in other activities outside of Bali itself, participating in some development projects (in Sulawesi Utara and Irian Jaya) and consulting in others (in Jawa Tengah and Sumatra Barat).

Additionally, a "sister-agency," the Lombok Tourism Development Corporation, is planning to develop tourism resorts patterned generally after the Nusa Dua concept, along five different beaches on the island of Lombok, roughly 100 kilometers from Bali. Whether responsible governmental officials can apply the Nusa Dua, Bali, experience to Lombok may well determine the future of that island.

Concentrated tourism development at Nusa Dua was created according to a government adopted plan in an area that was almost free of tourism 30 years ago. The challenges and opportunities for government direction and control are vastly different in *well-established* tourist destinations. While Canterbury chose a dispersal approach to alleviate the impacts of congestion, another medieval European city (discussed below) chose a concentration strategy, combined with traffic management techniques, to solve its congestion problems.

Case Study: Bruges, Belgium

Faced with an unacceptable influx of tourist automobile traffic in narrow roads originally designed for horsecarts, this medieval European city adopts a tourism concentration model, supplemented by a traffic control plan and shifts in its marketing focus.

Bruges is Belgium's eighth largest city, with approximately 130,000 inhabitants. (See Map 6-10.) Its principal noteworthy feature is a small, well-preserved medieval center city, char-

Map 6-10 Bruges, Belgium

Photo 6-6 Clock tower and statue in center of Bruges, Belgium (Courtesy of Deiter Dewulf, Toerisme Brugge)

acterized by interesting architecture, meandering canals, narrow streets and passageways, and a broad stock of restaurants, small shops, and cultural establishments. In the 1950s, writer Pamela Hansford Johnson lauded the qualities of Bruges in the pages of the prominent fashion magazine *Vogue:* "In Bruges you walk, you sit about, you lose time—not waste it, simply lose it, like a handkerchief or pencil out of your pocket. It is the quietest place under the sun; to slip within it is to slip within the pages of a Book of Hours."[42]

The center city functions well, both as a place for visitors and for the local population, in part because of early efforts at maintaining quality and historical authenticity. (See Photo 6-6.) In the article mentioned earlier, Johnson also remarked about the "restrictive laws to control dangerous flights of fancy: neon-light signs and enameled advertising plates are banned on facades within the periphery of the old city, and a shopkeeper contemplating a new awning must submit to the city authority a sample of the textile he has in mind. When they re-build, it is with care."[43] But the continued vitality and quality of the center city was placed in some doubt by the early 1990s, largely due to the yearly increases in visitor numbers and the resultant traffic.

1992 Study Identifies Serious Problems

By 1990, considerable local opposition had developed to continued tourism growth in Bruges. Two years later, a respected provincial planning organization, the Westvlaams Ekonomisch Studiebureau (WES), issued a comprehensive report on the fragility of the tourism sector and its impact on the quality of life of citizens of the city. The report noted the sharp increases of two types of tourists in Bruges: those who stay overnight for at least one night in the city, and day visitors. Overnight stays had more than doubled between

1975 and 1991; day-trips had increased by an alarming 370 percent during that same period. Additionally, 60 percent of these tourists traveled to Bruges by car. The WES report concluded that the growth and automobile-dependent character of tourism of all types undermined the quality of life, especially in the small, highly concentrated center city, whose street pattern had evolved in medieval times, long before the advent of motorized vehicles. Tourism and its traffic were having a "baleful" effect on the environment, inhibiting the mobility of both inhabitants and visitors to the city center and interfering with normal urban functioning.

The report also differentiated the socioeconomic impacts of the two types of Bruges tourists. Overnighters had different characteristics than day visitors. Although there were fewer overnighters (540,000 per year versus 2.2 million day visitors), overnighters tended to spend more locally, have a more positive employment impact (944 man-years versus 637 man-years for day visitors), be better spread over the entire calendar year (as opposed to day visitors, who tended to visit only at peak seasons), be somewhat less dependent on automobile use (thus creating fewer traffic and parking problems), and be more culturally oriented (day visitors tended to spend much of their time shopping). Additionally, the growth pattern for the overnight market was more stable than the booming, but erratically growing, day visitor market.

The WES report proposed a two-pronged strategy to manage the growth in tourism and its negative impacts. First and most importantly, the report identified a tourism concentration model that would ensure that tourism would remain largely restricted to the current tourist center, the cultural hub of Bruges, rather than spread to other residential areas of the city. A sophisticated traffic control plan would eliminate much of the existing congestion and safeguard the quality of life for inhabitants of the historical center. Second, the report proposed new marketing efforts to stimulate overnight tourism. This would achieve desired economic benefits while limiting actual tourist numbers.

Traffic Control Plan for a Concentration Model

The new traffic control plan, developed to promote the touristic concentration model, encompassed five aims: "The stimulation of the traffic flow within the city centre; the restriction of through traffic in the city centre; the discouragement of the use of the car as the best means of transport to reach the centre; the increase of the mobility of bicyclists; (and) the accessibility of administrative, socio-cultural and economic entities as well as the traffic within the centre for the inhabitants."[44]

The 1992 traffic plan completely changed the previous traffic system. Since 1978, Bruges had a loop system of traffic with its central connecting point, the Market Square, located in the city center. The new system, on the other hand, banned vehicles from the central Market Square. Five loops divert traffic from the center area, toward a number of previously existing parking lots on the periphery, as well as several newly constructed lots in strategically significant locations. These five loops are not interconnected; in fact, such interconnection is impossible by reason of one-way streets in some areas and extensive vehicular bans in others, with some limited exceptions for taxis and bicycles. An increased emphasis on public bus transportation to the city center supplements the traffic restrictions. There are now more bus stops, served by smaller, newer buses, with greater frequency.

Another necessary supplemental measure was the improvement and expansion of available parking spaces, so that visitors could easily and safely leave their vehicles outside of the concentrated central city, while enjoying its many amenities principally on foot or bicycle. Guarded underground garages now provide 4,300 parking spaces. This has allowed the city to implement a restricted on-street parking system in some neighborhoods where parking is limited to permanent residents. To deal with aesthetic and environmental drawbacks of large numbers of tour buses taking up above-ground parking spaces, the city created a 150-bus parking facility within walking and mini-bus distance of the city center. Day and other visitors without their own cars can arrive in a large tour bus, and then transfer to a less intrusive means of travel to the cultural and other attractions in the core area. Some connections between modes of transport are free. There have been moves to create a package of public transport (thus eliminating the need for private cars) between visitor origination points within Belgium and some other nearby countries. This idea has good promise in light of the fact that 70 percent of all visitors originate in these areas. Finally, public signage improvements are ongoing, directing visitors from the car or tour bus parking facilities to the center and also to sites within the center.

Marketing Efforts to Promote the Concentration Model

The traffic control plan is by far the most significant element of Bruges' concentration strategy because it enhances the aesthetic experience in the core and creates feasible ways of getting to and from that area. The second most important element is the increase in marketing efforts of inner city hotels, to target overnight tourists and convention and conference markets. The Bruges Sales and Meetings Guide is an elaborate, 53-page, multicolored, multilingual publication that emphasizes the many core city cultural and sightseeing opportunities. Admitting that many European "congress towns" offer convention facilities, the Guide asks: "What more does Bruges offer then? The unique character and the special charm of a historical city . . . with traditions!" The most well-equipped conference center in the city is billed as a "unique congress center right in the heart of the historic inner city"; a fine restoration of a nineteenth-century hospital is now called the "Art and Congress Center." Almost all of the three- and four-star hotels participating in the "Partners of Meeting in Bruges" program are in the central core area. The guide also appeals to the shopping interests of potential conference attendees, identifying the "main shopping streets . . . between the Market Square and the old city gates," creating an appealing image of quality preservation and reuse of historic structures. Several regularly scheduled "market days" in the central city are also highlighted, appealing to photographers and cooks, as well as shoppers.

The 1992 WES report proposed not only the encouragement of overnight visitors, but also the de-emphasis of day visitors as a marketing strategy. The report concluded that there were too many day visitors in the overall mix, who spent less, were car-dependent, and whose visits were seasonal. Overnight visitors would bring economic benefits, without significantly aggravating traffic problems, and without overwhelming the Center City at peak seasons. This decision not to promote day visits meant dropping participation in some promotions of the Flemish Tourist Board and the Belgian Railways.

Closing Comments

The Bruges concentration model was well thought out and has a few clear foci: discouragement of tourism that would spread into residential neighborhoods outside the old center city; traffic control measures; and marketing to generate more overnight stays and to reduce the number of day-trippers. One of its greatest strengths is the fact that the policy was based on clear data. Bruges knew more about the habits of its visitors than most destinations do. It was therefore able to develop a plan whose elements were designed to address specific patterns of behavior of particular types of tourists.

Whether the targeted marketing efforts will achieve the hoped for results is not yet clear. If not, then the traffic control mechanisms may not be sufficient either. Assessing the relative success of this well-crafted program must await more study. Three academics who spent time in Bruges in the mid-1990s, however, offered some sobering thoughts:

> Bruges has developed . . . (firm) spatial and programming policies based on a detailed knowledge of the visitor market. In doing so, it is creating a distinct product which will require a high level of investment, management, and regular upgrading. Although day visitors are not to be encouraged further, it is not clear how current overcrowding in central sites is to be diffused. It is also unclear whether disincentives will, eventually, be required to reduce the unfavoured day visitor.[45]

Nusa Dua was constructed under a national tourism plan, as a brand new, concentrated tourism location. Bruges combined management techniques and targeted marketing efforts to alleviate negative impacts of increasing tourism numbers. The situation facing New York City (see below) was drastically different. Years of physical deterioration, changed use, and sleaze had degraded its world famous Times Square. Here, revitalization efforts focused on recapturing concentrated tourist-related opportunities.

Case Study: Times Square, New York

Through a combination of zoning regulations, government financing, and the efforts of a voluntary organization of businesses, Times Square has been revitalized in its historic role as a concentrated center of tourism.

Times Square's self-adopted nickname of The Crossroads of the World seemed sadly self-mocking as recently as the late 1980s. Prostitutes, pimps, peep shows, three-card-monte scam artists, and XXX-rated stores lined the streets. Sleaze, drugs, and crime were the order of the day as well as the night; fewer and fewer native New Yorkers or tourists ventured through the area once known for its vibrancy and excitement. Times Square was in danger of dying.

Background

Following the real estate collapse in New York City in the late 1960s and the later recession, many owners of newly constructed high-rise towers around Times Square were forced into bankruptcy, and office and first floor retail space stood vacant. "Adult" establishments moved in, paying a higher rent than the owners of T-shirt shops could afford. Home-video technology made it possible for the sex-related retailers to sell cheap X-rated videocassettes, and Times Square now provided a new product for a very old demand. Theaters languished and many of their historic buildings deteriorated. Businesses catering to local residents and visiting families either folded or moved out of town to more congenial surroundings, while peep shows and massage parlors replaced them. Prostitutes walked the streets, drug use and crime increased, and the downward spiral continued.

Then in the early 1990s, a combination of private and public initiatives sparked what appears to be the successful revitalization of Times Square. In 1992, the Times Square Business Improvement District (BID) was formed; a few years later, New York City passed strong zoning laws prohibiting the clustering of sex-related businesses; the city worked with the Disney Company, offering incentives to lure the Magic Kingdom and its wholesome inhabitants to Times Square; and city and state funding is helping support new theatrical activity.

The Times Square Business Improvement District

The BID is composed of approximately 400 property owners and 5,000 businesses and organizations that have "voluntarily" joined together in a self-taxing agency that collects money from all the members to be used for the improvement of the district. (At least 51 percent of the owners and businesses in an area must sign a petition in order for a BID to be established.) The district itself stretches from 40th Street to 53rd Street on the West Side of Manhattan between Sixth and Eighth Avenues, encompassing the city's famous Broadway Theater District. (See Map 6-11.) Working in collaboration with city agencies, private businesses, community boards, and not-for-profit groups, and with an annual bud-

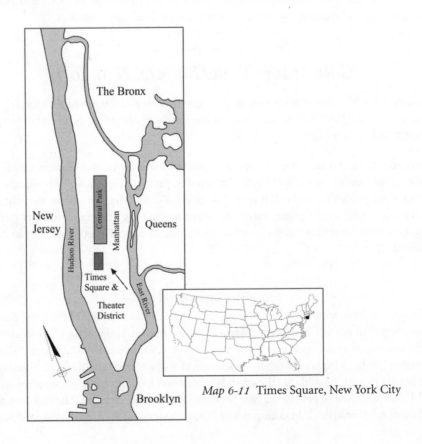

Map 6-11 Times Square, New York City

get of US $6 million, the BID has focused its efforts on making Times Square "clean, safe, and friendly."

Public Safety

One of the initial targets of the BID was improvement of public safety. The BID hired its own security staff of 40 officers who are connected by radio to the New York Police Department. These officers patrol the district streets from 10:00 A.M. to midnight, every day of the year. There are two security booths staffed by BID security people from 10:00 A.M. to midnight, a computerized watchman system at 45 different locations, daily jeep and bike patrols (weather permitting), and increased lighting near sidewalks and landmark buildings. The New York Police Department has increased its coverage of the district, and a special program allows NYPD officers to make arrests of alleged illegal peddlers on the basis of affidavits signed by BID security officers. Crime fell almost 47 percent between 1993 and 1996, and the notorious three-card-monte games decreased by 80 percent.

Although they did not necessarily pose a threat, the high number of homeless people on the streets who were also either abusing drugs or suffering from a mental illness did create a negative image. The BID secured federal and state funding for a pilot project developed by a social service agency operating in the Times Square district to address the needs of "service resistant homeless." Between this supportive approach and the more aggressive one occasionally adopted by some of the security officers of "encouraging" street people to move on a few blocks to another area, the number of visible homeless people has diminished.

Sanitation

A second focus of BID was on cleanliness of the district. The BID has hired, and dressed in designer uniforms with a Times Square logo, a sanitation force of 50 workers who work from 6:00 A.M. to 10:00 P.M. seven days a week, removing graffiti, painting street furniture, scrubbing sidewalks, and removing trash. They have even created a "sting" known as Operation Shutterbug: periodically photographic expeditions scour the district late at night to document "egregious" sanitation violations and, armed with picture proof, work with businesses to solve their garbage management issues.

Promoting Tourism

To make the Times Square district a friendlier spot for tourists, the BID established a Visitor and Transit Information Center, which was located in the historic Selwyn Theater on 42nd Street until the building collapsed late in 1997. It has recently been moved to the restored Embassy Theater, a 1925 movie theater complete with marble lobby and ornate woodwork, on Broadway between 46th and 47th Streets. The BID also provides a free, weekly walking tour of Times Square; produces the annual New Year's Eve celebration for which Times Square has been known for generations; offers a free annual summer concert of Broadway musicals; holds an annual Taste of Times Square with food from prominent restaurants; and publishes and distributes restaurant, hotel, and visitor guides.

The Role of Government

While the BID was becoming an increasing presence in the Times Square area in the early 1990s, the city government also became more active. The city condemned some of the buildings it had planned to bulldoze years before, and once again it tackled the problem of regulating the rampant pornography of Times Square. In 1993, the Department of City Planning did a study of the impact of "adult" uses throughout the five boroughs of the city. In 1965, only nine adult entertainment establishments existed in the city; by 1976, the number had increased to 151; by 1993, the number was 177. The BID had done its own study, which concluded that while the Times Square area could support some adult establishments, the increasing number of such uses and their concentration on Eighth Avenue posed a threat to "commercial prosperity and residential stability."

In November 1994, the City Council imposed a one-year moratorium prohibiting the establishment or expansion of stores selling adult books, videotapes, or magazines; topless or nude bars; and adult theaters showing films, videotapes, or live sex shows. Then in 1995, the city passed a new zoning law, prohibiting the clustering of porn purveyors by requiring a distance of at least 500 feet between any adult use and school, day care center, house of worship, residence, or other adult use. The law also imposes the 500-foot distancing requirement between adult uses and most zoning districts in which new residential use is permitted. The law thus effectively permits new adult businesses to locate only in the dense commercial and industrial zones that do not include residential uses.

The law also regulates adult uses in an attempt to limit the negative impact a single use can have on the immediate neighborhood. It restricts the maximum size of any adult establishment to 10,000 square feet; allows only one adult use per zoning lot; and regulates the size, placement, and illumination of signs, although not their content. Since the law's enactment, the number of porn shops in Times Square has dropped from 47 to fewer than 15.

Finally, the city adopted a unique regulatory approach to ensure that Times Square retains its "traditional" bright, flashy, neon glow. Buildings on 42nd Street and at Times Square are *mandated* to erect high-tech electronic billboards to maintain the glitzy image associated with Times Square.

Public Financing and Private Investment

Times Square was clearly changing its image, and nothing was a clearer symbol of that change than the move into the heart of the Times Square District of America's premier family entertainer, the Disney Company. Statues of Mickey and Minnie Mouse now grace 42nd Street, as does a four-story high mural of Dr. Seuss's Cat in the Hat down the street. Disney also refurbished, at a cost of US $34 million the Art Nouveau New Amsterdam Theater, original home of the Ziegfeld Follies, which now serves as the showcase for Disney movies and live productions.

All this was accomplished not only with Disney investment, but also with government financing as well. Times Square was in the process of revitalization, but it needed an anchor. Disney would attract other entertainment, retail, and corporate giants to invest in the area and lure the suburban families and visitors from Iowa who hadn't set foot in Times Square for years, back to the bright lights of New York. The city agreed to provide city-financed, low-interest loans to Disney covering approximately 75 percent of its project cost.

In a separate deal, US $18.2 million in city and state money went to New 42nd Street, a nonprofit agency that has a 99-year lease with the city to oversee redevelopment of some of the shabbiest buildings on the block. New 42nd Street renovated the New Victory Theater and is currently in the midst of planning for a new 10-story building that will house rehearsal studios and incorporate the old Selwyn Theater. The new structure will do its part to maintain the dazzling lights of Times Square: plans call for a façade of glass louvers with a computerized system of multicolored lights that will flash constantly changing patterns across the glass, as well as an illuminated tube rising 180 feet from the ground, through the façade, and projecting up from the roof line.

Closing Comments

This combination of voluntary efforts of the self-taxing association of businesses, strict zoning regulations, government financing, and private investment seems to have spurred the rebirth of Times Square, one of the world's most concentrated tourist destinations. The district is now home to over 668 retail establishments, including what is billed as the world's largest music store. There are over 220 restaurants in the area. Decaying theaters are being renovated, and ticket sales are the highest they've been in 15 years (over nine million theater tickets were sold in 1996). Corporate giants such as Morgan Stanley, Viacom, and Warner Brothers have moved in. Twenty million tourists visited Times Square in 1996; a million and a half people cross the streets in Times Square every day; over 45,000 people pass by on the sidewalks each hour.

Serious crime still occurs; peddlers, scalpers, and the homeless still roam the streets; the number of porn shops has diminished but not vanished; tourists still view the subway with foreboding. Some businesses feel they are being taxed by the BID to provide services for which the city government is responsible. Others fear the expanded role that private security forces are filling. Many taxpayers resent the generous terms the city gave Disney. But despite the problems, Times Square is once again being described as dynamic, bustling, hectic, noisy, glitzy, and brash—the image that attracts the many tourists it had almost lost.

Constraints of Concentration Strategies

One inevitable consequence of a concentration strategy is that the impacts of tourism development are intensified in a single area. This is, of course, often a primary goal of such a strategy. Unfortunately, when negative environmental impacts are exacerbated, existing mitigation measures may no longer be sufficient. Management techniques can often cope with heightened traffic congestion, noise, and air pollution. But increased demand for water and sewage disposal puts additional pressures on natural resources that they may not be able to bear. Before adopting any concentration strategy, a community should be especially mindful of potential environmental impacts. After adoption of a concentration strategy, a community needs to carefully and consistently monitor the environmental impacts of development, to ensure that mitigation measures are able to cope with the environmental impacts that result from intensified use.

Another unavoidable result of concentration strategies is that tourism uses will increase in the area. For Bruges, where there is a limited amount of residential use in the central area, this is not a particular problem. However, when single locations serve both residential and tourist needs, a concentration approach can shift that balance. Typically, when tourism becomes more economically profitable than other uses, rents go up, businesses catering to tourists displace those serving residents, the character of the neighborhood changes, and some residents start moving out. There is, of course, nothing inherently wrong with such a transformation. It is, though, an element of a concentration approach that should be included in any impact analysis.

A final constraint to concentration approaches is that they often fail to achieve some of the economic benefits that attach to other strategies. By intensifying tourism development in a single area, the immediate economic benefits of increased tourism tend to stay within a single, generally narrow area, rather than being spread out to a greater number of people and businesses. Both expansion and dispersal approaches, on the other hand, usually have as a goal the sharing of the economic benefits with local residents of small communities. Concentration strategies may result in highly successful tourism development that generates profits for an entire region or country; but it does not create the job opportunities in different communities that other approaches may generate.

Identifying New Tourism Resources

For communities eager to launch into tourism development for the first time, the strategies of expansion, dispersal, and concentration are premature. The primary consideration (once the community has decided upon venturing into tourism's terrain) is identification of the tourism resources—what assets of the community could attract a share of the tourist market? For Whistler and Yosemite, the resources center on the mountains and valleys; for Lake Tahoe and Milford Sound, the attraction lies in the water and rugged surrounding terrain; for Santa Fe and Oaxaca, it includes a blend of cultural heritage and contemporary crafts; for the Great Barrier Reef, it is the unique ecology; for places as diverse as Nusa Dua and Times Square, the appeal comes from the current style and mood of the place and its people. In the tourism industry, the resource is whatever is special about a destination, differentiating it from other places, and therefore capable of being separately described and marketed.[46]

Local communities and national governments throughout the world are working to develop new resources to attract tourists where they never thought to go. In some instances, communities are feeling new appreciation for natural resources that they've always enjoyed, recognizing their potential to attract visitors. Others are using whatever is idiosyncratic about their community as an attraction, relying on the appeal of the novel and unusual. (See Photo 6-7.) Still others are inventing wholly new attractions, relying on imagination and creativity to fashion an original product. The variety of attractions is

Photo 6-7 Creative, adaptive re-use of a French, later American, gun emplacement on highpass, Highway 1, north of Danang, Vietnam

breathtaking, and while each may not appeal to everyone, each seeks to find its own potential niche market and to build an identifiable and profitable new tourism product.

Natural Resources As a New Attraction

Generally the easiest type of tourist attraction to envisage is one that takes advantage of obvious and existing resources. For many communities, particularly in nonindustrialized nations, this translates into the physical setting and natural resources surrounding the community.

Toco Village Demonstration Project, Trinidad and Tobago

One nice recent example of new attraction planning occurred in the Caribbean island country of Trinidad and Tobago. Since the early 1980s, the national government stepped up its efforts to increase tourism, which nearby Caribbean island competitors had been doing for many years. Presently around 270,000 visitors arrive on Trinidad and Tobago each year, leaving behind approximately US $80 million in revenues. But many of these dollars are generated around the cruise ship dock in the capital, Port of Spain. Interior villages generally do not share in the benefits because tourists tend not to wander far from the coast.

In the 1990s, a small and poor (85 percent unemployment) interior village, 80 kilometers from the capital, formed a foundation to develop an ecotourist project. With a key US $23,000 grant from the United Nations Development Program's "Global Environment Facility" program and support from the central government (which wanted to create new opportunities for citizens living away from the coast), the foundation drew up plans for lush, bird-laden nature trails in the nearby mountains and visits to its "five living rivers." In the future, the residents' foundation hopes to build a lodge and offer some highly seasonal and disparate activities, such as surfing and turtle watching. Infrastructure is poor, however: electricity and potable water are inadequate, as is the road and telephone system. These are matters for the central government to address if this excellent concept is to become a model for other communities in the rural hinterland of Trinidad and Tobago.[47]

The Maya Forest of Central America

For many years, a number of projects have been launched to develop tourism in the rainforest areas of Central America populated by the indigenous Maya. The principal purpose of most of these efforts has been to provide for community development (i.e., economic benefit and infrastructure), although there are also at least ancillary purposes of natural and cultural conservation. Funded in a variety of ways (generally by nongovernmental organizations or international agencies) these initiatives focus on ecotourism, a small but growing niche in the tourism market that has attracted wide attention. Luckily, the area is rich in diverse elements that might attract visitors: various nature reserves; the ancient Mayan ruins of Tikal, Dos Pilas, Yaxchilán, and Caracol; jaguars, tapirs, quetzal, and toucans; and traditional Mayan crafts such as weaving and pottery.[48]

"Curiosity" As an Attraction

Especially for those communities lacking a spectacular setting or fascinating flora or fauna, other unusual assets may be turned into tourist attractions. Devonshire tea with scones and clotted cream has brought innumerable tourists to tea shops in the villages along England's southwest coast, while the castles of France's Loire Valley and the vineyards of Chianti attract their own devoted following. Other communities are discovering their own unique assets as well.

SHOWCASES OF PROSTITUTION IN KALGOORLIE, AUSTRALIA, AND FORT SMITH, ARKANSAS

In Kalgoorlie, a city in western Australia, many citizens support the renovation of a currently operating brothel, to include among its nonfleshly offerings a Museum of Prostitution. This would complement the existing attractions of a Goldfield Museum and a nearby working "Superpit" mine. The museum would be on the first floor (the prostitutes work upstairs and only at night) and would be open during the daytime for viewing of photographs, paintings, and historical objects to include a "working bed." Some support for the project comes from those who believe that it will promote continuation of the current concentration of the local (and illegal) sex industry; the mayor remarked that he wanted to avoid "take-aways"—freelance prostitutes offering cheap services outside the bordellos or call girls operating on the streets.

In another prostitution context, the city council of Fort Smith, Arkansas in 1997 approved $700,000 to restore its closed (but historically significant, National Register of Historic Places) bordello for use as the town's visitors' center. The glass transoms in the bedrooms are etched with the names of some of the former prostitutes, and a full-time hostess, dressed in the style of the bordello's founding madam, will greet visiting tourists. The project architect acknowledged a modest controversy over the suitability of using a restored bordello as a visitors' center but remarked, "You forget how vibrant it all was once. . . . Most people agreed this really gives us something pretty distinctive." That distinctiveness defines Fort Smith's new tourist attraction.[49]

A SPIRITUALIST CAMP IN CASSADAGA, FLORIDA

In 1894 George P. Colby, a medium from New York, founded a 55-acre spiritualist camp in Cassadaga, Florida, that flourishes to this day. An hour's drive from Orlando, Florida, and Disneyworld, the camp has a healing center, a church, a hotel, and bookstore and 25 camp-certified mediums and healers. On weekends, it offers classes in psychic development. Beyond the borders of the camp, various residents of Cassadaga offer "spiritual readings" and "past life regression, Tarot, and handwriting analysis."[50]

Cassadaga has always attracted people interested in spiritualism, but with the recent growth of the New Age movement, its popularity has grown. Hoping to lure some of those tourists enjoying Disneyworld to a different type of experience, the local West Volusia Tourism Advertising Authority now promotes Cassadaga in its brochure: "Looking for some place unusual?"

TOMB ROBBING IN ITALY

In an area of Italy west of Rome, there are ancient Etruscan tombs, most of which have been excavated by archaeologists or denuded of their treasures by "tombolari," who then sell the stolen artifacts. Many of the tombs have by now been emptied of their antiquities, and some of the tombolari have turned to a new source of income: forgeries. The enterprising tombolari put fake artifacts into tombs they've already cleared out, shovel the dirt back on the gravesite, and leave the tomb undisturbed for a few years. Then they find a tourist who's eager for a new and exciting experience. They lead the tourist to the site, "discover" the tomb, unearth the fake artifacts, and sell the "antiquities" to their tourist partner-in-crime.[51]

Cultural Tourism

Some communities may prefer not to be unique, but to be culturally distinctive. Most tourists in Paris visit the Louvre, even if they do not visit their hometown museum. The arts can be successful tourist attractions, as Ashford, Oregon (the home of a summer Shakespeare festival), and Nashville, Tennessee (the home of country music's Grand Ole Opry), have both discovered. Some communities may be lucky enough to have a cultural element they can develop into an attraction; others may have to create one to capture tourists' attention.

THE GUGGENHEIM MUSEUM IN BILBOA, SPAIN

Bilboa is a shipbuilding city in the northern Basque country in Spain that, until now, has never been on the tourist track. In an effort to secure its share of tourism's economic blessings, the city decided to use art as the draw. It convinced the Guggenheim Museum, headquartered in New York, to open a new modern art museum in Bilboa. The city hired the controversial architect Frank Gehry to design the new structure and spent over US $100 million to build it. Within little more than six months, it attracted over 400,000 visitors and the city hopes to be included on the "art tours" so popular with museum goers and college alumni.

Thus far, the plan seems to be working. As one magazine put it, "(e)very couple of years, one city emerges on the global itinerary as the newest hot spot, the one place that everyone seems to have just come back from, or is just heading off to . . . Now it's Bilboa. . . . The Guggenheim has transformed this sleepy—and rather ugly, if you must know—town into an arts mecca."[52]

THE EUROPEAN "BOOK VILLAGES"

In the early 1960s, the small village of Hay-on-Wye in Wales took advantage of the local interest in reading and buying books, turned itself into a book village, and now has a summer calendar filled with poetry readings, literary discussions, and book fairs. Following in its footsteps, a small village southwest of Brussels developed itself into a well-known European travel destination for visitors interested in specialty bookstores as well as expositions relating to books and art. Redu has 21 bookstores of many types, spread along its many appealing interconnected watercourses. Tourists stroll the attractive sidewalks and browse in these charming establishments, many of which carry rare books. Complementing this array of bookstores are approximately ten arts and crafts galleries, and eight restaurants within (and another eight nearby) the village. There are accommodations for visitors who remain overnight. Additionally, the village is the venue for a number of summer and fall meetings and festivals, many of which relate to books and regional folklore.

The success of the Welsh and Belgian "book village" format prompted a French bookbinder to try the same approach. He persuaded a book dealer from Redu and the initiator of the Hay-on-Wye transformation to open bookstores at what is now a thriving French book village of 800 citizens called Montolieu. Boasting 12 second-hand and rare bookstores, Montolieu is located near the famous walled city of Carcassonne in southern France. It had been experiencing population decline and poverty before the 1989 introduction of the first book stores, and it is now a very well-known destination (especially among those also visiting nearby Carcassonne), attracting almost 100,000 visitors in 1996. According to mayor Max Delperieur, "These are not polluting tourists. Book lovers are generally calm people, they don't throw plastic around, and they respect the landscape."[53]

Inventing New Attractions

For the truly imaginative, there is no need for tourism to be limited merely to existing natural or cultural attractions. With sufficient financial resources or with the benefit of high-technology, "virtual reality" techniques, some purveyors are venturing into the artificial, creating previously undreamed of attractions that are now within the realm of possibility.

AMUSEMENTS IN SAUDI ARABIA

In the remote Saudi Arabian region of Aseer, the ruling governor (a member of the Royal family) constructed mountain highways, power lines, and other infrastructure to some of the outlying valleys. He also worked with other royals and business affiliates to organize an amusement company to own hotels, amusement parks, and, most recently, a 3,200-seat theater especially for evening concerts. Another party is exploring the feasibility of winter sports complexes, complete with artificial snow, in the southern area of Aseer. In other regions of arid Saudi Arabia, there is a boom in vacation home developments on popular and lushly green golf courses.[54]

AT THE OUTER FRINGE: "SYNTHETIC TOURISM"

British journalist Mark Hodson, in his wonderfully titled Sunday Times article "Journeys in the Mind," from which this section is drawn, reported that the Royal Caribbean Cruise line operates a pretend tropical paradise on a private island, complete with "residents" who are actually cruise line employees and a fake underwater shipwreck. The purpose? The company believes that passengers want to avoid authenticity, especially such negative conditions as slums and hawkers on the beach. Two other Hodson illustrations come from Japan: a giant indoor ski resort and "the Phoenix Seagaia, near Miyazaki, an artificial-beach complex complete with palm trees, wave machines, and perfect white sand. When the weather turns nasty, a giant domed roof is simply drawn over the whole resort."

The use of "virtual reality" technology is making a new type of tourism experience available for the contemporary "armchair traveler." A British scientist is planning to recreate the experience of visiting Venice, by using a large room with shallow water on the floor and a full size gondola in which patrons sit while they absorb projection images, sounds, and even weather that will be "completely convincing." A somewhat similar program is being developed for England's Stonehenge. There, a visitors' center several hundred yards from the World Heritage Site will offer virtual reality presentations about the site, including "walks" through, and "flights" above, the mysterious giant stones, as well as summer solstice sunrise "watching."[55]

For most communities, the prospect of turning a desert into a golf course or creating Venice in a single room will not appeal as a practical solution. It is much more likely that communities will look at their existing assets with a new eye and fashion them into an attraction that appeals to a particular type of tourist, as much as it does to the residents of the community. This is what happened in a rural area in southwestern England.

Case Study: The Tarka Project, Devon, England

Various governmental bodies initiated a project with a literary theme as a marketing focus and identity for conservation, sustainable tourism, and economic improvement efforts in the North Devon area.

In 1927, Henry Williamson published his novel *Tarka the Otter* about the journeys and adventures in North Devon of an appealing otter named Tarka. The book reflected the author's attachment to the countryside and his experiences caring for an orphaned otter

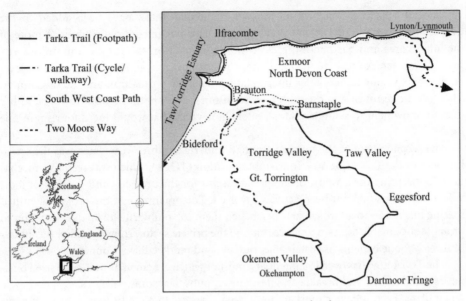

Map 6-12 Tarka Project, England

cub, and it became a much-loved English classic. Over 60 years later in 1989, Tarka was adopted as the identity for a 500-square-mile area of northern Devon, stretching from the dramatic cliffs of the southwest coast of England, through moorlands and river valleys to the north edge of Dartmoor.

The Devon County Council had issued a report in 1988 identifying a number of disturbing social and economic trends in this area. Agricultural incomes were declining; unemployment exceeded the national average; tourism was concentrated along the coast, where it had become the principal economic activity; the long-term viability of rural communities was in doubt; and the water quality of the rivers Taw and Torridge, which run through the heart of the area, was declining. To address these concerns, the report proposed what became the Tarka Project:[56] representatives of eight governmental entities developed initiatives aimed at conserving the wildlife, natural beauty, and special character of North Devon and promoting tourism, which together would contribute to the social and economic well-being of the area. Tarka the otter became the symbol of the project, and the area is now known, and marketed, as Tarka Country. (See Map 6-12.)

Tourism Strategy

The main focus when the project first began was on the creation of the Tarka Trail,[57] which traces the otter's fictional journey through the North Devon countryside. This loop trail winds 180 miles (290 kilometers) along the Taw Valley, through the forests of Eggesford and the moors of Exmoor, along the coastline to the estuaries of the Taw and Torridge Rivers, and then through the Torridge and Okement Valleys until it runs full circle to the northern fringes of Dartmoor. Designed primarily to attract the long-distance walker, the trail also includes over 30 miles of cycling path and links up with a branch line of the railway (now known as the Tarka Line) for part of the journey. The trail also intersects two other long-distance trails for those with greater energy and a longer vacation.

Since it was first designed, various short circular walks have been added to the trail, leading to some of Devon's small villages. This has introduced walkers to more of the inland area and has had a direct economic impact on the rural communities visited. Visitors tend to relax in the local pub, often stopping for lunch and shopping at local markets. Six visitor centers offer interpretative materials on the trail and Tarka Country. This was the result of a conscious effort to disburse visitors throughout the area, rather than to draw them to a single visitor center "honeypot" that would focus tourism in one locale.

The second phase of the tourism strategy, undertaken three years later, was the establishment of the Tarka Country Tourism Association (TCTA), which was seen as a mechanism for securing the support of the private sector for the project. Until then, most individual businesses had not been actively involved. The organizers of the project identified specific businesses to approach and persuaded them to voluntarily form an association to promote sustainable tourism practices among the private sector, convince other businesses of the economic benefits of sustainable tourism, and market Tarka Country.

The TCTA now has over 150 members, most of which are small or moderate sized businesses, such as bed and breakfasts, guesthouses, pubs, tearooms, village shops, and cycle rental firms. Each member must sign a "Green Charter" that confirms a long-term commitment to conservation of the area and minimal impact on the environment. TCTA now offers both business and environmental training to its members to enable them to fulfill the various elements of the charter.

There is also a "Producers Group" that enables local craft, food, and beverage producers to promote their wares to other members and market them to tourists. TCTA has taken on most of the marketing responsibility for the Tarka Project. It also established the "Friends of Tarka" group. Visitors are invited to make a voluntary donation to support local conservation and to go on a mailing list.

Conservation Strategy

Conservation and tourism have been intertwined in the Tarka Project from the beginning. The use of Tarka the otter as the symbol for the area implied a commitment to the protection of the natural beauty of the area and its wildlife. TCTA was established with a strong environmental orientation. Marketing of the trail has often blended with conservation goals, as it did with the Friends of Tarka scheme. As the Tarka Trail became a more popular tourist destination, more businesses adopted the Tarka name and identified themselves with the goals of the Project.

In 1996, the Tarka Project became one of five entities participating in a pilot project known as the Visitor Payback Project funded by the European Commission. This new program was aimed at demonstrating that tourists would voluntarily contribute funds for the conservation of areas they visited, thus providing badly needed funds for conservation efforts.

The Tarka Project has raised funds for this program in four different ways. The TCTA applied voluntary levies on various services sold by its members, such as overnight stays at hotels and bed and breakfasts; there was also a levy on merchandise sales by TCTA members; donation boxes with postcards were placed at strategic spots for voluntary tourist donations; and the Friends of Tarka was relaunched as a membership organization. The newly created Tarka Conservation Fund collects and uses the funds for a variety of conservation efforts, ranging from providing new tools for community volunteer groups working on conservation tasks, buying tree saplings that city children staying on a farm plant each spring, and supporting a program of educational and interpretative events for children.

Economic Strategy

The underlying assumption of the Tarka Project is that conservation of the natural environment will attract visitors, who can make a significant contribution to the economic well-being of the area. The statistics thus far seem to support this goal. While tourism declined throughout Devon between 1985 and 1995 by 1.5 percent, tourism increased in Tarka Country by 5.9 percent during that same period. There were almost half a million additional tourist nights spent in local accommodations. On the basis of surveys taken in 1994 and 1995, over 483,000 people used the Tarka Trail each year, and well over half of these were tourists from outside the area. The Devon County Council estimated that through 1995, the Tarka Project had generated an income of over £18 million and created over 500 jobs directly. Since much of the tourism and many of the overnights were spent in the interior hinterlands of Tarka Country, rather than along the coastline, much of the money and many of the new jobs came to an area suffering from declining agriculture and growing unemployment. Thus, tourism spending was being retained by the local economy where it was most needed.

Closing Comments

The success of the Tarka Project suggests that communities can develop new tourist markets based on conservation and environmental attractions that can bring economic improvement to an area. While the statistics indicate economic growth, those involved in Tarka have done their own evaluation and identified some areas where they need to, or in some cases already have, adapt their strategy.

When the steering group of the Tarka Project first developed the Tarka Trail, they assumed the market would be long-distance walkers. Therefore, the original advertising was aimed at that niche market. From the beginning, however, Tarka Country appealed to people who wanted a rural/coast holiday that included some walking or cycling. When the TCTA, composed of affected businesses, took over responsibility for marketing, advertising moved from what was a narrow focus to a broader and more mainstream one with the much larger audience of short-distance walkers. If the planners had included in their deliberations business people who had a greater awareness of the market, the original thrust of advertising and also the layout of the trail itself might have been different.

Other problems also arose because of the composition of the early decision-making body. The Tarka Project was initiated by the Devon County Council, which was then joined by seven other partners, all of them government-affiliated bodies. Neither businesses nor residents of North Devon were included in any of the original planning. As a result of the lack of direct public participation, the conservation efforts of the project were not actively supported by the tourism organizations and businesses, which did not see environmental issues as being in their self-interest. No one had done the necessary community education to convince all parties that their goals were compatible and interrelated. It was not until three years after the Tarka Project began that efforts were made to secure any degree of business involvement or support. The TCTA is now considered a highlight of the project, demonstrating that the private sector will adopt sustainable tourism concepts when it understands the economic benefits. Similarly, independent artisans and craftspeople agreed to the environmental orientation of TCTA as members of the Producers Group, when they realized that they would have a broader market for their goods.

Finally, the lack of public involvement meant that there was no groundswell of support for the project. Each partner in the project had one representative on the steering group, but there was no general membership, no active involvement by any group, and no representatives from the affected communities. The Tarka Project originally had only eight voices speaking in its favor. This resulted in a certain lack of political commitment, which weakens any program.

All these difficulties occurred in the early days of the Tarka Project, and have since been resolved. Looking to the future, the TCTA and the Tarka Country Trust (which oversees the Tarka Conservation Fund and the Visitor Payback program) are looking at their organizational structure and considering ways to expand the whole Tarka initiative. The continued involvement of so many of the important players in the development of the Tarka Project increases the chances for its long-term viability.

Another regional initiative, this one in Wales, has combined tourism development with overall economic development and environmental protection. Like the Tarka Project, it builds a tourist attraction based on the natural resources of the setting and the cultural history of the area. In this case, however, there was widespread community involvement from the outset and the active participation of organizations that provided expertise otherwise lacking. For that reason, it is a superb example of the benefits of partnerships and cooperation.

Case Study: South Pembrokeshire, Wales

A nongovernmental organization initiates an effort to improve the economic and social life of the local people and to enhance the environment in a disadvantaged area of Wales. The process encourages maximum community involvement in all stages of development and the use of expert "partners" to provide needed technical and financial resources to develop a rural tourism program.

South Pembrokeshire is located in the southwestern peninsula of Wales. It is a rural area comprising roughly 40 villages and towns and 400 square kilometers of land. (See Map 6-13.) The landscape is varied, including coastal and estuarian areas that are part of the Pembrokeshire Coast National Park, and rolling countryside and river valleys leading to the foothills of the Preseli Hills to the North. The "Landsker," a historic frontier line of castles and strongholds dating to the eleventh-century Norman invasion, divides the area into two culturally distinct parts: to the North, the Welsh culture and language predominate, while the area to the South has been anglicized. The surrounding countryside is picturesquely called the "Landsker Borderlands," whose villages and towns are interconnected by footpaths, bridle ways, and narrow lanes. (See Photo 6-8.)

Background

In 1992, the South Pembrokeshire Partnership for Action with Rural Communities, Ltd. (SPARC)[58] received European Union funding to extend a pilot project throughout the dis-

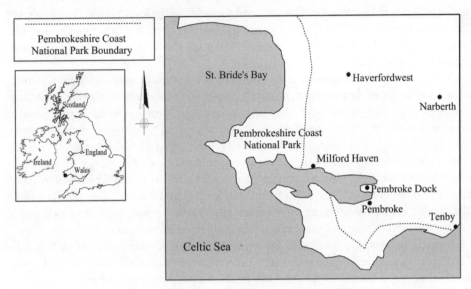

Map 6-13 South Pembrokeshire, Wales

Photo 6-8 Cyclists enjoying a cycling trail and the rich heritage of South Pembrokshire, Wales
(Courtesy of Joan Asby, coordinator, SPARC)

advantaged rural communities of South Pembrokeshire. Its goal was to develop an integrated program to improve the economic and social life of the local people and to enhance the environment. The SPARC effort is not focused solely on tourism but also includes interrelated environmental and agricultural strategies, which are seen as complementary components of the program.

Central to SPARC's approach is the encouragement of maximum community involvement in all stages of development: planning, implementation, and monitoring. First, local people in all 37 villages that have taken part in the SPARC program to date participated in an appraisal to identify the problems and opportunities of their own community. Next, they helped produce a local Action Plan, based on the appraisal. Most communities identified rural tourism in their Action Plans as a potential source of economic growth. They also, however, wanted a form of tourism "that was non-intrusive and which was based on the natural resources of the area, its landscape, heritage and culture." This translated into the SPARC goal of promoting environmentally sensitive rural tourism, which would respect the local culture and bring maximum local economic benefit.

Equally important to the SPARC approach is the assistance of a variety of what it styles "partners": educational organizations and experts who produced valuable data and assessments that they shared with the community and supportive public and private organizations that provided technical and financial assistance. SPARC, local communities, and these partners joined forces to determine a "product identity" for the rural tourism program: the theme of the "Landsker Borderlands." This offered a unified historic interpretation to the South Pembrokeshire district, accounted for the linguistic split between the Welsh speakers to the north and the English speakers to the south, and respected the cultural distinctions of the area.

As the tourism program developed, local citizens, "partners," and SPARC cooperated in virtually all aspects. Local citizens from the villages and towns were encouraged, again with the assistance of specialist "partners," to create leaflets providing information about their local heritage. Villages established or improved amenity centers, which provide car parking and interpretive panels in the heart of the community, and from which local footpath networks can be accessed. These footpaths were identified by local communities in conjunction with SPARC personnel, joining villages, providing access to historic sites when possible, and offering walks through the varied countryside. Walking, cycling, and fishing leaflets were also developed, in several languages. Local people identified special infrastructure projects that have become part of the rural tourism experience (e.g., transforming the medieval Hospice at Llawhaden into a local interpretative center). SPARC works with individual property owners to promote the provision of overnight accommodations, gives advice to individuals and groups that have identified an opportunity for business creation, and provides small grants for training small businesses. Finally, local citizens and organizations also work together in a Landsker Borderlands Tourism Association.

In 1994, SPARC established the Landsker Countryside Holidays Bureau to organize, promote, and market the Landsker Borderlands area. It has created visually appealing and informational brochures in English and Welsh (with a few in French and German as well), including large, interpretive fold-out brochures with maps and suggested itineraries. These cover a variety of recreational opportunities available to the tourist in South Pembrokeshire: walking, cycling, fishing, bird-watching, horseback riding, exploring local history, and historic sites. One of the newest offerings is the "Makers of Wales" heritage trails. This is a Wales-wide theme, which has been extended at the local level by SPARC, again with funding from the European Union. There are seven thematic itineraries in

South Pembrokeshire that visitors can follow (by car, cycling, or walking), each of which highlights a particular aspect of Welsh heritage, such as "Chieftains and Princes," "Arts and Literature," or "Makers of Wales." This regional tourism program has a number of objectives, including attracting more year-round visitors to South Pembrokeshire, interpreting and promoting Welsh heritage, restoring heritage sites, improving the local economy (especially through a need for increased accommodations and potential for more local shop purchases), and training local building workers in heritage restoration skills that can then be showcased to visitors.

The bureau also provides a booking service for visitors seeking overnight accommodations. This was designed in large part to minimize economic "leakage" of benefits outside of the South Pembrokeshire district. Accommodations include hotels, guesthouses, farmhouses, bed and breakfasts, self-catering cottages, static caravans, and sites for touring caravans and tents. Additionally, specially designed package holidays have been developed around walking, cycling, fishing, and painting holidays.

The final service offered by the Landsker Countryside Holidays Bureau is information on the Greenways "environmentally friendly transport initiative." This program, which was developed in partnership with the Countryside Council for Wales, is designed to develop additional opportunities for walking and cycling and to protect the environment by minimizing traffic. SPARC promotional materials clearly identify "walk and ride" opportunities, explaining the benefits of minimizing car use for the natural environment and the decreased impact of congestion and noise on the human environment. Various leaflets address "walk and ride" routes, road cycling routes, off-road cycling routes, and a "Hidden Heritage Miners Walk."

Noteworthy Features of the SPARC Program

One of the most significant features of the SPARC program is the extensive level of *citizen involvement*. The SPARC initiative involves local people in all aspects of rural tourism development: from the initial assessment of the community, through the planning process and implementation, to ongoing monitoring. The community has a role in all decision making, not merely in providing input to government officials or outside experts who then make the final determination. This has resulted in a tourism program that reflects the shared community vision, respects the community's concern for its heritage and environment, and thus increases the likelihood of local support and sustainability.

Although the local communities can provide commitment, the rural villages of South Pembrokeshire do not have the financial and technical resources necessary to develop successful, quality tourism programs without assistance. SPARC creates *partnerships* with a variety of public and private organizations to bring needed expertise to local communities, which they would not be able to attract on their own. SPARC has secured the assistance of educational institutions and scholars to do research, businesses to provide training to improve local skills, governmental units to provide funding, and a consortium of private and public agencies to cooperate with SPARC and local communities in all aspects of the planning and implementation of the tourism program. These partnerships, which appear to have been readily accepted by most community members, have brought a level of sophistication to the tourism program that would otherwise be lacking.

The SPARC initiative also involves strategies addressing three distinct elements: tourism, environment, and agriculture. Because of the *integrated approach,* there is not undue emphasis on tourism as the economic savior of the region. SPARC works on a variety of other community development projects, including the creation of credit unions, child care opportunities, computer training, and village enhancement schemes. Tourism is only one part of an overall approach to improve the economic and social life in South Pembrokeshire. Communities are developing the type of rural tourism that they are comfortable with and that respects their culture, lifestyle, and heritage. They might be less likely to place the restraints they do on their tourism development if they believed it was the only potential source of economic growth for their communities.

An additional benefit of the complementary strategies is that SPARC has created in the other components of its initiative ongoing mechanisms for developing leadership skills within the local community. SPARC has any number of training programs to ensure that the local capacity will exist for meaningful participation and real "empowerment" of the affected communities.

Although villages conduct their own assessment and create their own Action Plans, developing their own Tourist Centers and informational materials, much of the tourism program is regionally based. The Landsker Borderlands is a *regional concept* covering all of the South Pembrokeshire area. The extensive network of footpaths, cycling routes, and heritage trails encompass any number of communities. No single village, acting alone, would be able to attract a sufficient number of visitors to bring any significant economic benefit. However, working together to form a regional attraction, the villages and towns of South Pembrokeshire are developing into a successful rural tourism destination.

The pivotal role of SPARC, a nongovernmental organization with an agenda broader than rural tourism alone, has been crucial to the success of the initiative. Few small rural villages would have the resources to address the broader goals of improving their quality of life, developing a sophisticated process of planning and implementation, building citizen and governmental support, creating and coordinating networks of partnerships, ensuring the continued cooperation of all involved parties, developing a regional program, or securing funding and needed expertise. The same is often true of government officials and planners in rural communities. Businesses, no matter how altruistic and generous, typically have a narrower focus and an eye on profits. A special-interest nongovernmental organization can thus act as the convener and initiator of a successful tourism management process.

Efforts have been made to retain the economic benefits of the tourism program within the affected communities, rather than having them "leak out" to absentee owners of tourist-related businesses. The tourism program has not involved the development of large-scale hotels, restaurants, theme parks, or major attractions. Revenue from visitors largely stays in the local community, going to providers of accommodations, local restaurants, visitor centers, craftsmen, and local shop owners. SPARC has also secured funding for grants to small business owners for training to increase their skills, so that new business opportunities can be addressed at the local level rather than by entrepreneurs from outside South Pembrokeshire. Additionally, training in restoration skills is offered to local craftsmen, ensuring that most of the restoration work on historic sites and buildings can be performed by local artisans.

The tourism product itself has been diversified to extend both the timing and location of visits. The Heritage Trails program effectively extends the visitor season beyond the traditional "warm weather season" for most outdoor activities, thus building a stronger economic base over a longer period of the year and spreading visitor numbers, and therefore income, throughout the year. This diversification can have a significant impact on those members of the local community depending on tourism revenues. Similarly, the creation of the network of footpaths and cycling routes has reduced tourist pressure on the popu-

lar coastal paths and directed more visitors to the interior countryside, spreading the economic benefit of tourism throughout the area.

Closing Comments

The SPARC program is an excellent example of the leadership role a nongovernmental
organization can play in developing new tourism programs with an emphasis on community involvement and participation in all aspects of development. It is still too early to know
whether this regional program will, in fact, be able to attract sufficient numbers of tourists
over the years to make a significant impact on the local economies once the funding has
stopped. At this point, it seems to have made a successful start: SPARC estimates that in
1996, tourism brought in an additional £200,000 to South Pembrokeshire, mostly to accommodation providers, shops, restaurants, and pubs. If the rural villages can maintain these
numbers, if emerging entrepreneurs can master the skills necessary to run tourism-
oriented businesses, and if community members develop the leadership skills needed to
implement and monitor the tourism program they've developed, the chances are good for
long-term success.

Both the Tarka and the SPARC projects have been successful because of coordinated efforts
of various groups and constituencies. In the United States, the individual initiatives of
independent farmers in various locations are creating a new type of tourism with very targeted economic benefits. While both Tarka and the SPARC are regional in concept, farm-
based tourism in the United States has thus far remained largely dependent upon private
entrepreneurial efforts. Any economic leakage to a larger area is a corollary benefit.

Case Study: Agritourism in the United States

*Farmers across the United States are expanding the traditional scope of farms to include
tourism activities.*

Agritourism originally developed in several European countries, where it is a large and
growing phenomenon. A World Tourist Organization official estimates that as of 1998, it
generated between five and ten percent of the total US $218 billion European tourism rev-
enues.[59] Consisting largely of bed and breakfast operations on family farms, agritourism
has been heavily subsidized by 15 European Union governments (about US $2 billion since
1991) in an effort to replace rapidly diminishing agricultural price supports and to help
farmers remain on their land.

Keeping European farms economically viable has a positive effect on tourism in general. In Italy, "(a) populated countryside protects picturesque landscapes that attract
tourists. . . . The golden wheatfields around (a Tuscan farm) are, after all, virtually identi-
cal to those in fifteenth century paintings that attract countless tourists to the churches and
town hall of nearby Siena."[60]

In the United States, agritourism, or in some instances "agrientertainment," does not
rely on government support but on the idiosyncratic efforts of individual farmers who have
become independent tourism entrepreneurs in order to keep their family-owned farms

operating. Even world famous Cornell University in rural New York offers numerous courses and conferences to teach agricultural entrepreneurship to undergraduates, graduate students, and current farmers. Many farmers have earned educational degrees in marketing, and some have turned to the cyberspace Internet to advertise their fledgling businesses. There seem to be no reliable national statistics, but there are certainly thousands of such farms. For example, two recent state of Connecticut brochures listed 91 agritourism farms in just eight counties, and New York state alone has more that 1,500.

The appeal of visiting farms is increasing in the United States because many Americans are technology-oriented, bound to the indoors by computers, televisions, and video games. As more people live in urban environments, periodic trips to rural areas become more appealing; the "weekend in the country" is a relaxing antidote to the stresses of modern city and suburban life. Farm visits have increased in popularity in part because so many farms are now relatively close to population centers and thus involve short, convenient car trips. This has not gone unnoticed by savvy farmers.

Agritourism Attractions

Farm attractions have existed, and been used to supplement farmers' incomes, for many years: hayrides and sleigh rides, autumn pumpkin picking, and petting zoos. Farmers, however, have expanded their horizons well beyond those traditional offerings by adding other, less conventional, attractions in attempts to diversify and to lure additional visitors who want new experiences.

One type of new attraction is the "corn maze," a confusing, intricate network of winding pathways cut in large stands of tall corn. Corn maze owners typically invest a large sum of money to hire corn maze experts (itself a new field) to design and cut the attraction, which can bring high profits. Richard Hodgson of Hodgson Farm in Walden, New York, paid $100,000 to have the American Maze Company hand clear a corn maze in the shape of an *alien spaceship*. The shape and the concept seem odd, but in November 1997, Hodgson estimated that 30,000 people had visited the maze in the previous three months, with each person spending approximately $12 on admission and food. Similarly, Randall Hughes of Janesville, Wisconsin, planned to cut a 40-acre farmhouse-shaped corn maze in July 1998. He will charge a $6.00 admission and offer helicopter rides to allow visitors to see the shape from the sky. He will also sell T-shirts and offer a "VIP Tent" for businesses to hold picnics.

Farmers are also marketing the educational experience farm life can offer. This commonly attracts school-aged children who visit these farms on field trips. Many farmers offer tours focused on animals and their habits. These "show and tell" demonstrations allow visitors to touch the animals and see how the animals are cared for. Some farmers offer milking demonstrations, pony rides, and picnic spots. Many owners have capitalized on the successful educational draw by presenting exotic animals. For example, the imaginatively named "Amy's Udder Joy Exotic Animal Farm" in Crumble, Connecticut, boasts an eclectic mixture of "(l)lamas, fallow deer, tropical reptiles, wallabies, majestic peafowl, emu's and other avian species, Jacobs four-horned sheep, Tennessee fainting goats, prairie dogs, four-toed pygmy hedgehogs, tarantulas" and, of course "native wildlife." (With tarantulas and pygmy hedgehogs among the offerings, the owners ask "that all children be under adult supervision at all times.")

Some farmers have sought to diversify the educational elements of their sites by developing farming museums. One example is the Pomeroy Living History Museum, which memorializes life on the farm in the 1920s in the Pacific Northwest. Owners Bob and Jane Brink estimate that 6,000 school children came to their farm during the 1996–1997 school year. The farmstead, owned formerly by Mrs. Brink's grandparents, is now filled with antiques and depicts farm life during the troubled times of the Great Depression.

Farm tours can also provide an opportunity for families to spend time together. With this in mind, owners have developed marketing plans centering on family activities. For some years, Christmas tree farms have allowed families to select live trees to cut down themselves for the holidays. Other farmers have taken this "do-it-yourself" approach one step further by developing "U-pick" farms, which encourage people to enter the growing fields and select their own produce. (This can be particularly profitable, since wholesalers and their portion of the price are eliminated from the distribution chain.) Farmers have consciously expanded by diversifying the selection of pickable crops. Some farms feature high value U-pick produce such as asparagus, flowers, and raspberries. Other owners have developed niche attractions by specializing in wine, cheese, butter, or ice cream.

One highly entrepreneurial farmer is Mark Schnepf, mayor of the small western town of Queen Creek, Arizona. Schnepf Farms has developed a creative and extensive marketing and advertising program. A widely distributed, biannual newsletter features upcoming farm visit activities. Like a Disneyland flyer, each newsletter contains coupons for discounts on admissions and items for sale at the newly opened, on-site country store. The farm offers a walking trail, U-pick vegetables, a 250-acre campground, a petting corral, a park area, a country store, and a tree farm. Schnepf even hosts festivals such as an annual Sweet Onion Fest and a Potato Fest, complete with recipe contests, tugs of war over a mashed potato pit(!), arts and crafts, children's potato decorating, potato peeling contests, and potato sack races. Adding to that mix are summer barbecues and autumn pumpkin and chili parties, all of which feature such elements as country bands and dancing. Visitors flock to the farm: over 15,000 elementary school children and 30,000 festival attendees arrived at the farm in 1997. The farm is so popular that the Schnepfs now operate bus tours for out-of-state tourists.

Closing Comments

When properly and tastefully designed and operated, agritourism has considerable potential. By augmenting income and allowing farmers to maintain their land, it helps preserve open space and halt the conversion of prime farmland to residential subdivisions. Most agritourism sites actually produce food, as well, which of course is a farm's principal *raison d'être*. There is real opportunity for preservation of historic old farmsteads, together with the educational potential that comes from thoughtful interpretive/educational elements.

At the same time, the authenticity of farm life may also be undermined if farms become too commercialized and crowded. Neighbors who do not operate these types of activities and instead opt for more traditional farm life can find their roads clogged with vehicles and their livestock spooked by throngs of curious city folk. Environmental impacts can be significant, with increased noise and air pollution from vehicles, litter, and wastes. Additionally, since most agritourism develops from individual entrepreneurial activity, the economic benefits are not normally spread across a community but remain with the farm owner. Because agritourism tends to be so individualized, it can include enormous variations of attractions with enormously varying impacts.

The Tarka Project involved the direct and active participation of the business sector, with a level of government and citizen participation. The regional SPARC program grew out of the initial efforts of a nongovernmental organization. Agritourism tends to develop from individual entrepreneurial activity. In some instances, however, the impetus for creating new tourist attractions based on the tourism resources of the area comes from a centralized government body, that not only plans but also administers the tourism program.

Case Study: Bays of Huatulco, Mexico

An affiliate of the Mexico Ministry of Tourism has developed the tourism resources of the "Bays of Huatulco" on the Pacific coast to attract international visitors.

The Mexican state of Oaxaca is one of that country's poorest areas (p. 190). Until the 1990s, by far the most visited area in the state was the Spanish colonial style capital city of Oaxaca, about 200 kilometers across the Sierra Madre Mountains from the then largely undeveloped Pacific coast.

By contrast, new construction for tourism uses in the state is now focused principally on the coast itself, in a large, master-planned complex encompassing nine bays and picturesquely called the Bays of Huatulco. (See Map 6-14 and Photo 6-9.) The government preliminarily selected the area many years ago in 1969, but final conceptual planning occurred much later in 1984. Organized and implemented by FONATUR, the executive arm of the Ministry of Tourism, the project is designed to be a low-density beach resort with a tourism zone of 6,875 acres out of a total project area of 47,405 acres. The area was chosen primarily for its physical attributes: it offers both natural beauty and the attraction of sand beaches. An added benefit related to marketing potential: Huatulco could be mar-

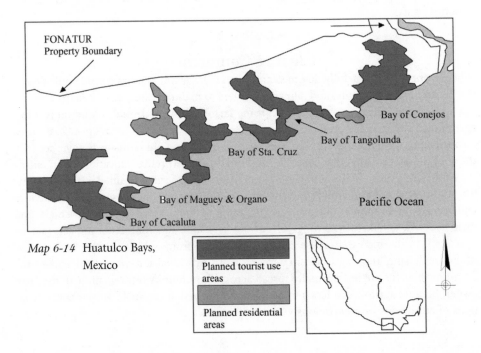

Map 6-14 Huatulco Bays, Mexico

Planned tourist use areas

Planned residential areas

Photo 6-9 Coastline of Huatulco Bays, Mexico (Courtesy of Lic. Salvador D. Anderson, Subdirector of Promotion and Publicity, Huatulco Bays)

keted as a complement to the archeological and cultural (both indigenous and colonial) attractions of the city of Oaxaca and its valleys. This could secure for the coast area a segment of the existing tourist market of the city of Oaxaca and potentially expand Oaxaca's market to those who also want a beach vacation.

The government expropriated the land it needed for the tourism development, compensating the communal landowners for the property. Residents displaced by the project were usually of Mixtec and Zapotec heritage, with a very low standard of living maintained by fishing and farming. One of the goals of the development was to bring the economic benefits of tourism to this area, creating jobs and improving the standard of living for residents.

Master Plan to Develop the Bays of Huatulco

The Master Plan, finalized in the mid-1980s, established timed stages for development from 1984 to 2018. Infrastructure was largely completed by 1986 and included a coastal road connecting the first three sub-areas selected for initial development.

The Master Plan called for 69 percent of the total acreage to be allocated for "ecological conservation." Most of this zone was located behind the nine bays, reaching into the green foothills, which visually complement the bright sun and blue Pacific. Almost 10 percent of the project was allocated to an "urban zone," primarily for employees of the tourist-oriented areas but for visitors as well. There was planned space for a large international airport (ultimately attractively designed in the "palapas" style common to the Pacific coast, with palm tree materials on the exterior walls and roof), which is now handling more than 3,500 flights per year.

Implementation of the Master Plan

FONATUR abandoned its early concept of building one "support city" for employees and a single, huge surrounding resort area, in favor of what it calls an "integrated tourist city" spanning a number of tourist centers that are linked by new roadways. The infrastructure was designed to (and does) benefit the local population as well as visitors.

FONATUR selected three of the nine bays—Tangolunda, Chahue, and Santa Cruz—for initial development. Using a staged marketing strategy, FONATUR advertised and offered for bidding those parcels deemed (by reason of their location, land use, and potential) most likely to trigger further private development. Most of the platted lots in those areas have by now been sold to private development companies. Tangolunda, which boasts five different beaches, as of this writing has one large deluxe hotel, five deluxe resorts, a golf course, a small harbor, and numerous restaurants and shops. A second resort area is not on the coast itself but instead is a village of about 7,000 people called La Crucecita with one four-star and many smaller hotels. The village includes an appealing and well-used traditional central plaza, or "zócalo." The La Crucecita village is only one mile from the beach—approximately ten minutes by taxicab from the Bay of Tangolunda. The third area selected for initial attention was the bay area of the village of Santa Cruz, which has about 1,000 inhabitants. Unfortunately, some of the residents were displaced into low-quality homes; according to Canadian tourism scholar Veronica Long "(t)he physical setting of palapas and gardens next to the ocean changed to cement houses aligned on dusty streets."[61]

This ambitious, multidecade program has necessitated governmental growth as well. There has been substantial upgrading of the interior town of Santa Maria Huatulco, the administrative headquarters of the municipality of Huatulco, which now has about 13,000 inhabitants. If the Master Plan projections are correct, that municipality will have a permanent population of 300,000 persons by 2018; 100,000 of whom will work in the tourism or allied industries. That level of local growth will, of course, produce great challenges to the government in terms of providing education, infrastructure, health services, and housing. There will also be significant challenges brought on by rapid change from a traditional way of life to the more modern lifestyle that generally accompanies growth in tourism.

FONATUR's Activities and Performance

Although the Bays of Huatulco is its newest large effort, FONATUR itself is no newcomer to mega-resort planning and development, having been responsible for the very large projects of Cancun and Los Cabos (aimed at international visitors), Ixtapa (appealing primarily to Mexican tourists), and the smaller Loreto. Created by the federal government, FONATUR's official name in English translation is "The National Trust Fund for Tourism Development." Its principal purpose is to develop the "integrally planned resorts" with infrastructure and urban construction activities, funded by sales of land, often acquired though expropriation with compensation to the individual or communal owners. It describes itself "as well as being the executive arm of the country's tourist policy and a leading company in its field, (it) is a business oriented body" offering consulting services to businesses and government units in Mexico but also abroad. FONATUR currently works in 11 Central and South American countries as well as outside the Americas.

Impressive as are the many accomplishments of FONATUR in the Bays of Huatulco project and elsewhere, at least one scholar has questioned its sensitivity to the needs of the local population in the Santa Cruz Bay community. Professor Veronica Long, who did field work in Santa Cruz Bay, asserts that local input into the Master Plan was accomplished only through public protest activities and that 61 percent of the affected citizens surveyed felt that "FONATUR treated the local residents poorly." At the same time (and perhaps contradicting the 61 percent figure), efforts to mitigate adverse social and other impacts (largely through community education) were viewed positively.

Closing Comments

The scope and timing of the Bays of Huatulco program are particularly noteworthy. The project area is vast, allowing construction to proceed in phases and in places selected as the most suitable at a given time, based upon such criteria as market conditions and infrastructure completion. The continual involvement of FONATUR in maintaining common areas, providing employment training, and a number of other responsibilities is also impressive.

Mexico has for many years been a leader in world tourism, especially of the "sun and sand" type. Its proximity to the United States and its affordability for many Europeans have provided a growing market. For some newcomers in the tourism world, eager to secure the economic benefits of tourism to improve the living standards, there is no built-in market. Our next case study explores one such example.

Case Study: Papua New Guinea

With tourism in an embryonic stage, Papua New Guinea is seeking to develop new attractions to improve economic conditions for the population, using a mapping strategy to protect its environment and population from negative impacts of tourism development.

Papua New Guinea is a diverse nation of approximately 4.3 million inhabitants located in the southwest Pacific Ocean, north of Australia. Its more than 600 islands stretch across some 500,000 square kilometers, with the largest concentration of land and population on the eastern portion of the island of New Guinea. (See Map 6-15.)

The environment is unusually diverse in flora and fauna, whose preservation is a major policy goal of the Papua New Guinea government. Scientists estimate that Papua New Guinea is home to some 1,500 species of trees; 9,000 species of "higher plants"; 700 bird species; and 200 species of mammals. Papua New Guinea participated in the 1992 United Nations Conference on Environment and Development (the "Rio Conference") and according to the Department of Environment and Conservation "is committed to developing an environmentally sound framework for resource use to mitigate (environmental problems faced in Papua New Guinea)."

The population of Papua New Guinea generally is sustained at a low standard of living. There are "strong cultural ties with the land and (the people) are highly dependent on it for their way of life. . . . Successful land management in Papua New Guinea is impossible without an understanding of the needs of the people and their cooperation." Textbook authors

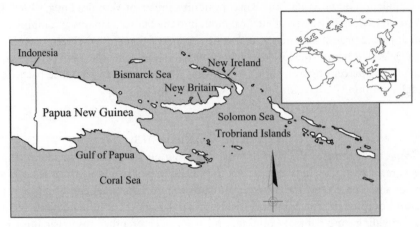

Map 6-15 Papua New Guinea

Peter Burns and Andrew Holden wrote that the government is "committed to preserving cultural heritage in the face of modernity,"[62] as reflected in a 1990s "Cultural Development Plan" that counseled:

> The people should be warned that large-scale development bring(s) with (it) certain destructive social habits. These habits confuse the members of old and new generations alike and lead to social disharmony in family units which are important bases of unity in a community and the society at large. . . . Furthermore, they should be warned that large-scale development will seriously affect the Cultural Heritage of the indigenous population.

Tourism Development Policies

The national government of Papua New Guinea is committed to improving the economic well-being of its citizens and is identifying tourism resources for that purpose. Recognizing that it is a "late starter" in encouraging tourism, the country adopted its first national tourism policy document in 1996. The key points of that pronouncement are economic: "This policy gives emphasis to coordinated and long-term sustainable development of tourism as a viable and growth-oriented industry sector. Principal ambitions in so doing are firstly, job creation and skills enhancement, and secondly, an increase in foreign exchange investment and trading receipts. Government revenue generation is not a priority."

In March 1996, the national government adopted as a "national priority" the "cohesive, controlled and sensitive development, growth, and maintenance of tourism." To further this broad national policy, the government also adopted goals to guide official decision making in a number of spheres: economic, social, political, and environmental. The principal preservation goals were social ("to preserve, protect and to promote a greater appreciation of the culture, heritage, history, and traditions of our country" (see Photo 6-10) and environmental ("to preserve, protect and sustain the biodiversity and the natural environment of our country"). All private proposals for development would be reviewed with the aim of protecting against environmental and cultural harm.

Of ten very broad categories of "Key Policies," the first listed (and presumably the most

Photo by Susan Turner

Photo 6-10 Papua New Guinea resident in traditional dress at a cultural tourism program (Courtesy of John Kambowa, Manager, Planning and Development, Papua New Guinea Tourism Authority)

important to planners and officials) was the creation of "Priority Tourism Zones" in four different regional districts: Central Province and Milne Bay; Highlands; Mamose; and New Guinea Islands Region. Historically, the country has been divided into these four regions for administrative purposes. The divisions were based on similarities in community history, culture, language, trade, geographical features, and former colonization. According to John Kambowa, Manager for Planning and Development of the Papua New Guinea Tourism Promotion Authority, these are the same criteria being used by many organizations and departments for planning purposes today.

The Papua New Guinea national government delegated the implementation of the tourism policy to an agency known as the "Tourism Promotion Authority" (TPA), which among other things is the liaison between the national government and the provincial governments. Regarding the four Priority Tourism Zones, the TPA will include representatives of each zone and will establish a physical presence in each zone. The TPA adopted an implementing "Corporate Plan" in 1996, which emphasizes assistance in the creation of a new visitor attraction. This contemplated assistance can take a variety of forms, including for example: "consolidating" development initiatives in the priority zones; assisting private industry; encouraging improvements in existing developments; promoting infrastructure enhancements; expanding existing markets; and identifying and targeting new markets. The use of the term "consolidating" in the types of assistance to be offered by TPA was amplified by manager John Kambowa, who explained that success will come only if all affected governmental offices act in a "collaborative and concerted spirit." Thus, progress in tourism development requires sustained and full cooperation among all of the "players," including ministries in charge of airports, seaports, electricity, water, roads, and other crucial infrastructure assets.

The Corporate Plan of the TPA includes a long section setting forth with impressive detail the goals, emphases, and operational strategies for tourism development. The plan calls for the TPA to "ensure availability" of hotels, resorts, and other service establishments to meet market demand; to encourage supplemental attractions (e.g., restaurants, hiking opportunities); to seek matches between "destination uniqueness" and the tourism development there; and to promote a high level of design and service. In order to accomplish these ambitious goals, the plan calls for the TPA to give primary emphasis within each of the four priority tourist zones to development of one or more "base anchors" (i.e., major tourist establishments associated with principal tourism resources). One example is the Ambua Lodge in the Highlands Region. That lodge is a community-based resort in the wilderness, offering cultural interaction with the Huli people of Tari, who design and wear elaborate costumes and unique, colorful, bird-feathered wigs. Perched high atop a hill at 7,000 feet, the traditionally designed lodge and the 40 bungalows are surrounded by a rainforest, trails, waterfalls, orchids, and ten species of birds of paradise. The lodge is a base for scenic bus tours, bird watching, and nature tours.

A Successful Tourism Project under the New Policy

An interesting example of a successful application for tourism development, justifiably regarded by the government as an "environmentally sensitive best practice (development) in a village setting," is the now completed, eight-unit Kumul development ("Kumul" means "paradise"). Promoted by local communal landowners (the Abonaom family of the Nenain clan) with the verbal "support" (a common traditional requirement) of the neighboring clans who communally own the adjacent land, the project application lists as indirect benefits to all local villages: increased cash circulation, employment for old and young, ancillary sales of artifacts and participation in entertainment, and sales of food produce to the lodge. Tourist attractions were listed as bush walking to waterfalls to see flora and fauna; participation in traditional ceremonies such as "bride price"; seeing traditional handicrafts, such as muumuu clothing styles; observance of lifestyles of nearby villagers; and sightseeing in the valley below the lodge. From the design standpoint, the main assembly building and also the individual bungalows follow the traditional style—high-peaked roofs with bundled kunai thatch, rubble stone and traditional, split yar studwork exterior wall areas. The lodge's site plan fully preserved the traditional ceremonial ground.

Future Activities of the Tourism Planning Authority

In the long term, the TPA seeks to encourage new and innovative tourism products that will be attractive to primary target markets; in the short term, it is encouraging improvement of existing attractions and facilities. Several of the operational strategies identified in the TPA Corporate Plan are quite common: (1) to consider alternatives for additional international air gateways in the four priority tourism zones; (2) to promote the development of meetings and convention facilities; (3) to promote coordinated activities among supplemental tourist-oriented businesses such as restaurants, entertainment facilities, and handicraft stores, especially within each of the priority tourism zones; (4) to encourage businesses to work together in packaging their products; and (5) to focus attention on ecotourism opportunities to take advantage of natural heritage assets. More unusual is another operational strategy set forth in the plan: *lobbying* both for product creation and for governmental incentives and concessions to secure product enhancement. Extensive lobbying for governmental incentives may not be necessary, because several incentives already exist regarding both income tax and employment/training. Many tourist projects already qualify for tax relief under the Pioneer Industry and Rural Development tax status statutes. Other forms of favorable treatment are also available: a double tax deduction for certain market development costs, a tourism plan deduction, an exemption from taxation of certain interest income, an import duty exemption, permitted repatriation of investment and profits, and a governmental contribution of a portion of the cost of project feasibility studies. Papua New Guinea also offers certain wage subsidies, taxation incentives, and a reduction in a training levy for employment and training of persons for the tourism industry.

Closing Comments

It is much too early to assess the success of Papua New Guinea's very recent planning efforts. The structure is impressive, however, as is the zeal expressed in the governing documents. The challenges will be to develop sufficient public and private infrastructure upon which a sizable tourism base could be built and to attract sufficient numbers of tourists to make the developments profitable, in a time of some considerable political instability and following the fatal 1998 tidal wave.

There is an inherent dilemma for Papua New Guinea: its two greatest attractions to tourists—the "exotic" aspects of its cultural traditions and the beauty and diversity of its environment—are the very two elements that it wishes to protect from tourist intrusion. New tourism developments and proposals have thus far met high standards, but it is too early yet to know whether they will bring the anticipated economic benefits without undue risks of environmental degradation and social harm.

Possible Difficulties Associated with Identifying New Tourist Resources

The most obvious problem associated with the identification of new tourist resources is the independence and relative speed with which they may sometimes be turned into tourist attractions. Often an individual entrepreneur can legally create a new attraction that may have an enormous impact on the broader community if successful. Yet there may be no impetus for consultation if there are no legal requirements for it, and if the entrepreneur is not an active member of the community, guided by local attitudes.

One of the most unusual examples of just such a new attraction is Althorp Park, the ancestral home of the late Diana, Princess of Wales. Her brother, the Earl of Spencer, has decided to open the 8,500-acre estate to the public from July 1 through August 30 every year. Visitors can tour some of the 122 rooms of the mansion; visit a museum with Diana's tiara and wedding dress and childhood memorabilia; walk the gardens; look across an ornamental lake to the Princess's burial site on a small island; visit a memorial to the

Princess and place floral tributes at an eighteenth-century temple; and then stop for a bite to eat in the café and look for souvenirs in the gift shop. Visitors are currently limited to 2,500 each day.

The estate is just outside the tiny village of Great Brington, population 220, which does not even boast a traffic light. Residents are fearful that every summer will see hordes of tourists descending on their erstwhile peaceful village, driving down the main road, searching for parking spots and restrooms. Many villagers are resentful that they were not consulted from the beginning. The Earl spends most of his time in Cape Town, South Africa, and so won't be particularly affected by the crowds and traffic. The villagers will be affected and fear that their community may turn into an English Graceland.

Final Observations

This chapter has presented alternative strategies that enable destinations to develop and enhance their resources to attract more tourists. Whatever approach is adopted—whether expansion, dispersion, concentration, or identification of new tourism resources—it is essential that destination communities consider the impacts of increased tourism. No community can afford to be sanguine about tourism growth. The impacts of twice as many visitors may grow exponentially, not merely double. Mitigating measures that may be sufficient to alleviate *existing* negative impacts may be incapable of coping with *additional* impacts from a heightened level of tourism. The infrastructure may not be able to support increased numbers of tourists, requiring massive public expenditures and a lot more concrete. The environment may not be able to sustain increased development without serious degradation. The ratio of number of tourists to number of residents may shift dramatically, with undesirable social and cultural consequences.

When destination communities choose a strategy for increasing tourism, they need simultaneously to consider quality control and quantity management measures to mitigate potential negative impacts from additional tourism development. The Republic of the Maldives, for example, recognized the need to preserve its environmental quality and therefore imposed the requirement that for each island devoted to tourist development, another three islands be set aside for preservation. Bruges instituted far-reaching traffic control measures to minimize the negative impacts of its concentration model. New York City imposed stringent zoning restrictions on adult uses to mitigate their negative impact on the Times Square area. Canterbury upgraded various spots along Queen Bertha's Walk and created new paths and terraces to improve the quality of its offerings. In Nusa Dua, extensive infrastructure construction preceded development to provide a measure of environmental protection; and strict architectural guidelines ensure consistency with established design criteria.

The case studies show that planning for new or increased tourism often occurs on a regional or even national level. Expansion and dispersal strategies by definition involve broadening the area that will be affected by tourism, often beyond jurisdictional boundaries. This necessitates either a cooperative and coordinated planning effort among multiple destination communities (which was the case in the Southern Lakes case study) or centralized planning by a regional or national government (as was the case in the Oaxaca Valleys, the Maldives, and in the development of Languedoc-Roussillon). Efforts to attract tourists for the first time also often include regional or national participants. When individual communities do not offer sufficient attractions to lure a meaningful number of tourists or do not have the resources to develop and market themselves, they may need to band together (as was the case in both the Tarka Project and South Pembrokeshire, Wales) or to rely on the efforts and resources of the government (as was the case in the development of the Bays of Huatulco).

The major challenge of regional planning in these instances is reaching consensus among disparate and diverse constituencies. The difficulties that the Southern Lakes Strategy group faced in trying to secure agreement on a solution to the congestion at Milford Sound is a classic example of the problems often encountered. There the boundaries were broadly drawn to include the entire Southern Lakes district. There was a well thought out and inclusive public participation process. Nevertheless, because the three original recommendations for new access to Milford Sound all had important economic and environmental impacts on different areas of the Southern Lakes, the multiple constituencies were unable to reach any consensus. The decision concerning access has been put on indefinite hold, while the parties reconvene to discuss their vision for the future of the Southern Lakes district.

Since location enhancement strategies all involve attracting more tourists, marketing plays an important role. The case studies suggest that destination communities will be better off if they are able (often through research efforts) to identify clearly their target market. Bruges studied the two types of visitors it attracted (overnight and day-tripper) and researched the impacts of each. It then decided to focus its efforts on increasing the number of overnight visitors and developed its concentration model, traffic control measures, and marketing with that category of tourist in mind. The Tarka Project, on the other hand, originally believed that the tourists who would be attracted to Tarka Country would be long-distance walkers. This turned out to be a misjudgment, and it took some years before the appropriate accommodations, trails, and promotional materials were prepared for the tourists Tarka Country was in fact attracting: families coming for a week-long rural vacation.

Oaxaca knew that tourists to the city were interested in local crafts, and its expansion model was developed with those tourists in mind. Nusa Dua has successfully built a high-end tourist enclave that concentrates those tourists in one small section of Bali, protecting the residents on the rest of the island from their influence. However, many tourists cannot afford Nusa Dua hotel rates and many others do not wish to be isolated from Balinese society, and so they choose to stay elsewhere on the island. The concentration model cannot mitigate the impacts of these tourists.

Another lesson from the case studies is the active and important role that the tourism industry can play in location enhancement strategies. The Tarka Project, Canterbury's creation of Queen Bertha's Walk, the New Zealand Southern Lakes Strategy, and the Times Square Business Improvement District measures were all initiated by private business associations and tourism councils. While these efforts resulted in well-planned and coordinated development (it is, after all, in the self-interest of the industry to develop sustainable tourism and not to kill the goose that lays the golden egg), this is not necessarily always the case.

Independent entrepreneurs, like the Earl of Spencer in England and some farmowners in the United States, can sometimes develop their own private resources into a completely legal tourist attraction that may have significant negative impacts on the shared assets of the broader community. When the law places inadequate restraints on development at the same time that the marketplace offers enticing economic incentives, the greatest protection from harmful individual developments may lie in the pressures of community norms and the expectations that development will conform to the community's shared vision rather than conflict with it.

7

Elements of Successful Strategies

The most successful strategies for managing tourism growth are those that address local goals, reflect the character of the destination community, and respond to local conditions. There is no "formula" that can be uniformly applied to all destination communities. Not only is any such formula likely to be out of date by the time the ink is dry on the plans, but it is also sure to ignore the special qualities of the place that give it its unique character. As destination communities consider how best to manage their own particular brand of tourism growth and resources, they should keep in mind the elements of both the *process* and *substance* of effective strategies and adapt them as needed to their own situation.

Process Elements

One of the best ways of ensuring that a strategy is tailored to the special resources and requirements of the destination community is to have that strategy evolve from an effective community planning process. Effective processes that lead to tailor-made strategies share common characteristics that emphasize the unique aspect of each destination community.

1. A careful definition of the boundaries of the planning area can help a community to identify the likely impacts, both positive and negative, of tourism growth and facilitate development of a strategy to minimize negative impacts in a sustainable manner.
2. An identification of all the parties who are likely to share in either the benefits or burdens of tourism growth allows their inclusion in the planning process and increases the likelihood that the final strategy will allocate the benefits and burdens in a way that the community perceives as equitable.
3. Community participation in establishing the goals and objectives of a management strategy and in making implementation decisions improves the chance that the final strategy will accurately reflect the values and vision of the community and then enjoy a high degree of compliance and widespread acceptance in the community.
4. Adoption of management techniques that address specific local objectives promotes the creative use of various mechanisms and discourages reliance on overbroad regulatory measures.
5. A continuing process of participation and the ongoing sharing of relevant information allow the community to rely on the long-term viability of the strategy to protect its tourism resources and its quality of life.

6. A system to monitor the effectiveness of the strategy in meeting its goals provides the community with data to determine whether the strategy needs to be amended to respond to changing circumstances and facilitates enforcement.

It is never an easy task to create a community planning process that is inclusive and fair. But the community may profit in the long run from such a process in ways that far outweigh the cost in time and effort. Strategies that develop with broad community involvement are most likely to secure those benefits that the community desires; avoid those impacts that the community deems harmful; share the benefits and burdens in an equitable way; and be adaptable to future changes in local conditions.

Substance Elements

The case studies in this book have been divided into categories according to the substantive management technique that they illustrate. There are ten categories, three each under the headings of quality and quantity, and four under the heading of location. Again, however, it must be emphasized that these are rough and overlapping categories. Many of the case studies could have been included in two or even more categories. Most of them use a variety of management techniques tailored to their own specific tourism resources.

The ten categories, therefore, might best be viewed as a checklist of opportunities that communities can review in analyzing where management of their particular resources is needed.

1. The identification of geographic areas where high quality should be created or maintained allows a community to focus its attention efficiently on the places where tourism resources can best be utilized without imposing inappropriate regulations on the community at large.
2. Performance standards that ensure high-quality tourism development can help ensure that the development enhances tourism resources in a sustainable manner while maintaining maximum opportunities for creativity and flexibility on the part of the developer.
3. Trade-off strategies that promote protection of high-quality tourism resources may promote a sense of both equity among members of the community and efficiency in the marketplace.
4. Preservation rules that strictly limit the quantity of development in sensitive areas may be necessary to allow tourists of future generations to utilize these resources.
5. Growth limitations that directly control the quantity of development may be needed where there is no efficient way by which an area can manage its current or projected rate of tourism growth without threatening the sustainability of the very resources that make tourism viable.
6. Incremental growth strategies that provide flexible standards to adapt the quantity of future growth to then-existing conditions are a form of adaptive management that may maximize the resiliency of a strategy to ongoing changes.
7. Expansion of a destination area may be an appropriate strategy if, for example, it can reduce congestion that is adversely affecting the efficiency or sustainability of existing tourism resources or if it can promote greater equity among the local beneficiaries of tourism.
8. Dispersal strategies, which try to spread tourists around to many locations and reduce concentration, are often used to distribute the benefits of tourism throughout

the community and to avoid overtaxing specific resources to a degree that may not be sustainable in the long run.

9. Concentration strategies that focus tourism intensively in specific locations are appropriate if the community's tourism resources are of the sort that can be most efficiently managed as a substantial, critical mass in a tightly confined area.

10. Strategies that identify and promote tourism resources that had not previously been targeted may sometimes be able to bring new economic benefits through adaptation to a changing market or environment in a resilient and efficient manner.

In considering these options, it should be remembered that management is not desirable for its own sake, but only to remedy perceived problems or to forestall future ones. Overenthusiastic micromanagement can diminish the creativity and entrepreneurship that have made tourism such a pleasurable activity for the participants. Management that selectively identifies and deals only with real problem areas is most likely to achieve the objectives of equity, efficiency, sustainability, and resiliency.

Notes

Chapter 1

1. World Travel and Tourism Council (1992). Quoted in William Theobald, "The Context, Meaning and Scope of Tourism," in Global Tourism: The Next Decade, ed., William Theobald, (London: Butterworth-Heinemann Ltd., 1994), p. 4.
2. See generally, "Home and Away," *The Economist*, 10 January 1998, pp. 3–4.
3. William Theobald, "The Context, Meaning and Scope of Tourism," in *Global Tourism*, William Theobald, p. 4.
4. B. Crossette, "Surprises in the Global Tourism Boom," *New York Times*, 12 April 1998, citing the World Tourism Organization.
5. E. Leed, *The Mind of the Traveler: From Gilgamesh to Global Tourism* (New York: Basic Books, 1991), p. 7.
6. One excellent resource book covering a wide range elements and issues produced by modern tourism is by Gareth Shaw and Allan M Williams, *Critical Issues in Tourism: A Geographical Perspective* (Oxford: Blackwell, 1994). Part IV of this book is particularly helpful, as it discusses a variety of "tourism environments": leisure environments, mass tourism, urban tourism, and rural tourism. Among the authors' useful predictions as to the future of tourism is that there will be an increased emphasis on sound planning in advance of tourism development. See also an interesting historical treatment of tourism in the western United States, Hal K. Rothman, *Devil's Bargains: Tourism in the Twentieth Century American West* (Lawrence, Kansas: University Press of Kansas, 1998). Rothman examines a number of areas, including some of the case study locations discussed earlier in this book: Aspen, Colorado; Jackson, Wyoming; and Santa Fe, New Mexico.
7. See, for example, *Agenda 21 for the Travel and Tourism Industry: Towards Environmentally Sustainable Development* (London: World Travel and Tourism Council and World Tourism Organization, 1995); *Awards for Improving the Coastal Environment: The Example of the Blue Flag* (Paris: United Nations Environmental Program and World Tourism Organization, 1996); *Guidelines: Development of National Parks and Protected Areas for Tourism* (Madrid: World Tourism Organization and United Nations Environmental Program, 1992). The World Travel and Tourism Council runs a worldwide environmental management and awareness program known as Green Globe that is open to travel and tourism companies of any size, type, and location. The International Hospitality and Restaurant Association is also active in promoting sustainable tourism. See *Environmental Good Practice in Hotels: Case Studies from the International Hotel and Restaurant Association Environmental Award* (Paris: United Nations Environmental Program and International Hospitality and Restaurant Association, 1997). *Condé Nast Traveler* magazine gives a yearly award for the best ecotourism business practicing "green" principles, as selected by a panel of leading industry representatives. Recognizing that awards can encourage environmentally sound programs, the European Union in 1995 created an

annual prize for tourism sites or destinations that respect the environment, based on many criteria including the degree of cooperation between private operators and public bodies.

Interested readers may wish to contact the Tourism Section of the Industry and Environment Division of the United Nations Environmental Program, headquartered in Paris, for information on international efforts in this area. UNEP has been a major proponent of "green" hospitality practices and has adopted a policy of working closely with tourism industry groups and professionals. A recent example is UNEP's 1998 study of voluntary approaches that promote environmental sustainability by awarding ecolabels to well-performing businesses. *Ecolabels in the Tourism Industry* (Paris: United Nations Environmental Program, 1998). See also the earlier *Environmental Codes of Conduct for Tourism* (Paris: United Nations Environmental Program, 1995). See also the excellent Suzanne Hawkes and Peter Williams, *The Greening of Tourism: From Principles to Practice* (Canada: Simon Fraser, 1993), which covers the programs of British Airways, the Chateau Whistler hotel, the Canadian Restaurant and Food Association, and the Hotel Uclivia. This book also summarizes some adventure tourism sustainability efforts.

8.   See Edwin McDowell, "Accidental Tourists Need Not Apply Here," *New York Times*, 5 September 1998, from which this account is drawn.

9.   Bapak Gede Arya, the District Leader for the villages in the Nusa Dua area, quoted in B.T.B.C., *Nusa Dua: Reflections of Bali* (Bali: Nusa Dua Development Corporation, 1995).

10. For example, travel writer and novelist Paul Theroux notes that logging has been banned on the island of Palawan in the Philippines archipelago, triggered in part by a policy to encourage tourism by protecting forest habitats. Now visitors can see pigs, bearcats, monkeys, and such unusual birds as the red-headed tree babbler in their natural setting. Paul Theroux, "The Essential Nature of Islands," *Outside*, September 1998, p. 110.

11. T. Patrick Culbert, "The New Maya," *Archaeology*, September/October 1998, p. 51.

12. A recent survey of their readers, reported in the September 1998 issue of *Condé Nast Traveler (Extra)*, p. 23, indicated that "(a)lmost 90 percent were interested in learning about the lifestyle and culture of the people who live where they're visiting, and 46 percent would like to live that lifestyle while on vacation. More than a quarter prefer culturally authentic accommodations; more than half have taken a short vacation that includes culture or history in the last year. . . .

13. Of course, familiarity with the ways of foreigners creates empathy only if the foreigners behave in a reasonably acceptable fashion. Traveling English soccer fans have done little to endear the English to the rest of Europe. And although the Woodstock Festival in the 1960s is now looked back upon with nostalgia, the reaction of local residents at the time widened the generation gap rather than narrowing it.

14. See Peter Burns and Andrew Holden, *Tourism: A New Perspective* (Hertfordshire: Prentice Hall, 1995), pp. 90–91, from which this account is drawn.

15. Steven Greenhouse, "Labor Eyes a Prize: Hotels of New Orleans," *New York Times*, 18 August 1998.

16. Peter Murphy, *Quality Management in Urban Tourism* (New York: John Wiley & Sons, 1997), pp. 47–49.

17. A small but important submarket of the tourism industry has received much attention in recent years: ecotourism. One of the best of many books on the subject is also one of the most practically oriented: Kreg Lindberg and Donald Hawkins, eds., *Ecotourism: A Guide for Planners and Managers* (North Bennington, Vt.: The Ecotourism Society, 1993). See also Elizabeth Boo, *Ecotourism: the Potentials and Pitfalls*, Vols. 1 and 2 (Washington, D.C.: World Wildlife Fund, 1990).

18. Dinerstein, Rijal, Bookbinder, Kattel and Rajinia, *Tigers as Neighbors: Efforts to Promote Local Guardianship of Endangered Species in Lowland Nepal* (Washington, DC.: World Wildlife Fund, 1997).

19. Much of the literature on adverse impacts of tourism stresses *environmental* impacts, which is discussed in two thoughtful and balanced books: Peter Johnson and Barry Thomas, eds., *Perspectives on Tourism Policy* (London: Mansell, 1992), especially Chapter 3; and Zbigniew Mieczlowski, *Environmental Issues of Tourism & Recreation* (Lanham: University Press of America, 1995).

20. Environmental Conservation Section of the Tourist Authority of Thailand, *An Outline of Problems and Remedies of Tourism Impact on the Environment,* 1993).

21. There has been a great deal of study on how nature is affected by tourism. An excellent source is Fred Kuss, et al., *Visitor Impact Management: A Review of the Research* (Washington, D.C.: National Parks and Conservation Association, 1990), covering especially well the impacts on vegetation and soils, water resources, and wildlife.

22. It is rare for a government to be as frank and forthcoming about the negative impacts of tourism as Thailand has been. Unfortunately, it is much more common for governments to deny problems and offer a positive spin on failures to mitigate adverse impacts. The island of Boracay, the Philippines' most popular tourist destination, is justly famous for its white sand beaches and clear water, attracting about 200,000 annual visitors. In July 1997, the national Environmental Department declared that the beaches were no longer safe for water activities due to elevated levels of coliform bacteria caused by several resorts that were dumping untreated human waste directly into the sea. The top tourism executive disputed the findings, asserting that the bacteria levels were normal for that time of year and that the level would dissipate with the onset of the monsoons later in the year. Tourism declined precipitously after the report was issued.

    In a move with all the earmarks of political motivation to protect the economically crucial tourism industry (US $2.7 billion in national revenues in 1996), the Environmental Department and the Tourism Department promptly released a joint statement declaring that the Boracay waters were *safe* for swimming, and the Secretary of the Environmental Department issued a public apology for his earlier "irresponsible statement" that the water was unsafe. Fortunately, the government has now adopted plans to step up monitoring of water quality and has created a fund for promoting environmental protection. See generally: "Cleanup of Infected Philippine Resort Underway," *Agence France Presse,* 7 July 1997; J. Grafilo, "Boracay's Feces-Infested Waters Trouble Tourism," *Japan Economic Newswire,* 8 July 1997; E. Jalbuna, "The Contamination of Boracay: Who's to Blame?," *Businessworld (Manila),* 16 July 1997.

23. Tourism Authority of Thailand, *An Outline of Problems and Remedies of Tourism Impact on the Environment,* July 1993. The TAT should be commended for its frank catalogue of difficulties and its goals of dealing with those problems, also expressed in the memorandum.

24. Some of these and related issues are addressed by K. S. Chon and A. Singh, "Environmental Challenges and Influences on Tourism: The Case of Thailand's Tourism Industry," in *Progress in Tourism, Recreation and Hospitality Management,* Vol. 6, eds., C. P. Cooper and A. Lockwood (Chichester: John Wiley & Sons, 1994), pp. 80–91.

25. Most of these "other negative impacts" involve private conduct that is difficult or perhaps inappropriate to regulate (for example, in the United States, the marketplace is the informal "regulator" of merchants charging higher prices than competitors, assuming no false misrepresentations or other prohibited conduct such as pricing collusion with other sellers).

26. *The Economist* magazine's well-regarded Intelligence Unit has very usefully categorized the fronts of "Tourism under Attack," illustrated typical problems in 20 countries, and posited a number of sensible action approaches Paul Jenner and Christine Smith, *The Tourism Industry and the Environment* (London: *The Economist* Intelligence Unit, 1992).

27. It would not be difficult to create a book-length compendium of serious negative impacts brought on by unrestrained tourism in various locations. However, while such an effort would be of some use, it could easily persuade many destinations to avoid tourism growth altogether. This would be very unfortunate, given that there are a number of approaches to mitigate most if not all of the potential problems and at the same time enjoy the many benefits of tourism. This book is an effort to help destination communities develop strategies that will, in part, minimize the negative impacts of tourism development. In any event, a listing of recent tourism challenges (some of which have been addressed by communities after the impacts have become apparent) include the following: (1) the overdevelopment of hotels around Victoria Falls, Zimbabwe that causes water supply, sewage, and waste disposal problems as well as undue stress of the wilderness by hordes of visitors; (2) the construction of too many lodges in the Serengeti National Park and the Ngorongoro Conservation Area, Tanzania that threaten significant cultural and environmentally fragile sites; (3) the adverse effect on wildlife caused by too many safaris in the Masai Mara Game Reserve, Kenya; (4) the tourism-related prostitution and pedophilia, together with rapid growth in visitor accommodations on the Indian island of Goa, creating adverse impacts on the resident population and the fragile ecology; (5) the refusal of the Australian government to allow desirable culling to control serious overpopulation of koalas, out of fear that tourists would object and/or boycott; (6) the Mexican national governmental approval of a cruise ship pier over Paradise Reef on the island of Cozumel, despite strong evidence that the project would seriously harm live coral; (7) the illegal and dangerous development of small hotels, bars, discos, and restaurants along the road leading to the gateway of Costa Rica's most beautiful national park, Manual Antonio; (8) the degradation of forests, valleys, and wildlife in the European Alpine countries, caused in part by tourism and second-home development; (9) the highly intense development patterns of high-rise buildings and sprawling settlements of year-round and second homes, most near the beaches of the tourism-dominated town of Calvia, Mallorca, triggering ecological damage to coastal areas and visual unsightliness; (10) the adverse ambiance and safety impacts on ancient cities and historical sites in England, generated by busloads of daytrippers (examples include Stonehenge, inundated by foot and vehicular traffic, and Cambridge, where the city introduced rickshaws to transport visitors along congested streets after a bicycle plan had failed); (11) the overbuilt, out- of-scale hotels at Ixia Beach, Crete, Greece, as well as illegally close, poorly designed small hotels along the northern coast of Crete; (12) the construction in Southeast Asia of more than 500 golf courses that use scarce water supplies, displace residents, and replace productive agricultural land; (13) the exchange of women's traditional costumes and jewelry, often representing their status in the tribe as well as their wealth, for westernized goods such as T-shirts and football jerseys in the hill tribes villages of the Golden Triangle of Thailand, Laos, and Myanmar; and (14) the proposal, later withdrawn as the result of protests led by a woman living in a shack on a sandbar, by a German company to build a large resort hotel on the Aegean coast of Turkey at Dalyan at a location that would greatly interfere with the ability of newly hatched loggerhead turtles to reach the safety of the sea.

28. J. Howe, E. McMahon, and L. Propst, *Balancing Nature and Commerce in Gateway Communities* (Washington, D.C.: Island Press, 1997), p. 34.

29. Kathleen McCormick, "In the Clutch of the Casinos," *Planning* (June 1997): p. 8.

30. Quoted in C. Lavery, "Bands Beat the Ban: Council Chiefs in Fort William Try to Stop Pubs from Playing Loud Gaelic Songs," *Sunday Mail,* 9 April 1995.

31. Quoted in M. Potok, "Fishing for Tourists, Moab Hooks a Shark," *The Denver Post,* 18 June 1995.

32. Alister Mathieson and Goeffrey Wall, *Tourism: Economic, Physical, and Social Impacts* (London: Longman Group Ltd, 1982), p. 1.

33. Thomas L. Davidson, "What are Travel and Tourism: Are They Really an Industry?" in *Global Tourism: The Next Decade,* ed., William Theobald (London: Butterworth-Heinemann Ltd., 1994) p. 23.

34. See the excellent discussion in Peter Murphy, *Tourism: A Community Approach* (New York and London: Methuen, 1985), pp. 7–8, referring to the work of other tourism scholars.

35. Murphy, *Tourism: A Community Approach,* p. 7.

36. An excellent and well-written general overview of a multitude of tourism development issues and analytical methodologies is the second edition of Douglas Pearce's well-known work *Tourism Development,* 2nd ed. (New York: Longman Group Ltd., 1989).

37. Professor Murphy has articulated a very interesting "ecological model of tourism planning," which readers might well find stimulating and conceptually useful. However, we do not ground our analysis on his model. See Murphy, *Tourism: A Community Approach,* pp. 166–176. See also Clare A. Gunn, *Vacationscape: Developing Tourist Areas* (Washington, D.C.: Taylor & Francis, 1997).

Chapter 2

1. Whistler, *Community and Resort Monitoring Program* (1995), p. 2.

2. One of the important elements of the Whistler monitoring program is the visitor satisfaction survey. Whistler recognizes that to maintain its position as a first-class tourist destination, it needs to understand why its visitors choose Whistler, whether their expectations have been met, and what steps it needs to take to ensure that it is offering a high-quality visitor experience, so that tourists will return.

3. Social indicators, for example, include population demographics, school enrollment, health data, social agency statistics, unemployment, crime statistics, and adult education opportunities and enrollments. Community facilities and infrastructure indicators include usage at community and recreational facilities, remaining water system capacity, remaining sewer system capacity, wastewater effluent quality and volume, energy consumption, length of bike trails and their usage, fire and other emergency calls, library use, and museum visitations.

4. Research into the nature of tourism resources has proceeded slowly, and "tourism researchers and theorists have yet to fully come to terms with the nature of attractions as phenomena both in the environment and in the mind," Alan A. Lew, "A Framework of Tourist Attraction Research," in J. R. Brent Ritchie and Charles R. Goeldner, *Travel, Tourism, and Hospitality Research: A Handbook for Managers and Researchers,* 2nd ed. (New York: John Wiley & Sons, 1994), pp. 291–304.

5. Tourism advertising typically focuses on the emotional experiences the tourist anticipates. See generally John C. Crotts and W. Fred van Raaij, eds., *Economic Psychology of Travel and Tourism* (New York: Haworth Press, 1994).

6. Of course, there are a few communities in which either public or private assets are so dominant that they seem to overwhelm everything else. In Washington, D.C., the federal museums and monuments are the dominant factor for tourism. In Disneyworld, at the

other extreme, private attractions dominate. But even in areas like these, tourism can be greatly affected by the way that shared resources are managed, as the examples cited in this chapter will show.

7. Different societies mean slightly different things when they use these terms, depending on whether they have inherited the common law or the civil law tradition, but these distinctions in terminology are not too important for purposes of the planning process.

8. See Susan Buck, *The Global Commons* (Washington, D.C.: Island Press, 1998).

9. Gunn, *Vacationscape*, p. 7.

10. On the obligation to future generations in land-use decisions, see Timothy Beatley, *Ethical Land Use: Principles of Policy and Planning* (Baltimore, MD: Johns Hopkins University Press, 1994), pp. 134–152.

11. Daniel W. Bromley, ed., *Making the Commons Work: Theory, Practice and Policy* (San Francisco: ICS Press, 1992), p. 229.

12. Bromley, *Making the Commons Work*, pp. 161ff.

13. Glenn G. Stevenson, *Common Property Economics: A General Theory and Land Use Applications* (Cambridge: Cambridge University Press, 1991).

14. Fikret Berkes, *Common Property Resources: Ecology and Community Based Sustainable Development* (London: Belhaven Press, 1989), p. 15.

15. Elinor Ostrom, *Governing the Commons: The Evolution of Institutions for Collective Action* (Cambridge: Cambridge University Press, 1990).

16. Richard W. Judd, *Common Lands, Common People: The Origins of Conservation in Northern New England* (Cambridge: Harvard University Press, 1997), pp. 55–56.

17. By empirical observation, we can determine which systems achieve these objectives and can identify their characteristics. At this stage, we can't realistically quantify that achievement, but as research proceeds, more precise evaluation is likely to follow.

18. Bromley, *Making the Commons Work*, p. 302.

19. Bonnie F. McCay, *Oyster Wars and the Public Trust: Property, Law, and Ecology in New Jersey History* (Tucson: The University of Arizona Press, 1998), p. 193.

20. Robert O. Keohane, *Local Commons and Global Interdependence: Heterogeneity and Cooperation in Two Domains* (London: Sage, 1995), p. 140.

21. Keohane, *Local Commons and Global Interdependence*, p. 166.

22. Berkes, *Common Property Resources*, p. 12.

23. Susan Hanna, *Property Rights and the Environment: Social and Ecological Issues* (Washington, D.C.: The World Bank, 1995), p. 94.

24. Mieczkowski, *Environmental Issues*, pp. 114–115.

25. Carol M. Rose, *Property and Persuasion: Essays on the History, Theory, and Rhetoric of Ownership* (Boulder: Westview Press, 1994), p. 190.

26. Bromley, *Making the Commons Work*, p. 51.

27. Ostrom, *Governing the Commons*, p. 87.

28. Bromley, *Making the Commons Work*, p. 13.

29. Hanna, *Property Rights and the Environment*, p. 97.

30. Hanna, *Property Rights and the Environment*, p. 21.

31. McCay, *Oyster Wars*, pp. 189ff.

32. Hanna, *Property Rights and the Environment*, p. 45.

33. Hanna, *Property Rights and the Environment*, p. 20.

34. Bromley, *Making the Commons Work*, p. 244.

35. Ostrom, *Governing the Commons*, p. 267.

36. Ostrom, *Governing the Commons*, p. 282.

37. Hanna, *Property Rights and the Environment*, p. 36.

38. Berkes, *Common Property Resources,* p. 11.

39. Keohane, *Local Commons and Global Interdependence,* p. 130.

40. Berkes, *Common Property Resources,* p. 49.

41. Hanna, *Property Rights and the Environment,* p. 19.

42. Stevenson, *Common Property Economics,* p. 75.

43. Ostrom, *Governing the Commons,* pp. 196ff.

44. Bromley, *Making the Commons Work,* p. 90.

45. Hanna, *Property Rights and the Environment,* p. 65.

46. McCay, *Oyster Wars,* p. 197.

47. Berkes, *Common Property Resources,* p. 31.

48. Berkes, *Common Property Resources,* p. 11.

49. Ostrom, *Governing the Commons,* p. 282.

50. Ostrom, *Governing the Commons,* p. 242.

51. Berkes, *Common Property Resources,* p. 42.

52. For a much more thorough discussion, see Jeremy Boissevain, "'But We Live Here!' Perspectives on Cultural Tourism in Malta," in *Sustainable Tourism in Islands and Small States: Case Studies,* ed., Luis Briguglio (New York: Pinter, 1996).

53. One practical difficulty that many communities face when seeking professional assistance is finding the money to pay for the needed services. Government funding (national and international) is one potential source. Peninsula Township received grants from the state Coastal Zone Management program, local foundations, a research institute, and Michigan State University. The Tarka Project in Devon and SPARC in South Pembrokeshire, Wales, both received some funding from the European Commission. The United Nations and the World Tourism Organization have both provided financial and technical assistance to numerous countries.

54. Norman Walzer, ed., *Community Strategic Visioning Programs* (Westport, Conn.: Praeger Publishers, 1996); Judith E. Innes, "Planning Through Consensus Building: A New View of the Comprehensive Planning Ideal," *Journal of the American Planning Ass'n* 62, 4 (Fall 1996): 460–472.

55. Monteverde cloud forest tourism issues are addressed in Chapter 7 of a well-conceived and executed series of articles combined in Martin Price, ed., *People and Tourism in Fragile Environments* (Chichester: John Wiley & Sons, 1996). The discussed destinations are all characterized by inherent fragility or by fragility due to human activities: the Zuni Pueblo, New Mexico; the Intuit area of Nunavut, Canada; the Aboriginal crea in Far North Queensland, Australia; Svalbard in the Northern Barents Sea; Richtersveld, South Africa; Flathead County, Montana; South Wales; the Masai areas of Kenya; Hwang National Park, Zimbabwe; and the Monteverde cloud forest, Costa Rica.

56. In the U.S.A., public participation has been required in the environmental arena by the Council on Environmental Quality regulations (1987), and many other federal agencies have similar public participation requirements. There are any number of books and articles evaluating those processes that might be helpful to those trying to set up their own model for community participation. See, for example, Larry W. Canter, *Environmental Impact Assessment* (New York: McGraw Hill, 1996), pp. 587–622.

57. See Steven Ames, ed., *A Guide to Community Visioning* (Chicago: APA Planners Press, 1998).

58. See Tazim Jamal and Donald Getz, "Visioning for Sustainable Tourism Development: Community-based Collaborations," in *Quality Management in Urban Tourism,* Murphy (Chichester: John Wiley & Sons Ltd., 1997), pp. 204–205; and John M. Bryson and Barbara C. Crosby, "Planning and the Design and Use of Forums, Arenas, and Courts," in

Explorations in Planning Theory, eds., Seymour J. Mandelbaum, et al. (New Brunswick, N.J.: Rutgers Center for Urban Policy Research, 1996), p. 462.

59.   Ritchie points out that the application of the current theory of "visioning" to planning for tourism destinations is complicated by the fact that (1) the diverse points of view of the many stakeholders may be hard to resolve and (2) the iterative process by which the visioning is conducted may continue indefinitely because it has no logical endpoint, yet it "tends to define the nature of extremely long-term major developments, many of which are relatively irreversible." J. R. Brent Ritchie, "Crafting a Destination Vision," in J. R. Brent Ritchie and Charles R. Goeldner, *Travel, Tourism, and Hospitality Research: A Handbook for Managers and Researchers,* 2nd ed. (New York: John Wiley & Sons, 1994), pp. 29–38.

60.   An interesting evaluation of the process undertaken in Atlanta, Georgia, known as VISION 2020, is by Amy Helling, "Collaborative Visioning: Proceed with Caution!" in *Journal of the American Planning Association* Vol. 64, No. 3 (Summer, 1998): 335–349.

61.   Patsy Healey, "The Communicative Work of Development Plans," in Mandelbaum, ed., *Explorations,* p. 263.

62.   For an interesting discussion of the impacts of such power imbalances, see Maureen G. Reed, "Power Relations and Community Based Tourism Planning," *Annals of Tourism Research* 24, No. 3 (1997): pp. 566–591.

63.   As of August 1997, Bangladesh had introduced some sightseeing and river excursions, created a nationwide package tour, commissioned a 75-seat riverboat, built miles of roads and bridges, developed two restaurants and two hotels with two additional ones under construction, and purchased two 18-seat tourist boats.

64.   Diana Jean Schemo, "2 Brazil Towns Fight for Road," *New York Times,* 7 April 1998.

65.   George Ridge, "Island Paradise Grapples with Infrastructure," *International Herald Tribune,* 9 October 1995.

66.   Hotel and restaurant owners, many of whom operate their own in-house training programs, have identified the need for additional carpenters, bricklayers, and electricians. Bonaire, known for its snorkeling and scuba diving opportunities, also needs more dive masters, almost all of whom are foreign. To address these issues, the plan recommends an increase in the work permit fees for expatriates to encourage the hiring of Bonaireans where available; efforts by the private sector to develop a training scheme for dive masters; and endorses a proposal that any company bringing in senior personnel would need to agree to fund or run a training program on senior management skills in order to receive work permits.

67.   A 1993 work that grew out of a Canadian conference is a good beginning source for information on monitoring in tourism contexts. J. G. Nelson, R. Butler, and G. Wall, eds., *Tourism and Sustainable Development: Monitoring, Planning and Managing* (Canada: University of Waterloo, 1993).

68.   World Tourism Organization, *What Tourism Managers Need to Know: A Practical Guide to the Development and Use of Indicators of Sustainable Tourism* (Madrid: World Tourism Organization, 1996), pp. 39, 62–63.

69.   Marion Jackson and David Brice, "Monitoring and Evaluating a Tourism Development Programme: A Study of Chepstow," in *Perspectives on Tourism Policy,* eds. Peter Johnson and Barry Thomas (London: Mansell, 1992), pp. 105–119.

70.   See K. Michael Haywood, "Creating Value for Visitors to Urban Destinations" in *Quality Management in Urban Tourism,* Murphy, pp. 175–179.

71.   In October 1998, this hotel chain received certification by the prestigious International Organization for Standardization in Geneva, Switzerland, for excellence in environmen-

tal protection, as reflected in compliance with published ISO rules. The hotel understandably uses that and other environmental awards in its promotional program.

72. Berkes, *Common Property Resources*, p. 52.
73. Robert C. Ellickson, *Order Without Law: How Neighbors Settle Disputes* (Cambridge, Mass.: Harvard University Press, 1991).
74. Berkes, *Common Property Resources*, pp. 125ff.
75. Keohane, *Local Commons and Global Interdependence*, p. 61.
76. Hanna, *Property Rights and the Environment*, p. 53.
77. Ellickson, *Order Without Law*, p. 285.

Chapter 3

1. For a current analysis of the law of growth management in the United States, see Julian C. Juergensmeyer and Thomas E. Roberts, *Land Use Planning and Control Law* (St. Paul, Minn.: West Group, 1998), pp. 365–410.
2. Godschalk, Brower, et al., *Constitutional Issues in Growth Management* (Washington, D.C.: Planners Press 1979), p. 8.
3. A survey of growth management measures in California found no correlation between the adoption of such programs and a reduction in growth rates. Madelyn Glickfeld and Ned Levine, *Regional Growth . . . Local Reaction: the Enactment and Effects of Local Growth Control and Management Measures in California* (Cambridge, Mass.: Lincoln Institute of Land Policy, 1992).
4. On the "environmental roots" of growth management, see John M. DeGrove, *Land, Growth & Politics* (Washington, D.C.: Planners Press, 1984), pp. 371–376.
5. "Risk analysis" and "risk assessment" are the terms used to describe an analytical process in which the odds against some unfavorable event happening are calculated. If some degree of the unfavorable circumstances is inevitable, then we might more accurately call the process "harm analysis." For example, if tourism development will increase traffic at the airport, increased noise is not a risk but an inevitable harm. Airplane accidents, however, will not inevitably increase, but the risk of them will increase by at least some small amount. As a practical matter, risk analysis treats both risks and harms as part of a common equation. See generally John D. Graham and Jonathan Baert Wiener, *Risk vs. Risk: Tradeoffs in Protecting Health and the Environment* (Cambridge, Mass.: Harvard University Press, 1995). The engineering profession has led the way in developing risk analysis methods. Increased public concern about the risks associated, for example, with the building of dams or power plants, or with the introduction of new chemicals, has spurred a search for a reliable way of calculating the risks associated with these developments. The process begins by identifying a particular hazard or hazards; say drowning while swimming at a beach. Using historical data, an estimate of the likelihood that any individual would drown while swimming could be created. The second step would be to consider how the hazard could be avoided through various safeguards, such as breakwaters, lifeguards, etc. The computation of risk is the amount of the hazard divided by the value of the safeguards, or $R = H/S$. Once the risks are analyzed, the nature and extent of the risks must be communicated to the public. See National Research Council, *Understanding Risk: Informing Decisions in a Democratic Society*, Paul C. Stern and Harvey V. Fineberg, eds. (Washington, D.C.: National Academy Press, 1996). Government often faces difficult decisions whether merely to inform the public of the degree of risk or to establish standards minimizing the risks. See Beatley, *Ethical Land Use*, pp. 155–169.
6. 42 U.S.C. §4321 *et. seq.*
7. In a relatively short period of time, the idea was incorporated in the legal systems of the

European Community and many of the other developed nations. The World Bank and other international institutions began to use the idea in their internal decision-making processes. The scope and technique varied greatly, but the jargon of environmental assessment became used around the world. See generally, Daniel R. Mandelker, *NEPA Law and Litigation: The National Environmental Policy Act* (New York: Clark Boardman Callaghan, 1984).

8. When public health is involved, the uncertainties of medical knowledge often require the input of public health professionals. In the developed world, the history and severity of patterns of common diseases may be relatively easy to estimate from historical patterns. But new information constantly becomes available. Britain's experience with "mad cow disease" represents a hazard for which estimation would be impossible because of the almost complete uncertainty about the means by which the disease is transmitted. This uncertainty becomes much more common in more remote areas that have no long history of an influx of travelers from other parts of the world. Are the local people carrying rare viruses that could spread widely? Do they lack immunity to diseases carried by travelers? Both the likelihood of damage and the degree of harm may be very difficult to predict.

9. David Takacs, *The Idea of Biodiversity: Philosophies of Paradise* (Baltimore, MD: Johns Hopkins University Press, 1996).

10. Mark S. Dennison and James F. Berry, *Wetlands: Guide to Science, Law and Technology* (Park Ridge, N. J.: Noyes Publications, 1993).

11. Norman Williams, Jr., *American Land Planning Law*, Vol. 1, pp. 311–314 (rev. ed. 1988).

12. For a discussion of the application of environmental economics to tourism planning see Mieczkowski, *Environmental Issues*, pp. 360–367.

13. Mandelker, *NEPA Law and Litigation*.

14. Arthur C. Nelson and James B. Duncan, *Growth Management Principles and Practices* (Chicago: APA Planners Press, 1995).

15. The history of the judicial acceptance of growth management is set out in Juergens-meyer, *Land Use Planning*, at 369–379.

16. Since the 1970s, there have been few legal challenges to growth management, reflecting the fact that "growth management has become a widely accepted practice which . . . generates few constitutional challenges." Rutherford H. Platt, *Land Use and Society: Geography, Law, and Public Policy* (Washington, D.C.: Island Press, 1996), p. 314.

17. Juergensmeyer, *Land Use Planing*, at 371.

18. Porter, *Profiles in Growth Management* (Urban Land Institute 1996). See also James A. Kushner, *Subdivision Law and Growth Management* (New York: Clark Boardman Callaghan, 1991). Chapter 2 contains an extensive catalogue of growth management techniques.

19. Porter, *Profiles in Growth Management*, p. 6.

20. Mieczkowski, *Environmental Issues*, p. 416.

21. By summarizing the techniques that are often used in the United States, there is no intent to suggest that these are superior or inferior to other techniques that are available under the laws of other countries. For a comprehensive guide to local growth management techniques that includes many case studies and examples, see Michael Mantell, Stephen Harper, and Luther Propst, *Creating Successful Communities: A Guidebook to Growth Management Strategies* (Washington, D.C.: Island Press, 1989).

22. The idea has great promise, but many applications of it have failed for the lack of a perception of permanence. People will invest meaningful sums in development rights only if they are convinced that the rights will not be made available more cheaply within a

reasonable time. The fluidity of local politics in many communities means that a prospective buyer must always weigh the cost of buying a TDR against the chance that the next election will bring in elected officials who will give the rights away. See Norman Williams, Jr., *American Land Planning Law*, Vol. 5, pp. 556–558 (rev. ed. 1988).

23. For a recent description of the problems with the conservation of reef fish in the Western Pacific, see Carl Safina, *Song for the Blue Ocean: Encounters Along the World's Coasts and Beneath the Seas* (New York: Henry Holt and Company, 1997), pp. 303–407.

24. Fred P. Bosselman, "Limitations Inherent on the Title to Wetlands at Common Law," 15 *Stanford Environmental Law Journal* 247 (1996).

25. For an interesting discussion of the potential impact of global climate change on ski resorts, see Paul Jenner and Christine Smith, *The Tourism Industry and the Environment* (London: The Economist Intelligence Unit, 1992), pp. 22–24.

26. On the extent to which local communities have an obligation to consider impacts of their land-use decisions beyond their borders, see Beatley, *Ethical Land Use Planning*, pp. 227–240. Claims by tourism industry groups about environmental sensitivity need to be evaluated cautiously. See Alex Markels, "The Great Ecotrips: Guide to the Guides," *Audubon*, Vol. 100, No. 5 (September–October 1998).

Chapter 4

1. Economists continue to debate the extent to which increased development costs are passed on to customers or are passed back to the landowners from whom developers buy property (and pay less for).

2. Mapping is also an essential element of any location enhancement strategy (see generally chapter 6) and often of quantity management strategies as well (see generally chapter 5).

3. Once the map and text are legally enforceable, landowners who wish to develop their property are able to study the uses permitted (or sometimes permitted after receiving a special permit) and the regulated aspects of development (such as minimum lot size, density, and height limitations). In addition to regulating use and other aspects of development, the enactment may also require participation in a specified process (perhaps attending a public hearing on the proposal and receiving a favorable vote by an elected or appointed group) before a developer can legally proceed with a project.

4. Districting is a technique that ensures a degree of quality in tourism development by restricting development in areas where its impacts would be largely negative and promoting development in areas where it would further community goals. See Chapter 7.

5. World Tourism Organization, *Sustainable Tourism Development: Guide for Local Planners* (Madrid: World Tourism Organization, 1993).

6. These two programs were America's first, but there are now many hundreds, if not thousands in the country. (1990 estimate of 1,500 to 2,000 historical preservation ordinances. Carmella, "Landmark Preservation of Church Property," *Catholic Law Journal* 34 (1990): pp. 41–43.

7. *Vieux Carré Ordinance*, Sections 65–68.

8. Applications must "conform with the quaint, traditional architecture of the Vieux Carré," *Vieux Carré Ordinance*, Sections 65–66.

9. Quoted in Sharon Donovan, "Tourists, Residents Battle over Historic French Quarter," *Reuters North European Service*, 11 January 1987.

10. Elizabeth Mullener, "T-shirts: Critics Don't Cotton to Gift Shops," *The Times-Picayune*, 15 May 1994.

11. Bruce Eggler, "Proposal Tightens Quarter Growth," *The Times-Picayune*, 10 May 1993.

12. The Commission rejected that imaginative proposal, partially on the grounds of privacy of those being televised. Colman Warner, "TP Request for Camera in Quarter is Rejected," *The Times-Picayune,* 20 December 1995.

13. This example relies heavily on the interesting discussion found in Edward Inskeep, *Tourism Planning: An Integrated and Sustainable Development Approach* (New York: Van Nostrand Reinhold, 1991), pp. 293–295.

14. Murphy, *Tourism: A Community Approach,* pp. 62–64.

15. Murphy, *Tourism: A Community Approach,* p. 64.

16. For destination communities, districting can be used to direct the location of tourism development so that the desired benefits will be maximized and its unwanted impacts mitigated. See Chapter 7.

17. As a country of islands, Indonesia faces some special problems and opportunities. Published case studies of island tourism development include those in a useful volume, Lino Bruguglio, ed., *Sustainable Tourism in Islands and Small States: Case Studies* (New York: Pitner, 1996). The case studies cover the Shetland Islands, Zanzibar, Sri Lanka, Guadeloupe, Martinique, Barbados, St. Lucia, Belize, Dominica, Mykonos, and in great detail, Malta. A considerably more theoretical companion volume is Lino Bruguglio, ed., *Sustainable Tourism in Islands and Small States: Issues and Policies* (New York: Pinter, 1996).

18. These national planning efforts included regional and local components as to some locations of particular attractiveness for tourism. One example is the plan for Nusa Tenggara, the sociocultural element of which is briefly discussed in Chapter 26 in a useful work of the World Tourism Organization and Edward Inskeep, the author of an excellent reference text, *Tourism Planning: An Integrated and Sustainable Development Approach* (New York: Van Nostrand Reinhold, 1991). The joint work, *National and Regional Tourism Planning* (London: Routledge, 1994), recommends tourism planning methodologies and concludes with a brief, but helpful, discussion of components of tourism plans in a number of diverse destinations: Malta, Oman, Goa, Zanzibar, Bhutan, Bangladesh, Cyprus, Mongolia, Uganda, Philippines, Mexico, Senegal, Tibet, Maldives, Nusa Tenggara, Sri Lanka, Belize, and Ethiopia.

19. City of Santa Fe, *General Plan Draft* (September 1997): p. 3.

20. City of Santa Fe, *Working Paper: Urban Area and Extraterritorial Zone Evaluation and Planning Issues* (June 1995): pp. 1–10.

21. City of Santa Fe, *Working Paper,* pp. 1-13–1-15.

22. In December 1998, city planners presented the comprehensive proposed plan revisions, which include a new urban-growth boundary. Mayor Larry Delgado, whose principal campaign promise was to secure approval of the plan so as to manage growth, announced his goal of City Council approval by mid-1999. The plan has already engendered acrimonious debate. A proposed "community impact statement ordinance" designed to mitigate negative impacts on neighborhoods from large projects was the subject of a divisive controversy between neighborhood groups and developers. It was defeated in December 1998 by a 5-to-3 vote of the City Council.

23. John Barnett, "Redesigning the Metropolis: The Case for a New Approach," *Journal of the American Planning Association* 55 (1989): p. 131.

24. *Reimer v. Upper Mount Bethel Township,* 615 A.2d 938 (Pa. Commw. Ct. 1992).

25. Lane Kendig, et al., *Performance Zoning* (Chicago: Planners Press, American Planning Association, 1980).

26. World Tourism Organization, *Sustainable Tourism Development: Guide for Local Planners* (Madrid: World Tourism Organization, 1993).

27. New Zealand Tourism Board, New Zealand Tourism Industry Association, and the Ministry for the Environment, *Tourism's Guide to the Resource Management Act* (June 1996).

28. The guide includes such practical suggestions as allowing adequate time for the consultation process, since the Maori will respond in a time frame that is appropriate to their culture, rather than the time demands of a developer. It also suggests arranging for consultation in a place and in a format that is culturally comfortable for the Maori. Developers are advised to recognize that it may take several meetings before the proposed development is even mentioned, and that silence does not necessarily imply approval.

29. Interview with two of the authors, December 1997.

30. These principles also gave rise to a number of related initiatives, including acquisitions of thousands of acres of land through purchase for open space, entryway protection, land-banking for affordable housing, and historic preservation and by receipt of conservation easements that bar development for a number of purposes.

31. *Park City General Plan* (20 March 20 1997): p. 67.

32. *Jackson/Teton County Comprehensive Plan* (17 October 1994): p. 6-6.

33. At the time of writing, the transfer mechanisms in the TRPA program are under considerable (and well-funded) criticism as violating certain provisions of the United States Constitution.

34. See Martin Jaffe, "Performance Zoning: A Reassessment," *Land Use Law and Zoning Digest* (March 1993): p. 3.

35. See Christopher J. Duerksen, "Modern Industrial Performance Standards: Key Implementation and Legal Issues," *Zoning and Planning Law Report* 18 (May 1995): p. 33.

36. See generally the excellent article on TDR programs, from which this section is partially drawn, Edward H. Ziegler, "The Transfer of Development Rights," *Zoning and Planning Law Report* 18 (September 1995): p. 61.

37. Readers of this book could contact program administrators at a number of locations to learn more. Agricultural protection plans have been adopted in Montgomery County, Maryland; Buckingham Township, Pennsylvania; Marin Country, California; and the Pinelands of New Jersey. Among those communities adopting TDR programs to protect environmentally sensitive lands are Nantucket, Massachusetts; Island County, Washington; Anchorage, Alaska; Collier County, Florida; and the Lake Tahoe Regional Planning Agency (a TDR program currently under legal attack for allegedly violating the United States Constitution). Finally, several cities have utilized TDR plans to preserve historically significant buildings and/or landmarks: New York, Los Angeles, San Diego, San Francisco, Denver, Pittsburgh, and New Orleans.

38. *Teton County Land Development Regulations, Section 4330(B)(1),* 1998.

Chapter 5

1. For interesting discussions of the changes in approaches to carrying capacity analysis, see John Glasson, Kerry Godfrey, and Brian Goodey, *Towards Visitor Impact Management* (Aldershot: Avebury, 1995), Chapter 4; Peter W. Williams and Alison Gill, "Tourism Carrying Capacity Management Issues," in *Global Tourism,* Theobald, pp. 174–187; Harry Coccossis and Apostolos Parpairis, "Tourism and the Environment—Some Observations on the Concept of Carrying Capacity," in *Tourism and the Environment,* eds. Helen Briassoulis and Jan van der Straaten (Dordrecht: Kluwer Academic, 1992), pp. 23–33; Peter W. Williams and Alison Gill, *Carrying Capacity Management in Tourism Settings: A Tourism Growth Management Strategy* (Canada: Simon Fraser University, 1991).

2. George H. Stankey, et al., *The Limits of Acceptable Change System for Wilderness Planning* (Ogden: U.S. Department of Agriculture, 1985).

3. F. R. Kuss, A. R. Graefe, and J. J. Vaske, *Visitor Impact Management: A Review of Research,* Vol. 1 (Washington, D.C.: National Parks and Conservation Association, 1990).

4. See, for example, Peter E. Murphy, "Tourism and Sustainable Development," in *Global Tourism,* ed., Theobald, pp. 274–291; Bruguglio, *Sustainable Tourism: Issues and Policies;* Coccossis and Nijkamp, *Sustainable Tourism Development* (Aldershot: Avebury, 1995); World Tourism Organization, *Indicators of Sustainable Tourism and the Environment* (Madrid: WTO, 1994).

5. Another good source for information on environmentally sensitive practices in the tourism industry is the United Nations Environmental Program/International Hotel and Restaurant Association, *Environmental Good Practices in Hotels: Case Studies from the International and Restaurant Association Environmental Award* (Paris: UNEP, 1997).

6. C. Honchin, Great Barrier Reef Marine Park Authority, *Planning for Latent Capacity: A Case Study in Managing Increasing Tourism Use in the Great Barrier Reef Marine Park* (April 1998).

7. The designation of "World Heritage Sites" under an elaborate program administered by the United Nations agency UNESCO began in 1972 with the signing by many nations (and many more since that date) of a Convention whose "primary mission is to define the worldwide natural and cultural heritage and to draw up a list of sites and monuments considered to be of such exceptional interest and such universal value that their protection is the responsibility of all mankind." (*The World Heritage,* UNESCO1994.) Nations that are party to the Convention promise to conserve World Heritage Sites within their borders.

    As of January 1998, there were 552 identified sites in 112 countries. This list is continually updated by a committee of experts from 21 of the signatory nations, who themselves are assisted by the International Council on Monuments and Sites and the World Conservation Union. Nations receive assistance, financial aid, and technical help provided by the affiliated World Heritage Fund, which receives moneys from member states and from voluntary contributions from others, to help them conserve their designated sites.

8. Allan Williams, Tourism Coordinator of the Great Barrier Reef Marine Park Authority (letter to the authors), 18 August 1997.

9. Williams (letter to the authors), 18 August 1997.

10. Claude Filion, Director of the Saguenay-St. Lawrence Marine Park (letter to the authors), 2 October 1997.

11. Filion (letter to the authors), 2 October 1997.

12. Terry Pindell, *Yesterday's Train: A Rail Journey Through Mexican History* (New York: Owl Books, 1997), p. 242.

13. Tim Padgett, "The Battle for the Beach," *Newsweek* 1 July 1996, p. 58. The owners quoted in the article, Dan Vallejo and Susan Bohlken, also allege that the Mexican government has begun to delay building permits and raise immigration questions: "It's like open season on us because they need beaches for casinos and marinas." Padgett notes in his article that the family of former Mexican President Salinas "declines to comment" on reports that they own "massive concealed investments on the Cancun Corridor."

14. Pindell, *Yesterday's Train,* p. 243.

15. Mark Ottoway, "Beyond Cancun," *Sunday Times* 1 December 1996.

16. Pindell, *Yesterday's Train,* p. 245.

17. For an interesting discussion of the economic impacts of preservation zones on abutting communities, see Jim Howe, et al., *Balancing Nature and Commerce.*

18. Oxford's challenges and initiatives are nicely covered in Glasson, Godfrey, and Goodey, *Towards Visitor Impact Management,* pp. 121–145. This work is a successful attempt to address European programs to manage tourism numbers in heritage cities.

19. See James Mak and James E. T. Moncur, *Sustainable Tourism Development: Managing Hawaii's "Unique" Resource—Hanauma Bay,* presented to the 2nd Global Conference on Tourism: Building a Sustainable World Through Tourism, Montreal, Canada, 12–16 September 1994.

20. *The Comprehensive Land Use Plan of the City of Sanibel* (5 August 1997), p. 4.

21. *The Comprehensive Land Use Plan of the City of Sanibel,* p. 5.

22. *The Comprehensive Land Use Plan of the City of Sanibel,* p. 155.

23. In tourism parlance, a "bed" does not refer to a piece of furniture but to a quantified measure of capacity to house tourists.

24. *Draft Yosemite Valley Implementation Plan, Yosemite National Park, California* (November 1997), p. 3.

25. *Draft Yosemite Valley Implementation Plan,* p. 164.

26. A well-written and well-conceived recent addition to the literature of tourism development patterns focuses on islands both in the developed and the developing worlds. Douglas Lockhart and David Drakakis-Smith, *Island Tourism: Trends and Prospects* (London and New York: Pinter, 1997). In that work, contributing scholars from a variety of countries and disciplines effectively address a broad range of issues and destinations: Orkney and Shetland Isles, Scotland; Channel Islands; East Frisian Islands, Germany; Smögen, Sweden; Balearic Islands; Malta; Cyprus; Jamaica; Barbados; Mauritius; Singapore; Bali and Lombok, Indonesia; Fiji; and the South Atlantic Islands.

27. Tourism Planning and Research Associates, 52 High Holborn, London WC1V 6RB, England.

28. *Whistler Comprehensive Development Plan* (1988), p. 19.

29. Professor Alison Gill has studied Whistler and offers useful perspectives on its development, concerning types of residents in resort communities and "territorial competitiveness, in "Competition and the Resort Community: Towards an Understanding of Residents' Needs," in *Quality Management in Urban Tourism,* Murphy, Chapter 5.

30. Whistler, *Community and Resort Monitoring Program Report* (1996), p. 2.

31. *Pitkin County Housing Study,* 1990, cited in Bill Hedden and Luther Propst, *A Profile of the Roaring Fork Valley* (Tucson, Arizona: The Sonoran Institute, 1998), p. 6.

32. *Aspen Area Community Plan* (January1993), p. 5.

33. Hedden and Propst, *A Portrait of the Roaring Fork Valley,* p. 19.

34. According to Planning Officer Imani Fairweather, this legal situation of not having the Master Plan formally adopted by law has generated both benefits and problems: "The main disadvantage has been that the planning criterion for approval has been used mainly as guidelines for approval and approvals have been granted for variances from the guidelines. (In some cases, the variances granted by the committee have been significant.) On the other hand, being able to be flexible with approval has had its benefits in that any subdivision done prior to the master plan may have lot sizes much smaller than what's recommended in the master plan. It is obvious then that this would affect the ability of the developer to meet with the other setback requirements. . . . Being able to be flexible with such requirements has been good in some instances." (Letter to the authors) 4 March 1998.

35. Growth during the 1990s was far stronger than estimated by the planners who prepared

the master plan. Martin Alegria, a professional in the Department of Environment, offered these statistics:

POPULATION INCREASE FOR SAN PEDRO

Year	Population
1991	2,001
1192	2,052
1993	2,002
1994	3,250
1995	3,250
1996	3,325
1997	3,275

TOURISM-RELATED STATISTICS FOR SAN PEDRO

Year	Room Nights Available	Room Nights Used	Bed Nights Used
1994	239,171	90,751	130,417
1995	205,883	80,861	113,030
1996	234,224	78,118	96,220
1997	244,520	83,052	124,830

Mr. Alegria also explains that "the room nights and bed nights" is the parameter used by the Belize Tourist Board to estimate the amounts of nights a room or bed was used during the year. To estimate the actual rooms and beds available in San Pedro, these numbers should be divided by 4 (the average number of nights that a tourist stays in Ambergris Caye).

36. The Belize Water and Sewerage Authority conducted these deep well tests in the late 1980s, but the results were not encouraging, even though the tests did reveal limited fresh water in many interconnected cavern systems.

37. Planning Officer Imani Fairweather reports that the Planning Committee has implemented these guidelines for three low-density developments and that the protective approach has worked well. The lowest density area of the three is the most environmentally sensitive, primarily wetlands with mangroves. Enforcement of the guidelines has been politically feasible because citizens and committee members recognize that the protected areas ensure the presence of natural amenities that attract tourists for birdwatching, fishing, and similar activities. (Letter to the authors) 4 March 1998.

38. Belize, *Master Plan for Ambergris Caye—Summary* (1988), p. viii.

Chapter 6

1. See Christopher Smith, "Moab's Natives," *New York Times,* 11 March 1998, from which much of this information is drawn.

2. Quoted in V. Dion Haynes, "Lake Poisoned and Town Withers," *Chicago Tribune,* 16 April 1998.

3. Martin Ruiz Camino, Minister of Tourism Development of Oaxaca State (letter to the authors), 14 April 1998.

4. Pindell, *Yesterday's Train,* p. 218.

5. New Zealand Tourism Board, *Southern Lakes Tourism Strategy: Directions and Opportunities for Sustainable Tourism Development,* (February 1998): p. 4.

6. New Zealand Tourism Board, *Southern Lakes Tourism Strategy,* p. 46.

7. New Zealand Tourism Board, *Southern Lakes Tourism Strategy,* p. 38.

8. New Zealand Tourism Board, Southern Lakes Tourism Strategy, p. 38.

9. The nature and impacts of regional tourism patterns in Europe are of increasing interest, particularly with the formation of the European Union. An excellent recent compendium of analyses offers valuable insights concerning the Alpine area, central/eastern Europe, Mediterranean regions, the British Isles and Scandinavia, as well as discussions of a variety of topics of particular relevance in Europe. Armando Montonari and Alan Williams, eds., *European Tourism: Regions, Spaces and Restructuring* (London: Wiley & Sons, 1995).

10. Ann Louise Strong, Planned Urban Environments (Baltimore, MD: Johns Hopkins University Press, 1971), pp. 366–377.

11. Fred P. Bosselman, *In the Wake of the Tourist: Managing Special Places in Eight Countries* (Washington, D.C.: The Conservation Foundation, 1978), pp. 60–63.

12. Mary Klemm, "Sustainable Tourism Development: Languedoc-Roussillon Thirty Years On," *Tourism Management* (June 1992): p. 169.

13. Strong, *Planned Urban Environments,* p. 367.

14. Pearce, *Tourist Development,* 2d ed.

15. Melvin Bernarde and Anita Bernarde, *Beach Holidays from Portugal to Israel* (New York: Dodd, Mead and Co., 1974), pp. 91–92.

16. Glasson, Godfrey and Goodey, *Towards Visitor Impact Management,* pp. 136–138.

17. G. J. Ashworth, and H. Voogd, *Selling the City* (London: Belhaven, 1990), p. 73.

18. Readers wishing more information on this study can refer to G. Dann, "Sociocultural Issues in St. Lucia's Tourism," in *Sustainable Tourism,* Briguglio, pp. 103–121.

19. One of the best recent books addressing the complex and multifaceted aspects of tourism in urban areas generally is Murphy, ed., *Quality Management in Urban Tourism.* It is divided into three parts: management issues, heritage and cultural commercial links, and management partnerships.

20. Hotel developers are often international; one of the most recent development was by the Four Seasons, which included such amenities as private spas for each of its secluded cottages.

21. Quoted in P. Ghate, "Maldives: Tourism Booming but Environment, Culture Still Safe," *Inter Press Service,* 23 May 1997.

22. Quoted in P. Ghate, "Maldives," 23 May 1997.

23. Douglas Pearce, *Tourism Today: A Geographical Analysis* (New York: Longman Group Limited, 1987), p. 164.

24. Glasson, Godfrey, and Goodey, *Towards Visitor Impact Management,* p. 151.

25. This discussion draws heavily from the early study of Cancun included in Bosselman, *In the Wake of the Tourist,* pp. 37–57.

26. Quoted in Bosselman, *In the Wake of the Tourist,* p. 40.

27. Quoted in Bosselman, *In the Wake of the Tourist,* p. 46.

28. *Michelin Guide to Mexico,* (1989), p.63.

29. Larry Rohter, "What's Doing in Cancun," *The New York Times,* 8 March 1998.

30. Both tourists quoted in staff and wire reports, "A Bit of Home on the Beach at Cancun: Resort Offers Comfy Slice of Tourist U.S. in Mexico," *The Plain Dealer,* 15 February 1998.

31. Christine Riccelli, "Cancun," *The Des Moines Register,* 11 January 1998.

32. Molly Moore, "Spring Breakers Drink in Cancun's Excess: Mexican Resort is No.1 Party Spot," *Washington Post,* 3 April 1998.

33. "Cancun PR Campaign Curbs Rowdy Tourists," *O'Dwyer's PR Services Report* (August 1996): p. 8.

34. Michael Herzfeld, *A Place in History: Social and Monumental Time in a Cretan Town* (Princeton: Princeton University Press, 1991).

35. Herzfeld, *A Place in History,* p. 39.

36. Herzfeld, *A Place in History,* p. 41.

37. Pearce, *Tourism Today,* p. 153. Sometimes resorts themselves are such enclaves. The world famous Hotel Mamounia, where Sir Winston Churchill often vacationed, is a walled world set amidst the teeming streets of Marrakesh, Morocco.

38. The description of Bali life draws from Canadian geographer Professor Geoffrey Wall, University of Waterloo, Canada, who is a leading expert on tourism development in Bali. He contributed a great deal of assistance in designing its sustainable tourism strategies. Among his writings in the area are "Toward a Tourism Typology," in *Tourism and Sustainable Development,* Nelson, Butler, and Wall, pp. 45–58; and "Bali and Lombok: Adjacent Tourism Islands with Contrasting Tourism Experiences," in *Island Tourism,* Lockhart and Drakakis-Smith.

39. Bette Duke, "Bali Sigh," *Travel and Leisure,* March 1993: p. 130.

40. See generally Duke, "Bali Sigh," March 1993.

41. Molly O'Neill, "Mystical Bali, Refined," *New York Times,* 19 April 1998.

42. Pamela Hansford Johnson, "Bruges," reprinted in *Travel in Vogue* (New York: DaCapo Press, 1981), p. 153.

43. Johnson, "Bruges," p. 154.

44. Dieter Dewulf of Toerisme Brugge (letter to the authors), 5 December 1997. Mr. Dewulf also wrote a useful summary document published by Toerisme Brugge in 1998 titled *A Structural View on City-Planning and Touristic Development in Brugge.* Mr. Dewulf and Hans Vancompernolle provided invaluable information for the Bruges Case Study.

45. Glasson, Godfrey, and Goodey, *Towards Visitor Impact Management,* p. 101.

46. Hundreds of tourism marketing texts and articles discuss the creation, maintenance, and marketing of various sorts of tourism products. Because it is beyond the scope of this book's purposes, we do not pretend to cover this complex field.

47. Readers wishing to learn more about developing nature tourism programs can consult Tensie Whelan, ed., *Nature Tourism: Managing for the Environment* (Washington, D.C.: Island Press, 1993).

48. The complexity and diversity of these most interesting efforts are beyond the scope of this introductory section. Readers should consult the excellent Richard B. Primack, et al., eds., *Timber, Tourists, and Temples: Conservation and Development in the Maya Forest of Belize, Guatemala, and Mexico* (Washington, D.C.: Island Press, 1998), particularly "Community-Based Ecotourism in the Maya Forest: Problems and Potentials," pp. 327–342.

49. See F. X. Clines, "Bordello as Visitor Center," *New York Times,* 1 December 1997.

50. See Mireya Navarro, "A Beacon for Those Seeking Answers from Beyond the Grave," *New York Times,* 26 April 1998.

51. This account is based on an interview by Giovanni Lattanzi with a tombolaro reported in *Archaeology,* May/June 1998.

52. D. T. Max, "Basque Magic," *Smart Money,* September 1998, p. 187.

53. Quoted in M. Simons, "Montolieu Journal: A Dying Village Is Fertile Soil for Bookworms," *New York Times,* 30 July 1997.

54. Readers wishing to learn more about any of these activities could read D. Pearl, "Tour

Saudi Arabia: Enjoy Sand, Surf, His-and-Her Pools," *Wall Street Journal,* 22 January 1998, from which this account draws.

55. For further information, readers may consult M. Hodson, "Journeys in the Mind," *Sunday Times,* 15 June 1997.

56. The Tarka project was discussed briefly but effectively in a fine book for general readers, Jonathan Croall, *Preserve or Destroy: Tourism and the Environment* (London: Gulbenkian Foundation, 1995). This short work also briefly discusses a number of community partnerships in other parts of the United Kingdom, as well as some initiatives in Greece, the Himalayas, India, France, and Senegal.

57. Britain's long history of common law protections afforded the pathways and byways that make up the miles of criss-crossing trails that Britishers "ramble" on during their holidays, allows tourism development dependent upon hiking.

58. John Asby, coordinator of SPARC, provided factual verfication of this case study.

59. See J. Tagliabue, "Preserving a Heritage via Bed and Barns," *New York Times,* 13 August 1998, from which this account is drawn.

60. Tagliabue, "Preserving a Heritage," 13 August 1998.

61. Veronica Long, "Techniques for Socially Sustainable Tourism Development: Lessons from Mexico," in *Tourism and Sustainable Development,* Nelson, Butler and Wall, p. 210.

62. Burns and Holden, *Tourism: A New Perspective,* p. 116.

Index